BEHAVIORAL ISSUES IN OFFICE DESIGN

BEHAVIORAL ISSUES IN OFFICE DESIGN

JEAN D. WINEMAN, Editor

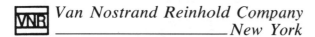 *Van Nostrand Reinhold Company*
New York

Printed in the United States of America

Designed by Christopher Simon

Van Nostrand Reinhold Company Inc.
115 Fifth Avenue
New York, New York 10003

Van Nostrand Reinhold Company Limited
Molly Millars Lane
Wokingham, Berkshire RG11 2PY, England

Van Nostrand Reinhold
480 La Trobe Street
Melbourne, Victoria 3000, Australia

Macmillan of Canada
Division of Canada Publishing Corporation
164 Commander Boulevard
Agincourt, Ontario M1S 3C7, Canada

16 15 14 13 12 11 10 9 8 7 6 5 4 3 2 1

Library of Congress Cataloging in Publication Data
Main entry under title:

Behavioral issues in office design.

   Bibliography: p.
   Includes index.
   1. Office layout—Psychological aspects—Addresses, essays, lectures.   2. Office decoration—Psychological aspects—Addresses, essays, lectures.   I. Wineman, Jean D.
HF5547.2.B43   1985   725'.23   85-7339
ISBN 0-442-29181-7

Contents

Preface

Are the needs of office workers important to organizational effectiveness? Is worker satisfaction relevant to productivity? How do the design and management of the physical setting contribute to worker satisfaction and job performance? As the number of office workers grows, these and other questions relevant to the professional effectiveness and productivity of the white-collar work force have spurred designers, office managers and administrators, and other professionals to search for better information to guide office planning and design. The work presented in this volume represents a compilation of some of the current thinking in the field.

The intent of *Behavioral Issues in Office Design* is both to provide a theoretical understanding of the role of human values and behavior in the planning, design, and management of work environments and to present specific research results on current issues in the field. The work is introduced by a chapter that attempts to shed light on the complex question of how the designed environment influences organizational effectiveness and worker productivity. The first section of the book addresses conceptual and methodological issues concerning behavioral inputs to workplace planning, design, and management. The second major section reviews results from several office setting evaluations and presents a theoretical basis for understanding and interpreting these results. The third section addresses specific aspects of office design: the open-office concept, privacy and communication, status support, lighting, and office automation. The volume concludes with a chapter that reviews significant issues in the field and provides recommendations for office design.

It is hoped that the work contained within this volume will encourage a reassessment by design practitioners, office-planning and management personnel, researchers, and others of the importance of workers' needs and values to the success of the work process, and the contribution of the often overlooked resource, the physical setting, to worker productivity and organizational effectiveness.

Introduction

The Importance of
Office Design to Organizational
Effectiveness and Productivity

JEAN D. WINEMAN

College of Architecture
Georgia Institute of Technology
Atlanta, Georgia

The growing percentage of workers employed in office settings has resulted in a rapid increase in this sector of the U.S. economy. In fact, it has been projected that by 1990 there will be 20 million new jobs, of which over 50% will be in white-collar work (Working Women 1980). Managers and administrators in the private and public sectors are understandably concerned with office workers' professional effectiveness and productivity as they affect the competitive position of American industry and the comparative efficiency of our government's bureaucracy.

With growing nationwide interest in organizational effectiveness, the design and management of work environments and workers' responses to them are receiving increased attention. Renewed research efforts have focused on the contribution of the workplace to worker satisfaction and productivity, communication and interaction, and other job-related behaviors. This renewed research interest is probably not unrelated to the expanding market for open-plan office systems and increasing organizational concern regarding their effectiveness.

The assessment of productivity among office personnel is a long-standing problem. With some job types, such as clerical work, a measurable output does exist. For nonclerical workers, however, quantity and quality of product are difficult to measure because many of the tasks are mental and there are no standards available against which to measure output quality. The applicability of measures used for one job type or task to other types of office work is clearly questionable.

Productivity is a broad concept, which includes not only employees' work performance but also associated organizational costs, such as employee turnover, absenteeism, tardiness, required overtime, vandalism, grievances, and mental and physical health. Because of the difficulty of obtaining a satisfactory measure of employee performance or product output in office settings, these associated organizational costs, which are more easily quantified, are often used as measures of productivity.

PRODUCTIVITY AND SATISFACTION

Historically, much of the research on productivity has relied on using measures of employee satisfaction as indicators of productivity (S → P). The assumption has been that if employee satisfaction is high, motivation is high, and therefore one can expect a high level of performance. "The happy worker is a productive worker." Based upon this model, if one could positively affect satisfaction, one would expect to see an increase in productivity. Research efforts have, therefore, focused on the identification of correlates of job satisfaction.

The S → P model has some validity. Research indicates a strong relationship between employee satisfaction and the factors of absenteeism and turnover (Lawler and Porter 1967). But the relationship to productivity is not as strong as might be expected. As described by Lawler and Porter (1967), research of the 1950s indicated such a low level of relationship between employee satisfaction and performance that this assumption was considered to be incorrect. However, Lawler and Porter cited three major reviews of the literature (Brayfield and Crockett 1955; Herzberg, Mausner, Peterson, and Capwell 1957; Vroom 1964) that presented evidence to suggest that a consistent but low positive relationship exists between satisfaction and performance. These findings raise questions about the appropriateness of relying on satisfaction as a primary predictor of productivity and suggest that there may be alternative avenues of research that may be as fruitful if not more so.

Because of the low level of relationship between satisfaction and performance, Lawler and Porter sought a more powerful explanation. They hypothesized that "the relationship found between satisfaction and performance comes about through the action of a third variable—rewards. Briefly stated, good performance may lead to rewards, which in turn lead to satisfaction; this formulation would then say that satisfaction, rather than causing performance, as was previously assumed, is caused by it'' (Lawler and Porter 1967, 23). This theoretical model, as shown in figure 1-1, also distinguished two kinds of rewards: *extrinsic rewards* (those controlled by the organization, such as pay, promotion, status, and security) and *intrinsic rewards* (those self-administered for good performance, such as the feeling of accomplishment of a task well done). The authors suggested that the relationship between rewards and satisfaction is moderated by an individual's expectations concerning those rewards: that is, what the individual feels he or she *should* receive for a certain level of performance. Statistical tests of this model indicated that it provides a good explanation of the hypothesized relationships (Lawler and Porter 1967).

As suggested by Lawler and Porter, this model has significant implications for evaluating the effectiveness of office organizations. If, as this model suggests, satisfaction results from intrinsic and extrinsic rewards for performance, a strong positive relationship between satisfaction and performance would suggest that employees find their work intrinsically rewarding and that extrinsic rewards, such as pay or promotion, are perceived as being distributed appropriately. Furthermore, since turnover and absenteeism are related to satisfaction, a strong relationship between satisfaction and performance suggests that "the poorer performers rather than the better ones are quitting and showing high absenteeism" (Lawler and Porter 1967, 27).

On the basis of this model, one could posit that organizational effectiveness and productivity can be leveraged more effectively through improvements to the match between satisfaction and performance, rather than simply by addressing satisfaction per se. The key to this match appears to be perceived equitable distribution of rewards (Lawler and Porter 1967).

Herzberg (1976) concluded from surveys of 1,685 workers representing a range of job levels and job types that there was a distinct difference between aspects of the work environment that generally contribute to satisfaction and those that contribute to dissatisfaction. Herzberg's research revealed that satisfaction and dissatisfaction are not extremes of a single continuum, but that, in fact, they are separate aspects of workers' responses to the work environment. "The opposite of job satisfaction is not job dissatisfaction but, rather, *no* job satisfaction; and, similarly, the opposite of job dissatisfaction is not job satisfaction, but *no* job dissatisfaction" (Herzberg 1976, 69). Factors that Herzberg labeled "motivators," such as achievement, recognition, work itself, responsibility, and advancement, contribute to job satisfaction, whereas such aspects of the work environment

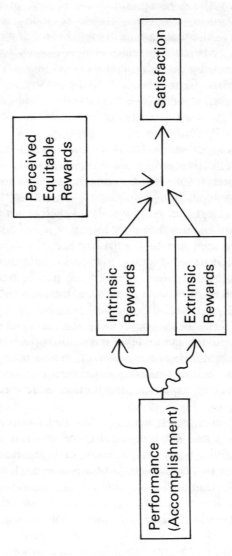

1-1. The relationships of performance and satisfaction (Lawler and Porter 1967, 23)

as company policy and administration, supervision, relationships with others, and work conditions (labeled by Herzberg as "hygiene factors") contribute to job dissatisfaction.

Herzberg's "motivators" are aspects of the work setting related to the rewards for work performance. Such motivators as achievement and work itself provide intrinsic rewards, while others, such as recognition and advancement, provide extrinsic rewards. According to the Lawler and Porter model (1967), it is these kinds of intrinsic and extrinsic rewards that affect job performance. "Hygiene factors," in contrast, are characteristics of the organizational setting in which the work is performed.

In their review of the literature, Lawler and Porter (1967) found a strong relationship between employee satisfaction (considered as a single continuum) and the factors of absenteeism and turnover. If this finding is considered in light of Herzberg's (1976) distinction between satisfaction and dissatisfaction, a revised model of the performance-satisfaction relationship could be proposed in which characteristics of the organizational setting influence both job performance and job dissatisfaction (fig. 1-2). Job dissatisfaction may lead to absenteeism and turnover, whereas rewards for performance ("motivators") influence job satisfaction and, ultimately, future job performance.

CONTRIBUTIONS OF THE PHYSICAL SETTING

In terms of dollar outlay over the 40-year life cycle of an office building, 2–3% is generally spent on the initial costs of the building and equipment; 6–8% on maintenance and replacement; and 90–92% is generally spent on personnel salaries and benefits. These data suggest that if an investment in physical planning and design could be made that would favorably influence organizational effectiveness and therefore reduce personnel costs, total life-cycle costs could be substantially reduced (*see also* Brill, Mandell, and Quinan 1982).

In attempting to understand the contribution of the physical setting to organizational effectiveness, it appears on the basis of the previous analysis that physical characteristics have both direct and indirect effects. Clearly, the physical setting has a direct effect on individual task performance and the work process as a whole. If the work environment hinders the successful completion of tasks—disruptive noise when a worker is trying to concentrate, for one—one might expect either a lower level of performance or a less effective performance (that is, it takes longer).

On the individual (worker) level, work process involves the individual's ability to accomplish work tasks. Environmental characteristics that in-

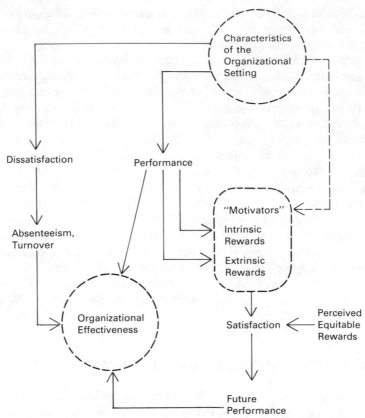

1-2. Revised model of performance-satisfaction relationship

fluence this level of the work process include what has been defined by Archea (1977) as both architectural properties and architectural attributes. Architectural properties are such aspects of the physical environment as size of office, number of walls, ambient conditions (heating, ventilation, air conditioning, lighting), ergonomic factors, and relationships to support services. Architectural attributes are people's attitudes and perceptions related to those properties, for example assessments of openness, noise, enclosure, lighting, and temperature (*see* Marans and Spreckelmeyer, this volume; Ferguson and Weisman, this volume).

On the organizational level, work process involves the capacity of the organization to support the accomplishment of work. Here again, a distinction can be made between organizational properties or structure and organizational attributes. Organizational properties include the traditional measures of bureaucracy defined by Duffy (1974), including degree of participation, hierarchy of authority, centralization, job specificity, and complexity and routinization. Organizational attributes reflect the social dimensions of organizations, such as patterns of communication (frequency and occurrence of various kinds of inter- and intradepartmental, formal and informal, interactions), perceptions of participation in decision making, and job autonomy. Properties of the physical setting that affect both these aspects of the organization include space sizes, shapes, and boundary controls, structural capacity to accommodate various configurations, and space flexibility (Duffy 1974).

Characteristics of the physical setting have indirect effects on organizational effectiveness through their role as rewards for performance. The design and management of the physical environment and factors such as job design provide opportunities to reward employees outside of salary and promotion decisions. Aspects of the physical setting have symbolic status value in organizations (see Konar and Sundstrom, this volume). They are perceived as part of the external reward system reflecting a worker's position and performance.

Locke (1970) identified a number of the intrinsic, or what he terms "task-related," rewards of work. Among these are the value of simply engaging in a task activity and the rewards of successful performance or achievement of particular qualitative and/or quantitive goals. He suggested that "individuals value jobs which allow them to control their own work pace and work methods, to exercise their skills and abilities, and to learn new things" (Locke 1970, 487). These task-related rewards of work are similar to Herzberg's factors of "achievement" or the "work itself" (factors that contribute to job satisfaction). Characteristics of the physical setting may indirectly affect the attainment of these intrinsic rewards through their influence on the ability of the worker to accomplish work tasks. If, for example, aspects of the physical environment such as disruptions, distractions, or perceived lack of control compromise or prohibit the accomplishment of tasks, the intrinsic rewards of a job well done will be minimal.

Finally, the work environment is a significant factor affecting worker dissatisfaction. Characteristics of the physical setting, components of Herzberg's "work conditions," are factors that contribute to job dissatisfaction (Herzberg 1976). Dissatisfaction with work conditions may then lead to worker absenteeism, turnover, and other behaviors that reduce organizational effectiveness.

RESEARCH DIRECTIONS

What, then, does this perspective suggest for research on office settings? First, it suggests that the focus of most environment-behavior research on employees' satisfaction is not inappropriate, but should be considered in light of its relationship to other significant aspects of the work process. Employee satisfaction appears to be an important concern for four reasons: (1) the clear relationship between satisfaction and employee absenteeism and turnover; (2) the low but positive relationship between satisfaction and performance; (3) humanitarian considerations for employee well-being; and (4) the role of rewards as mediators of the relationship between performance and satisfaction.

This perspective suggests a second productive research approach: focus on task performance. Given the widely accepted satisfaction-productivity model, little attention has been paid to interpreting environment and behavior relationships in terms of task performance. Past research has tended to treat job level as a measure of job responsibilities and task complexity, rather than to explore actual use patterns or the perceived effectiveness of design features in supporting task performance. The work of Brill and his associates (1982) suggests that, in fact, aspects of the work environment related to job satisfaction (floor area, temperature/air quality, lighting, safety/security, noise and ease of communication) are, in general, different from those related to job performance (lighting, control of access, visual access).

Through an intensive analysis of employees' tasks, task complexity, and organizational work patterns, the objective of this approach would be to identify ways of improving the fit between the physical setting and the work process, both at the individual and at the organizational level. This improved fit would not only improve performance directly, it would also enhance the intrinsic rewards of a job, "satisfaction with a job well done," and indirectly contribute to future successful job performance.

RECOMMENDATIONS

The research perspective described here provides a number of directives for the planning, design, and management of office settings.

First, and perhaps most important, the office setting provides support mechanisms for the completion of work tasks. Ease in accomplishing work affects productivity directly, but also appears to affect motivation and, therefore, performance through its influence on intrinsic rewards. Engaging in work tasks, accomplishing tasks, and perceptions of task control have all been identified as intrinsically rewarding aspects of work. To the extent that the individual workspace and the organizational context are designed to assist the work process and provide workers with real and perceived control, the intrinsic rewards for performance will increase.

Second, the office setting embodies a range of symbolic indicators of status. To reward productive workers appropriately, it is important that extrinsic rewards, including environmental factors such as status symbols, be allocated in accordance with the quality of performance.

Last, it is important that work conditions, including aspects of the physical environment (such as ambient conditions, office size, and organization) and people's attitudes and perceptions related to those properties (such as assessments of noise, enclosure, and temperature), do not contribute to dissatisfaction.

The work that is further described in this volume elaborates on this complex multidimensional system in which characteristics of the workers, the job, the organization, and the physical setting interact in a dynamic way to influence organizational effectiveness and productivity.

REFERENCES

Archea, J. 1977. The place of architectural factors in behavioral theories of privacy. *Journal of Social Issues 33* (3): 116–137.

Brayfield, A. H. and W. H. Crockett. 1955. Employee attitudes and employee performance. *Psychological Bulletin LII* (September): 396–424.

Brill, M., D. Mandell, and M. Quinan. 1982. *The office environment as a tool to increase productivity and the quality of work life.* Buffalo, NY: BOSTI.

Duffy, F. 1974. Office design and organizations: 2. The testing of a hypothetical model. *Environment and Planning B* 1: 217–235.

Herzberg, F. 1976. One more time: How do you motivate employees? In W. R. Nord (ed.), *Concepts and controversy in organizational behavior.* Santa Monica, CA: Goodyear Publishing Co.

Herzberg, F., B. Mausner, R. O. Peterson, and D. F. Capwell. 1957. *Job attitudes: Review of research and opinion.* Pittsburgh: Psychological Service.

Lawler, E. E., III, and L. W. Porter. 1967. The effect of performance on job satisfaction. *Industrial Relations* 7: 20–28.

Locke, E. A. 1970. Job satisfaction and job performance: A theoretical analysis. *Organizational Behavior and Human Performance* 5: 484–500.

Vroom, V. H. 1964. *Work and motivation.* New York: John Wiley & Sons.

Working Women. 1980. *Race against time: An overview of office automation.* Cleveland, Ohio: Working Women Education Fund.

SECTION 1

OFFICE DESIGN, OFFICE ORGANIZATIONS, AND HUMAN NEEDS

The design and management of office settings affect work processes at both the individual and organizational levels. The three chapters that follow describe the close relationship between design and worker behavior. Significant human values and methods of responding to them are discussed in light of the planning and design of work settings.

The chapter by Moleski and Lang focuses on the premise that the corporate environment must be supportive of organizational needs within the context of human values. To be effective, corporate office planning must go beyond the recording of organizational needs and user preferences to examine the environmental planning process by which the organization determines its environment. Environmental planning for changing organizations is concerned with organizational effectiveness, destiny, and quality of the work environment. Solutions to the first two can be derived through the analysis of the organization and its determinant conditions. The third requires a more thorough examination of planning principles. To be responsive to organizational changes, user-needs research and corporate space planning must be redefined to recognize the importance of freedom of choice in determining behavioral patterns and involvement in the planning and research process by individuals and work groups.

Davis and Szigeti describe processes for determining user-oriented design requirements in the planning and programming of office facilities. Constraints and opportunities inherent in the process approaches commonly

1

used in Canada and the United States are discussed. Organizational
characteristics that may affect the choice of process are identified. The
authors predict an increase in participatory approaches to planning and
design.

Steele discusses the effects of setting design and use on power behavior
and other organizational dynamics. Typical problems experienced by
organizations with regard to facilities design are reviewed. To improve
the functioning of organizations, Steele suggests improving the match of
physical and social structure needs. Organizational needs should be considered as a system rather than the sum of individual needs.

As described in this section, organizational effectiveness is dependent
upon both physical design and social processes. The planning and design
effort must be responsive to these facets of the workplace and their
interrelationships at both the individual and organizational levels.

Organizational Goals and Human Needs in Office Planning

WALTER H. MOLESKI

JON T. LANG
ERG Environmental Research Group
Philadelphia, Pennsylvania

In today's dynamic world, corporate organizations are faced with massive changes, affecting their nature, the work they perform, and their members. Changes occurring in the social environment, office technology, business climate, and human values have brought about a radical redefinition of organizational structures and process, restructuring work tasks and, perhaps more important, reordering priorities for meeting individual needs. It has long been evident that new managerial strategies are required to cope with these changes (Ackoff 1981). To enable these strategical changes to take place, it is also necessary to make innovations in the design of corporate workspace, including the restructuring of the environmental-planning process (Pava 1983). The major thrust in corporate office planning must be the integration of organizational objectives and the individual needs of the worker.

Conditions forcing change in corporate planning processes and user-needs research are numerous and far-reaching. The business environment has become more dynamic and more interdependent; business enterprises have increased in scale, complexity, and diversification. To cope with this, corporate organizations have become larger and temporarily organized around project groups rather than around role expectations of its members and the corporations' hierarchical structures. Organizational goals reflect

3

an increased concern for adaptation rather than for standard procedures (Beckhard 1969; Bennis 1969).

Workers have become better educated, have more job mobility, and are more professionally and technically oriented (Beckhard 1969). Concomitant changes in work values have also occurred: Workers are more intellectually committed to their jobs and professional/peer groups, are less committed to the work organization and traditions, and demand more involvement and participation in the decision-making process (Bennis 1969). Also, tasks have become more technical, complicated, and unstructured and require more collaboration and group problem solving. Worker motivation has become the product of self-actualization and satisfaction with meaningful tasks, as well as the product of monetary reward (Kahn 1973). Social structure has developed around short, intense relationships with the worker's immediate, but temporary, work group within an ambiguous and unstructured organizational framework (Bennis 1969). Because of these changes, corporations and employees have become more concerned with the quality of work life, which includes, in part, the quality of the office environment (Ford 1976).

Environmental planning was simple for yesterday's mechanistic, bureaucratic organizations in a stable business environment with an other-directed work force. It was based on the development of static solutions that would fulfill the organization's needs. User-needs research consisted of an articulation of the management's aims for the facility and an understanding of the organization's hierarchical structure, with its division of labor and the resultant task requirements. This research was conducted with an impersonal quality and with concern only for the scientific management and human-engineering aspects of a work organization's efficiency (Bach 1972). Only occasionally would an organization be more humanistic and consult its employees on their preferences for particular solutions.

Planning for today's adaptive, organic organizations in a dynamic business environment with an inner-directed population requires that user-needs research go beyond the cataloging of management goals and procedures and the recording of worker preferences. Corporate environmental design must also include an in-depth analysis of the corporation as a social organization, the behavior of the individuals within it, and the physical setting that houses it—a total system of interrelated parts.

• THE CORPORATION AS A SOCIAL ORGANIZATION

A corporation is a complex social organization consisting of a system of structural, functional, and social components. Within this system, people behave in an interrelated fashion according to the norms, values, and roles that are formed by the goals of the organization and accepted by its members. A social organization reduces the variability of human behavior by three types of pressures: task requirements in relation to satisfying an individual's needs; demands arising from shared values and expectations; and reinforcement of accepted rules (Katz and Kahn 1966). The nature of an organization is defined and its boundaries are determined by the relationships and patterns of behavior involved in the process of achieving its goals (Kahn 1969).

An organization establishes sets of roles by which its members perform organizational tasks and relate to each other. These sets of role behaviors formalize the expected interdependent behavior of the members and represent standardized forms of activity (Katz and Kahn 1966). Most members of social organizations have strongly held expectations about their role set and the role set of others, which includes the physical setting in which the role behavior is to take place. Overtly, they will attempt to communicate their expectations of the roles to be played and will exert pressures upon the individuals involved to conform to this role set, exhibiting stress if these expectations fail to be met (Katz and Kahn 1966). To ensure that these role behaviors are established, a task-oriented organization will exert influence on the behavior of the individual members by dividing the work among them, establishing standard practices and systems of authority, providing channels of communications, and training new members (Simon 1945). By doing so, the organization develops a set of norms that makes explicit the forms of behavior considered appropriate for its members and a set of values that rationalizes these normative requirements. Major determinants of an organization's system of norms are the type of activity in which the corporation is involved (Katz and Kahn 1966) and the form of its corporate culture (Deal and Kennedy 1982).

By instituting a normative pattern of behavior to achieve its goals and establishing a value system that supports its goals, the organization begins to develop a culture that provides a sense of common meaning and purpose to its members. Through the control of the tempo of its activities, the interaction among its members, the training of new members, and rewards, the organization's culture is reinforced and becomes the means by which it communicates its essential nature to outsiders and insiders. In this way, the organization defines its relationship to the contextual environment in which it exists. A corporation's culture creates its corporate identity by institutionalizing the appropriate patterns of behavior, establishing a belief system that ties the employees to the company, and defining the corporation within its business environment. The purpose of the organization's culture is to symbolize the company to the outside world, preserve what makes the company special, set a standard of performance, and motivate its employees (Deal and Kennedy 1982).

Within the boundaries of the corporation, behavior occurs that is not involved with organizational context but nevertheless exerts some influence on the design of the physical environment. This includes the social behavior of secondary organizations, informal groups, and individuals. Because members of the primary organization may belong to other organizations, such as professional, special interest, or recreational groups, these over-lapping secondary organizations become an adjunct component of the corporate environment. Another level of behavior within this category involves those social interactions that are not directly concerned with the output of the organization. Since people do not devote their entire fund of energy to the pursuit of organizational goals, the environment must allow them to pursue behaviors other than those required in task performance. Finally, people will also attempt to organize their environment to provide freedom in choosing their individual patterns of behavior (Proshansky, Ittleson, and Rivlin 1970). These extra-organizational behaviors must be identified and analyzed as part of the whole environmental system.

♦ ORGANIZATIONAL ACTIVITY SYSTEMS

Because of the purposeful and goal-directed nature of an organization, it must divide its activities into a set of specialized units to achieve optimum efficiency. In terms of the corporation, these subsystems include departments, work groups, and task forces. To maintain its equilibrium and control the outcome of its activities, the organization develops both formal and informal processes that link these subunits together. These processes become the matrix of the activity system by forming the trans-actional environment for each of the subunits (Galbraith 1973). The organizational processes provide the flows of work, the paths of communication, the means of collaboration, the channels of authority, and the methods of coordination that enable the organization to meet its goals. In old bureaucratic business organizations, the corporation could be described by its static hierarchical structure. In light of today's changing demands and the needs for adaptation, organizational description must consider the dynamic nature of the organizational process (Beckhard 1969).

The organization determines its environment by controlling the activities taking place within its boundaries by distributing activities spatially and by prescribing the regions in which these activities are to take place. It also controls behavior by segregating one behavior from another and by establishing normative behavior for each setting. Organizations set the rhythm and the tempo with which activities take place and control the time sequence of these activities (Hawley 1950).

These ecological processes construct the activity system of the organization both temporally and spatially. An activity system develops when a behavioral unit such as an organization, a social group, or an individual exhibits regularities in the content and ordering of its activities in time and space (Chapin and Brail 1969). The activity system consists of those discrete behavioral episodes that have meaning because they are purposeful to the organization and are influenced by environmental constraints. Because an organization locates its activity system spatially and temporally, ongoing behavioral patterns can be studied in relation to their physical setting. This relationship between behavior and its setting can be studied further by analyzing its dynamic structure and identifying characteristic behavioral patterns.

Since behavioral patterns must be compatible with, and are closely related to, the physical place in which they occur, components of that physical setting should be studied in relation to their effect on these behavioral patterns. This active and continuing process in which the components of both the physical and the behavior systems are defining and being defined by each other establishes a meaningful system of feedback between these environmental elements. It is in this manner that the physical environment supports the organizational system as well as the patterned behavior of its members.

THE RELATIONSHIP BETWEEN BEHAVIOR AND THE ENVIRONMENT

The complex relationship between the built environment and human behavior confounds both the designer who creates it and the behavioral scientist who studies it. Since both the *deterministic* view that behavior is completely controlled by the layout of the physical environment and the *free-will* position that behavior exists without reference to the physical setting have been equally refuted, the question is not so much whether behavior is influenced by the environment, but to what degree. Psychologist Roger Barker states that the ecological environment does not demand behavior but, rather, permits some behavioral patterns to take place, supports certain activities, and restricts others from taking place (Barker 1968). The environment does so by acting in an instrumental fashion, providing the facilities and space for the users to achieve their goals; in a mediational role, interceding with the users and causing them to adapt their behavior to the setting; and in a symbolic mode, providing a series of messages that convey information about the appropriate form of behavior. As sociologist Herbert Gans points out, the designer can provide only a potential environment permitting possibilities and clues for behavior; the effective environment is the totality of all significant varieties of behavior, including how people perceive and adapt the environment to their use (Gans 1968).

The physical setting functions in three ways to support behavior. First, it provides the physical elements required to sustain the physical states necessary for an individual to satisfy his or her needs. These elements are light, heat, sound, sanitation, firmness of surface, and smell. The physical setting can be conceived as the man-made container of behavior, which acts as the filter between people and the natural environment. Second, the physical environment goes beyond containment to provide physical facilities and spatial arrangements that aid specific activity patterns and hinder others. Part of this function is the capability of the built environment to facilitate the formation of social groupings, to ease communication and movement, and to provide desired levels of privacy. The variables of this function are the dimensional and geometrical properties of the setting, the spatial relationships between spaces, the formal arrangements within the spaces, and the components available within the spaces. The final functional aspect of the built environment is that it generates and maintains mental and emotional states necessary for need satisfaction by fulfilling symbolic, aesthetic, and ambient functions. The ambience of the setting refers to overall expressive qualities that project an emotional feeling. This communication function works by expressing self-images, cultural symbols, and aesthetic concepts of the users, clients, and designers.

The relationship between physical setting and behavior is modified by three elements: the goal structure of the organization, the values of the workers, and the demands of the future. The corporation's objectives and goals must be understood to provide the administrative context for the solution. Before the human context for the solution can be established, there must be a humanistic interpretation of the workers' values and needs. Finally, the future demands placed on an organization by its external environment must be filtered through the beliefs of the corporate culture to establish the symbolic context of the solution. Three major categories of office-planning problems can be distilled through this systems analysis: organizational effectiveness, organizational destiny, and quality of work life.

ORGANIZATIONAL EFFECTIVENESS

Problems of organizational effectiveness are those involved with achieving the organization's mission and are usually concerned with work activities, intergroup processes, and communication patterns. Analysis of these problems investigates the workers' behavior in accomplishing their organizational tasks. The procedure for such analysis can be outlined as follows (Moleski 1973). The work organization is divided into a system of activity sites in which specific extraindividual, organizational activities take place and are tied together by a matrix of organizational processes. These sites can be analyzed by their recurrent patterns of behavior, their sociophysical performance characteristics, or their physical structures. Based on this approach, a set of genotypical office function descriptions has been developed that simplifies the analysis and generation of design criteria. For the corporations that the Environmental Research Group (ERG) has studied, six categories have evolved: executive, operations, planning, administrative, production, and service.

Office Functions

Each of the above-mentioned categories has its own particular spatial, organizational, and physical requirements. The executive group serves the function of managing the organization and establishing the thrust of the organization. The operations groups carry out the activities that produce the corporation's product or service; depending upon the corporation, functions in this group may include manufacturing, construction, or engineering. The planning groups perform the problem-solving and tactical operations that provide information for the continued operation of the system; functions in this category may include marketing, corporate planning, corporate training, and research. The administrative groups record and store information for the organization; functions that fall within this category may be accounting, human resources, auditing, and purchasing. The production groups are involved with the processing of material that is used by other groups; functions that could be included are information processing and records management. The service groups provide support to the other groups; this may be building services, printing, security, communications, or food services.

Corporate Activity Systems

The behavior of activity sites can be analyzed along three components: task-related, social, and organizational behaviors. Task-related descriptors include those behavioral components created by a work group's performance. A simple, concise definition of the activity taking place gives a very general indication of the ongoing behavior within its activity site and can be further delineated by characteristics of the task, including the level of physical activity, the intensity of problem solving, the amount of repetition, and level of selective attention required to perform the task.

The social considerations of the activity system describe those elements that tie individual members within the activity site together into social groups, forming the first level of the social structure of the organization. These components include the level of explicit rules and formalized roles that define the interdependent behaviors, the characteristics of task-related interactions, the exercise of authority, and the social focus of the group.

Organizational considerations are those components that describe how the organization controls behavior. These descriptors include the value system that the leaders hold, behavioral norms, the outcome of the group's work in relationship to the primary product of the corporation, how members are rewarded for their task performance, and the management style of the corporation.

The sociophysical characteristics of these activity sites are described by concepts that have both physical and social connotations. These performance elements serve as a means to translate the behavioral requirements into a description of the supportive physical environment. Sociophysical scales include privacy, social focus, proximity, accessibility, interference, structure, stimulation, clarity, interdependence, and constancy factors.

Analysis of the physical structure of the activity sites should explore systematically alternatives that can achieve the required site performance to support the behavior of the workers. The physical environment is described by four general categories: spatial organization, environmental components, environmental attributes, and perceptual qualities. The spatial organization category describes the large-scale elements that control the overall environmental envelope, such as the size and scale of the spaces, the visibility of activities in the space, and the boundaries and configurations of the space. The environmental components are those smaller-scale elements that occupy space; these descriptors include the arrangement of furniture and screens, the organization of work areas, the control of circulation and traffic, and the location of individuals. The environmental attributes are those elements that give the activity site its character and mode; these include lighting, temperature, color, materials, and acoustics. The perceptual elements are those characteristics of the site that encode it and transmit messages to the users; the image of setting is conveyed by symbols and signs, visual dynamics of spatial form, and organizational cues.

Corporate Processes

Since an organization divides itself into functional subsystems and distributes activities within its boundaries, the organizational environment consists of a myriad of activity sites linked together by various ties of communications, work flows, roles, and authority systems. The type of links existing between activity sites and the strength of these links is a function of the type of activity that takes place within the sites. Some linkages are networks that span the entire organization, whereas others will only connect several sites together. Linkages can be analyzed in terms of character and strength, giving each a weighting that will establish the geographic distribution of the activity sites across the organization.

The most common linkage is the communication network, which ties one site to another by the flow of information required to perform the task of that site. These networks are usually established across the organization in relation to its character and the nature of the activities. Two types of communication networks exist within a corporate environment: a formal one, which is defined by organizational policy; and an informal one, which develops outside that policy.

The performance characteristics of some activity systems require that other forms of connection take place between sites. One classification is the functional connections of work flow, material flow, and paper flow. In a situation where the activity is part of a longer ongoing system, or uses material that is produced within another site, or passes a large volume of work to other sites, the most important locational criterion is the ease with which the work material flows between sites. Another classification is the human process of collaboration and group problem solving; this occurs when the activity system requires that people from different organizational components form project teams to work on a single project or task forces to provide expertise to the management. The most important locational criterion for these connections is the ability to come together and share information, insights, and experience. The location of other activity sites may be based on status because organizational values may deemphasize functional concerns and emphasize symbolic meanings. In order to increase the status of an activity site to reach some organizational objectives, it can be located within the perceptual sphere of a high-status site so that it will share its perceptual identity. In addition, activity sites can be connected by power networks generated by the hierarchical organizational structure.

The final means of locating activity sites within the organizational territory is according to compatibility of activities, physical settings, or populations. This category of linkage operates when there are no other criteria to locate sites. It is also used to modify the strength of other connections. Two sites may have a communication requirement that represents a tie between them; however, if the activity patterns are incompatible, some dysfunction may result if this is not taken into consideration.

ORGANIZATIONAL DESTINY

Within the second problem area of corporate office design, the concern with organizational destiny, two key planning issues have emerged: predictions of future development and identification with the organization.

Both require the complete understanding of the organization's objectives, culture, and the conditions facing its long-range planning.

Growth and Aspiration

An analysis of problems of organizational destiny involves the study of growth predictions, adaptation needs, and organizational revitalization. Problems of growth can be analyzed through the use of critical path methods in conjunction with mathematical projections and trend analysis. Since the organization's development is determined by the conditions affecting its nature, the solution to the problems of adaptation and revitalization can be predicted through the analysis of the corporation's long-range and strategic planning, its business environment, technological forecast, and economic and social predictions. To simplify strategic planning and forecasting for organizational growth and change, the complexity of data can be reduced without losing its reliability by selecting and examining key variables in the data to serve as representatives of the others, identifying a relatively small number of significant change indicators, and establishing recurring patterns of change. It must be understood that the more future planning and forecasting move from the current temporal base line, the more uncertain and hypothetical the predictions become. Since planning for growth and change can only make use of correspondence between current and past events, it is important to include the potential of new factors in the forecasting and planning method.

Corporate Culture and Identity

The second element of the destiny analysis concerns how people identify with the organization and its goals. An organization communicates messages about its character and values to both its staff and the public through the design of its physical setting. The symbolic qualities of the environment go beyond the placement of the firm's logo across the building as part of a corporate identity program. The choice of office layout, planning concepts, spatial organization, and environmental design style all contribute to the organization's identity and the individual's perception of his or her place within the organization. Problems in this sector are created by the complexity and diversity of roles that face individual members and the ambiguous, temporary structure of the corporations; these are directly related to the physical environment through symbolic properties that communicate information about the social structure of the organization.

Misunderstanding the symbolic qualities of the environment, disregarding the users' experiences with and interpretations of symbols, and placing emphasis on currently fashionable images of office design can cause a number of identity problems. First, the selection of an office planning system such as open-office landscaping without reference to the organizational climate may foster a perception of the organization as being unconcerned with individual needs and a perception of lost status by those people formerly in private offices. The anonymous and impersonal visual character of modern design can create a cold and dehumanized image of the organization. The use of a current fashion without consideration for the organization's culture may create a loss of identity with the organization and its efforts.

The problems in planning or designing environments that support the corporate culture are more difficult to solve because they deal with "soft" issues rather than the "hard" concerns of organizational effectiveness. This results from the undefined nature of corporate cultures, the elusive descriptions of corporate value systems, and the pervasive quality of environmental symbols. Analysis of the corporate culture with its concomitant value system requires the investigation of the organization's social structure and the corporation's business environment.

Analysis of the cultural structure should examine the historical development of the firm, the values and beliefs that hold the corporation together, and the means by which these are communicated to new members. Historical development encompasses how the organization was formed and identifies the important elements of its identity; descriptors of this level of analysis include the size of the firm, its stage of development, its form of organizational structure, and the driving force of its development (Tregoe and Zimmerman 1980).

The value system of the organization provides control of its members' behavior and establishes standards by which success can be achieved. The value system at this level should be analyzed along five dimensions: the style of management, the reward system, the beliefs about business conduct, and the presence of informal social structures. The manner by which the organization organizes itself communicates its values to its members. Analysis should examine the degree of formalization of the social structure, including the role system, the division of labor, communications, and collaboration.

The greatest influence in shaping the corporate culture is how the firm fits into the reality of its marketplace (Deal and Kennedy 1982). The products a company offers, the markets it serves, the technology it employs, the method of sales it uses, the competition it faces, the natural resources it consumes—all describe the corporation's business environment. The manner by which the corporation elects to deal with these issues forms a large component of its cultural system and provides the framework for its values and beliefs.

To be successful, the corporation must communicate its culture to its workers, its customers, and its competitors. The physical environment forms an important aspect of the development of a strong culture. Its spatial organization, environmental components, environmental attributes, and perceptual qualities all form a symbolic system that conveys more information about the culture of the firm than does the corporate logo. The layout of offices, through its spatial configurations, will express information about how the management views the workers and the tasks they perform and what is important to the organization. The size, materials, number of environmental components, character of lighting, control of environmental systems, and level of sound will convey messages about status and recognition of the occupants within that space as well. The incorporation of visual symbols, including the corporate products, logo, photographs of corporate heros and scenes of historic company endeavors, furniture style, and artwork, add the final level of meaning to environment. The selection of design features must be consistent with the culture of the company and should be appropriate to the messages it wants to convey.

The analysis should not only include an examination of the management's concept of the corporate culture and business concerns, but also investigate how the staff and public view the organization, because their perception of the corporate image is important. To communicate an image, the sender of the message must understand the visual language of those receiving it. Therefore, the analysis has to include a knowledge of what meanings various users, that is, staff, management, investors, consumers, and the public, give to environmental design elements. An organization should spend as much attention on developing the spatial image of its facilities as it does on creating its logo and advertising slogans.

THE QUALITY OF THE WORK ENVIRONMENT

Solutions to the first two categories of office design problems can be derived easily through an analysis of the organization and the conditions that determine its form. But these solutions are incomplete, solving only the environmental needs of the organization, not the human needs of the individual within it. In fact, these solutions often raise problems that generate dissatisfaction, alienation, and stagnation. For example, the staff must learn to live with ambiguity and adaptation, more intense temporary social relationships, and must become self-directed.

When viewed in terms of the life cycle of a corporate office environment, the importance of solving the problems of human development and satisfaction becomes critical. When a cost analysis is done over the 30-year life of a building, the building system itself costs 2% of the money spent, maintenance costs 7%, and salaries and benefits to the staff consume over 90%. The inconspicuous cost of a building not conforming to the human values of the user is much greater than the conspicuous cost of the building construction.

Solutions to the problems of quality of the work environment require response to two issues: first, the development of planning concepts that relate managerial behavior and environmental design to the humanistic interpretation of human needs; and second, a redefinition of user-needs studies and their relationship to the environmental planning process. To achieve these goals, the environmental needs of the people must be understood.

Environmental Needs

The complexity of human needs and the processes that people follow to satisfy them have some very important implications to design. Because of the complexity and diversity of needs, office design must go beyond solutions for the so-called physiological and task needs and provide for more complex social and psychological needs. Both needs and the manner in which they are satisfied are the product of the person and the society of which the person is a member. Needs are diverse and complex—so much so, that endless lists of environmental needs based on worker behavior could be drawn up.

To be able to develop buildings that fit the needs of the occupants, some form of classification structure must be developed. Psychologist Abraham Maslow presented a very useful model that classified not only needs but also the manner in which they are satisfied (Maslow 1943). He proposed a hierarchical structure of needs, the basis of which is that lower-order (more basic) needs must be fulfilled before higher-order (more complex) needs. As the lower-order needs become satisfied, the higher-order needs become salient. What this means is that only after a person finds a secure shelter will he or she be concerned with higher-order needs of belonging and establishing identity. The structure, in the order of the lowest level to the highest, is as follows: physiological needs to carry out bodily functions; safety needs, such as security and protection from physical and psychological harm; belonging and love needs, which concern being a member of a group; esteem needs, or those desires of a person to be held in high evaluation by self and others; actualization needs, which represent the desire to achieve one's full potential; and aesthetic and cognitive needs, which give sensory and nonfunctional pleasure to the individual, such as a beautiful place in which to work.

Environmental needs can be given priorities according to Maslow's hierarchy. Physiological needs could include the need for shelter, sensory stimulation, and special accommodation for the handicapped. Safety needs include personal territory, defensible and personal space, and privacy for solitude. Belonging needs, when taken in an environmental context, refer to such needs as privacy for intimacy, maintaining social interaction, and establishing group identity and community. Esteem needs are the expression of self-identity and status through symbols. Self-actualization needs involve personalization and the freedom of choice in determining behavior and environment. Aesthetic and cognitive needs refer to intellectual understanding of environmental structure and beauty. Obviously, the needs listed are very general. To be useful, they require further definition.

Privacy, for example, is not a simple response to a single need level; it may be a need for security from unwanted intrusion, or for belonging in terms of intimacy, or for the esteem of holding private territory, or actualization for pursuing one's own creative goals. The behavioral variables that define privacy can also be derived from individual, group, and cultural variations of behavior. Privacy can be defined by the person's ability to filter out unwanted stimuli, the person's concepts of what constitutes privacy, the social context in which the person is involved, the norms of the culture, and the situation in which the person finds himself or herself. The role of the physical environment in supporting privacy can be achieved by isolating the person, by controlling stimuli, by structuring space to limit the activity that can take place, and by presenting symbols that communicate the occupant's desire for privacy.

The thorniest problem facing designers is one of needs versus desires. A person transacts with the environment in two ways: experientially and mentally. Experientially, a person, through behavior, learns the reality of setting and whether it supports behavior and satisfies needs. Mentally, a person thinks how the environment will accommodate needs and what the important facets of the environment are in need satisfaction. The environment's ability to facilitate or impede the efforts of a person to reach a goal has actual properties that exist in reality as well as perceived properties that are assigned by the person. It is, therefore, important to consider that a worker may be motivated by personal preference rather than by homeostatic needs. For example, a person may feel that it is important to have an office that expresses a certain symbolic image rather than one that performs optimum physical functions. Need satisfaction is largely determined by three factors: the strength of the need and intensity of gratification; the socialized behavior patterns in conjunction with the person's previous experience of need gratification; and perceived importance of the need.

Satisfying the functional and aesthetic needs of a diverse set of people is extremely difficult and the assumption that the environment can be planned as a closed system that is frozen at the time of design conception is erroneous. Users change with time, new behavioral repertories develop, new activity patterns are introduced, and the values of the work groups or organization shift. To be successful, the environment must be conceived as being in a constant state of adaptation to permit the maximum freedom of choice of desired behavioral patterns and to order the setting to support these patterns; it must also have the potential for the expression of the personal identity of future users as well as current ones.

Comfort Versus Development

Fitting the environment to the needs of the users presents another problem. The architect has the choice of creating environments that are familiar and reflect the behavioral ecology of the user population or of designing environments that are new and reflect a challenge for improvement. It must be noted that not all adaptive behavior has a negative effect on the person: Learning, for example, is a form of positive adaptive behavior. The designer must ascertain whether the environment should be planned to achieve the maximum comfort or to achieve maximum development for the users. Psychologist M. Powell Lawton has developed a concept of environmental competence, which is "the ability that enables an individual to function" (Lawton and Nahemow 1973, 25). He uses this concept in conjunction with environmental press, which includes "those aspects of the environment that act in concert with a personal need to evoke behavior by the individual" (Lawton and Nahemow 1973, 26), to investigate the fit of the environment. There is a varying level of adaptation in which the competence of the person is equal to the press of the environment. If the person has moderately more competence than the environment has press, the person will be comfortable and will experience positive affect and positive adaptation. If the environment has moderately more press than the person has competence, then the person will be challenged to develop new behavior responses and to increase the level of performance. However, if the environment has too much press or too little press in relationship to the user's competence, negative affective and maladaptive behavioral situations are created, thereby producing stress or atrophy within the user. The goals of the corporation in conjunction with the nature of its culture will establish whether the design should compel the workers to adapt to the new office environment (such as office landscaping) or allow the workers to retain familiar work habits. However, the designer should ensure that proposed solutions are within the behavioral experience of the users or near enough to that experience so that they can recognize the solution and not be overwhelmed by the environment.

Social Enrichment

To solve the problems generated by short, intense social relationships within temporary work groups, by the lack of individual identity in the larger corporate organizations, by the lack of enduring social contacts among members of the organization, and by a stronger orientation to outside professional groups than to the work organization, office planning must socially integrate the individual with fellow workers. These problems, coupled with managerial programs such as job enrichment, job nesting, and work modules (Ford 1976), force the physical planning for work groups to concentrate on the needs, dynamics, and character of small-group relationships. This planning concept seeks to provide a sociopetal focus (a means to draw people together) to these groups in order to maintain required social contact between members, give positive feelings about belonging to a small group, and provide more efficient exchanges of information in problem-solving activities.

Personalization

Another planning issue results from the problems caused by the ambiguity of the organizational environment and the worker's temporary location within it, coupled with the worker's need for a pleasurable environment. Corporate office design must consider appropriate means by which a worker may personalize the work environment, communicate an expression of self, and indicate his or her position in the organization. Since workers maintain multiple membership and engage in extra-organizational social activities, consideration should be given to providing space in which chance, informal, social contacts can be made. This arrangement provides an additional benefit to organizational efficiency by creating the potential for workers to exchange task-related information with people outside their immediate work environment.

Although these concepts of small-group planning, personalization of work environments, and extra-organizational social spaces solve certain aspects of the problems of the quality of the work environment, they do not solve the major problem of fitting the environment to the individual's personal needs. To accomplish this, the environmental planning process must be restructured to provide a transactive exchange between the user, the designer, and the space.

Several approaches have been developed to respond to these problems of fit between personality and the corporate environment. The first of these approaches involves the analysis of the individual personalities to form a set of criteria by which the environment can be structured. Since organizational requirements force individuals to move about and work groups to restructure, this type of planning develops only short-range satisfaction and does not appear to be useful for realistic planning of large-scale organizations.

A more useful general approach is the analysis and generation of an organizational personality profile (Argyris 1954) and the development of the environment to meet the needs ascribed to this corporate personality. The question of what happens to those workers who do not fit within this personality construct arises, since the complexity of today's organizations and their diverse activities include a myriad of personalities.

A third approach appears to be far more useful and significant. This is the procedure of permitting the user to have the freedom of choice. This means that the user determines what behavioral pattern or work style should be adopted to reach an objective. Part of this determination involves being able to structure the physical setting to support that behavior pattern. The design of an environment must allow the user options and must be transactive with the user's needs.

User-needs analysis of an office setting is a multistep process, involving specification of the range of options open to the user and the continuous evaluation of environmental changes and resulting behavior changes. Unfortunately, office situations that permit change are not used to their full potential to create high-quality work environments. This occurs for several reasons. First, management control of the environment may prohibit the workers from manipulating the environment; second, designers may inhibit significant changes to the environment by design; and third, users, because of their lack of experience in environmental manipulation, may not recognize alternative solutions. This blindness to environmental manipulation illustrates the reason mere cataloging of user preferences is not an adequate indication of user needs. To increase the competence of the user to articulate his or her environmental needs, there must be considerably more involvement of workers in shaping their environments. Competence or growth is developed by learning from experience, storing relevant knowledge, acquiring and using feedback on performance and manipulation, and realizing that one can direct one's own destiny.

SUMMARY

A more effective organizational environment can be planned if obstructions to work performance, such as the poor location of critical materials and information, noise and interference, and poor lighting and ventilation are identified and designed out of the activity system. This identification involves viewing the work environment as a system of interrelated activity sites in which task and social behaviors take place within an organizational context. These behaviors are supported by the sociophysical environment created by the environment's own spatial configuration, arrangement of furniture and equipment, environmental ambience, and symbolic properties. To be completely effective, the office planner has to respond to problems of organizational destiny by designing the physical environment to meet its future activities, its growth patterns, and its culture. For an organization to be effective, its physical image should enable the staff to identify with the organization and view it as being sympathetic to their needs.

However, only when users have the opportunity to choose their own patterns of behavior, to organize their physical environment, and to realize the effects of their actions will the design of the office environment be able to satisfy the problems involved in satisfaction and development.

As organizational psychologist Fred I. Steele (1973) has pointed out, the planning process by which the environment is determined has a more powerful influence on employee satisfaction than perhaps the setting itself. Warren Bennis states: "What I think most people in institutions really want and what status, money, and power serve as currency for is affection, acceptance, a belief in their growth, and esteem. I think you can create changes and innovations if you succeed in not losing the affection for the people who, on the face of it, seem to be losing it" (Bennis 1971, 11).

REFERENCES

Ackoff, R. L. 1981. *Creating the corporate future: Plan or be planned for*. New York: John Wiley & Sons.

Argyris, C. 1954. *Organization of a bank*. New Haven, CT: Labor and Management Center, Yale University.

Bach, F. W. 1972. Analysis of communications and work flow. In Carl Heyel (Ed.), *Handbook of modern office management and administrative services*. New York: McGraw-Hill.

Barker, R. 1968. *Ecological psychology*. Palo Alto, CA: Stanford University Press.

Beckhard, R. 1969. *Organizational development: Strategies and models*. Reading, MA: Addison-Wesley.

Bennis, W. G. 1971. Everything you always wanted to know about change. *Environment/ Planning and Design* (Summer): 4–11.

Bennis, W. G. 1969. *Organizational development: Its nature, origins, and process*. Reading, MA: Addison-Wesley.

Chapin, W., and F. S. and R. K. Brail. 1969. Human activity systems in metropolitan United States. *Environment and Behavior* 1(2): 107–130.

Deal, T. E., and A. A. Kennedy. 1982. *Corporate culture: The rites and rituals of corporate life*. Reading, MA: Addison-Wesley.
Ford, R.N. 1976. Job enrichment: Lessons for AT&T. *Harvard Business Review* 54: 96–106.
Gans, H. J. 1968. The potential environment and the effective environment. In H.J. Gans (Ed.), *People and plans*. New York: Basic Books.
Galbraith, J. 1973. *Designing complex organizations*. Reading, MA: Addison-Wesley.
Hawley, A. H. 1950. *Human ecology: A theory of community structure*. New York: Ronald Press.
Kahn, R. L. 1973. The work module: A tonic for lunchpail lassitude. *Psychology Today* (February): 35.
Kahn, R. L., D. M. Wolfe, J. D. Snoek, and R. A. Rosenthal. 1964. *Organizational stress: Studies in role conflict and ambiguity*. New York: John Wiley & Sons.
Katz, D., and R. Khan. 1966. *The social psychology of organizations*. New York: John Wiley & Sons.
Lawton, M. P., and L. Nahemow. 1973. Towards an ecological theory of adaption and aging. In W. F. Preiser (Ed.), *Environmental design research, Vol. 1, Selected Papers*. Stroudsburg, PA: Dowden, Hutchinson and Ross.
Maslow, A. H. 1943. A Theory of Human Motivation. *Psychological Review*, pp. 370–98.
Moleski, W. H. 1973. Behavioral analysis and environmental programming for offices. In J. T. Lang (Ed.), *Designing for human behavior*. Stroudsburg, PA: Dowden, Hutchinson and Ross.
Pava, C. 1983. *Managing New Office Technology*. New York: The Free Press.
Proshansky, H., W. Ittleson, and L. Rivlin. 1970. The influences of the environment on behavior: Some basic assumptions. In H. Proshansky, W. Ittleson, and L. Rivlin (Eds.), *Environmental psychology: Man and his physical setting*. New York: Holt, Rinehart & Winston.
Simon, H. A. 1945. *Administrative behavior*. New York: The Free Press.
Steele, F. I. 1973. *Physical settings and organization development*. Reading, MA: Addison-Wesley.
Tregoe, B. B., and J. W. Zimmerman. 1980. *Top management strategy*. New York: Simon & Schuster.

Planning and Programming Offices: Determining User Requirements

GERALD DAVIS
Harbinger Group Inc.
Norwalk, Connecticut

FRANÇOISE SZIGETI
Institute for User Studies
Norwalk, Connecticut

In recent decades, it has become progressively more difficult to establish performance requirements for the physical setting for office work. The process of planning, programming, designing, and construction of physical environments has been increasing in complexity (Glover 1976). The introduction of many new building materials and construction methods has had unforeseen consequences, sometimes resulting in degradation or failure of the building fabric (Mill, cited in Ellis 1981) and sometimes impairing the health of building occupants (National Research Council 1981).

At the same time, more stringent performance requirements for the office work environment result from the introduction of new technologies for office work. For instance, special illumination requirements follow the introduction of microfiche readers and video display terminals; similarly, open-plan layouts often require new forms of acoustic treatment if an acceptable degree of voice privacy is to be achieved.

A large proportion of office space has been constructed in the last two decades to accommodate the growing number of white-collar workers, but the occupants of such space are often dissatisfied with the way these spaces function and meet their needs. As a result, the effect of the office work environment on its users has recently become a focus of attention.

The problems affecting users of the office work environment fall into the following major categories: (1) those causing physical health hazards; (2) those affecting people's relationships to each other and to their environment; and (3) those that impede the work effectiveness of individuals and groups.

Problems in the design, management, and use of the physical setting for office work occur because the values and objectives for a project are rarely clearly stated and understood by all the participants; because the values and objectives for various participants in a project are often in conflict; and because the needs of the office users are often poorly defined.

There are many ways of uncovering and clarifying the values and objectives for a facility and the needs of its occupants, and for developing functional and technical performance requirements for the physical environment that will meet the needs of the users. There is no real consensus as to which way works best for each particular type of situation, but it is clear that no one approach, method, or process is appropriate for all types of office-planning situations. This chapter focuses on the determination of those performance requirements that directly affect the users of office work environments.

DETERMINING USER-ORIENTED DESIGN REQUIREMENTS

Sims (1978) discusses six methods for determining user-oriented design requirements. The first five (user characteristics, social functions, behavior circuit, behavior setting, and postoccupancy evaluation) rely mainly on appropriately trained technical specialists and professional programmers, with the users being involved only passively, or not at all. In the sixth method (various forms of user participation), users are directly involved in the process. For each of these six methods, Sims outlines basic steps and summarizes inherent strengths and difficulties. The degree of user involvement likely to occur in each method is shown in Table 3-1.

User Characteristics Method. Design requirements are derived from a detailed picture or profile of the expected users, including their behavioral patterns, environmental needs, vulnerabilities, and other characteristics. This method is particularly useful when planning general-purpose office space, before the specific occupants have been identified. It is the principal method used, explicitly or implicitly, by many developers of commercial office space.

Social Functions Method. In this method, one determines which characteristics of the physical environment would support or suppress specified

Table 3-1. User Involvement in Each of Sims' Six Methods

DEGREE OF USER INVOLVEMENT

Methods	Mainly Users[a]		Mainly Specialists[b]
	‹---------------------------------›		
User Characteristics	• =======		
Social Functions	• • • • • • • ============== • • • • • • • •		
Behavior Circuit	• • • • • • • ============== • • • • • • • •		
Behavior Setting	• • • • • • • ============== • • • • • • • •		
Postoccupancy Evaluation	• • • • • • • • • • =============		
User Participation	========== • • • • • • • • • • • • •		

a. With little involvement of specialists
b. With little involvement of users
• • • • •   Partial user involvement
====   Full user involvement

social/psychological/physiological functions, such as supporting friendship formation or suppressing vandalism. We have found this method to dominate in some office projects, such as for clients engaged in research and development who wish to facilitate interaction and discussion among research scientists, and for a university administration that wanted to provide student counseling facilities that would be seen as inviting and open, yet allow the student, once inside, to feel private and secure.

Behavior Circuit Method. Design requirements to support or discourage behavior at a particular setting are derived from systematic analysis of the predominant sequences or chains of overt behavior of individual users.

Behavior-Setting Method. Overt patterns of behavior within a setting or area are systematically disaggregated in this method. It is then possible to generate setting characteristics logically that will provide a specified level of support to the behaviors identified, using a checklist of environmental attributes.

(We have found these two last methods to have only limited use in the programming of offices, because of the large (and therefore expensive) amount of data gathering required and because we have never worked with an organization whose principal behavior circuits or behavior settings were expected to continue unchanged until move-in, much less to endure for an extended period in the future offices. Indeed, the very act of moving into new facilities typically creates so many unforeseen opportunities that substantial changes in the ways that people go about their work are inevitable, even when operating systems and work flows have been studied and planned in detail.)

Postoccupancy Evaluation[1]. In this method, the problems and assets of a particular physical environment are identified and analyzed; and programmatic data are gathered for later use when remodeling the environment, when planning for a new set of activities within the existing environment, or when refining the design of subsequent projects for the same organization. Although findings from one formal postoccupancy evaluation are rarely transferable directly to a project for a different organization, insights and inferences from the literature are useful in suggesting issues for consideration during planning and programming. For each of our assignments to program an office, we have conducted an assessment of existing facilities as one of the first tasks: In the 1960s, the assessment was treated as one component of the overall programming study; in recent years, these assessments have grown into formal evaluations, with special reports to senior management. Although these findings have usually been shared with the office workers, through presentations to them or to their union representatives, the findings have not been formally published because of management's typical desire to present the most positive public image. Firms that specialize in space planning and interior design of offices rarely conduct formal postoccupancy evaluations. They often work within a tightly competitive fee structure that forces them to limit evaluation of existing facilities to a walk-through, a few interviews, and, in some cases, an inventory of furniture, equipment, and telephones. Furthermore, their staff members usually lack the training and skills for investigations oriented to environment and behavior considerations.

User Participation.   Sims's sixth method differs from the others in that the users themselves determine objectives and establish programmatic requirements, although professional expert programmers and designers do contribute skills of group facilitation to the process. Sims uses a typology by Lynch (1971) to show the complications that may arise in this method when suitable conditions (users available, informed, and so on) are not present.

PROCESSES FOR PLANNING AND PROGRAMMING OFFICE FACILITIES

The overall process of creating physical environments is a composite of many other processes: approvals, strategic planning, programming (or briefing), procurement, design, construction, evaluation, and so on. Determining user-oriented requirements, which is a part of strategic planning and programming, is only one activity within this overall process.

The processes used in most office planning for determining user-oriented requirements in North America can be classified within a four-part typology, including self-help, joint, directed, and traditional. A major difference between these four kinds of processes, as shown in Table 3-2, is the degree of involvement of the users and of technical specialists and professional programmers. Another key difference, as noted below in the descriptions of each process and in Table 3-3, is that facilities administrators and line managers have different kinds of roles in each of the four processes.

Each of the six methods described by Sims may or may not be useful in a particular situation, depending on the process that is used for determining user-oriented requirements. Sims points out that these six methods are often complementary; that is, no one method will be wholly adequate and the weaknesses of one are often the strengths of another. As a general principle, multiple methods are recommended for environment and behavior research to avoid the biases inevitable in any one method of investigation, to enhance validity, to control for side effects, and to produce more usable results (Sommer and Sommer 1980, 7–10; Zeisel 1981, 228–229).

In our experience, the process of investigating and determining user-oriented requirements always necessitates the adoption of several methods. Although aspects of two or more methods are used on every project, one method usually dominates because of the particularities of each situation.

Table 3-4 contains our assessment of the likely use of the six methods identified by Sims for office planning when using the self-help, joint,

Table 3-2. User Involvement in Each of the Four Processes

DEGREE OF USER INVOLVEMENT

Process	Mainly Users[a]	Mainly Specialists[b]
	‹---›	
Self-help	============= • • • • • • • • • •	
Joint	• • • • =================== • • •	
Directed	• • • ============= • •	
Traditional	• • =============	

a. With little involvement of specialists
b. With little involvement of users
• • • • •   Partial user involvement
= = = =   Full user involvement

Table 3-3. Likely Roles for Planning and Programming of User Requirements for an Office Facility, Using Each of the Four Processes

Group	Traditional Process	Directed Process	Joint Process	Self-help Process
Staff and first-line supervisors of user groups	Respond with information only if asked	Respond with information only if asked	Delegates make main planning and programming decisions	Collaborate or inactive
Line and program managers of user groups	Request that facilities be provided, and respond with information when asked	Varies: May give direction or may only respond with information when asked	Grant mandate and resolve conflicts	Make main planning decisions
Corporate and line-planning groups	Provide overall planning context	Varies: May direct facilities planning and programming	May coordinate facilities planning and programming	Provide overall planning context
Administrators of facilities	Direct facilities planning and programming	Provide technical knowledge	Provide technical knowledge	Execute decisions
Facilities programmers and technical specialists	Provide facilities programming	Provide facilities planning and programming	Provide expertise and informed facilitation	Little or no involvement

directed, or traditional process. As explained below, each of these four processes may be more or less suitable for a particular situation, depending on such factors as how the organization is structured (Mintzberg 1979); the environmental competence (Steele 1973) of the various groups in an organization; the style of senior and middle managers (Fiedler and Chemers 1974; McGregor 1960; Steele 1975); the role of planners in staff and line groups; and the perceived effectiveness of the facilities administrators.

Self-help Process

Office planning is sometimes undertaken without outside participation by the unit that will occupy an office. A line manager may make the main planning decisions, perhaps delegating detailed layout to supervisors. Subordinate staff may collaborate, or may have little participation. The essential difference between this and the other processes is that professional experts, such as interior designers, space planners. programmers, technical

Table 3-4. Likely Use of the Various Methods for Generating User-oriented Requirements in an Office Planning Project

FOUR PLANNING PROCESSES

Methods[a]	Traditional	Directed	Joint	Self-help
User Characteristics	High	High	Moderate	Moderate
Social Functions	Low	Moderate	Low	Low
Behavior Circuit	Low	Low	–	–
Behavior Setting	Low	Low	–	–
Postoccupancy Evaluation	High	High	Moderate	Moderate
User Participation	Low	Moderate	High	High

a. Sims 1978

specialists, or facilities administrators, have little or no involvement until the main planning decisions have been made, the layout has been determined, and sketch drawings are complete in essentials and ready to be converted into working drawings and specifications. Only then is the plan presented to the facilities administrators who will manage construction and installation.

To be successful, this process requires that the users have access to information and self-help aids. It also assumes that they have a certain environmental competence (Steele 1973): that is, that they know their requirements; understand what is practicable and how it is likely to be planned and built; and that they can guide and monitor the work of technical specialists who carry out their instructions.

Self-help is nothing new. It goes back to the direct control most people used to have over their immediate surroundings, before the Industrial Revolution. It is analogous to the way that we observed farm buildings being built and remodeled in villages of Switzerland, France, and England before and after World War II. Farm families decided what was needed and what they could afford. When the main choices and budget had been set, they called in the carpenter or builder from their own or a nearby village to help them with construction and finish the woodwork and trim. Self-help continues as common practice in the older residential neighborhoods of North America, as home owners remodel and rehabilitate their homes, doing most of the work themselves.

This approach to planning office facilities does not require that an organization reorganize its facilities management staff, but it does require acceptance on the part of facilities administrators and initiative from line managers. The necessary environmental competence is not widespread among office managers and staff, but some organizations are working to remedy this. For instance, self-help guides can be prepared to teach line managers and staff how to make things better in the physical setting at work.

Joint Process

A form of Sims's (1978) sixth method, user participation (for example, Sanoff 1977, especially pp. 6–17; Davis 1978) is often applicable for office planning because the users, in most cases, are known and present, and often understand the needs and priorities relevant to their work environment. In practice, however, it has been unusual for the occupants of an office to be involved in decision making about their new offices and rare, indeed, for them to be involved in preparing the actual detailed layouts. There are many reasons for this: for example, the management style of the particular corporation or organization; a manager's lack of confidence in participatory or delegated decision making; the perception that consideration of the physical work environment does not influence effectiveness or profitability and, therefore, is insignificant; the need to follow preexisting union channels to obtain staff involvement; or the need to comply with guidelines of the public service or the corporation involved.

In the 1970s, drawing on experiences in many countries, a movement developed to enhance the quality and effectiveness of working life, in part by involving workers in decision making about aspects of their work and its context (Davis 1979; Davis and Cherns 1975; Trist 1973; Trist, Higgins, Murray, and Pollock 1963). Joint design of a new organization and its physical setting has been used for the planning of industrial facilities, such as oil refineries, meat-packing plants, and automobile factories. Joint planning for the physical work environment of an office is a subset of joint design for a total work environment.

In joint planning, the basic planning decisions and later the detailed planning are done by a coalition that includes not only technical experts such as architects, engineers, and space planners but also actual users, often acting as delegates of their work groups. The technical specialists and professional experts provide knowledge and experience and later execute the decisions of the coalition (which may be called the *joint planning group*).

A facilities programmer, or an organizational development specialist, may serve the group as *informed facilitator*. This role involves facilitating group process; ensuring not only that what a participant communicates is correctly heard, but also that the facts are technically valid and are understood; and helping the participants to apply principles of decision theory and design methodology (Wise 1979) to their decision making.

No technical specialist or professional expert has the authority to overrule the joint planning group, even within his or her area of expertise; instead, she or he must convince the joint planning group and abide by their decision.

In some situations, the joint planning process appears to offer substantial benefits to the organization and to the individual workers, as compared to the traditional planning process. Steele (1973, 91–92) emphasizes the value to the organization of having its staff develop skills in working together by using group processes to design their work settings. This can enhance people's awareness of their physical work environment, and can lead to a heightened sense of esprit de corps and personal effectiveness. Furthermore, staff members who have participated in the joint planning process are in fact exercising control over their environment and becoming environmentally competent (Steele 1973, 113–144).

The joint planning process can also be a component of an organizational development effort, such as the environmental change technology described by Conyne and Clack (1981, 117–149), who offer an environmentally based model of action research that builds upon several prior models. It involves a continuing flow of steps from initiation, through environmental assessment, change planning, change implementation, monitoring, modification, stabilization, to withdrawal. Conyne and Clack have broadened the meaning of the concept of environment to include organizational structure, characteristics of the setting and inhabitants, the social climate, and the reinforcement contingencies that exist in those settings. It is a conception that views human problems as located not exclusively in individuals or in their environments, but in the interaction between the two. Their concept of a *change agent* and a *change team* is congruent with the concept of a joint planning group described above.

Evaluations are needed of the joint planning process and the physical work environments that result from it. Our experience with joint planning for the office work environment for government employees has been consistent with Steele's assertions (Davis, Gray, and Szigeti 1981), and has resulted in plans significantly different from those that have been provided by design professionals. For instance, in a large open-plan office building, the designers had decided that main circulation routes should run along the windows so everyone would have access to a view to the outdoors while walking around, and that no middle managers or supervisors should have office space at the windows. The staff delegates reversed this and developed a plan that gave almost all subordinates and managers better access to a view, and moved all main circulation to the interior. This plan also saved space and provided a more "legible" environment, with group territories clearly defined and bounded.

We concur with Palmer's assessment (1981, 276) that the use of participatory processes will tend to increase. Among clients we have served, this kind of process has been endorsed by senior management and lower levels of staff, but has often been resisted by middle managers, particularly those with responsibility for buildings and facilities administration. This resistance at the middle levels is becoming recognized in the business press (for example, Burck 1981) and by researchers. Miller (1980) found that perception of personal and organizational effectiveness in decision making was affected by whether a supervisor or middle manager was a subordinate who had been allowed to participate or was a superior who had allowed such participation. When in a subordinate role to a higher authority, a supervisor was likely to view participation favorably, but a supervisor acting as manager of other subordinates did not.

Directed Process

Directed planning is a process in which an organization's corporate planners and operating managers direct activities such as strategic planning for facilities and functional programming. In response, the organization's facilities services group provides or commissions technical and design programming (Davis and Szigeti 1979), space planning and interior design, working drawings, specifications, and construction or remodeling.

The extent to which occupant managers and staff are interviewed, observed, and given questionnaires varies widely, depending on such factors as the preferred working methods of the programmers and planning/design consultants; the wishes of occupant management and of the facilities services group; and the amount of fee and elapsed time available for the work. A significant difference from joint planning is that the majority of occupant staff typically have minimal involvement in the process. An important difference between directed and traditional planning is that corporate planning for facilities is under the purview of the organization's corporate and operating managers, rather than under the facilities service group. In directed planning, it is the corporate and operating managers who lead the process and work with the line managers to define and set the user requirements for a facility.

We have found that this is another process that is gaining acceptance. For instance, one major bank is grouping its facilities and realty operations into a separate operating corporation, and is then providing special consulting services to corporate planners and operating managers to assist them in directing the planning and programming of the facilities for their groups.

Traditional Process

For the last several decades, there have been two archetypal situations for decision making about what the physical office environment should be: Professionals (programmers, architects, space planners, and/or interior designers) establish user requirements and develop layouts and designs; or a manager in the user groups sketches out what she or he wants and directs someone to "draw it up and make it happen."

In large organizations, the key decisions about what the users require and about design and cost have traditionally been made by only a few executives, who themselves have little involvement in the day-to-day activities of the majority of office workers (Bobrow 1974). If these executives expect to occupy space in the completed facility, they normally have offices with features and comforts not available to the majority of the occupants in the building; often, they do not occupy space in it at all. These executives are typically much less sensitive to the needs of the office workers than are the operating executives and staff who will occupy space about which decisions are required (Davis and Szigeti 1979).

When these decisions are made solely by a central services group, such as a facilities operations unit, or a plant engineering group, or a central government agency, then the pressures for inappropriate decisions are even more prevalent than when a few key senior executives are responsible. As noted previously, this happens because a facilities manager is rewarded for reducing the costs of facilities, or reducing energy consumption for building operations or the like, without incentive to consider explicitly effects on the whole organization. As a result, the overall operating costs or energy consumption of the organization may be increased or productivity reduced.

VARIABLES AFFECTING THE CHOICE OF PROCESS

In our experience, the most important variables affecting the choice of process adopted to determine user needs and requirements for an office facility are: (1) control of the decision-making process, and (2) size, complexity, and style of the organization.

Locus of Control of Decision Making about the Physical Office Environment

For a large group of occupants, and for smaller groups that are part of a complex organization, the processes used are usually different from those used in situations that do not involve large organizations and that, therefore, do not involve specialist facilities service units (Davis and Szigeti 1979).

At the present time, planning for a large organization usually requires authorizations and approvals from several levels of management; professional programmers, space planners, and/or interior designers are often engaged or are available in-house; either the organization or its professionals and technical specialists may set norms and standards for the amount of floor space allowed to each worker; and few, if any, of those who will actually work in the future facilities have significant involvement in the planning process. By contrast, in the planning of offices for a very small business with only one or two levels of supervision or management, all or most workers may have an opportunity to make their needs and wishes known, at least informally; and many of the workplaces may be tailored not only to the requirements of specific jobs, but also to the preferences of particular individuals.

As indicated in Table 3-5, if the group that will occupy a facility is itself fairly large or is part of a larger organization, then space planning and design are typically provided or obtained by a group specializing in the provision of facilities services. These specialist groups normally have broad responsibility for obtaining (building, leasing, or renting), managing, and servicing the physical office environment. Most managers and professional staff members of these service groups have a background in engineering, in interior design or architecture, or in financial management or real estate appraisal. In 20 years of professional practice, every one of our corporate, institutional, and government clients in Canada and the United States has conformed to this pattern.

Not only do the manager and staff of a group occupying office facilities have different backgrounds from the facilities service people responsible for providing office space in moderate-sized and large organizations, but they also have different objectives, values, incentives, and rewards with regard to office facilities.

For instance, people who will actually occupy a work environment tend to give highest priority to achieving organizational objectives; they are likely to make decisions about what features should be provided by assessing whether the cost of a particular feature can be justified because it will improve the effectiveness of their work group, or enhance the quality of working life, or support other management objectives.

Table 3-5. Provision of Planning and Design for Office Projects

PLANNING AND DESIGN PROVIDED BY

Approximate Group Size	*Overall Organization's Facilities Service Group*		*Occupants of the Space*	
Several Thousand	Typical		Rare	
500–1,000	Typical		Rare	
100–250	Typical		Occasional	
	Part of Larger Organization	*Independent Unit*	*Part of Larger Organization*	*Independent Unit*
40–70	Typical	Common	Rare	Common
15–35	Typical	Rare	Rare	Typical
2–12	Typical	Never	Occasional	Typical

Source: Based on a working paper by the authors prepared during 1976–78, as part of an assignment for Public Works Canada.

People in the specialist role of facilities manager or planner, on the other hand, generally do not occupy the office facilities under their purview and, therefore, are affected only indirectly by the characteristics of the physical environment that is provided. Instead, they usually earn rewards and promotion by controlling the overall costs of facilities and by ensuring compliance with organizational standards. Therefore, even though they nominally act as a service organization, they often function in the conflicting role of "corporate policeman," enforcing rules and seeking to cut costs. Also, they need to maintain effective continuing working relationships with the central service agency or with their space planning, design, and engineering consultants, with whom most share a common professional background and value system. Therefore, they frequently negotiate with occupant groups on behalf of their technical consultants, rather than representing the values and objectives of the users in negotiation with those consultants.

In our experience, decision makers who will occupy space in a proposed office facility (that is, operating managers), taken as a group, are much more receptive to giving high priority to environment-and-behavior factors (when they are adequately informed about them) than are managers of an organization's facilities services group. Even when a facilities manager expresses strong support for "humane" behavioral objectives, these objectives are still likely to be in conflict with the "policeman" part of his or her mandate and, therefore, to receive lower priority than such values as economy and efficiency.

Size, Complexity, and Style of Organization

Until the beginning of the 1980s, two major factors affecting the choice of process for office programming, space planning and design, and the role of the actual office occupants in decision making about their physical work environment were: the size of the group occupying an office, and whether the group was part of a larger organization. Although these factors will continue to have an impact on the way a project is implemented, it is becoming apparent that the factors affecting the choice of process are more and more varied.

Size and Complexity of the Organization to Which the Occupants Belong. Most large organizations have a separate facilities group, which establishes and controls formal standards and procedures for the procurement, allocation, and use of facilities. The facilities group often takes possession of the process—indeed, their mandate may be to do that. Typically, these groups either provide consultant specialists from their own staff or obtain outside consultants who then assist user groups. Either way, users are often prohibited from directly engaging consultants to assist them in programming or planning their work environments.

Size of the Occupant Groups. Managers are often less sensitive to the environmental needs of those workers with whom they have little contact than they would be for workers with whom they have frequent, face-to-face contact. Therefore, in small organizational units, the manager or decision maker is closer to the lower staff levels than in large groups and is more likely (or less unlikely) to make sensitive decisions that reflect actual user objectives and needs. The scope of planning for a large group also requires the intervention of more levels of management. A small relocation in which one small unit of a large organization is moved into an existing building may be arranged informally and quickly, with relatively few approvals required, whereas the complete rearrangement of a large corporate headquarters within its own building, following an organizational reshuffle, might involve all levels of management and the board of directors.

Complexity of the Approvals Process. The more levels of management through which a decision must be passed in order to get final approval, the more opportunities for frustration and estrangement between users and deciders. Each approver has his or her own criteria and objectives, which may be quite different from those of the users. Indeed, granting or withholding approval over decisions about facilities is often a useful weapon for intracompany politics.

Extent and Flexibility of the Organization's Norms, Regulations, and Standards Applicable to the Project. Many large organizations have made explicit their objectives for image, function, and cost as they affect the work environment. Standards and regulations for facilities may become a straitjacket that constrains organizational effectiveness or may leave room for maneuver by facilities planners. Armies and post offices are among the organizations that typically prescribe precisely how facilities are to be provided, planned, programmed, and designed. Planning and programming for corporations with major real estate programs or for the public sector, where system-wide norms and standards and regulations apply, is typically much more constrained than planning and programming for a unique organization in the private sector, such as a research-and-development group, which may occupy a purpose-built, one-of-a-kind facility.

Management Style and Image. The management orientation and social culture of the occupant groups and of individual managers are usually major determinants of what processes will be acceptable in a particular organization. An open organization (Steele 1975) is much more likely to permit user involvement in facilities planning and programming than a top-down, "theory X" (McGregor 1960) type of organization. In our experience, "person-oriented" managers (Coffey, Athos, and Raynolds 1975; Fiedler and Chemers 1974; Little 1976) are more likely than "thing-oriented"[2] managers to respond to insights about the physical work environment that are derived from the behavioral sciences. Individual organizational groups often have a distinct social culture. For instance, among our clients for office planning and programming, every engineering group tended to be thing-oriented, whereas some industrial design and personnal services groups have been strongly people-oriented. In the physical environments they chose, the difference might be symbolized by the conference rooms of two units within one of our client organizations. A group of engineers furnished their conference room with stacking steel chairs and folding tables on a vinyl asbestos tile floor. In contrast, a group of product designers chose to confer while reclining on huge beanbag chairs on a carpeted floor.

Access of the Occupants to the Office Planners and to the Office Planning Process. When office planning is conducted by a group physically or organizationally located remote from the office users for whom they are planning, the collaborative attitudes needed for joint and directed planning are often hard to achieve. For instance, in some large corporations, facilities planning is a headquarters function. When the facilities planning staff deals with a field office, the potential for misunderstandings is high.

Amount of Information about the Occupants.   Some processes are impractical if information about the prospective occupants is not available. For instance, planning and programming for the new headquarters building of a large organization would implicitly or explicitly be consistent with its corporate strategic plan and with the action plans of its component units; whereas planning and programming for a developer's general-purpose building is frequently conducted without any knowledge of the specific group(s) that will eventually move in.

We expect that during the next few years, there will be a significant increase in the use of the self-help, joint, and directed planning processes by moderate-size and large organizations (with a consequent shift away from the traditional planning process). This will be a result not only of the increased use of participatory approaches, as noted earlier, but also of the growth and maturation of corporate planning, both at long-range (strategic) and short-term (action) time frames, within operating groups. In consequence, the relationships listed in Table 3-4 are likely to be transformed.

In most cases, senior managers implicitly determine the range of processes that will be permitted within their organization when they establish the relationship between corporate planning, operating units, and facilities services. They further constrain the margin for choice when they appoint staff to the different units concerned with facilities and approve the selection of consultants. They do so because they usually lack any knowledge of the potential opportunities and consequences, benefits and costs, inherent not only in each of the above-mentioned processes themselves, but also in the resultant environments that support or constrain the office work of their organizations.

The resistance of middle managers to changes in the traditional planning process and to the use of participatory approaches needs to be explored and explained. Practitioners need to understand this, so that they can help such middle managers to avoid possible unfavorable consequences of using participatory approaches. Research and generalized theories are needed about the range of consequences of participatory processes for the various categories of participants, and for others who are affected by this type of approach.

There is a dearth of comparative empirical data about the physical work environments that result from each of the approaches described. Comparative evaluations are needed of the office work environments that have resulted from the use of these different approaches and processes and of the environments that were developed using various combinations.

Their impacts on the attitudes and perceptions of the occupants need to be observed over a period of time. A manager recently reported on the use of a participatory approach for the design of a new building. His perception was that, whether the resultant physical environment was in fact different and/or better because of the use of such a participatory approach, the gain in the occupants' support and the improvement in their environmental competence were sufficient to justify the participation of the staff.

These comparative evaluations of office environments that take into account such factors as the type of process and approach used, the categories of managers and participants, and other aspects of interest to behavioral scientists can also contribute to the understanding and assessment of the complete ecological system at the workplace. A subcommittee of the American Society for Testing and Materials was recently established to address the need for understanding, and the development of standards for "total building performance"[3]. This is conceived as a transdisciplinary effort, one that should draw not only on engineering and the "hard sciences," but also on the insights and data from environment-and-behavior research. Efforts such as those of the society and the Centre International du Bâtiment[4] provide encouraging signs that the value of environment-and-behavior research is being recognized.

At this time, building performance standards apply only to components and assemblies of the parts of a building. The development of standards and norms for total building performance is only beginning. Environment-and-behavior studies, including evaluations such as those mentioned above, drawing on data from the field, should be a significant component of the knowledge base underlying standards for the office work environment.

NOTES

1. The term *postoccupancy evaluation* is not to be taken literally; that is, it does not refer to evaluation post- (after) occupancy, when the space has been vacated, is empty, or destroyed. Instead, it is understood to mean *during occupancy*, that is, *post- (after) completion* of a facility and after move-in. Other terms have been used or suggested over the years and we hope that the meaning of the terminology used in this respect will be clarified in the future.
2. Since 1975, our assessments of management vis-à-vis this family of dimensions have coincided, in every instance, with the assessments of the organization's senior personnel executive.
3. The American Society for Testing and Materials has established Subcommitee E6.25, Overall Performance of Buildings, under E-6 Committee on Performance of Building Construction. The Chairman of E6.25 is Gerald Davis, Principal, Harbinger Group Inc., 17 North Avenue, Norwalk, CT, 06851.
4. In 1982, the Environment Design Research Association received a request to nominate

a representative to the U.S. National Commission of the Centre International du Bâtiment. The CIB has a Working Group on Building Performance.

REFERENCES

Bobrow, P. D. 1974. Experimental changes to the architectural process. *Industrialization Forum* 5: 5, 9–20.

Burck, C. G. 1981. What happens when workers manage themselves. *Fortune* (July 27): 69.

Coffey, R. E., A. G. Athos, and P. A. Raynolds. 1975. *Behavior in organizations: A multidimensional view*. Englewood Cliffs, NJ: Prentice-Hall.

Conyne, R. K., and R. J. Clack. 1981. *Environmental design and assessment: A new tool for the applied behavioral scientist*. New York: Praeger Publishers.

Davis, G. 1978. A process for adapting existing buildings for new office uses. In W. F. E. Preiser (Ed.), *Facility programming*. Stroudsburg, PA: Dowden, Hutchinson and Ross, 27–53.

Davis, G. and F. Szigeti. 1979. Functional and technical programming when the owner/sponsor is a large or complex organization. *Proceedings of the 4th International Architectural Psychology Conference, 1979*. Louvain-La Neuve, Belgium: Universite Catholique de Louvain.

Davis, L. E. 1979. Optimizing organization-plant design: A complementary structure for technical and social systems. *Organizational Dynamics* (Autumn): 3–15.

Davis, L. E., and A. B. Cherns. 1975. *The quality of working life*. Vol. 1: *Problems, prospects and the state of the art*. Vol. 2: *Cases and commentary*. New York: Macmillan.

Ellis, L. (Ed.). 1981. *Proceedings of the Montebello Conference*. Ottawa: Architecture and Building Science Directorate, Public Works, Canada.

Fiedler, F. E., and M. M. Chemers. 1974. *Leadership and effective management*. Glenview, IL: Scott, Foresman & Co.

Glover, M. 1976. Alternative processes: Building procurement, design and construction (IF Occasional Paper Number 2). Montreal: Industrialization Forum, University of Montreal. Champaign/Urbana: University of Illinois.

Little, B. R. 1976. Specialization and the varieties of environmental experience: Empirical studies within the personality paradigm. In S. Wapner, S. B. Cohen, and B. Kaplan (Eds.), *Experiencing the environment*. New York: Plenum Publishing, 81–116.

Lynch, K. 1971. *Site planning*, 2nd Ed. Cambridge, MA: MIT Press.

McGregor, D. 1960. *The human side of enterprise*. New York: McGraw-Hill.

Miller, J. 1980. Decision-making and organizational effectiveness: Participation and perceptions. *Sociology of Work and Occupations*, 7(1), 55–79.

Mintzberg, H. 1979. *The structuring of organizations: A synthesis of the research*. Englewood Cliffs, NJ: Prentice-Hall.

National Research Council. 1981. *Indoor pollutants*. Washington, D.C.: National Academy Press.

Palmer, M. 1981. *The architect's guide to facility programming*. Washington, D.C.: The American Institute of Architects. New York: McGraw-Hill.

Sanoff, H. 1977. *Methods of architectural programming*. Stroudsburg, PA: Dowden, Hutchinson and Ross.

Sims, B. 1978. Programming environments for human use: A look at some emerging approaches to generating user-oriented design requirements. In W. E. Rogers and William H. Ittelson (Eds.), *New directions in environmental design research*. Washington, D.C.: Environmental Design Research Association, 489–498.

Sommer, R., and B. B. Sommer. 1980. *A practical guide to behavioral research: Tools and techniques*. New York: Oxford University Press.

Steele, F. I. 1973. *Physical settings and organization development*. Reading, MA: Addison-Wesley.

Steele, F. I. 1975. *The open organization: The impact of secrecy and disclosure on people and organizations*. Reading, MA: Addison-Wesley.

Trist, E. L. 1973. Task and contextual environments for new personal values. In F. E. Emery and E. L. Trist (Eds.), *Towards a Social Ecology*. New York: Plenum Publishing, 182–189.

Trist, E. L., G. W. Higgin, H. Murray, and A. B. Pollock. 1963. *Organizational choice: Capabilities of groups at the coal face under changing technologies*. London: Tavistock Publications.

Wise, J. A. 1979. Decision theory and design methodology. In W. Gasparski, D. Miller, and A. Strzaleckiego (Eds.), *Zagadniena Psychologii Projektowania*. Proceedings of the Conference, Design Methodology and Related Researches on Design, Radziejowice, Poland, 1977. Warsaw: Polish Academy of Sciences. (Reprints are available from the author.)

Zeisel, J. 1981. *Inquiry by design: Tools for environment-behavior research*. Monterey, CA: Brooks/Cole.

The Dynamics of Power and Influence in Workplace Design and Management

FRITZ STEELE
Partners Consulting Group
Boston, Massachusetts

Everyone connected with workplace design and management knows that power and influence are facts of life in any organization. Issues of status, power, control, participation, and freedom loom large in working out and implementing the design of office settings.

In the reverse direction, patterns of power and influence are, in turn, affected by the features of settings and how those settings are used. The impact of physical settings on these patterns is sometimes planned, sometimes accidental, but almost always a factor in shaping events and who influences them within the organization. This chapter will examine some of these effects, including the following: settings as symbols of power and status; gaining power through the use of settings; settings as power elements in themselves; settings as an influence on events; the effects of physical features on organizational dynamics; and some typical power problems related to organizational settings.

First we should consider a few general assumptions that underlie much of the discussion in this chapter[1]:

1. *Organizational power,* as used here, simply means the ability to influence events in an organization in the directions desired. Power may be related to formal position in the system, although it is not synonymous with it.
2. Hard-and-fast rules about what something "means" in terms of in-

dications of power standing in the system are likely to be wrong at least as often as they are right. Context and situation make a big difference, as does the history of how something got the way it is today.

3. In most organizations, members tend to make frequent inferences about what physical symbols mean, and these inferences can cause problems by being overly rigid or self-serving.

4. Settings can be *indicators* of power differences and dynamics; *media* for influence and control; and *cues* for an observer diagnosing the dynamics and issues in a system.

5. Settings can be used consciously as a support for power moves; they may be used unconsciously to aid in influence or control; or they may influence events through patterns they cause, without any individual's having chosen to do it.

6. To diagnose settings problems and potential from a human system point of view, one must look at both how people make places that help or hinder functioning (including altering them); and how they use the settings that exist. The effects of settings are almost always a result of two complementary forces: the physical qualities of the place, and the social system structure and norms of the people who are using it.

In short, I would like to counter a tendency today for the general public to seek simplistic hard-and-fast rules about what an element of a setting *means* in power terms, or what one *must* do in order to be powerful in an organization. The area is more complex and deserves to be approached with some thoughtfulness and curiosity, rather than with dicta that usually hold true only when people with much positional power can force these rules on those around them.

SETTINGS AS SYMBOLS OF POWER AND STATUS

One of the most familiar connections between settings and system dynamics is the manner in which people read messages into the places that different people and groups own or control within the organization. Being aware of these messages can help one be more sensitive to the roles that different people play in influencing people and events, as long as one is also aware of the limitations in this language: It is approximate, sometimes vague, and often unintentional (unplanned) and can mean more than one thing at the same time. Additionally, it is important not to make too many inferences without getting some confirmation from other sources.

With this in mind, let us look at a few of the dimensions or qualities used in our culture to symbolize a person's or a group's power in an organization.

Luxury Features and Trappings

An obvious indicator of organizational status is the degree of luxuriousness of a setting: fine materials, comfortable furniture, expensive accessories, large spaces for a given use, high-quality art works, and so on. Whether or not this is an indicator of power in the organization, however, is a different story. One has to know more about the situation, since there are cases in which status and power are not synonymous. For instance, a senior executive may be provided with a plush office but given very little to do (be "put out to pasture"). He or she has been given trappings in lieu of the actual power needed to influence events in the organization.

There are also settings where luxury does signify power, at least the power to provide oneself with fine things when others cannot make that decision unilaterally. The executive who takes such action often justifies it as expected of someone in his or her position ("I really don't care myself") or necessary to functioning in a high-powered mode ("It sets a tone that helps exert authority"). This may or may not be the case in terms of actual effect, but the argument has had its desired result of justifying their self-indulgence.

Locations

There are certainly different messages associated with different locations in an organization. Closeness to the acknowledged power center (person or group) is used as one measure. There is some justification for this, since those who are close are more likely to have regular contact with the top people. Locations near the highest activity areas are another type of indicator. Many personnel departments are seen as low power because of their backwater locations away from crucial management actions, and if they have agreed to be placed there, they are tacitly agreeing to reduce their own perceived (and real) clout in the system.

The location of a workplace within a given area can also carry messages about power. The usual factors have to do with being near the boss, near a window, near a corner, or on the way to important people, but not too accessible (for example, executive-row layouts).

In a given building, location by floor level is sometimes a clear indicator of standing in the corporate hierarchy. Simple height off the ground is a surprisingly common indicator of status, with career progress being measured by how high up in the building one has risen. This kind of gauge will be thrown haywire if a new boss decides that he or she wants to move down to the ground floor to be more visible to the troops: It could make sense as an experiment and might increase the executive's awareness of what is happening in the system, but the move confuses all the middle-management people who have faithfully played the climbing-the-building game. The language has been confused and is no longer to be completely relied upon.

Security

Keys, locks, doors, barriers, and other control devices can indicate power for those who control their use. One can sometimes measure the importance of an executive by the number of tests one has to pass in order to gain access to him or her, such as how many receptionists must be satisfied by credentials or the right to enter into the inner regions of power.

Doors and locks do not have to be closed in order for their owners to be seen as powerful: They just have to be available for the closing and be seen as controlled at the person's discretion.

Seating in Meetings

A common power indicator is seating location in meetings of all kinds, from small office sessions to large conference center gatherings of whole departments or larger collections. The messages here are harder to state unequivocally, but they tend to relate to three areas: where one chooses to sit, where one is allowed or instructed to sit, and group norms about who sits where in a given event. Location around a meeting conference table is probably the simplest example, with nearness to the boss being a measure of standing in the meeting. This may be misleading, in fact, since a relatively equal rival may choose to sit opposite the boss as a way of focusing the confrontation between them. This is a high-impact location in terms of getting the boss's attention (and it is easier to make eye contact than when sitting side-by-side), even though it is not typically called a high-status location. The most extreme examples are at formal events such as stockholders' meetings, with the inside power people sitting at the front of the room on a raised platform and everyone else sitting as the "audience" (that is, passive receivers of leaders' pronouncements), although activist stockholders may not play this expected passive role no matter where they are seated.

In summary, there are a number of qualities that are part of the language of power standing in an organization. Some of these are typical of most systems (luxurious trappings, for one), and some are particular to a given organization (such as a particular building whose history in the development of the firm makes it *the* place to have one's office). They all have an element of the self-fulfilling prophecy: When people believe that a person's setting speaks of power, they tend to treat that person with more deference and concern, thus conceding him or her more power and influence. It is sometimes hard to know which comes first: Do people acquire power symbols because of their clout, or do they acquire clout as their power symbols increase? One thing we should always keep in mind is that there are no universal messages consistently sent by a given setting. Hard-and-fast interpretations usually have a self-serving element on the part of the interpreter. It is usually to his or her advantage that a particular arrangement be thought of as having only one possible meaning.

POWER ACQUIRED THROUGH MODES OF USING SETTINGS

Another interesting effect on power relations in settings comes not from what the setting is like, but from how it is used. There is great latitude for using settings to enhance personal power, influence, dramatic impact, and so on, and some people are quite good at consciously using this latitude for their own desired effects.

For instance, if there is a choice of possible settings for a crucial meeting that is likely to be confrontational, an attempt can be made to have one's home territory selected so that one can legitimately play the role of host or hostess while others are in the role of guests. This is not the only role influence in the session, but it is a factor that might as well be working for you rather than against you.

People who use settings for influence are, as a rule, also more likely to make conscious choices about where events should be held, whereas those who are not as aware of this process tend to take what is available or usual as their scene for events. (In a small survey of consultants, most had not thought much about where they chose to do different activities, or even about their processes for choosing such sites.)

During an event in a given setting, people often make influence moves by their selection of where they place themselves in the setting. If everyone is sitting down, it can be useful to remain standing as a way of differentiating oneself from the rest. And, vice versa, if everyone is standing, a person can gain the spotlight by being the only one sitting down. Where one places oneself in a room can have a similar effect: under a light, at a corner position that draws peoples' eyes, near a door that is the only entrance or exit, at the "head" of the table (if the head of the table is

OFFICE DESIGN AND HUMAN NEEDS

evident), and so on. One thing that should be remembered is that there is no single rule (such as always standing or sitting to control attention) that holds for every occasion. The choice depends on the situation, the structure of the setting, and personal goals.

A similar process, dubbed "the positive power of puttering," is the use of props in a setting to focus attention, draw the conversation, or control the flow of time and pace of the event. An obvious example is the way pipe smokers may begin a statement and then putter with the relighting of their pipe while still maintaining a claim to the floor. If done well, they can control the total pace of the conversation that way. Similar moves can be made with almost anything that is handy in a setting: pointers, flip chart pads, coffee cups and pots, magazines, or whatever. Anything can be used to putter with and draw attention (often without others' being conscious of the way their attention is focused by the moves) to a particular person or spot at a particular time. We could even say that standing up and pacing in a conference room at a crucial moment is a way of puttering with the available free space.

These considerations also suggest that a setting that has an array of "stuff" in it is richer in puttering possibilities than one that does not. One thing that provides high-power bosses with extra clout when they hold meetings in their own offices is that they have many of their own things to tinker with during the meeting; it is legitimate for them to do so, but would be considered intrusive for guests to do the same. An office that is very thin in personal items is a harder setting in which to do this, from the owner's point of view, and is a meager contribution to focusing attention and making dramatic moves.

SETTINGS AS POWER ELEMENTS

Our third topic concerns situations in which a setting is not just a symbol or message, it is also a power element in and of itself. In such a case, the setting has the power to influence the behavior of users, and those who understand this will use that quality to their own advantage. Settings are often established consciously as a means of control so that managers do not personally have to make visible attempts to influence others. For example, signs with rules and instructions can be displayed visibly so that those who are responsible (or feel responsible) for seeing that these rules are obeyed will not have to explain them to each person who comes in. And, if they should see someone disobeying the rules, they can merely point to the sign, as if to say, "It's nothing to do with me, the rules are right there for all to see."

Another example is less tangible but no less powerful. The history of a particular setting sometimes builds an atmosphere that controls the behavior of people who use it. A board room may have been the setting of famous events that people recall each time they use it for a meeting, just as Yankee Stadium is a potent setting for many baseball players since so much of the history of American baseball has taken place there.

Settings are also designed to have selective power over certain people. The most obvious example is the typical courtroom, which is structured to exert considerable power over defendants and other noninsiders (such as the audience) while allowing a fair amount of freedom for the insiders (such as judge, police, clerks, and lawyers).

Territorial boundary markers create a certain type of power for settings, mainly that of allowing or blocking movement or access between parts of an organization. An office complex in which most groups are hidden away behind blank doors has an almost tangible power over the movements of employees. It will usually constrain movements, except in times of high stress, when people feel they really need to see others face-to-face; then, the layout requires much more movement and coming and going than would another plan. People cannot see from their own spot whether someone else is in, so they have to go through the doors (or airlocks) and find out, often repeating this three or four times before they succeed.

Visibility in a setting can be a powerful medium of control, depending on who is visible to whom. The classic example of this is the open bull pen arrangement in the old-style insurance office, with all desks in rows facing the same direction and the supervisor on a slightly raised platform at the back where he or she can see everyone without being observed.

Settings literally provide a place to be, a structure in space, so that a person can function for a period of time without having to find another spot. This is power of a sort, but it is usually taken for granted by most of us until, for one reason or another, we find ourselves in a powerless situation where we have no place (such as being broke in a big city). Then we realize how restricted we feel without a setting in which to operate freely. (I see the results of this each winter morning in the group of vagrants gathered around the hot-air vent at the hotel down the street. This spot gives them a warm place to be where they can survive, as long as the police tacitly agree that they are free to stay there.)

An interesting organizational example of the same phenomenon was observed at a military training institute that occupies space on a large, permanent base. The institute has approximately 150 students per program, most of whom live on the base. These students have no place of their own within the institute's territory: They are either in the main classroom (the auditorium), in discussion rooms (in the administration building), or wandering on the base, since there is no community space designated as their own. They have no formal place to gather and spend time. This condition is both disempowering and unlikely to help them develop any shared identity as a group. It also tends to restrict their influence in relation to the staff. The system pays a price in terms of its product, since, as a result, the shape and content of the program is influenced mostly by the staff and very little by the students. If the students had a common space where they could get together and talk about what was going on and how they liked or did not like it, they might develop a common consciousness of their position, and of the possibilities that concerted action would have on influencing the staff. The present layout suggests that the staff would not want this to happen, but there are still high costs to the system because program content can become unrealistic without being challenged. The layout tends to skew influence distribution in favor of the staff, not the students; so the students tend to remain a collection of individuals rather than becoming a group with a shared identity and perceptions of similar concerns, interests, and rights.

Settings and Events

A special case of the power of settings is the way that they can influence the character of particular events in an organization. It was previously noted that layouts in which groups are near to or far from one another have an effect on the interaction patterns of the two groups and help determine whether they ever get together to discover common interests and concerns. Similarly, when a crisis hits an organization, it is a different event if the system is laid out in an open-office plan than if everyone is dispersed in private offices that are hidden from one another. The news travels much faster in the open plan, the whole mood of the place can be affected in one day, and people can see that mood change in the way others are moving about or talking with one another, for example. This is not to say that one layout is better than the other—that depends on how fast one thinks the mood *should* spread and on the capacity of the members to respond to the crisis without panicking.

Another example of influence on events is the conference area that is very tight for space, with overlapping group areas impinging upon it. Meetings to diagnose problems of one group, when held there, may be much more constrained than they would be in a more private space, where there would be no fear of being overheard. The whole mood of the session would be different and less publicly oriented.

Where events are held influences power balances and the overall tenor of events, especially regularly recurring ones. In a major corporation's large manufacturing complex (with several smaller factory areas making up the total), all meetings called by the complex's manager with his staff were held in the conference room of the administration building. This room was next to the complex manager's office, and across the hall from those of the personnel and finance managers. The department heads of the different plants (who came from their own areas for the meetings) seemed to take little interest in the discussions of site-wide issues, and most of the talking was done by the complex manager and the personnel and finance managers.

It seemed that this pattern might be caused partly by the unintended and unnoticed effect of holding all the meetings in the territory of the most talkative threesome—that this was one reason they were most talkative, being on their home turf and therefore more comfortable (and feeling first class or one-up compared with the operations managers). When the meetings were switched, as an experiment, to a rotation of locations around the complex so that different people hosted it on different weeks, the meetings became much more lively, with the plant managers becoming more verbal about issues in the complex. The managers had not changed, but their feelings about themselves in the meeting were more positive. This strategy also gave the complex manager much more of a feel for what was happening around the complex, not just in his own administration building. The personnel and finance managers became less verbally dominant and more interested both in what others had to say and in what was going on in areas other than their own.

Another potent feature of settings is lighting. The nature and level of lighting can have a great effect on the character of an event, no matter what the intentions of the people who set it up. Lighting can make the mood intimate (if low), public (if bright), festive (if varied and playful), and so on. Spotlights can focus attention on one or more people; house lights in a theater can raise audience members' awareness of themselves and their numbers. Variable lighting is often underutilized as a device to shape events.

The symbolic messages that settings hold can influence specific events as well as people's perceptions of the influence of others. An example already mentioned is the board room that has pictures of the founders around the walls, and is also used as a conference and training room. The pictures carry a very high message value about continuity, permanence, stability, and traditional values of the organization. This setting can be perfect for certain events, but it can also set a tone of conservatism and stability, which makes it very hard to explore new directions or to get people to think for themselves about what the system could be like in the future. The very walls say, "Follow the people and norms that made us what we are today," and there is pressure to seem grateful for this past leadership by not rejecting what they stood for.

Finally, the weather can be the controlling force in what occurs in a setting. If the weather is cold and icy, outdoor rallies are hard to start. If the weather is hot and sticky, meetings held outside may degenerate into lethargic get-togethers, as many training directors have found after scheduling winter sessions in Florida or the Bahamas: Not much energy is brought to bear on the issues. Bad weather can also be a catalyst, as, for example, when it spurs people who control no sheltered workplaces of their own to unite and demand more from those who have control. In a good climate, people can get by with fewer resources, so their threshold of frustration tends to be higher, or slower to be reached.

SETTINGS AND HUMAN SYSTEMS DYNAMICS

The effects we have been considering here can be brought together by viewing them from another interesting angle: the impact of physical setting features on the dynamic events and behaviors taking place in an organization. This is particularly relevant if power is defined as the ability to influence organizational dynamics in desired directions.

Because the number of possible effects to consider is enormous, they have been organized in the form of a large summary table (4-1) that provides examples of the typical impacts of six physical feature categories of office settings on twelve areas of organizational dynamics and behavior. First, let us define each of the organizational dynamics categories:

1. *Boundary management:* the kinds of controls people exert over movement of people, information, money, materials, and so on among organizational units and between the organization and its environment.
2. *Energy management:* the stimulation and direction of human energy to various activities and ends (not to be confused with physical energy management, such as heat and lighting).
3. *Controlling resources:* the use of various desirable resources (money, information, time, and so on) to produce something or influence events.
4. *Positional behavior:* the influence of peoples' positions (social and physical) on their behavior and on others' perceptions of them.
5. *Controlling structures:* the influencing of the various formal (responsibility and reporting relationships) and informal (regular groupings, temporary teams) structures that influence behavior in the system.
6. *Differentiation of units:* sharpening differences of style, responsibility, capability, and so on among the various units of the organization.
7. *Integration of units:* the connections of the units to one another

through information sharing, coordination of actions, joint decisions, and so on.

8. *Face-to-face influence:* people's attempting to influence each others' opinions, ideas, or readiness to act; and doing this when physically in each others' presence.
9. *Symbolic messages:* the large mass of information communicated in the organization in an informal manner through signs, symbols, and other graphics.
10. *Controlling events:* trying to shape the occurrence, nature, or sequence of events that take place within the system.
11. *Physical coercion:* influencing people's behavior in the organization through the use of physical threats or constraints.
12. *Subunit power:* the relative ability of an organizational unit to influence other parts of the system.

The six physical feature categories that have been selected for illustration are as follows:

A. Locations of offices, departments, personal workplaces, and so on.
B. Design of entrances, exits, and accessways.
C. Furniture arrangements.
D. Signs and graphics.
E. Trafficways, aisles, and corridors.
F. Lighting arrangements and level.

Table 4-1 contains examples of the effects of each particular physical feature on the particular category of organizational behavior. This is not meant to be an exhaustive survey; rather, it is meant to suggest patterns that readers can look for in their own organization or take into account when designing new office settings. Many of these effects have been mentioned in some form in the preceding discussion, and are merely summarized here.

Table 4-1. Effects of Physical Setting Features on Organizational Behavior

ORGANIZATIONAL DYNAMICS

Physical Features	*1. Boundary Management*	*2. Energy Management*
A. Locations	Adjacency increases contact Distance decreases it Visibility leads to less mystery Choice of mixing vs. separating units Dispersal vs. concentration changes experience pattern	Visibility can make enthusiasm contagious Hassle factor if separation distance is large Overcrowding, stress, tension, action? Communication equipment needs

Table 4-1. (Continued)

Physical Features	1. Boundary Management	2. Energy Management
B. Entrances and Exits	Clear vs. hidden access "Insider"–"outsider" feel if hidden or difficult Visitors' first experience Possible visual distractions Controlling access—easy or difficult	Distractions break concentration Channeling people to right place without energy drain Regular outside inputs can stimulate thought and action
C. Furniture Arrangements	Defining areas with furniture arrangements A "screening person" must be in right spot Furniture styles can sharpen differences among groups	Making easy visual and audial contact possible Having right type and size of furniture for tasks Visibility tends to promote sense of common concerns Controlling interferences with productive work
D. Signs and Graphics	"Enter" or "keep out" messages Help in finding access or exits Temporary signs to open or close boundaries Styles in decorations and art works for units	Visual reminders of issues or concerns needing action Directing people to right place for their purposes Posted rules about activity accepted or not Stimulating vs. soothing colors
E. Trafficways	May need to block a path to close a boundary Passing through a group's area or to the side Are there easy links between groups?	Paths affect energy needed to get from A to B Different modes of movement possible with different path With easy movement, people can pass excitement on to others (vs. dissipate)
F. Lighting	Different intensities can signal different zones Dark spots often act as a barrier to free movement Different styles of fixtures identify groups' areas	Different light levels tend to stimulate energy or reduce it Dimness or glare can induce fatigue in high-concentration tasks

	3. Controlling Resources	4. Positional Behavior
A. Locations	Doling out high-quality, high-status locations Deciding who can be where and what can be done in different locations	Being in a spot where one does not see what is happening Being ceded authority because of one's location

Table 4-1. (*Continued*)

Physical Features	3. Controlling Resources	4. Positional Behavior
	Determining adjacencies and therefore opportunities	Department members' concern for certain issues because their location induces certain experiences
B. Entrances and Exits	Who has access to resources (stock room, computer, copier, etc.) Are resources visible or hidden? Access to facilities at nonstandard times may be tightly controlled	People tend to be put in space-guardian role due to location of their work spot (e.g., secretary near a door) Role expectations set by cues from entrances and exits
C. Furniture Arrangements	Variations in what items one has to work with Formal rules about acceptable arrangements Control harder without visibility of what you are trying to control	Certain arrangements (and therefore work modes) that are supposed to go with a position Desk arrangements that increase/decrease visible activity (and awareness)
D. Signs and Graphics	Control of graphics—degree of personal choice Signs that delineate ownership of facilities Signs that declare who can use what	Indicators of position and status in the system Titles, names, and functions displayed directly Informal status language: type and quality of art, decorative arrangements, etc.
E. Trafficways	Path control helps control access to materials Who can use which paths (such as executive elevator) can shape what people can do easily Freedom of movement is a resource itself	People may skip making face-to-face contact because path is muddled or difficult People on trafficways often seem irritable, due to pattern of interruptions (not to personality)
F. Lighting	Making an area unlighted restricts its use Power people can program lighting patterns over the course of a day if there is a centrally controlled system	Lighting arrangements appropriate to one's position may be poor for one's work style preferences Personal task lighting choices vs. uniform general lighting affects choices about different work modes at different times

Table 4-1. (Continued)

Physical Features	5. Controlling Structures	6. Differentiation of Units
A. Locations	Configurations often determine where events can be held, or if they can Being located centrally can help one see patterns and know when to let go of old structure/create new	Very different types of locations tend to sharpen differences between groups People can move their desks away to make statement about differentiation Groups in separate buildings
B. Entrances and Exits	Are entrances right for flow when important meetings are held? Are exits right? Groups may play different functions based on their access to other groups	Clear exclusion of some groups from contact with others Insiders-outsiders setup sharpens differences Groups may use poor access as an issue to establish separate identity
C. Furniture Arrangements	Setting up special arrangements to control the flow of meetings, conferences, and the like Setting rules about arrangements, as a means of controlling relationships	Different styles of layout signal group differences in outlook, values, etc. Furnishings for a whole building may be uniform, to minimize difference, or tailored to different groups to heighten it
D. Signs and Graphics	Rules, constraints, and procedures visibly displayed Are there clear messages in right places about expectations for events?	Identifying signs for groups' territories Banners used to identify group areas (in open-plan layouts) Distinctive decorative elements, colors, etc.
E. Trafficways	Rules about who can use which paths, and when Creating new paths can help create new bonds between formerly separate groups or individuals	Passageways tend to separate groups when they run between them Lack of a path joining two groups tends to accentuate differences
F. Lighting	Controlling policies about lighting (type, time of use, etc.) can shape which events can occur and when	Differences in style or intensity set different moods for different groups Big difference/contrast in lighting level tends to sharpen awareness of different group territories

Table 4-1. (*Continued*)

Physical Features	7. Integration of Units	8. Face-to-Face Influence
A. Locations	Putting units in same building Mixing up groups, not totally separate location Adjacency with easy access Communication equipment when distances are great	Adjacency provides unplanned moments of contact and influence Being central allows one to be around and act when an issue is hot
B. Entrances and Exits	Inviting entrance to a group's area can draw others for better communication Clear access speeds contact in emergencies	Designs can control who has access to power people, and who gets a chance to influence them Choices of exits from an office or area allow people to escape face-to-face contact if not desired
C. Furniture Arrangements	Workspaces arranged for easy sharing of information Trading of items among groups Similar settings that make members of different groups feel comfortable	An office set up to place resident in dominant mode over visitors (imposing desk, light source behind resident, poor seating for visitor, etc.) Visibility of subordinates to boss
D. Signs and Graphics	Integrated decoration of system Signs encouraging visits from one group to another Maps and charts showing locations and paths for different groups' areas	Visible instructions about who to see for various pieces of business Certificates, plaques, etc., displayed at personal workplaces to establish credibility
E. Trafficways	Paths can link groups together; absence of clear paths encourages independent actions	Trafficways provide settings for impromptu chats and influence (if they are wide enough to allow stopping and chatting) Visible, open paths allow one to spot passersby
F. Lighting	Common lighting systems or patterns tend to tie groups together Common switches or controls require groups to coordinate decisions about lighting	Level of lighting can set mood of intimacy, conspiracy, public posturing, etc. Lighting can focus people's attention on each other or on surroundings

Table 4-1. *(Continued)*

Physical Features	*9. Symbolic Messages*	*10. Controlling Events*
A. Locations	Who is up/down in status shown by location Some locations hold more territorial messages than others do (based on the system's history) Closeness to power centers (e.g., president's office) implies standing	Putting people near one another can spark issues or confrontations High densities of people in same area can raise tensions and aggression Holding events in own turf can provide control over them
B. Entrances and Exits	Thoughtfulness about entrances and exits says something about welcomeness of visitors Design implies who counts, who does not	Access can be used as an issue to draw people together to take common action Entrances shape how people get to events, and how they feel at the start
C. Furniture Arrangements	Seating arrangements tell others about one's desired interpersonal style Style of furnishings may reflect personal style Layouts imply what activities are acceptable in a setting	Setups for meetings, conferences, etc., shape the processes that can happen Special arrangements are institutionalized to control events (e.g., courtrooms) Layout scheme affects contact (e.g., open vs. closed layout)
D. Signs and Graphics	Status indicators such as titles, colors, etc. Taste in art may be communicated if occupant chose it Basic functions of different groups shown by graphics in their areas	Can be visible messages that set mood, influence awareness and feelings Can create zones or areas with graphics—special spot for special events
E. Trafficways	Freedom of use of different paths is sign of insider or power status Freedom from trafficways in own area can also be a sign of high status (one rates an enclave)	The movement of people, spontaneous gatherings, chance meetings are all influenced by the structures of paths and access Shutting off access to path can keep events from happening
F. Lighting	Lighting level sets a mood, speaks about nature of contact that someone desires Being nearer to natural light often taken as sign of high status	Climate and mood of an event influenced by nature and intensity of light Light can focus members' attention (e.g., a spotlight)

Table 4-1. (*Continued*)

Physical Features	11. Physical Coercion	12. Subunit Power
A. Locations	Placing people so they are visible to the controller Secure locations that cannot be entered without identification or keys Isolated locations that make users dependent on authority figures	Powerful units tend to be in central spots where they can easily get and give information Locations that were chosen by the group often reflect power just through the freedom to choose
B. Entrances and Exits	Entrances can be blocked and exits as well, so that they are only usable when controller decides Fortifications designed so access can only be gained through entrances	Careful entrances provide units control of their own turf Entrances within a group area can provide members with freedom of movement, which builds self-esteem
C. Furniture Arrangements	Jail cells and work cubicles both imply rules about restricted movement Freedom to choose arrangements (or lack of it) is communicated by settings to those who can read them	The typical facilities management group controls other groups' actions by setting policies about use of furniture and space Power images may be projected by style and placement of furnishings
D. Signs and Graphics	Visual directives about permitted and forbidden actions Warnings, visual reminders of past punishments, etc.	Clear, strong identity may be projected by the graphics in a group's area Directives to steer unwanted traffic away or draw desired traffic through a group's area
E. Trafficways	Degree of security (walls, fences, etc.) determines their usability Paths that are busy may be safer than those that are isolated	Locations near many paths or nodes tend to strengthen a unit's power; backwater locations tend to reduce it
F. Lighting	Spotlights in areas where surveillance is desired Light as a weapon, as in "the 3rd degree" Ability to cut off light source	Which groups have the right to deviate from standard system or set up one of their own

TYPICAL POWER PROBLEMS IN RELATION
TO SETTINGS

As a final topic for this chapter, let us consider some of the most typical systemic problems that seem to be caused or contributed to by the nature of work settings.

Organizations often retain a physical structure that was right for a certain phase in their development but is no longer appropriate. Locating divisions in separate buildings or different towns may have been necessary or very useful at one time, for example, but now this setup costs a great deal in terms of lost influence and sorely needed integration. Yet the leaders talk about the unnecessary costs of moving when they still have perfectly usable space (meaning that each body fits in a spot). They do not calculate the costs to the system: separations and major inconveniences (travel time, making appointments, carting materials around) in order to accomplish any kind of face-to-face influence compared to a structure in which groups are easily accessible to one another in the same building.

Middle managers often have a power problem in relation to settings: They are expected to get their mission accomplished, but they do not have control over many of the settings they must use to accomplish this mission. They cannot make space decisions, they cannot allocate specific offices to people, and they may not have enough meeting areas (without distractions) to hold the kinds of larger events they see as useful to overall management of their effort. There are extreme cases where middle managers have no place to get together as a group to talk about the common concerns and problems associated with that level. Higher-level people have personal meeting rooms; lower-level people have largish work areas or lounges; but the people in the middle have neither, so they remain fragmented and function solely as individuals trying to deal with the higher and lower levels of the system. It is not just the lack of an appropriate setting that keeps them fragmented, of course; they generally do not even recognize that it would be worthwhile to get together, or they do not want to risk looking insubordinate by making a collective move.[2] But not having a space makes it even less likely that any sort of common identity will develop.

Implied in this example is the situation where managers do not control the settings in which they work: They are supposed to manage in a structure that is set by someone else while being held accountable for the results. This is quite common, and yet it is somewhat surprising that managers will accept this situation as a natural or necessary part of organization life. They allow top management to have it both ways: that is, to talk about how they "manage by results" while at the same time to dictate many features of the physical and social structure that influence those results. It is an indicator of deep feelings of powerlessness that middle managers would allow these mutually contradictory situations to exist.

Another problem pattern is that facilities issues are often treated as inconveniences or necessary evils rather than as continuing opportunities or media for influencing system dynamics. As is implied by the variety of entries in Table 4-1, there are many opportunities to change boundaries, social structures, the flow of energy, and the use of resources by altering physical layout. These influences can come both from the content of the project and from the process—how the data are collected, needs diagnosed, and decisions made and implemented. When this opportunity is not clear in leaders' eyes, the task of design gets delegated to facilities management, often made up of former military or cost-accounting people who are more interested in discipline and costs per square foot than in the impact of design on the organization's functioning. The leaders make their inputs in terms of cost parameters and of their own personal preferences and biases about design; but they do relatively little setting of standards and expectations for the systemic impact that the new setting should promote, nor do they indicate how to get there from the present state.

Finally, confusion about the crucial purposes of settings often leads to both a weaker impact and dilution of effectiveness. When members of a system over-interpret physical features in terms of status and power language (what each element "means" and therefore must mean if being replanned), there are several consequences: (1) Leaders feel constrained to avoid spatial innovations out of fear that members will be upset or "take something the wrong way"; this fear becomes a controlling element in the rich use of resources. (2) Rigidity about acceptable space assignments (such as someone being in too large an office for his or her level) leads to lowered flexibility and adaptability. (3) Lower-quality settings become the norm, with less "zip" to them and more blandness. (4) Mediocre task settings are tolerated, with status symbol considerations driving out effective work design concerns.

A conscious, periodic evaluation and review of the quality of an organization's work settings would help to sort out the effects of the settings themselves from the effects of the way settings are managed, controlled, and designed, so that interventions could take place on either end. Opportunities exist for much more powerful uses of settings than most organizations ever realize in practice.

CONCLUSIONS

This chapter has attempted to explore some of the many aspects of the relationship between organizational power dynamics and various aspects of the organization's settings: how workplaces are structured, the impact they have on events in the organization, how they are used as a power language, who can use them and in what ways, and who has the power to shape these work settings for their own purposes. As stated earlier, this is a very complex area and is not amenable to simple rules about what elements always *mean* or what one *must* do in order to exercise desired influence through physical facilities. Nor can the topic really be summed up in a single short chapter. My intention has been, rather, to provide some themes to help readers look at the relationships (actual and potential) between physical settings and power dynamics in their own organizations.

What we can say with some certainty is that positional power, perceived power, influence over events, and control over the shape and use of facilities are inextricably bound up with each other, so that anyone who wants to improve the functioning of an organization by improving the match of physical and social structures needs to be able to look at these factors in a clear, open-minded, problem-solving manner. One of the most important issues to keep in mind when trying to assess these factors is the difference between focusing on getting the facilities one personally wants as an *individual* (for example, a certain type of workplace, furniture, or location) and focusing on the facilities that the *system* needs in order to function effectively (such as how many separate workspaces and how many combined ones). My observations suggest that, in many organizations, once managers get past very rudimentary choices such as size of total office area and overall layout, they tend to deal with facilities design issues as simply a collection of individual concerns and preferences. It should be clear from this chapter that facilities design decisions and use patterns are also important because of their effects on the dynamics of the organization and its subgroups. Individuals need to have some degree of satisfaction with their personal workplaces or their resentment will block productivity in the long run. This satisfaction is a necessary but not a sufficient condition of organizational health. Poor layouts from the point of view of the organization's patterns of action may occur even when the individual members like their workplaces. Designers and users must remain aware of both personal and systemic effects in order to create settings that influence power behavior and other organizational dynamics in a positive manner.

NOTES

1. My appreciation and understanding of power dynamics in organizations have been heavily influenced by my work over a number of years with Barry Oshry. His points of view are well summarized in papers such as "Organic Power," "Power and Position," "Middle Power," and "The Success of a Business/The Failure of Its Partners." These are all available from PST, Inc., P.O. Box 388, Prudential Station, Boston, MA 02199.

2. Oshry has dealt very well with the fragmentation pattern and what can be done about it in a recent paper, "Middles of the World, Integrate!" available through PST, Inc., P.O. Box 388, Prudential Station, Boston, MA 02199.

SECTION II

EVALUATION OF OFFICE SETTINGS

Office setting evaluations provide an understanding of how the work environment supports human behavior and work processes. In this section, conceptual frameworks for office research are presented and discussed with respect to the results of a number of evaluation studies.

Marans and Spreckelmeyer indicate the need for a more comprehensive and systematic approach to examining the human response to the built environment. In an attempt to overcome limitations characteristic of past evaluations, a conceptual model is presented as a guide to evaluators in collecting and analyzing data on office environments. A number of components of the model are then examined using data from a study of a new federal office building. Findings corroborate those reported by others in showing that conventional offices are viewed more favorably by people occupying them than by workers in either open or pooled office arrangements. The amount of workspace available to the worker is the most important factor associated with work station satisfaction, even after taking into account the type of work station and the workers' ratings of specific work-station attributes. It is also demonstrated that people's feelings about the ambience of the agency within which they work and the architecture of the building influence their reactions to the immediate workspace. It is suggested that space planners and designers who want their work to be appreciated by the user should concern themselves with the details of the workspace as well as with the larger-scale environment.

A theoretical model presented by Ferguson and Weisman, tested in eight organizational settings, focused on understanding the privacy needs of office workers. Results support the importance of workers' attitudes and perceptions of physical environmental factors to workspace and job satisfaction. The authors demonstrate the advantages of the *structural model* approach over the *estimation model* techniques of office evaluation. They contrast two analysis techniques. The more traditional analysis identifies a number of critical issues affecting workplace satisfaction, including distractions, privacy, openness, and job level. An alternative approach to analysis, *path analysis,* modifies these conclusions. Openness and job level now appear to have largely indirect effects, with the factors of distractions and privacy emerging as the more powerful influences on workplace satisfaction.

The research of Goodrich emphasizes the need to view the designed environment of an office, as experienced and used by people, as part of a dynamic system that influences users' performance and well-being. Research results reported in this chapter are based upon extensive interviews, questionnaires, group interviews, and observations at 14 companies representing a variety of physical environments. These case studies document some of the ways in which the designed environment affects, both positively and negatively, morale, communication patterns, perceived privacy, and workers' relationships with others. Similarly, social processes and task variables influence a user's perception of and reaction to the environment in which he or she works.

The perspectives presented in this section identify the multiple interacting forces that influence worker responses in the workplace. It is clear that problem solutions must be responsive to a range of environmental factors. Both the organizational context and objective job characteristics emerge as factors that require consideration in office evaluation research.

A Conceptual Model for Evaluating Work Environments

ROBERT W. MARANS
College of Architecture and Urban Planning
Institute for Social Research
University of Michigan
Ann Arbor, Michigan

KENT F. SPRECKELMEYER
School of Architecture and Urban Design
University of Kansas
Lawrence, Kansas

In a period in which office technology is rapidly changing, the issue of performance on the job and how it is affected by the physical environment has attracted the attention of corporate executives and space planners alike. Concurrently, isolated findings from a number of studies have supported the contention that the design of the workplace can serve to impede job performance (for example, Allen and Gerstberger 1975; Harris 1978) and enhance the satisfaction of workers on the job (Lunden 1972). In their efforts to develop a better understanding of the relative importance of the physical setting, a number of environmental researchers and designers have sought to isolate relationships between specific attributes of the workplace on the one hand, and satisfaction and performance on the other. Several have done so within the framework of empirically based postoccupancy evaluations. Although many interesting and sometimes useful findings have resulted from these efforts, this chapter suggests that comprehensive and more systematic approaches are needed for examining relationships between the built environment and people's responses to it.

There are indications that in the future, systematic evaluations of workplaces and other types of built environments will become an important part of the planning, design, and building process. The U.S. government, for example, has considered the need for evaluation as a requirement of all major public works projects (*Architectural Record* 1978). Our earlier

* Robert W. Marans and Kent F. Spreckelmeyer, "A Conceptual Model for Evaluating Work Environments," *Environment and Behavior*, vol. 14, no. 3 (May 1982), pp. 333–51. Copyright © 1982 by Sage Publications. Reprinted by permission.

research has been in response to the National Bureau of Standards' interest in establishing an overall framework for evaluating built environments.[1] Private organizations have also taken positive actions toward evaluating people's responses to the workplace. A pair of studies, prepared under the sponsorship of a major furniture manufacturer, has examined a range of attitudes of office workers, drawn from national sample surveys (Harris 1978, 1980). Although the studies make a contribution to our understanding of people in the workplace, their significance lies in their national data, which can serve as a basis for comparison of data from other studies of office environments.

Several past evaluations show ingenuity and are worthy of examination by those who wish to conduct further research on built environments: nevertheless, many are inherently weak in both execution and theoretical foundation. A major shortcoming, for example, has been their failure to specify the criteria to be used in determining the degree to which an environment is successful. Even if criteria are specified, valid and reliable measures of success are rarely used. Another failing has been the lack of a carefully developed conceptual link between physical environmental attributes and various levels of worker responses to those attributes. Furthermore, the attributes that are to be measured in the workplace, both objectively and subjectively, have been either poorly or incorrectly specified and measured by evaluators. Finally, numerous evaluations are characterized by their informality of execution and lack of clarity in communicating findings. Often, efforts at disseminating information are limited, so that the research seldom benefits anyone other than the individuals involved in conducting it.

In an attempt to overcome some of these problems, this chapter presents a conceptual model for guiding evaluators in the collection and analysis of data on office environments. The model suggests the kinds of environmental conditions, and subjective responses to those conditions, that should be considered in studying work environments and proposes the manner in which they are interrelated and linked to job satisfaction and worker performance. A number of components of the model are then examined using data from studies of two new office buildings. Although the findings are useful in that they corroborate findings of other researchers, our central purpose is the presentation of a model that can serve as an organizing framework for thinking about and performing evaluations of work environments in other settings.

CONCEPTUAL MODEL

An underlying purpose of any environmental evaluation should be to develop a better understanding of how the physical environment or place contributes to or impedes the goals or purposes of individuals or groups of individuals operating within that place. Specifically, the evaluation should attempt to clarify and supplement what is currently known about specific attributes of the physical environment as they relate both independently and together to people's behaviors and subjective responses to that environment. Within any environmental context, there is clearly a multitude of interrelationships that require examination if this basic objective is to be fulfilled.

The conceptual model presented here is a mechanism for understanding the interrelationships among data collected as part of any evaluation. It serves two additional purposes as well. First, it provides the reader with a map showing how different sets of variables covering workers and their actions, feelings, and environmental settings might be interrelated. Second, it serves as an organizational framework for guiding the collection and analysis of data as part of the evaluation.

The conceptual model is derived in part from a framework previously developed by one of the authors for use in conducting research on relationships between objective conditions, subjective experiences, and residential satisfaction (Marans and Rodgers 1975). Basically, that model suggests that satisfaction with the residential environment, as expressed by an individual, is dependent upon his or her evaluation or assessments of several attributes of that environment. How a person evaluates a particular attribute, in turn, is dependent on two factors: how that person perceives it and the standards against which he or she judges it. An individual's perception of a particular attribute is dependent on but distinct from the objective environmental attribute itself. The possibility of bias, inaccuracy, or simply differences in perceptions among individuals in the same environment is recognized explicitly. Finally, the characteristics of an individual are seen as affecting his or her perceptions and assessments of environmental attributes and the standards for comparisons that are used.

It has been posited as an extension of this framework that satisfaction with the residential environment together with satisfaction with other domains of life can influence the quality of life as an individual experiences it. Similarly, residential satisfaction is seen as contributing both to selected behaviors of residents and to the extent to which those behaviors occur within the residential setting.

From the perspective of the environmental designer, the core of the model is represented by the direct and indirect links between objective environmental attributes, people's subjective responses to these attributes, overall environmental satisfaction, and a specific behavior or sets of behaviors.

Of course, not every evaluation of a physical environment or place would operate with the same set of variables. Places differ in their purposes, and the variables to be considered are usually determined after these purposes are identified and prioritized. Nor, for that matter, are all evaluations undertaken for the same reasons or with the same level of funding and/or sophistication. Nonetheless, place evaluations conducted from the perspective of users can operate from a common analytical framework, irrespective of the type of physical environment being evaluated. Evaluations of each type of physical environment have operated under the assumption that any particular place is made up of component parts or environmental attributes. Furthermore, each attribute can be assessed by people who use that place, and the sum of any individual assessments contributes both to an overall evaluation of the place and to specific behaviors that take place within it. The kinds of overall evaluations and specific behaviors to be considered differ, depending on the type of place being evaluated and the particular outcomes or indicators of success that are considered important. For example, in evaluations of residential environments, outcomes may have to do with dwelling satisfaction, neighborhood satisfaction, or the desire to move from a particular locale. Or in an evaluation of hospital wards, outcomes may be related to patient comfort or the ability of doctors and nurses to give care to patients (for example, Canter, Kenny, and Rees 1980).

The issue of appropriate outcomes or indicators of success in work environments has received considerable attention in recent years. At the same time, research on the quality of working life, whether conducted in office or industrial settings, has viewed the physical environment as one of several factors contributing to that quality. Much of this research has treated overall job satisfaction as a key outcome measure, whereas organizational studies of work environments have considered worker performance as an indicator of success (Seashore 1974; Steele 1973).

In evaluations of work environments, it seems reasonable to consider both job satisfaction and job performance as appropriate outcome measures. No doubt other criteria could be identified in evaluating any particular work setting, and their selection generally reflects factors such as the purposes of the study; the interests of the client; who the evaluators are and who the study sponsor is; and what resources are brought to bear on the work.

Figure 5-1 graphically depicts a conceptual model for evaluating work environments. In this model, three key outcomes are suggested: overall environmental satisfaction, job satisfaction, and worker performance. As noted above, overall environmental satisfaction is the common ingredient of all place evaluations; it is the outcome of greatest interest to architects and the one receiving the most attention in this work. The model suggests the manner in which conditions or attributes of the workplace are linked to the satisfactions and experiences of workers.

Overall environmental satisfaction for an employee is dependent upon

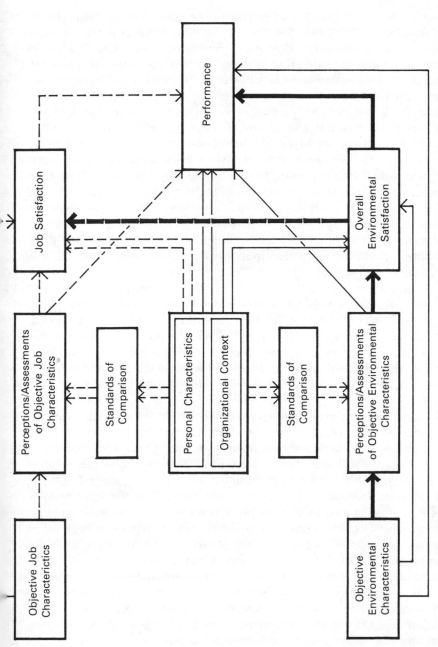

Note: Bold lines suggest relationship important to environmental designers. Broken lines represent relationships that were not examined within the case study in this article. Double lines denote characteristics of organizations and their individual workers.

5-1. Conceptual model for evaluating work environments

four factors. First, the characteristics of the employee, including his or her position or job type, influence how he or she evaluates a work environment. A clerical worker and a manager both working in an open office may have very different feelings about their work environment. Second, overall environmental satisfaction is dependent upon the organizational context in which employees operate. This context encompasses, but is not limited to, the mission of the organization, the activities that take place within it, the morale of the organization, and the general nature of employee/employer relations. An employee requiring privacy may not view the workplace favorably if the organizational requirements also necessitate its being used for group meetings. Third, overall environmental satisfaction is dependent on the individual's perceptions and assessments of a bundle of specific attributes. Finally, the objective attributes themselves contribute to overall environmental satisfaction. Excessive noise and stuffy air, aside from a person's perceptions of these attributes, could influence that individual's feelings about the office in which he or she works.

The model also shows that an individual's perception and assessment of a particular attribute is dependent on two factors: the standards against which he or she judges that attribute, and the objective attribute itself. The standards for comparison may include the previously experienced level of a particular attribute (less noise); the level of the attribute assigned to co-workers (closer to the boss); or the level of the attribute to which he or she aspires or expects to receive along with a promotion (more space).

As noted above, an individual's perception or assessment of an environmental attribute is related to but distinct from the objective attribute. For example, an employee operating in a very dense workspace may not necessarily feel crowded or lacking in privacy. From the point of view of researchers and the environmental designer, a central purpose of evaluation research is to explore such connections between specific environmental attributes and people's perceptions of them. By understanding these relationships, the designer will ultimately be in a better position to judge the ways in which prospective users of the built environment are likely to respond to his or her creation.

Individual perceptions and assessments of specific environmental attributes and the attributes themselves also contribute to a worker's job performance. High noise levels and feeling crowded can be distracting and can affect the quality and quantity of work produced. At the same time, the characteristics of the individual and his or her organizational context are likely to have some bearing on job performance. Another set of relationships implied by the model and suggested by the literature dealing with the quality of work life has to do with specific job characteristics as they relate to the worker's perceptions and assessments of them and to overall job satisfaction. One specific job characteristic and the responses to it centers on the quality of the physical environment. In our model, this is represented by the box labeled *Overall Environmental Satisfaction* and is seen as providing a unique contribution to overall job satisfaction. Finally, job satisfaction—like job performance—is apt to be influenced by the characteristics of the individual worker, such as age and seniority, and the organization within which he or she operates.

Although it is possible to develop appropriate measures for each element of the model within the context of any work environment evaluation, limitations will no doubt be placed on the researchers which prevent them from doing so. In our study of a federal office building, we were unable to measure the full range of employee job characteristics or the ways in which these characteristics were assessed by individual employees. Nor were we permitted to measure their overall job satisfaction. In part, these limitations were imposed by individuals whose cooperation was essential to the successful completion of the research. Similar limitations were placed on the researchers in their efforts to measure worker performance. Finally, the identification of specific characteristics of each organization within the building was considered to be beyond the bounds of our investigation. At best, we were able to differentiate between organizations by indicating the particular agency in which the individual employees worked.

TESTING THE MODEL: TWO CASE STUDIES

A new federal office building (Case Study 1) in Ann Arbor, Michigan, offered one opportunity to test the conceptual model. The building was built under new federal guidelines calling for architectural excellence and has been recognized by the architectural profession for its design. Within the first few years of completion, it received numerous design awards and extensive publicity in newspapers and in the architectural press. Nevertheless, it was reputed to have problems and had been the focus of controversy in Ann Arbor since its downtown site was announced in the early 1970s. An evaluation of the building also offered the potential for adapting both the findings and the approach used to the evaluation of other built environments, including those built under federal sponsorship.

A second opportunity to test the model was presented as part of an evaluation of a privately built office building (Case Study 2), used as a data processing center. The second evaluation used a survey instrument similar to the one developed for the federal building study. The evaluation was undertaken under private sponsorship by the owners and users of the facility in an attempt to measure its impact on the work force. Many design features within this second building were similar to those incorporated in the federal building, especially the use of three types of office arrangements: conventional, pool, and open. (A major locational change from a previously established geographic area was also a feature of both buildings.)

At the time the federal building evaluation was initiated (Fall 1979), the facility housed 14 separate government agencies and approximately 270 federal employees.[2] Except for the post office located on the ground floor, the interior contained large open-office spaces with north windows and had continuous overhead lightwells. All floors were connected to one another with an open lightwell located below the overhead skylight. The building represented one of the first attempts by the federal government to plan for flexibility by instituting an open-office arrangement. However, several conventional private offices and pool arrangements were also planned as part of the design.[3]

During the evaluation of the second office building (Summer 1982), there were 150 employees at the facility. As in the federal building, a high degree of flexibility was sought by the planners and managers, which resulted in the use of open-office arrangements that shared common amenities and public facilities among several separate work departments. Unlike the federal building, however, almost all the open-office furniture specified by the designers was installed at the time of occupancy.

Both evaluations were made from the perspective of the building users. The major users in the first evaluation were the federal employees who worked in the building; the residents of Ann Arbor and its surrounding communities were the second group. Information about these two groups and how they interacted with the building was obtained through questionnaires administered to all federal employees and to two samples of community residents, one representing visitors to the building and the other representing the community-at-large.

Similarly, the primary user group in the second evaluation was the employees, with opinions again being registered through self-administered questionnaires. For both studies, measures of a number of specific environmental characteristics or attributes of the building were also taken. Additionally, systematic and impressionistic observations were made of all users and the manner in which they interacted with the physical environment. The self-administered questionnaires for both sets of workers focused on their activities; their feelings about their particular building as a place to work; and their ratings of specific environmental attributes of the workspace.[4]

Findings of the two case studies are reported in the following section. For brevity, the federal office building evaluation is referred to as Case Study 1; Case Study 2 denotes the evaluation of the privately built office building.

RESULTS

The two case studies produced a number of significant findings, many of which support relationships suggested by the conceptual model. One of the more general findings from both studies, and perhaps the most important, is that people's assessments of the larger environmental settings are influenced by their feelings about their immediate workplace. In Case Study 1, these feelings were mixed: More than one-third of the federal employees expressed some level of dissatisfaction with their office environment.[5] In Case Study 2, only 10% of the workers were dissatisfied with their work stations. In both buildings, assessments of overall architectural quality and the functional arrangement of the larger office settings were strongly related to these assessments of the workplace.

It was also found that people with a greater degree of control over their immediate environment were more satisfied than those having a diminished amount of control. Occupants of conventional private office space expressed greater satisfaction with their workspaces than those working in open or pool arrangements.

Differences in response were also related to the kinds of offices people had previously experienced. Among the workers in the federal building in an open or pool office arrangement who previously had worked in a conventional office, three-quarters of the workers said their new workspace was worse; fewer than one-third (29%) of the workers in private offices who previously occupied an open office said their new work station was worse.

In Case Study 2, none of the employees had moved from conventional offices in the old building to open or pool arrangements in the new one. In fact, 15% had moved from a pool arrangement to an open arrangement with partitions, a fact that may help to explain the more positive ratings for this case study group.

Specific attributes of open and pool office arrangements were also rated poorly relative to attributes found in conventional offices. As seen in figure 5-2, workers in conventional offices in both case studies were

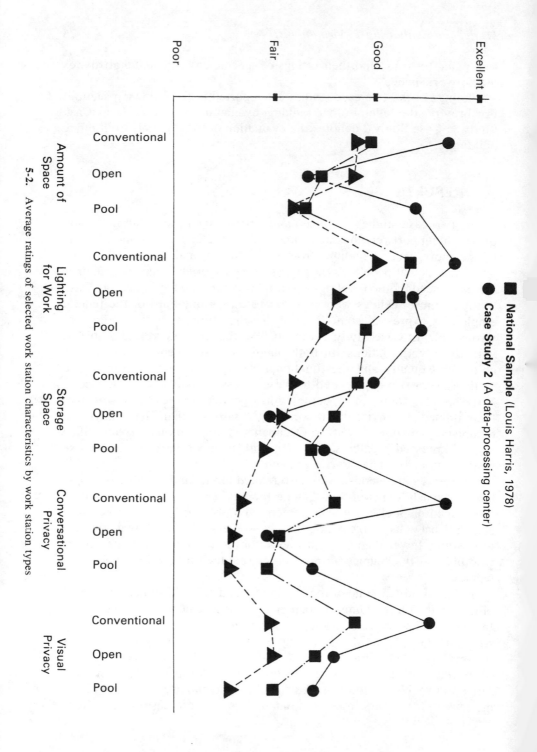

5-2. Average ratings of selected work station characteristics by work station types

Poor   Fair   Good   Excellent

■ **National Sample** (Louis Harris, 1978)
● **Case Study 2** (A data-processing center)

Amount of Space — Conventional, Open, Pool

Lighting for Work — Conventional, Open, Pool

Storage Space — Conventional, Open, Pool

Conversational Privacy — Conventional, Open, Pool

Visual Privacy — Conventional, Open, Pool

consistently higher in their ratings than workers in either the open or pool arrangements.

A comparison between our data and those from the first Harris study (1978) shows that the profiles of responses to specific work station characteristics are generally consistent (see fig. 5-3). However, the federal employees in Case Study 1 were generally more dissatisfied than the office workers in the national sample or in Case Study 2. This latter finding can be explained, in part, by the fact that governmental workers generally tend to be more critical of their work environment than are those in private sector (Harris 1978).

It can be seen from figure 5-3 that the most negative ratings of the workspace are those related to conversational and visual privacy. This is especially true of office workers occupying open or pool offices in all samples. In order to explore more fully these relationships, several specific attributes of the work station were examined vis-à-vis employee evaluations. Figures 5-4 and 5-5 show bivariate relationships for three types of worker evaluations and the amount of workspace and the specific type of work station.

As seen in figure 5-4, worker evaluation of conversational and visual privacy and the amount of workspace increases, logically, as the amount of actual workspace increases. In Case Study 1, this relation holds for work stations with *more* than 40 square feet of space; for very small work stations, a relatively higher rating was found for each of the three evaluative items. When the structure of our conceptual model is taken into account, these relationships are not anomalous; in fact, they are predictable. Our model has suggested that individual evaluations depend as much on job characteristics—such as job content—as on environmental attributes. In other words, the relationship between privacy and the amount of space cannot be viewed in isolation from the functions or tasks that are performed in that space. In the case of the federal building, work stations with less than 40 square feet were concentrated in the post office and were occupied only periodically during the day. Conceptually, therefore, one would not expect limited space to be as critical for postal workers, many of whom are carriers, as for people who perform more desk-related clerical or technical tasks. This hypothesis is reinforced in figure 5-5, where the responses of the postal workers to the privacy question are compared to those of people working in conventional, open, and pool arrangements.

In order to further examine the relationship between a global assessment of the work environment and specific worker evaluations of individual work stations, several multivariate analyses were performed with data from Case Study 1. In a model predicting work station satisfaction 41%

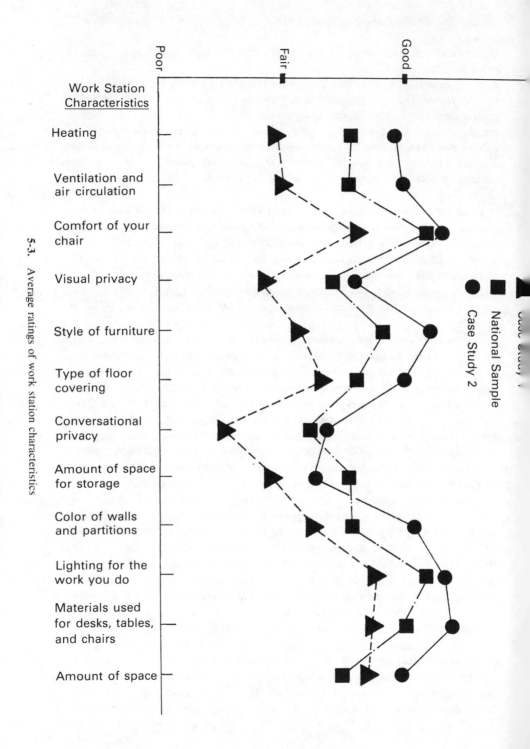

5-3. Average ratings of work station characteristics

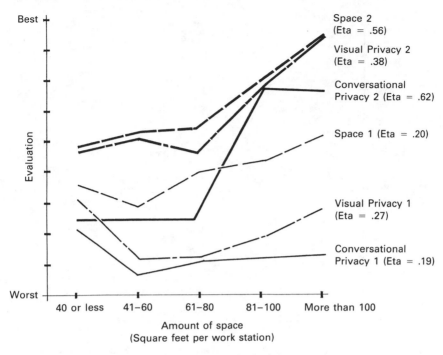

(1 indicates Case Study 1, 2 indicates Case Study 2)

5-4. Relationships between the amount of space and evaluations of space, conversational privacy, and visual privacy

of the variance was explained using a number of objective environmental attributes, subjective evaluations, and employee characteristics. Although the actual amount of workspace, the type of work station, and the agency in which the station was located were the most important predictors, workers' ratings of several environmental attributes were also important to the prediction of work station satisfaction (Table 5-1). As implied by the model, the extent to which federal employees were satisfied with their work stations was a function not only of who they were and where they worked, but of the level of specific environmental attributes available to them *and* how they evaluated these attributes. In another multivariate analysis predicting workers' responses to the larger environment (that is, the ambience of their agency), satisfaction with the individual work station was the predominant predictor, accounting for two-thirds of the total variance explained (46.6%).

In Case Study 2, a high degree of association was found among several predictors of work station satisfaction. For instance, ratings of the aesthetic quality of the workspace were related to ratings of its size ($r = .45$) and

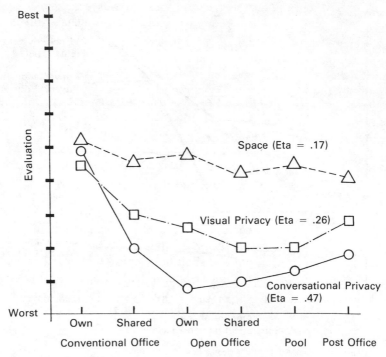

5-5. Relationships between type of work station and evaluation of space, conversational privacy, and visual privacy (Study 1)

to conversational privacy ($r = .32$). These ratings were also associated with people's assessments of overall architectural quality, providing additional support for our contention that the immediate workspace and its attributes can have a significant bearing on global environmental evaluations.

Finally, in order to understand more fully relationships between environmental attributes of the work station and feelings of workplace satisfaction, the building occupants in Case Study 2 were asked to rank 18 attributes in terms of their respective degrees of importance in helping them perform their jobs. As shown in figure 5-6, the attributes with the highest and most uniform rankings are those that most directly affect the immediate work environment, such as the amount of working surface, the size of the work area, task lighting, and storage space. Attributes associated with the macroenvironment of the job—the functional location in the building, travel distance to work, and proximity of outside amenities— were judged to be of lesser importance by the workers, especially those occupying open and pool arrangements.

Table 5-1. Satisfaction with Work Station, Predicted by Objective Work Station Attributes and Evaluation of Work Station Attributes*

Predictors	Eta Coefficient	BETA COEFFICIENT (RANKING OF IMPORTANCE)			
		Employee Characteristics Only	Employee Characteristics and Attribute Ratings	Employee Characteristics and Objective Attributes	Employee Characteristics, Objective Attributes and Attribute Ratings
EMPLOYEE CHARACTERISTICS					
Agency	.28	.34(1)	.17(5)	.20(3)	.39(2)
Job Classification	.24	.26(2)	.28(5)	.20(4)	.27(5)
OBJECTIVE ATTRIBUTES					
Amount of Workspace	.39			.49(1)	.50(1)
Chair Type	.33			.19(5)	.16(8)
Work Station Type	.25			.25(2)	.36(3)
Window Condition	.26			.14(6)	.31(4)
ATTRIBUTE RATINGS					
Aesthetic Quality	.38		.18(4)		.15(9)
Space	.33		.29(1)		.26(6)
Conversational Privacy	.30		.15(6)		.14(10)
View Outside	.21		.19(3)		.17(7)
Percentage of Variance Explained**		11.2	30.6	25.5	41.1

*Multiple classification analysis, 194 employees.
**Adjusted multiple R^2.

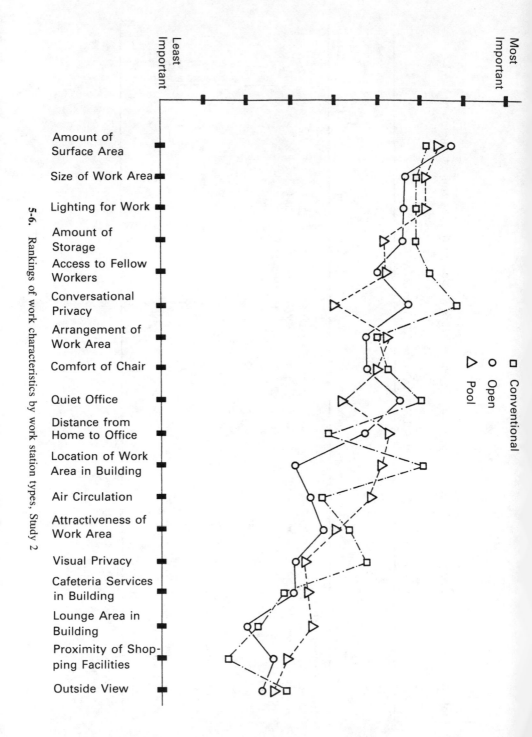

5-6. Rankings of work characteristics by work station types, Study 2

□ Conventional
○ Open
▷ Pool

Most Important

Least Important

Amount of Surface Area

Size of Work Area

Lighting for Work

Amount of Storage

Access to Fellow Workers

Conversational Privacy

Arrangement of Work Area

Comfort of Chair

Quiet Office

Distance from Home to Office

Location of Work Area in Building

Air Circulation

Attractiveness of Work Area

Visual Privacy

Cafeteria Services in Building

Lounge Area in Building

Proximity of Shopping Facilities

Outside View

Again, in terms of the model outlined earlier, the findings from the two case studies suggest that global measures of environmental satisfaction are strongly related to and dependent upon the success of immediate work station. Although many relationships within the model remain untested, especially with respect to the organizational purposes and arrangements (context), a number of indirect measures of this component of the model are seen to indicate the validity of our conceptualization. For example, data from Case Study 1 show that a major predictor of work station satisfaction is the organizational affiliation or agency of the worker (Table 5-1). In terms of further improvement and validation of this conceptual framework, we suggest that other studies focus on the connections between the nature of the organization and the work that takes place within it, and the physical setting of the office environment.

SUMMARY

This chapter has posited that most postoccupancy evaluations of office environments are inherently weak in both execution and theoretical foundation. In an attempt to deal with the latter problem, we have presented a conceptual model for guiding evaluators in the specification, collection, and analysis of salient data covering office environments. The model suggests the kinds of environmental conditions and subjective responses to those conditions that require consideration when studying job satisfaction and office worker performance.

Selected relationships suggested by that model have been examined using data from two case studies. Specifically, consideration has been given to the extent to which satisfaction with the individual workspace is a function of a number of environmental attributes, the worker's assessments of those attributes, and characteristics of the worker and his or her organization. Findings corroborate those reported by others in showing that conventional offices are viewed more favorably by the people occupying them than either open or pool office arrangements are. Furthermore, the amount of workspace available to a worker is the most important factor associated with satisfaction, even after taking into account the type of work station and the worker's ratings of specific work station attributes. It has also been shown that people's feelings about the ambience of the setting within which they work and the architecture of the building are a function of their reactions to their immediate workspace. Under the circumstances, space planners and designers who want their work appreciated by the user should concern themselves with the details of the workspace as well as with the larger-scale environment.

NOTES

1. The study was supported by a grant from the Center for Building Technology, National Bureau of Standards, U.S. Department of Commerce, Grant G8-9020.
2. Since the completion of the evaluation, several major changes in the building design and occupancy have taken place. For a complete discussion of the building, the changes, and the entire evaluation, see Marans and Spreckelmeyer (1981).
3. A *conventional* office is defined as a space surrounded by full-height, fixed partitions and occupied by one or two workers. An *open* office is one that is separated from the surrounding workspace with head-high, movable partitions. A *pool* arrangement houses workers in a large, open space with no visual separation between workers.
4. A total of 239 questionnaires in the federal office building evaluation were returned; the study of the private office building yielded 137 questionnaires. Response rates for the two surveys were 88.5% and 93%, respectively.
5. Despite their relative low assessments, office workers in the federal building are no different from government workers nationally. According to the first Harris study (1978), one-quarter of all office workers were not very or not completely satisfied with their individual work stations; among government workers, one-third were dissatisfied.

REFERENCES

Allen, T. J., and Gerstberger, P. G. 1973. A field experiment to improve communications in a product engineering department: The non-territorial office. *Human Factors* 15 (3): 487–498.

Architectural Record. 1978. The new buildings: Those guiding principles, pp. 110–111.

Canter, D., C. Kenny, and K. Rees. 1980. A multivariate model for place evaluation. Unpublished paper, Department of Psychology, University of Surrey, England.

Louis Harris and Associates. 1980. Comfort and productivity in the office of the 80s. Grand Rapids, MI: Steelcase, Inc.

Louis Harris and Associates. 1978. *The Steelcase national survey of office environments: Do they work?* Grand Rapids, MI: Steelcase, Inc.

Lunden, G. 1974. Environmental problems of office workers. *Build International* 3: 24–29.

Marans, R. W., and K. S. Spreckelmeyer. 1981. *Evaluating built environments: A behavioral approach.* Ann Arbor, MI: Institute for Social Research and Architectural Research Laboratory, the University of Michigan.

Marans, R. W., and W. Rodgers. 1975. Toward an understanding of community satisfaction. In A. Hawley and V. Rock (Eds.), *Metropolitan American in contemporary perspectives.* New York: Halsted Press.

Seashore, S. E. 1974. Job satisfaction as an indicator of the quality of employment. *Social Indicative Research* 1: 135–168.

Steele, F. I. 1973. *Physical settings and organizational development.* Reading, MA: Addison-Wesley.

Alternative Approaches to the Assessment of Employee Satisfaction with the Office Environment

GLENN S. FERGUSON
Buffalo Organization for Social and Technological Innovation (BOSTI)
Buffalo, New York

GERALD D. WEISMAN
School of Architecture and Urban Planning
University of Wisconsin–Milwaukee
Milwaukee, Wisconsin

The office environment, and the open office in particular, have emerged as settings of considerable interest to both academic and professional audiences. Reports on the movement toward the open office—as well as apparent employee dissatisfaction with such settings—have received national attention in the business press (such as, "The trouble with open offices," *Business Week* 1979; Rout, *Wall Street Journal* 1980). At the same time, the office setting has become the focus of substantial academic research within the fields of organizational behavior (for example, Oldham and Brass 1979), environment-behavior studies (Wineman 1982), and architectural planning and design (Duffy 1974a, 1974b).

For those who study, plan, and/or design such settings, however, many critical questions regarding the relationship between the office environment and employee attitudes and behavior have yet to be answered. The reasons for this lack of relevant theoretical and pragmatic information are numerous. Because the extant research literature reflects a variety of disciplinary perspectives, key relationships between organizational, psychological, and architectural variables are not always considered: progress toward integrative theory-building remains quite limited. Furthermore, since few studies deal with specific features of the physical setting in a detailed operational fashion, the generation of guidelines for office planning and design remains problematic.

This chapter, and the study it reports, endeavors to address these limitations of existing office environment research.[1] Building upon a broadly based conceptualization of the office "environment," a range of variables relevant to its organizational, behavioral, and physical components are briefly reviewed. An integrated model, based upon a subset of these variables and linking the office environment to employee satisfaction, is developed. Alternative approaches to the statistical testing and interpretation of such models are then examined. The chapter concludes with a discussion of implications for both office research and design.

Defining the Office Environment

The conduct of office environment research requires, of course, that one first define what constitutes "the office." Since such research has been carried out within a variety of disciplinary perspectives, it should not be surprising that the office itself has been conceptualized in a variety of ways, often quite limited in scope. Both the behavioral sciences and the traditional planning/design fields have in the past failed to deal with the environment in comprehensive and theoretically meaningful terms (Archea 1977; Ittelson, Proshansky, Rivin, and Winkel 1974). Thus, in office research, as in other facets of environment-behavior studies, there exists a need for what Moos (1973) has characterized as better conceptualizations of human environments.

The conceptualization of the office environment used in this chapter builds upon a succession of earlier models developed in the programming/design literature over the past decade (for example, Building Performance Research Unit 1972; Sanoff 1977). It likewise parallels the model of the environment more recently advanced by Moos and his associates (Moos 1973; Moos and Igra 1980) in their research on institutional settings. Thus, in this chapter the office is conceptualized as an "environment-behavior system" (Weisman 1981) composed of three interacting subsystems: organization, individuals, and physical setting.

To date, only a limited number of office environment studies have taken such a systems perspective; little attention has been directed toward organizational and individual factors as they interact with more frequently studied physical setting variables. Review of both the organizational behavior and management literatures, however, is suggestive of a range of variables that might profitably be explored in the context of office research. By way of example, Oldham and Brass's (1979) study illustrates the mediating role of organizational variables in linking office openness and employee satisfaction. Other potentially interesting organizational variables include task interdependence (Van de Ven 1980) as well as structural characteristics such as size, configuration, formalization, and centralization (Oldham and Hackman 1981). Familiar psychological concepts are also beginning to appear in the organizational literature in an effort to understand the role of the individual employee within the work environment. Thus Schuler, Ritzman, and Davis (1980) report findings regarding employee needs for privacy and autonomy, and Sims and Szilagyi (1976) suggest the potential value in exploring variables such as sense of personal control and need for personal fulfillment or self-actualization.

Variables related to the physical setting have been the focus of considerably more attention in office research. These variables include: room size (Canter 1968; Nemecek and Grandjean 1973b); density of people (Schuler et al. 1980; Szilagyi and Holland 1980); ambient conditions such as noise and light (for example, Beranek 1956; Brookes 1972; Nemecek and Grandjean 1973a); and office openness/enclosure (see Canter 1972; Duffy 1969; Justa and Golan 1977; Riland and Falk 1972).

Properties and Attributes

The environment-behavior systems model used here categorizes variables in a second way as well. In addition to grouping by organizational, individual, and physical setting subsystems, components of the system may be conceptually distinguished as either *properties* or *attributes* (Archea 1977; Weisman 1981).

Properties represent "those intrinsic, defining characteristics of a thing or class of things that make it what it is" (Archea 1977, 119). Thus, the size, shape, or temperature of an office may be characterized as objective, measurable, and (in some cases) enduring properties of its physical setting. Attributes, by contrast, are "those extrinsic, relational characteristics of things or class of things that relate them to other things for specific purposes" (p. 119). Thus crowdedness or privacy are most accurately characterized as contextually defined attributes of the environment as experienced.

Furthermore, attributes typically reflect interactions among organizational, individual, and physical setting components of the total environment-behavior system. An attribute of the environment such as crowdedness is in part a function of specific features and properties of the physical setting such as presence of doors and size of the workspace. However, it is also likely to be influenced by organizational and individual variables—group norms or the nature of the tasks performed, for example. The qualities people attribute to an environment are thus a product of such interactions, and these environmental attributes in turn influence patterns of behavior within the setting.

Recognition of this distinction between properties and attributes can provide greater conceptual clarity in the classification and interpretation of variables used to define the office "environment." Thus Marans and Spreckelmeyer's (1982, 340) distinction between "the individual's perceptions and assessments of . . . specific environmental attributes . . . and the specific attributes themselves," (such as excessive noise and stuffy air) might be characterized more precisely as a distinction between contextually defined attributes and objective properties. Such a distinction would likewise clarify the concepts of "psychological and architectural privacy" as employed by Hedge (1982) and Sundstrom, Burt, and Kamp (1980).

Finally, it may be suggested that exploration and understanding of the linkages between objective properties and subjective or experiential attributes constitute a central concern for theory building in office research and in environment-behavior studies more generally. Attributes such as privacy, crowdedness, and meaning, which are the products of interactions among the components of environment-behavior systems, are at the center of much of the environment-behavior research literature. As Kaplan and Kaplan (1982) argue, "It turns out that many of the important and interesting topics that concern environmental psychologists are based upon amorphous, hard-to-define, rather abstract concepts" (p. 209), which in the context of research are often characterized as *constructs*. Within the present discussion, attributes of the environment as experienced are viewed as such constructs, which require further definition in terms of the objectively defined properties that contribute to them.

Such relationships between properties and attributes assume importance for pragmatic reasons as well. Behaviorally based programming and design, such as that now conducted for office settings, is typically directed toward the creation of environments with particular qualities of privacy, meaning, or stimulation deemed relevant to desired behavioral outcomes. The office designer, however, can intervene only in terms of creating a setting with a specific set of properties—size, shape, color—which in interaction with other components of the total system will contribute to the attribution of desired qualities to the environment.

THE PRESENT STUDY

The considerations and conceptualizations described above serve to shape the study presented in this chapter. This research is directed toward a clearer understanding of the relationships between individual, organizational, and architectural variables within the office environment. Study variables, methods, and results are detailed in the following sections.

Study Variables

To the extent possible, variables selected for inclusion in the study are those past research has demonstrated as having significant relationships to other components of the total office system.

Job Level

A range of organizational variables are clearly relevant to office environment research; however, as described previously, few have been incorporated in such studies to date. For purposes of the present study, employees' job level (clerical, managerial, or executive, for example) is included as an organizational variable of interest.

As reviewed below, previous office research has demonstrated significant relationships between job level and facets of workplace satisfaction related to privacy (Sundstrom, Herbert, and Brown 1982a). More generally, it appears that job level is related to the next variable to be discussed— office openness—with enclosed offices often representing a perquisite of higher job levels.

Office Openness

Although the general movement toward open offices is quite clear-cut, the question of just what defines an "open" office, or what constitutes "openness" itself, remains more problematic. Open offices may include a range of different configurations, including multicellular, landscaped, and systems settings (Lorenzen and Jaeger 1968; Shuttleworth 1972). Likewise, the concept of openness has been defined and operationalized in a variety of ways in recent office environment research.

In general terms, openness may be seen as related to the presence or absence of visual and/or acoustic barriers within a space, as well as a more subjective sense of enclosure. Thus, measures used in previous research that might be viewed as relevant to the concept of openness include: number of workers within a room (Canter 1972; Nemecek and Grandjean 1973b), and the extent to which each individual within a space sees and can be seen by others (Archea 1974; Riland and Falk 1972). The concept of "architectural privacy" as employed by Sundstrom and his associates (1980) likewise appears to be related to openness as dealt with in the present research:

Architectural privacy refers to the visual and acoustic isolation supplied by the environment. A work area completely enclosed by soundproof walls with lockable doors embodies a high degree of architectural privacy; a large room in which many people occupy an undivided space would give minimal privacy (p. 102).

For the present study, data on office openness were gathered primarily through investigator observations of the various study settings. Descriptive information was recorded for such features and properties of the workspace as number of enclosed sides, presence or absence of a door, number of other employees sharing the space, and number of people visible from a normal seated position. Additional questionnaire items included Likert scale ratings of employee perceptions of office openness and conspicuousness, as well as satisfaction with these attributes of their workspace.

Perceived Privacy

It seems intuitively reasonable to hypothesize that office openness, as described above, should be related to the experience of privacy, as an attribute of the total system. Thus, Sundstrom and associates (1980) differentiate architectural from psychological privacy and posit a relationship between the two: "Architectural privacy may contribute to psychological privacy because people in private quarters can control their accessibility to others more easily than in open and visible places (p. 102)." Support for this relationship is provided by a number of office environment studies that demonstrate a negative relationship between perceived privacy and openness (Hundert and Greenfield 1969; McCarrey, Peterson, Edwards, and von Kulmiz 1974; Sundstrom et al. 1980; Sundstrom et al. 1982a).

Perceived privacy of employee workspaces was assessed through 13 questionnaire items. Items reflected both facets of the bidirectional nature of privacy (see Altman 1975). Thus one subset of questions tapped the extent to which respondents felt information about themselves was being disclosed to others, such as sense of being on display or freedom to speak freely at one's workspace. The second subset focused upon the unwanted intake of information from others: for example, hearing and understanding the conversations of others.

Distraction Due to Noise

In addition to office openness, one might also posit a relationship between perceived privacy and distraction due to noise. Thus, the extent to which noise in the office serves as a source of distraction has been studied directly by Mercer (1979), Nemecek and Grandjean (1973a), and Sundstrom and associates (1982a). Previous research has likewise demonstrated bivariate relationships between reported distraction due to noise and a range of other variables, including: office openness, number of individuals within a space, and perceived noise level (Sundstrom et al.

1980); ability to concentrate in open-plan offices (Nemecek and Grandjean 1973b; Ives and Ferdinands 1974); and satisfaction with the workspace and ratings of workspace utility (Sundstrom et al. 1982a). A recent national survey by Steelcase (1978) also suggests that substantial numbers of office workers perceive distraction due to noise to be a problem in their work environments.

In the present study, noise distraction was measured by ten questionnaire items assessing whether employees were annoyed by noise, found it difficult to concentrate or talk on the phone, or found their concentration disrupted.

Satisfaction

Two facets of satisfaction—satisfaction with the work environment and job satisfaction—are included in the present study as outcome measures and are viewed as two specific sources contributing to more general life satisfaction (Rice, Near, and Hunt 1980). Previous research has demonstrated relationships between a range of office variables and one or both of these measures of satisfaction; the demonstration of relationships directly tying the office environment and measures of global satisfaction or employee productivity, however, have yet to be supported by the research literature.

Previous research has defined bivariate relationships between *satisfaction with the office environment* and various facets of openness. These include: presence of partitions and doors (Sundstrom et al. 1980); relocation to an office landscape setting (Sundstrom et al. 1982a; Ives and Ferdinands 1974); and number of employees within a space (Canter 1972). Relevant questionnaire items included in the present study assessed satisfaction with specific features and properties of the workspace such as size, location, and furnishings, as well as satisfaction with the workspace in general. Employees were additionally queried regarding their desire to change aspects of their present office environment, or to change workspaces completely, along with their perceptions of the impact of their present space upon job performance.

The final variable[2] to be considered is *job satisfaction*. This is obviously a significant concept within the organizational literature (for example, Locke 1976; Schwab and Cummings 1970) and, as a more general form of satisfaction, has been found to bear a positive relationship to employees' satisfaction with their work environment (Canter 1972; Sundstrom et al. 1980). Job satisfaction has likewise been related to various facets of office openness, including: visibility (Schuler et al. 1980); relocation to office landscape settings (Oldham and Brass 1979); number of workers within a space; office size (Canter 1972; 1968); and Sundstrom and associates' (1980, 1982a, 1982b) concepts of architectural and psychological privacy. Relevant items included in the study questionnaire assessed employees' desire to change jobs as well as satisfaction with their daily routine and their work in general.

Methods

Settings and Subjects

As suggested at the outset, the clarification of relationships between objective properties of the physical setting and both attributes of the office as experienced and resultant behavioral responses constitutes a central challenge to environment-behavior studies in general and to office research in particular. The analysis of such relationships, however, will require moving beyond the case studies that constitute so much of the current office research literature (see Wineman 1982) and the very real limitations that such research designs impose. As Sommer (1977) argues, an investigation of any one setting, even if it involves hundreds of interviews and observations, "is still basically an $n = 1$ study" (p. 201). To assess adequately the impact of properties and features of the physical setting requires that the setting itself (for example, an entire office or individual work stations) serve as the unit of analysis, rather than individuals or groups, as more commonly employed in behavioral research. Thus the sampling of settings (Kaplan and Kaplan 1982) becomes an essential component of office environment research, providing some measure of variance in the design features of interest and maximizing the subsequent generalizability of a study.

To meet this desire for sampling of settings, office workers in eight different organizations participated in the research project. These organizations provide management and administrative support for banking, manufacturing, educational, research, and publishing activities. A variety of office types, ranging from traditional private spaces to large open areas housing 40 to 50 employees, were provided by each of the participating organizations.

Between 20 and 66 employees at each organization participated in the project, yielding a total of 360 respondents. These employees work at all levels in their organizations and fill many of the functional roles typically associated with office work.

Materials and Procedures

A questionnaire including 3 to 13 items for each of the six variables described in the previous section constituted the primary data-gathering instrument for the present study. Individual items were developed on the basis of relevant conceptual and methodological discussions in the architectural, environment-behavior, management, and psychological literatures. Response formats for the questionnaire items were predominantly 5-point Likert scales, with some additional multiple response questions. Instructions as well as a letter of introduction from an executive in each organization (from a personnel director or company president) were distributed to participating employees along with the eight-page questionnaire booklet.

Employees received the questionnaire early in the day at their workplace. After distribution of the booklets, the objective openness measures described above were recorded for each respondent's workplace. This procedure was relatively unobtrusive and took about five minutes per workplace. To assure confidentiality, the questionnaires were collected personally near the end of the work day.

Results

Complete and usable questionnaires were returned by 288 (80%) of the 360 employees asked to participate in the project. These questionnaires, along with the observational data for openness, were used in all analyses. Questionnaire items for each of the six study variables were evaluated in terms of both item-total and inter-item correlations, and items with low correlations (that is, below .40) were deleted from subsequent analyses. Cronbach's standardized coefficient alpha was then employed to assess the reliabilities of the resulting six composite variables. Alpha values ranged from .74 to .94, with a mean value of .82. Each of the final composite scales included from 2 to 10 items, for a total of 48 of the original pool of 57 items included in the questionnaire. These 48 items, as well as relevant statistics for each composite scale, are displayed in Table 6-1.

Measures employed to assess the degree of openness of the study settings were also evaluated using a factor analytic approach to better understand the facets of openness that were being assessed. Principal components analysis with varimax rotation yielded two components accounting for 59% and 10% of the variance, respectively. The first of these two factors included seven items related to the presence or absence of physical barriers in the office (such as number of walls, presence of a door, and size of room within which workspace is located). Visibility to others was assessed by five items with high factor loadings on the second component (number of others in the office, number of others visible from workspace, and visual exposure). Given the close relationship between these two components, as well as the high value of coefficient

Table 6-1. Scale Items and Statistics

SCALE STATISTICS

Items	Corrected Item-Total Correlation	Mean Inter-Item Correlation	Standardized Coefficient Alpha
JOB LEVEL			
Type of job	.59	.59	.74
Number of persons supervised	.59		
OPENNESS OF THE WORKSPACE			
Visibility to others	.44		
Ability to see others	.52		
Workspace very open	.53		
Number of walls around workspace[a]	− .74		
Door on workspace[a]	.55		
Type of workspace[a]	.75		
Number of persons in room[a]	.89	.55	.94
Degree of enclosure[a]	.72		
Visual access[a]	.45		
Size of workspace[a]	− .48		
Size of room workspace located in[a]	.64		
Number of persons in 400 sq ft area[a]	.62		
Visual exposure[a]	.81		
Distance to nearest neighbor[a]	− .44		
AURAL DISTRACTIONS			
Concentration frequently distracted	.74		
Frequently annoyed by noise	.84		
Noise interferes with job performance	.80		
Noise level too high	.80	.67	.94
Noise makes talking difficult	.80		
Workspace usually quiet	− .72		
Satisfied with noise level	− .82		
Ability to concentrate	− .83		
PERCEIVED PRIVACY			
Feel like on display to others	− .62		
Very little privacy	− .80		
Very few activities unknown to others	− .77		
Can hear other's conversations	− .47		
More private than other workspaces	.55	.48	.90
Have time to myself	.67		
Others know little about my conversations	.68		
Low visibility to others	.52		
Satisfactory level of privacy	.78		
Ability to have private conversations	.76		

Table 6-1. *(Continued)*

Items	Corrected Item-Total Correlation	Mean Inter-Item Correlation	Standardized Coefficient Alpha
SATISFACTION WITH WORKSPACE			
Would like to change workspace	− .76		
Difficult to do job in workspace	− .71		
Like my workspace	.70		
Like a different type of workspace	− .79		
Satisfied with workspace	.82	.55	.92
Satisfied with size of workspace	.75		
Like arrangement of workspace	.67		
Like location of workspace	.55		
Satisfied with workspace furnishings	.63		
JOB SATISFACTION			
Several things I dislike about my job	− .54		
In general I like my job	.57		
Would like to change jobs	− .52	.45	.80
Satisfied with daily job routine	.60		
Satisfied with the work I do	.65		

a. Measures recorded by the investigator. All other measures reported by respondants on questionnaire.

alpha for the entire openness scale, it was decided not to segregate these two components in subsequent analyses.

Correlations among the six composite variables used in the study are presented in Table 6-2. Statistically significant relationships exist among most variables. Particularly strong relationships exist between perceived privacy and openness, aural distraction, and satisfaction with the work-

Table 6-2. Correlation Matrix

VARIABLE NUMBERS

Variables	1	2	3	4	5	6
1. Job Level	−					
2. Openness	− .36*	−				
3. Distractions	− .11	.45*	−			
4. Privacy	.29*	− .66*	− .71*	−		
5. Satisfaction	.09	− .40*	− .71*	.64*	−	
6. Job Satisfaction	.18*	− .20*	− .20*	.36*	.35*	−

*p < .01

space; there is likewise a strong relationship between aural distraction and satisfaction with the workspace. Job level had the fewest significant relationships to other variables; specifically, aural distraction and satisfaction with the workspace appear to be unrelated to job level.

To gain further insight into the relationships among these variables, stepwise multiple regression analyses were also performed. Job satisfaction was used as the dependent variable in the first analysis, and the remaining five variables accounted for a total of 19% of the variance (multiple R = .45). A second equation, predicting satisfaction with the workspace from aural distraction, privacy, openness, and job level, yielded a significantly higher multiple R of .74, accounting for 54% of the variance in satisfaction with the workspace. The stepwise regression procedure selected aural distraction as the first variable for inclusion in this model, indicating that it was the "best predictor" among the set of four variables employed.

Discussion

A number of conclusions regarding the process and substance of office environment research may reasonably be drawn from these data. First, traditional psychometric scale construction techniques can be used to create reliable measures of physical, organizational, and individual dimensions of the office environment. By clearly identifying the components of these dimensions prior to questionnaire development, it is possible to create measures that discriminate among closely related variables.

The sampling of workers employed in a number of businesses, holding a range of job levels, and occupying a variety of office settings provides variance in the variables of interest. In much of the existing office research, often only a single subset of employees (for example, clerical staff), a limited range of organizations, or dichotomous characterizations of the office (open versus closed, for one) have been employed. Expanding the range of variance on variables assessing these several dimensions of the office environment, as was the case in the present study, should decrease the likelihood of erroneous generalizations from the data.

Finally, results of the data analyses provide useful evidence regarding correlates of the open-plan office. Relationships between degree of openness and perceived privacy, aural distraction, and job satisfaction, as demonstrated in previous research and reviewed earlier in this chapter, were replicated in the present study. In addition, satisfaction with both workplace and job was found to be related to openness of the office environment. Thus, open-plan settings may influence employees' work by decreasing satisfaction with both the work setting and the job in general. Although the analytical techniques used preclude interpretation of cause-and-effect relationships among these variables, the significant, and in some cases rather large, correlations among variables certainly justify further research to clarify underlying processes and causal orderings.

AN ALTERNATIVE APPROACH

The presentation of the above study completed, this chapter might well end at this point. Indeed the reader may be surprised to find that it does not. The study, after all, appears to be a perfectly reasonable and moderately successful investigation of behavioral issues in the office environment. The correlation coefficients reported are quite substantial, accounting for what in behavioral research constitutes a credible percentage of variance. The results likewise replicate and support findings from previous office research.

Further examination, however, reveals additional, and unnecessary, limitations that serve to constrain the theoretical as well as pragmatic value of this and comparable studies of the office setting. Survivors of any introductory statistics course know that correlation does not imply causation; however, it is all too often assumed that an understanding of causal relationships can be obtained only through the use of traditional experimental designs, often ill-suited to field research. Thus, authors of correlational studies describe how variables "appear" to be related to one another, and what "seem" to be causal ties between them, much as was done in the preceding discussion section.

Limitations of this sort, however, are not inevitable. Even with non-experimental data, one is not necessarily limited to "estimation model" techniques, such as correlation and regression, which are directed toward estimation of the proportion of variance for which a variable or set of variables is able to account. There are also "structural models" (Heise 1968) that can be used to "permit prediction of how a *change* in any one variable in the system affects the values of [all] other variables in the system" (p. 41).

Thus, the study reported in the preceding section will be recast into a structural model framework to illustrate the process, output, and presumed benefits of such an alternative approach to office environment research. Study settings, methods, and instruments will all remain as before; only the approach to conceptualizing and analyzing relationships among variables will differ. This section will conclude with a consideration of some of the contributions, both theoretical and pragmatic, of this alternative model.

Structural Models and Path Analysis

One of the most common techniques for the analysis of structural models is provided by path analysis (Duncan 1966; Wright 1934). Among its benefits, path analysis allows the investigator to break down the correlations in a relationship and to predict the outcome of the hypothesized change without directly manipulating the variables (Heise 1968). Although path analysis does not allow one to "prove" causation, it does provide a statistical means of testing a model in which a causal ordering is hypothesized, "and thus of making quantitative an interpretation which would otherwise be merely qualitative" (Wright 1934, 175).

To realize these benefits of path analysis, two basic assumptions must be met: (1) One must have knowledge of, or be able to hypothesize, the causal order among a set of variables; and (2) the relationships under study must occur in a closed system (Kim and Kohout 1973).[3]

To meet these demands of path analysis, it is first necessary to integrate the six variables defined previously into a structural model that posits causal orderings among them. Direction for the construction of this model can be derived from the discussion of environment-behavior systems at the outset of the chapter. Thus, an adequate model should reflect the three interacting components of such systems—organization, individuals, and physical setting—as well as the fact that the office environment, as people perceive it and act within it, is defined by the interactions among these three components of the total system.

In general terms, it might be suggested that organizational variables influence decisions about the physical setting that the organization occupies. Organizational variables likewise influence employees' perceptions of and responses to the office setting. Finally, the physical setting exerts an influence upon employees' perceptions, which, in turn, shape behavioral and affective responses to the office. This general model is depicted in figure 6-1.

Figure 6-2 corresponds to the general environment-behavior schema depicted in figure 6-1, but incorporates the six variables used in the analyses reported in the first section of the chapter. *Job level,* which is included as an organizational component of interest, is frequently a determinant of one's office setting and may also influence one's response to open-plan settings (Sundstrom et al. 1982a). *Degree of openness* represents that aspect of the physical setting of most immediate concern and is defined primarily in terms of properties of the individual employee's

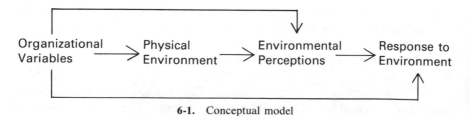

6-1. Conceptual model

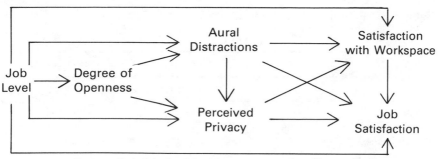

6-2. Structural model of employee responses to the office environment

workspace. Experience or perception of the work environment are represented by both *distraction due to noise* and *perceived privacy.* Finally, *satisfaction with the workspace* and *job satisfaction* are viewed as outcome measures. Hypothesized causal relationships among these variables are as depicted in figure 6-2.

Evaluation of the Structural Model

Tests for linearity and additivity—assumptions of path analysis—were carried out prior to performing the actual analyses (Billings and Wroten 1978). No violations of the assumptions were detected.

The "theory trimming" approach to path analysis (Heise 1968) was employed to test the structural model depicted in figure 6-2. This approach involves statistically analyzing a model in which causal paths between all possible pairs of variables are specified (that is, a "completely specified" model). Path analysis provides a statistical basis for deciding which, if any, paths to delete from the completely specified model in order to produce a more parsimonious or "reduced model" (Kerlinger and Pedhazur 1973) while still reflecting the relationships among variables. The reduced model is then evaluated to determine if any paths critical to the model have been deleted. If not, the reduced model may be compared to the hypothesized structural model to determine the similarity between the two.

Path coefficients for the completely specified model corresponding to Table 6-2 are shown in Table 6-3. These coefficients may be interpreted in roughly the same way one interprets correlation coefficients. However, path coefficients reflect only the *direct effect* of one variable on another. Path coefficients thus differ from correlation coefficients, which are indicative of: (1) *direct effects;* (2) *indirect effects* transmitted from one variable to another through other variables in the model; and (3) correlations

Table 6-3. Path and Correlation Coefficients

VARIABLE NUMBERS

Variables	1	2	3	4	5	6
(a) PATH COEFFICIENTS						
1. Job Level	–					
2. Openness	−.36	–				
3. Distractions	.05[a]	.47	–			
4. Privacy	.10[a]	−.39	−.53			
5. Satisfaction	−.05[a]	.01[a]	−.50	.31	–	
6. Job Satisfaction	.10[a]	.10[a]	.28	.38	.33	–
(b) CORRELATION COEFFICIENTS						
1. Job Level	–					
2. Openness	−.36	–				
3. Distractions	−.11	.45	–			
4. Privacy	.29	−.66	−.71	–		
5. Satisfaction	.09	−.40	−.71	.64	–	
6. Job Satisfaction	.18	−.20	−.20	.36	.35	–
(c) ESTIMATED CORRELATION COEFFICIENTS						
1. Job Level	–					
2. Openness	−.36	–				
3. Distractions	−.17	.47	–			
4. Privacy	.23	−.63	−.71	–		
5. Satisfaction	.09	−.43	−.72	.67	–	
6. Job Satisfaction	.07	−.25	−.23	.41	.39	–

a. Paths deleted from the completely specified model.

between two variables of interest and a *third variable* not included in the model. Also, the path coefficient for A → B will not be the same as that for B → A, as would be the case for the A–B correlation coefficient.

The theory-trimming procedure resulted in the deletion of six paths. The path from job level to openness was retained, whereas paths from job level to all other variables were deleted. Two additional paths—from openness to the two satisfaction variables—were also deleted. The reduced model (i.e., the structural model after deletion of these six paths), as well as the path coefficients for the remaining paths, are shown in figure 6-3.

Statistical evaluation of the reduced model is possible using correlation coefficients. If correlations computed for the reduced model adequately reproduce the actual correlations among the six variables, there is reason to believe that the reduced model accurately reflects the obtained data

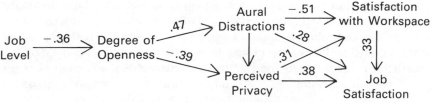

6-3. Reduced model and path coefficients

(Duncan 1966); the model may then be assumed to accurately portray the true relationships among the variables. In Table 6-3, the correlations estimated from the path coefficients are shown below the actual correlations. Comparison of these values indicates that the reduced model adequately reflects the data collected in the project (likelihood ratio = 2.82, $p > .05$).

Discussion

Inspection of figures 6-2 and 6-3 reveals them to be quite similar; thus the plausibility of the model of employee response to the office environment developed at the outset of this section is to a considerable extent supported. Primary revisions that appear necessary consist of deletion of the four paths that originate with the organizational variable, job level. The remainder of the structural model is confirmed by the data.

On the basis of the existing research literature, relationships, as displayed in figure 6-2, were hypothesized between job level and the other five variables within the model. Path coefficients, however, indicate that although the relationship between job level and openness is relatively strong ($p = -.36$), the strength of the remaining four relationships— distraction, privacy, workspace satisfaction, and job satisfaction—is minimal. This suggests that job level has a greater influence upon the type of workspace to which an employee is assigned than it does upon the individual's perceptions of the work environment.

These results would also seem to contradict the belief of many designers and managers that people at higher job levels are less satisfied with open offices. The symbolic value of a closed office as an indicator of status and job level may be quite important (see Konar, Sundstrom, Brady, Mandel and Rice 1982), but as figure 6-3 illustrates, job level alone produces little influence on employee perceptions or satisfaction with the office. This suggests that individuals at different job levels may be equally satisfied with open offices.

Given the primary concerns of the overall study, the relationship between openness and satisfaction with the office is clearly of particular interest.

As figure 6-3 illustrates, this relationship is mediated by both distraction due to noise and perceived privacy. Path coefficients for these indirect effects are computed by multiplying and summing the path coefficients for alternate paths between these two variables (see Duncan 1966). The coefficients for these indirect paths demonstrate that although openness does not directly influence satisfaction with the workspace, it has an indirect effect on satisfaction by influencing aural distractions ($p = -.23$) and perceived privacy ($p = -.12$). By comparison, the path coefficients for the *direct* effect between openness and satisfaction, displayed in Table 6-3(a), is .01, demonstrating a negligible direct influence.

This distinction between direct and indirect effects is of particular salience in contrasting the conclusions of the path analytic approach employed here with the correlational approach used earlier in this chapter and in much of the office research literature. By way of example, in the present study a correlation coefficient of $-.40$ was obtained for the relationship between office openness and workspace satisfaction. This is consistent with values ranging between $-.25$ and $-.50$ previously reported in the literature (for example, Sundstrom et al. 1980; Sundstrom, Town, Brown, Forman, and McGee 1982b). However, given the negligible direct effect of openness on satisfaction reported above ($p = .01$), it becomes clear that the relatively high correlation coefficient is due almost entirely to indirect effects. Thus, it is likely the case that confusion about the sources of dissatisfaction with the open office has continued unnecessarily because previous correlational studies have not been able to separate out direct and indirect effects; as a consequence, it has been incorrectly assumed that the openness of offices directly influences employee satisfaction with these settings.

Careful examination of figure 6-3 reveals what appears to be one anomaly: a positive path coefficient for the aural distraction/job satisfaction path. Such a relationship would seem counterintuitive, since one would more likely expect that as distraction increases, job satisfaction would decrease, as is the case for satisfaction with the workspace. Two explanations for this phenomenon are plausible: (1) A third variable, not included in the present model, may be correlated with both distraction and job satisfaction; or (2) the positive direct relationship between these two variables may be offset by large negative indirect effects.

With regard to the first of these two possible explanations, the presence of a correlated third variable would result in an undetected indirect causal path between aural distraction and job satisfaction. Two pieces of evidence, however, suggest that such an extraneous variable is *not* responsible for the anomalous positive path coefficient. First, as discussed in the Results section, no violations of the additivity assumption of path analysis were detected; the presence of a third variable would likely be demonstrated by a nonadditive relationship between distraction and job satisfaction.

Second, that part of the correlation between these two variables that is due to common or correlated causes is $-.05$, not a statistically or logically significant value.

The second proposed explanation for this anomalous relationship—indirect effects that offset the direct effect—appears to be the more likely one. Significant *negative* path coefficients are present for the indirect path by way of privacy ($p = -.20$) and also via satisfaction with the workspace ($p = -.16$), indicating that the net effect is negative ($-.14$), as would be expected. Thus, we can assume that, considering the model as a whole, higher levels of distraction will result in lower job satisfaction by reducing perceived privacy and satisfaction with the workspace.

A final set of conclusions that may be drawn from figure 6-3 concerns the *strength* of the relationships among the variables included in the model. For a direct effect, one may square the relevant path coefficient to determine the proportion of variance of the latter variable directly accounted for by the causally prior variable. For example, satisfaction with the workspace accounts for 11% of the variance in job satisfaction ($.33^2 = .11$), whereas 28% ($-.53^2 = .28$) of the variance in perceived privacy is accounted for by aural distractions. Determination of strength of relationships in situations involving multiple paths (that is, indirect effects or multiple causes of one effect) require more complex analyses.[4]

The multiple paths of most interest are those from openness to both satisfaction with the workspace and job satisfaction. Openness accounts for 19% and 6% of the variance in these two variables, respectively. While the reader may at first be somewhat surprised, or even disappointed at how little of the variance in these satisfaction measures is explained by openness, two fundamental issues must be kept in mind. First, it is the case that myriad other variables in addition to openness likely influence employee satisfaction and must, therefore, account for some proportion of the variance in these measures. Second, the environment-behavior system perspective outlined earlier in the chapter posits that the effects of openness are mediated by other variables within the system rather than being transmitted directly to satisfaction with both workspace and job. In keeping with this systems viewpoint, the model in figure 6-3, which incorporated organizational and individual as well as physical variables, is able to account for fully 54% of the variance in multidimensional satisfaction with the office.

CONCLUSIONS AND IMPLICATIONS

Having presented these two alternative approaches to the assessment of employee satisfaction with the office environment, what conclusions and implications can now be drawn? In brief, it is hoped that this direct comparison of estimation and structural models has served to illustrate and highlight a number of issues viewed as central to further development in the field of office research. These issues deal with both substance and methodology and, perhaps most important, with the relationships between the structuring of a study and what one can potentially learn from it.

It is likely that the key substantive conclusion concerns the lack of a direct relationship between those physical features and properties that contribute to office openness and employee satisfaction with either work-space or job. Thus, attempts to increase employee satisfaction through reduction of office openness may not be as effective as interventions that alter perceptions of aural distraction and/or perceived privacy are. The utilization of sound-masking systems, selection of furnishings with low acoustical reflectance values, or reorientation of employees' desks to improve visual and auditory privacy may therefore all serve to enhance satisfaction, even though they do not represent a change in openness of the work setting.

Furthermore, as defined at the outset of the chapter, distraction and privacy are both attributes of the environment as experienced and are potentially influenced by all components of the environment-behavior system. Thus, organizational and individual factors, as well as those related to the physical setting, may represent appropriate means of inter-vention in the office. Organizational policies that clearly define employees' rights to both quiet and privacy within their workspace or educational programs that enhance awareness of nonverbal privacy cues may be infrequently used but effective approaches to increased satisfaction with both office and job.

The primary methodological implications of this chapter clearly relate to the utilization of path analysis as an approach to office environment research. Since much attention was given in the preceding section to the identification and testing of causal orderings among a set of variables, it is essential to clarify the value and limitations of such a concern with causation. As noted earlier, path analysis does not allow one to prove causation in a definitive fashion. On both pragmatic and epistemological grounds, it is not reasonable to assume that one could ever identify and measure all the variables that interact in a complex system such as an office environment.

At the same time, as Kerlinger (1973) notes, "path analysis and related methods can help to clarify theoretical and empirical relationships" (p. 393). The initial construction of a causal model requires that one articulate on theoretical and/or empirical grounds what seems to be a reasonable set of relationships among a set of variables. Path analysis, in turn, provides a means of testing the adequacy of this particular modeling (and sim-plification) of reality.

The estimation model techniques, such as correlation and regression, more commonly employed in office research, might be seen as taking something of a black box approach in which no attention is given to the interrelationships among variables. By contrast, the structural model approach illustrated here is seen as contributing to the construction of a conceptualization of the office as a system. Such a model can provide a rich set of hypotheses for further empirical research. Furthermore, to the extent we are able to better understand the relationships among components of the office system, we should have a better basis for confident and informed decision making. Thus, both research and design can contribute to the provision of facilities appropriate to the tasks that must be performed and to the social and psychological needs of office workers.

NOTES

1. The empirical portions of this chapter are based upon a doctoral dissertation carried out by the first author in the Program in Man-Environment Relations at Pennsylvania State University.
2. See Ferguson (1984) for a discussion of the variables not considered here.
3. In the context of structural modeling, a closed system is one in which the variables of primary conceptual and theoretical interest are included.
4. An addendum to Duncan (1966), which appeared in H. M. Blalock (Ed.), *Causal Models in the Social Sciences*, Chicago: Aldine, 1971, corrects errors in the earlier discussion of the computation of indirect effects. This addendum also reviews the decomposition of correlation coefficients into direct effects, indirect effects, and correlation due to common or correlated causes. The strength of a complex relationship may then be determined by squaring the appropriate indirect effect for indirect paths, or by squaring the multiple R to determine the variance accounted for by multiple causes of a dependent variable.

REFERENCES

Altman, I. 1975. *The environment and social behavior: Privacy, personal space, territory, crowding*. Monterey, CA: Brooks/Cole.

Archea, J. 1974. Identifying direct links between behavior and its environment: Toward a predictive model. In T. O. Byerts (Ed.), *Environmental research and aging*. Washington, D.C.: Gerontological Society of America.

Archea, J. 1977. The place of architectural factors in behavioral theories of privacy. *Journal of Social Issues* 33(3): 116–137.

Beranek, L. L. 1956. Criteria for office quieting based on questionnaire rating studies. *Journal of the Acoustical Society of America* 28: 833–852.

Billings, R. S., and S. P. Wroten. 1978. Use of path analysis in industrial/organizational psychology: Criticisms and suggestions. *Journal of Applied Psychology* 63: 677–688.

Brookes, M. J. 1972. Office landscape: Does it work? *Applied Ergonomics* 3(4): 224–236.

Building Performance Research Unit. 1972. *Building performance.* New York: John Wiley & Sons.

Canter, D. 1968. Office size: An example of psychological research in architecture. *Architects' Journal* (April 24): 881–888.

Canter, D. 1972. Reactions to open plan offices. *Built Environment* 1(October 1972): 465–467.

Duffy, F. 1969. A method of analyzing and charting relationships in the office. *Architects' Journal* 149(11): 693–699.

Duffy, F. 1974a. Office design and organizations: 1. Theoretical basis. *Environment and Planning B* 1: 105–118.

Duffy, F. 1974b. Office design and organizations: 2. The testing of a hypothetical model. *Environment and Planning B* 1: 217–235.

Duncan, O. D. 1966. Path analysis: Sociological examples. *American Journal of Sociology* 72: 1–16.

Ferguson, G. S. 1984. Evaluation of a causal model of the office environment. Unpublished doctoral dissertation, Program in Man-Environment Relations, Pennsylvania State University, University Park, PA.

Hedge, A. 1982. The open-plan office: A systematic investigation of employee reactions to their work environment. *Environment and Behavior* 14(5): 519–542.

Heise, D. R. 1968. Problems in path analysis and causal inference. In E. F. Borgatta (Ed.), *Sociological methodology 1969.* San Francisco: Jossey-Bass, 1968.

Hundert, A. T., and N. Greenfield. 1969. Physical space and organizational behavior: A study of an office landscape. *Proceedings of the 77th Annual Convention of the American Psychological Association* 4: 601–602.

Ittelson, W. H., H. M. Proshansky, L. G. Rivlin, and G. H. Winkel. 1974. *An introduction to environmental psychology.* New York: Holt, Rinehart & Winston.

Ives, R. S., and R. Ferdinands. 1974. Working in a landscaped office. *Personnel Practice Bulletin* 30(2): 126–141.

Justa, F. C., and M. B. Golan. 1977. Office design: Is privacy still a problem? *Journal of Architectural Research* 6(2): 5–12.

Kaplan, S., and R. Kaplan. 1982. *Cognition and environment: Functioning in an uncertain world.* New York: Praeger Publishers.

Kerlinger, F. N. 1973. *Foundations of behavioral research,* 2nd ed. New York: Holt, Rinehart & Winston.

Kerlinger, F. N., and E. J. Pedhazur. 1973. *Multiple regression in behavioral research.* New York: Holt, Rinehart & Winston.

Kim, J. O., and F. J. Kohout. 1973. Special topics in general linear models. In N. H. Nie, C. H. Hull, J. G. Jenkins, K. Steinbrenner, and D. H. Bent (Eds.), *Statistical package for the social sciences,* 2nd ed. New York: McGraw-Hill.

Konar, E., E. Sundstrom, C. Brady, D. Mandel, and R. W. Rice. 1982. Status demarcation in the office. *Environment and Behavior* 14(5): 561–580.

Locke, E. A. 1976. The nature and causes of job satisfaction. In M. D. Dunnette (Ed.), *Handbook of industrial and organizational psychology.* Chicago: Rand McNally.

Lorenzen, H. J., and D. Jaeger. 1968. The office landscape: A "systems" concept. *Contract* 9: 164–173.

Marans, R. W., and K. F. Spreckelmeyer. 1982. Evaluating open and conventional office design. *Environment and Behavior* 14: 333–351.

McCarrey, M. W., L. Peterson, S. Edwards, and P. von Kulmiz. 1974. Landscape office attitudes: Reflections of perceived degree of control over transactions with the environment. *Journal of Applied Psychology* 54: 401–403.

Mercer, A. 1979. Office environments and clerical behaviour. *Environment and Planning B* 6: 29–39.

Moos, R. H. 1973. Conceptualizations of human environments. *American Psychologist* 28: 632–665.

Moos, R. H., and A. Igra. 1980. Determinants of the social environments of sheltered care settings. *Journal of Health and Social Behavior*, 21: 88–98.

Nemecek, J., and E. Grandjean. 1973a. Noise in landscaped offices. *Applied Ergonomics* 4(1): 19–22.

Nemecek, J., and E. Grandjean. 1973b. Results of an ergonomic investigation of large-space offices. *Human Factors* 15(2): 111–124.

Oldham, G. R., and D. J. Brass. 1979. Employee reactions to an open-plan office: A naturally occurring quasi-experiment. *Administrative Science Quarterly* 24: 267–284.

Oldham, G. R., and J. R. Hackman. 1981. Relationships between organizational structure and employee reactions: Comparing alternative frameworks. *Administrative Science Quarterly* 26(1): 66–83.

Rice, R. W., J. P. Near, and R. G. Hunt. 1980. The job satisfaction/life satisfaction relationship: A review of empirical research. *Basic and Applied Social Psychology* 1(1): 37–64.

Riland, L. H., and J. Z. Falk. 1972. *Employee reactions to office landscape environment.* Rochester, NY: Personnel Relations Department, Eastman Kodak Company, April.

Rout, L. 1980. Designers modify the open office to meet complaints of workers. *Wall Street Journal* (November 5): 1.

Sanoff, H. 1977. *Methods of architectural programming.* Stroudsburg, PA: Dowden, Hutchinson and Ross.

Schuler, R. S., L. P. Ritzman, and V. Davis. 1980. *Merging prescriptive and sociopsychological approaches for office layout* (WPS 80-27). Columbus, OH: Ohio State University, College of Administrative Science, April.

Schwab, D. P., and L. L. Cummings. 1970. Theories of performance and satisfaction: A review. *Industrial Relations* 9(4): 408–430.

Shuttleworth, G. N. 1972. Convertible space in office buildings. *Building Research* 9(2): 9–15.

Sims, H. P., Jr., and A. D. Szilagyi. 1976. Job characteristic relationships: Individual and structural moderators. *Organizational Behavior and Human Performance* 17: 211–230.

Sommer, R. 1977. Action research. In D. Stokols (Ed.), *Perspectives on environment and behavior: Theory, research and applications.* New York: Plenum Publishing.

Steelcase Inc. 1978. *The Steelcase national study of office environments: Do they work?* Grand Rapids, MI: Steelcase Inc.

Sundstrom, E., R. E. Burt, and D. Kamp. 1980. Privacy at work: Architectural correlates of job satisfaction and job performance. *Academy of Management Journal* 23(1): 101–117.

Sundstrom, E., R. K. Herbert, and D. W. Brown. 1982a. Privacy and communication in an open-plan office: A case study. *Environment and Behavior* 14: 379–392.

Sundstrom, E., J. P. Town, D. W. Brown, A. Forman, and C. McGee. 1982b. Physical enclosure, type of job, and privacy in the office. *Environment and Behavior* 14(5): 543–559.

Szilagyi, A. D., and W. E. Holland. 1980. Changes in social density: Relationships with functional interaction and perceptions of job characteristics, role stress, and work satisfaction. *Journal of Applied Psychology* 65: 28–33.

Business Week. 1978. The trouble with open offices. (August 7): 84–88.

Van de Ven, A. H. with M. A. Morgan. 1980. A revised framework for organization assessment. In E. E. Lawler, III, D. A. Nadler, and C. Cammann (Eds.), *Organizational assessment: Perspectives on the measurement of organizational behavior and the quality of work life.* New York: John Wiley & Sons.

Weisman, G. D. 1981. Modeling environment-behavior systems: A brief note. *Journal of Man-Environment Relations* 1(2): 32–41.

Wineman, J. D. 1982. Office design and evaluation: An overview. *Environment and Behavior* 14: 271–298.

Wright, S. 1934. The method of path coefficients. *Annals of Mathematical Statistics* 5: 161–215.

The Perceived Office:
The Office Environment as
Experienced by Its Users

RONALD GOODRICH
Building Programs International
New York, New York

The office environment, unlike the factory environment, has not been the focus of much psychological research. As a benign, safe, and clean workplace, it was not seen as having significant impact upon users and user performance. This is no longer considered true. Now, as a result of the growing importance of office work, the introduction of office automation, the changing character of work, and the economics of office buildings, the office environment is becoming more intimately linked to the psychological needs, performance, and well-being of its users. We are creating environmental conditions that support or even enhance the work experience of individuals as well as the performance of organizations.

Office work continues to grow in importance, both in terms of the numbers of people involved and the nature of the work conducted. In the past, the office was organized as a support function to the manufacturing process, to record sales transactions and monitor the production process. Office tasks were primarily those of paper handling. For this passive mode, office design needed only to provide an acceptable, functional workplace. Today, office work is increasingly concerned with the generation and communication of ideas. Using vast databases, workers analyze, conceptualize, and communicate. The office is being called upon to support a new range of activities and is no longer an adjunct to the factory.

* Ronald Goodrich, "The Perceived Office: The Office Environment as Experienced by Its Users," *Environment and Behavior,* vol. 14, no. 3 (May 1982), pp. 353–78. Copyright © 1982 by Sage Publications. Reprinted by permission.

Office functions have become an integral part of the organization, and productivity in the office has become an important issue. Now, office design needs to provide a responsive environment—interior spaces that encourage productivity by facilitating task performance, by supporting user needs, by allowing for meaningful communication and work relationships, and by providing a stimulating organizational climate.

The rapid introduction of automation into the office also portends a radical restructuring of work, with jobs becoming more technical and more complex than ever (*Business Week* 1981). In the process of creating a machine environment, we are introducing some of the same problems (stress; boredom; loss of control over the work, the work pace, and environment; depression) into the office that resulted in dehumanization, reduced productivity, and low morale in the factory. Recent studies also suggest that some office equipment may have negative impacts on the health and psychological well-being of the worker (National Institute for Occupational Safety and Health 1981).

Work that is performed in offices is becoming more cognitive in character. Increasingly intelligent machines are "doing" the work in the sense of actually producing tangible output. People, on the other hand, are "thinking" the work. They analyze, reflect, conceptualize, and communicate. To do the work requires high levels of involvement, sustained attention, creative thinking, and communication with others. These kinds of internal, psychological processes need to be supported by the design of the work environment. To be functional now, office design must support not only the physical activities of workers, with furniture, space, and equipment, but also users' perceptual, cognitive, and social activities.

The economics of office buildings is also focusing more attention on the impact of the designed environment on its users. Over the life of a typical office building, about 90% of the costs incurred are employee costs (mainly salaries and benefits), with the other 10% being for the creation, construction, and operation of the building itself (Building Programs International 1980). Every day, people have to work in a physical environment that affects their ability and desire to work. The building, then, regardless of its initial costs, aesthetics, or other considerations, must facilitate the utilization of human resources. Research that explores the relationships between user needs and characteristics of the designed environment is necessary if we are to achieve a supportive office environment.

In summary, the office environment is more than just a static setting that has little psychological impact upon its users. The physical environment is one component of an integrated system, which also consists of people, activities, organizational and personal relationships, and technology. Changing the work activities, the technology with which we do them, the organizational structure, or the way people work together creates new user needs and environmental requirements. This dynamic environment, as *perceived and experienced by the user,* is the focus of the studies reported here.

THE STUDIES

The projects (Table 7-1) from which the results are taken and categorized are similar in some important ways. Each project (except Citibank) has involved the planning or evaluation of a new corporate headquarters building or complex. Each of the buildings (except for Nestle and TRW, which are campus plans) is a high-rise office building located in a central business district of an urban area. Each building is between 30 and 60 stories tall, except for the Senate Office (Russell A. Hart) Building, which is restricted by city ordinance, and the Guardian Life Building, which is 20 stories tall. Each project has been planned to house large numbers of users in general office and highly specialized work areas (computer rooms, trading floors, laboratories). Given the size and complexity, each has been planned and implemented by a team of professional specialists collaborating to create a particular solution to satisfy the client's requirements.

In the studies presented here, the office environment is conceptualized as a *dynamic sociophysical system,* to differentiate it from the office as a place, a physical setting, or an organizational unit. This is also to highlight the interdependency between the physical systems (that is, the designed environment, the technology, work requirements and activities, and so on) and the social system (people, their values, expectations and needs, people's relationships to co-workers, work perceptions and meaning, the organization's culture). This interdependency is complex and relationships between the two systems are often indirect and counterintuitive.

Six distinct subsystems or dimensions can be identified within this overall sociophysical system. Each is relatively independent, with its own set of problems, procedures, and expertise. In the office environment (environment being understood here as the total surrounding context of influences and forces proximate to the individual user and not just the physical setting), these six subsystems mediate the criteria a person uses, and the judgments he or she makes in evaluating the physical environment.

The six subsystems are:

1. *People:* the kind of people who work in the office, their psychological characteristics, and their needs, perceptions, and expectations
2. *Work:* the work system, its organization and requirements, and the tasks these people perform

Table 7-1. Projects Profile

Project	Type of Study[a]	Sample Size[b]	Methods	Project Size (Personnel)	Project Completion
Amoco	DCD	36	Interviews with cross section of users, observation	900	1980
Anaconda	POA	551	Questionnaire, interview user sample, observation	700	1979
Arco	POA	185	Questionnaire, interview user sample, observation	1400	1975
Citibank	POA	154	Questionnaire, observation	1100	1977
Dome	DCD	36	Interview with cross section of users, observation	2000	[f]
Duquesne	DCD	53	Questionnaire, observation	1000	1982
Guardian	REP	26	Interviews with department heads	600	[e]
Mellon	REP	60	Interviews with department heads	3300	[e]
Nestle	DCD	32	Interviews with cross section of users, observations	1500	1981
Petro-Canada	DCD	38	Interviews with cross section of users, observations	2100	[f]
Procter & Gamble	REP	33	Interviews with cross section of users, observations	3600	[e]
TRW[c]	–	–	Interviews	800	[f]
U.S. Senate[d]	DCD POA	180	Questionnaires, interviews, observations	1500	[f]

a. Design criteria development (DCD) is part of programming and consists of creating performance criteria for individual workspace in a new building; postoccupancy audit (POA) assesses user reaction to the designed environment after move-in; real estate planning (REP) entails the development of a strategy for handling a corporation's space requirements over a 30-year period.

b. Sample size for DCD studies was determined by job function and type of individual workspace. Sample size for POA studies was number of questionnaire respondents.

c. The TRW project will involve various user education programs in addition to design criteria development and postoccupancy analysis.

d. The U.S. Senate project involved both a pre- and postoccupancy analysis.

e. Project completed with program report.

f. Project in process.

Source: Goodrich 1982

3. *Social processes:* communication, relationships, group processes, and what is usually described as the informal organization
4. *Organization:* the organization itself, including its culture, resources, business plan, and competitive environment
5. *Technology:* the technology that is used by people to perform their work activities
6. *Environment:* the designed environment (including various building and interior systems) itself

All of these subsystems impact upon, and are impacted by, each other. Significantly changing one subsystem necessarily has consequences for the others. Introducing new technology into the office, for example, is changing how people work (tasks), their communication patterns with others, the organizational structure in which they work, the kind of physical environment that is needed, and even the kind of people who do office work. Similarly, in designing or evaluating a new office environment for an organization, a designer/researcher is intervening in this complex, dynamic sociophysical system. Focusing only on one subsystem, and neglecting the others can inadvertently cause problems in the overall system. There is no best design or physical environment in and of itself. The best designed environment needs to be seen in the context of the overall system. The best design solution recognizes, respects, and optimizes the other subsystems.

The perceived office concept also assumes a user-centered perspective. The user is *in* and a *part of* the dynamic system as described above. This involvement influences the subjective criteria against which a person compares and evaluates the actual physical environment. Thus, even though a secretary and a professional may work next to each other in the same physical environment, they may (and usually do) perceive the environment very differently.

The studies summarized here (see Table 7-1) are organized into six sections representing six of the subsystems already described.

PEOPLE AND THE DESIGNED ENVIRONMENT

People possess unique personality characteristics that influence their desires for particular kinds of work environments. In the Senate study, more shy, introverted types of people desired work areas that provided isolation and quiet, whereas more gregarious types seemed to enjoy opportunities for meeting others and social interaction. Yet in spite of their importance, the influence of personality and other psychological factors on the evaluation or the design of work environments has not been adequately addressed.

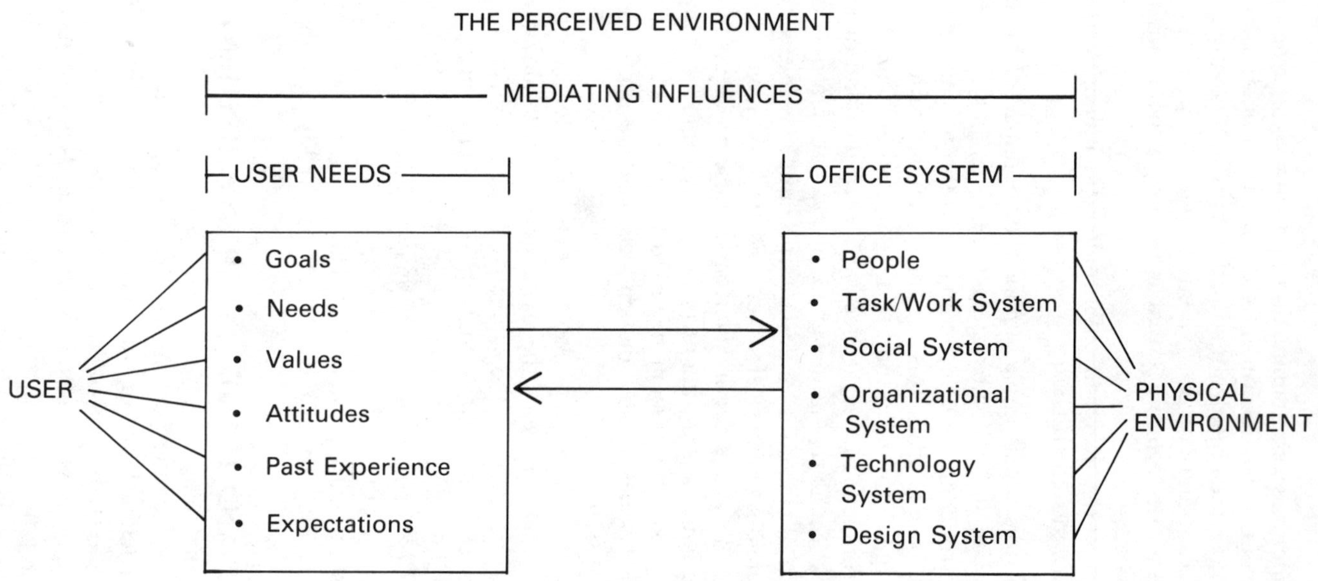

THE PERCEIVED ENVIRONMENT

|— MEDIATING INFLUENCES —|

|— USER NEEDS —| |— OFFICE SYSTEM —|

USER NEEDS box:
- Goals
- Needs
- Values
- Attitudes
- Past Experience
- Expectations

USER

OFFICE SYSTEM box:
- People
- Task/Work System
- Social System
- Organizational System
- Technology System
- Design System

PHYSICAL ENVIRONMENT

7-1. Factors that mediate and influence user's evaluation of an office environment

In one study, the Anaconda postoccupancy evaluation, personality differences seemed to account for user reaction to the colors used and the characterization of the new work environment. The prominent colors in the award-winning, very attractive office space were gray carpet tiles with small details of blue, white wall panels with gray tinted glass panels, and blond wood furniture. Task/ambient lighting was used and light was reflected off the ceiling into the private offices and adjacent open office space. Only a few chrome lighting fixtures were suspended from the ceiling and these were clustered in open areas. Most of the workspaces on a floor were private offices with floor-to-ceiling partitions. Artwork was used extensively throughout. The look of the environment was modern and stylish, yet it felt warm and pleasant to be in.

In the study, respondents were asked to use their own words to characterize the new environment. Of the 551 respondents, about half (268) provided some descriptors. Two themes emerged from the data. Theme one characterized the new setting as pleasant, attractive, nice to work in, modern, and functional. Theme two characterized it as cold, mechanical, hospital-like, sterile, hard, and antiseptic. Each theme focused on different aspects of the same environment, suggested different meanings attributed to it, and indicated different emotional reactions as a result.

An analysis of responses by job type also revealed consistent differences. Secretaries, geologists, and geophysicists were more likely to characterize the environment in theme-two terms, whereas engineers were more likely to characterize it in theme-one terms. Further analysis also revealed that the former group rated the amount and choice of color used negatively, whereas the latter group rated it positively. Of the individuals from these job categories who responded, there was little overlap and little correlation between these characterizations and their ratings of satisfaction with and liking of the new environment.

The Type-A personality is also likely to be an important factor that mediates users' response to their work setting. The Type-A personality refers to a cluster of psychological and behavioral dispositions, including heightened competitiveness, high arousal levels, time pressure, a compulsive drive, and an inability to relax. In the U.S. Senate Office Study, those individuals who scored high on the Sales Type-A Personality scale (Caplan 1971) rated levels of crowding, frequency of distractions, and lack of privacy more negatively than did others. They also rated the open office plan more negatively. This suggests that these people may be more sensitive to external (environmental) stimuli or may react more adversely to them.

Another study, the Atlantic Richfield (ARCO) Centre Square evaluation, investigated a relationship between a newly designed environment and self-esteem. Anecdotal evidence has suggested that when in this environment, people dress better, have more pride in themselves, their work, and the workplace, and show other signs indicating an increase in self-esteem. The questionnaire for the postoccupancy survey contained several items that asked employees to rate the effect of the new office environment on various dimensions of self-esteem. A total of 65% believed that the new environment enhanced a person's self-image and status. Half (49%) of the professionals reported that it enhanced a person's self-worth, whereas two-thirds (67%) of the secretaries and 70% of the executives reported that it did. Similarly, 75% of these people also believed that the new office environment fostered a climate of respect and dignity in the office.

In summary, these studies lend support to the belief that a new office design has a positive psychological effect on its users. This effect is likely to be experienced somewhat differently, depending upon one's status within the organization. In the ARCO study, and in most other cases, secretaries received the greatest improvement to their work environment, which may account for the more positive attitudes. But it is also clear that psychological variables mediate a user's response to the environment. The person brings with him or her certain subjective criteria that are based upon previous experience and personal disposition.

WORK AND THE DESIGNED ENVIRONMENT

Office work, depending upon the job, places certain cognitive, emotional, and behavioral demands upon the person. To perform the various tasks that make up a job, the individual needs an environment that supports not only the physical activity but also thought processes and emotional well-being.

Different tasks have different mental and physical demand characteristics. In the Amoco study, geologists spent a good deal of time reflecting on information and formulating hypotheses. Managers reported spending most of their time communicating and responding to external requests. Financial professionals reviewed computer printouts and performed numerical calculations. Each job made distinct demands upon the individual and required different environmental conditions to support them.

Office technology changes the way a person works. Interacting with a video display terminal (VDT) is very absorbing and focuses the user's attention. The user requires less privacy, is less distracted by nearby activities, and needs greater environmental variety compared with a person who is using paper-and-pencil technology. Workers at Amoco and Dome reported that terminal work is structured differently from paperwork so that interruptions are not as disruptive. The worker can reengage the information needed or reconstruct a logical sequence by simply pressing a few buttons.

Use of electronic office equipment demands its own environmental solutions. According to interview responses of workers who were intensive users of video display terminals in the Dome and Anaconda studies, greater intensity of involvement with the VDT increases fatigue, muscular tension, and monotony. To offset these effects, they left their workspace and walked around to obtain a more varied environment; within their own workspace, this would include regions of different light intensity and varied visual distances so that they could look away from the machine and out into these spaces to relax. The use of more color, lower ambient light levels, lighting regulated by the user, better air conditioning in private office areas to compensate for the additional heat thrown off by the equipment, and physical fitness facilities were also suggested.

Results of these same studies suggest that office equipment and task differences influence a user's preference for windows. Both machine users and workers engaged in paper-and-pencil work reported that having a window is psychologically important. One feature that several workers described was the ability to look away from their immediate work, look out into the distance through the window, and gain a psychological as well as a perceptual vista. Being able to look out into space, they could daydream, reflect, and disengage their thinking from the immediate demands of the task on which they were working. They reported that being able to look out provided them with more mental freedom, a chance to get away from the problem to gain new insight, and a broader perspective. It also reduced fatigue and stress. Terminal users, although they appreciated these benefits, complained bitterly because they could not adequately regulate the amount of light in the room. Sunlight produced glare, low visual contrast on the VDT screen, and heat gain in the space.

People also develop characteristic work styles that influence their evaluation of the environment. In the Senate study, several styles were observed. Some workers rely more upon the visual processing of information, whereas others rely more upon auditory means. The former need to read and see things, so they have more paper to work with and store. The latter seem more comfortable with conversation and discussion, issuing and storing paper only as necessary to document something. A second style concerns the organization of work. Some organize their work horizontally and laterally; others use a vertical style. The former place piles of work on available surfaces around the space and use it as needed. Those with a vertical style use shelves and tacking surfaces to organize their work. A third style reflects how people organize their personal workspace. Strict organizers keep their area neat and orderly; they know where things are and like to keep their space uncluttered. They use files, shelves, and other storage systems. Relaxed organizers keep their space cluttered and disorderly in appearance. They use shelves and other organizing elements in the environment in their own unique way. A fourth style concerns storage needs. "Pack rats" feel compelled to save things. They have difficulty throwing anything away and report feeling insecure without their things under their control. They typically are involved with technical detail and complain that as soon as they release something to file or throw it away, someone wants it. "Neat rats," on the other hand, save hardly a thing. They do not want to keep files around and report feeling some discomfort and mental disorganization when there are too many things around them. They prefer fewer objects and like a sense of space in their workplace. A fifth style involves a rigidity-flexibility dimension. Some workers territorialize their space to a significant degree. They mark their chair, personalize their workspace to make it fit their work style, and report feeling annoyed when others used their personal space. Other workers do not feel this way and seem to be more flexible in how they set up and use their space.

Work is more than just doing tasks efficiently. A lack of variety in task performance will create the same dehumanization, alienation, and boredom produced by the assembly line. The emotional, playful, and social sides of the person need to be respected. In the ARCO study, observations and interviews suggested that a new open-plan environment, with its indirect task/ambient light, plants, and kitchen areas on each floor, created the image of a neighborhood. People leaned on the work station partition as if it were a backyard fence and casually spoke with the user, thereby facilitating informal working relations. At Nestle, a relaxed, suburban, residential kind of office with kitchens, coffee, refrigerators, and other similar "household" amenities helped to sustain the image of the work group as a "family." Informal conversations with workers suggest that this encouraged an entrepreneurial climate and reduced status distinctions within the work group. In the Anaconda study, secretaries and earth-science professionals responded more negatively to the character and the "feel" of the space. They described it as gray, sterile, and cold because of its colors and hard surfaces.

In summary, the designed environment needs to support the mental and physical work that people do in offices. Work, however, is not merely the specific tasks people perform in their personal work area. The work people do in offices includes the mental activities and operations that are required for doing work; the organization, tempo, variety, pace, and other psychological dimensions of the work; work styles and manner in which people do their work; the project nature of work and how people interact; the demand characteristics of different kinds of tasks; and the overall climate of work, including morale, productivity, and job satisfaction. Taking only a functional approach and designing only for things that people do in their own work area often leads to the unintended effects of creating boredom, stress, work dissatisfaction, low morale, and employee turnover. Design solutions need to respond to a fuller conception of work and how people do it if they are going to address the physical and psychological needs of the individual and organizational user of the environment.

SOCIAL PROCESSES AND THE DESIGNED ENVIRONMENT

The designed environment influences our social relations in many ways, including our contact with others (Festinger, Schachter, and Back 1950); the type of interaction (Hall 1966); the amount and quality of interaction (Sommer 1969); and the interaction process itself (Scheflen 1972). People modify the physical environment to support desired transactions, and experience stress and discomfort when these conventions are violated (Scheflen 1976).

Individual design features can act singly or cumulatively to inhibit desired relationships. In the Anaconda study, the absence of a dining room or some other common-use facility, together with a card-entry security system and a creative but irregular office layout, had the unintended effect of keeping people on a floor in their own work area. This discouraged individuals from getting to know workers in other departments and encouraged identification with a single work group rather than with the entire company.

The Senate Office study showed that office layout also affects morale, group involvement, and communications. One layout, with desks around the perimeter of the room so that people faced outward away from an empty center area, encouraged cooperation and teamwork among the four professionals and three secretaries. The close quarters, the minimal acoustical privacy, and the spatial arrangement of the furniture supported close working relationships. Secretaries could overhear professionals' conversations, had a real sense of what they were working on, and could answer outside inquiries themselves instead of disturbing the professional each time. They reported feeling highly involved in their work, a sense of professionalism, personal responsibility for the work that they did, and high morale. Professionals reported feeling like members of a team with high morale and a strong sense of group purpose. They also said that they had adequate visual privacy and that the openness and close proximity encouraged the sharing of information among individuals.

At Procter and Gamble, this type of communication and interdependency between managers and secretaries was encouraged by the physical design of offices. In some departments, following the example of one of the founders (Procter), secretaries worked within the manager's private office. This was done to encourage teamwork and administrative efficiency. Those who worked in this type of configuration reported that it did encourage teamwork but at the expense of some privacy and personal freedom.

Office layout can negatively affect identification with one's work group, group involvement, and morale. In the Senate Office study, one design treatment necessitated the use of a public hallway as a connecting aisleway between five adjacent rooms, each of which was occupied by a small group of five to seven persons. Before the design change, individuals from the farthest room could walk through each of the other three suites to get to the reception area and entrance at the other end. With the change, they had to leave their suite, walk along the public corridor, which was outside the other suites, and reenter the reception area. All reported feeling isolated from others they worked with, a loss of morale, and reduced group involvement.

Group cohesion and involvement can be negatively affected even when design treatments provide the individual with more privacy and better working conditions. In the Senate study, one group of five legislative assistants, professional personnel who research legislative issues for the senator, worked in the open in one suite. They communicated with each other a good deal and reported high morale. With the introduction of masking sound into the suite to provide added acoustical privacy, they could not overhear each other, felt more physically and psychologically separated, and reported reduced morale. They also complained that communication did not seem as spontaneous as before and that it required greater effort on their part to sustain a comfortable level of interaction.

On the other hand, group involvement, high motivation, and organizational norms can minimize the negative impacts of environmental problems and poor working conditions. At Procter and Gamble, a company renowned for its business success and marketing prowess, groups of five or six persons worked in a crowded (approximately 70 square feet per person), open, bull pen type of environment. The setting was crowded, noisy, and unattractive. In spite of this, these teams were very productive. Their own high achievement standards, the excellent training that they were receiving, the deserved marketing reputation of the company, and their own intense involvement in their work sustained high levels of motivation and performance. Working in this crowded bull pen became like a fraternity "hazing": It served as a test of one's ability and encouraged group identification.

The amount and type of spatial privacy that a person has affects social processes, especially face-to-face communications, group involvement, and a sense of belonging to the group. An interior designer usually tries to achieve an optimum balance of these, depending upon task requirements and work style. Privacy is defined primarily in physical terms with solid walls, sound-absorbing partitions, masking sound, and physical separation. From the point of view of the user, however, the experience of privacy, *perceived* privacy, is more complex and is influenced by more than spatial parameters.

In the ARCO study, many individuals who worked in private offices reported that they did not have adequate privacy because sound leaked through the walls and the ductwork. Another factor was the grouping of private offices with secretarial work stations immediately outside them. Although managers trusted their own secretary to keep their work private, they felt somewhat inhibited because of the proximity of the other secretaries, whom they did not know. At Anaconda, professionals in private offices did not have adequate acoustical privacy because secretaries were clustered in open areas along the aisle. The shape of the aisle and the hard wall surfaces in the corridor funneled the sounds down the hallway and into offices some distance away. At Dome, some managers who worked in private offices explained that they did not have privacy because the background sound levels were too quiet; sounds they made stood out in contrast to the surroundings. Having a private space does not necessarily mean that a user has privacy.

Perceived privacy is multidimensional (Laufer, Proshansky, and Wolfe 1974) and depends upon more than just the physical environment. Other research has shown that it depends upon norms regarding how a private office should be used and when signaling the need for privacy is appropriate (Golan and Justa 1976). A person's definition of accessibility to others also influences how a private office will be used. In one study, female managers, more than male managers, believed that they had to be very accessible to their staff. This belief prevented them from closing the door to their office to attain privacy, even when that was necessary to do work (Josefowitz 1980).

Social variables also influence a person's need for and experience of privacy. In the U.S. Senate study, individual's working in cohesive work groups reported less need for privacy. Similarly, individuals who worked in the open, in a bull pen type of arrangement where the individual's space was not symbolically separated from other spaces, also reported less need for privacy. (This was observed for some groups at Procter and Gamble as well.) The size of the work group is another factor. In the Petro-Canada study, people who shared an office with one or two other individuals reported that they experienced very little privacy because whatever they or the other person did stood out and called attention to itself. People who worked in larger, open, undifferentiated spaces, on the other hand, reported that they had a real sense of personal privacy because of the anonymity of the space.

Task variables are also involved. Worker reports (Anaconda study) suggest that individuals who are engaged in jobs that require creative thinking, reflecting, and developing a logical train of thought are more disturbed by environmental distractions. After the distraction is over and they return to their task, they must reconstruct their thought series to some degree. On the other hand, individuals typing or engaged in less demanding cognitive activity can return to the point where the distraction occurred and continue from there. It was found that with routine, repetitive, and mechanical jobs, too much privacy isolated an individual from his or her co-workers and increased reports of job stress, errors, perceived fatigue, and boredom. Reports of reductions in both attention and group morale also increased.

Demographic factors play a role. In interviews at Petro-Canada and at Amoco, older employees (those over 40 years of age) desired higher levels of privacy than did younger ones, although status considerations may be the reason. In the Dome, Anaconda, and TRW studies, female secretaries who sat alone or clustered in the open complained that they had no privacy. They felt exposed, uncomfortable, and vulnerable and spoke about being constantly on display with no place to hide. Nonsmokers wanted more privacy so that they could control their own workspace and keep it free from cigarette smoke.

Symbolically defining the boundaries of the space encourages or discourages one's sense of privacy as the two examples indicate. At ARCO, individuals working in open-plan work stations that had clearly defined boundaries on only three sides (the fourth side was completely open on a secondary aisle) reported that they had little privacy. They complained that people would penetrate what they defined as their personal workspace and walk right up to their desk. This was experienced as an intrusion, a breach of their personal space, and an invasion of their privacy. They also felt some powerlessness because of their inability to control access to and the use of their space.

Round tables served as desks in this same three-sided workspace, and this did provide adequate privacy for meetings. A group assembled around the table for a discussion provided a clear visual signal to passersby that a meeting was in session. The roundness of the table organized the group into a circle, with individuals' backs defining a boundary to the outside, focused attention inward across the table, and allowed people to lower their voices as they spoke to each other at a close, intimate distance. Users reported that they had adequate privacy for these meetings.

Interviews suggest that (1) the boundary must provide a clear distinction between the inside of the workspace and the outside; (2) it must surround the individual and give him or her a sense of being enclosed and within; and (3) it should provide only one entrance. Without adequate boundary definition, users generally felt more susceptible to interruptions, vulnerable, and unprotected. They were unable to control their own space, complained of a lack of privacy, and desired more personal privacy in a future environment. While some sense of privacy can be achieved through anonymity in large, open, bull pen areas, it does not seem to develop once an individual workspace is defined unless these conditions for boundary definition are met.

The use of large plants appears to increase the individual's sense of privacy. Workers concurred that the office was more pleasant and informal with plants, and that these qualities seemed to reduce their need for a high level of privacy. Lighting is another important factor. Reduced light levels in the ARCO and Senate studies induced individuals to speak more quietly, according to many who were interviewed. Task/ambient systems that provide higher light levels on the primary work surface but reduce the overall ambient light levels create an unevenly lit space surrounding the workspace. This unevenness, with pools of illumination rather than a homogeneous volume of light, produces an atmosphere similar to residential space that is lit by table lamps. This quality seems to increase informality, to reduce status distinctions, and to create a more relaxed working climate, all of which increased their sense of perceived privacy.

Some design solutions may have the unintended effect of reducing *perceived* privacy by creating more *spatial* privacy. When partitions are used for visual privacy, the individual is "blind" to his or her surroundings. Noises and movements outside are sudden, unanticipated, and surprising. They are more likely to stand out from surrounding sound levels and to be more distracting. In the Senate study, where the spatial density of a suite was high, this was especially true. Once people heard a sound outside of their workspace, it was difficult to tune it out. They reported that they felt almost compelled to pay attention to it.

Private offices with interior glass panels create a fishbowl for their users and may reduce perceived privacy more directly. In the Dome, Petro-Canada, and Anaconda studies, professionals in this type of office complained that they felt exposed, vulnerable, and constantly distracted. The glass invited passersby to look in—almost like looking at television. If eye contact was established, they usually stopped to chat. Users said that they could also sense outside movements with their peripheral vision. They would either look up to investigate the movement or experience an urge to do so, even if they did not act upon it. They felt on display and experienced some pressure to be always available to others. Since interior glass is usually used to open up the interior space to the outside, design solutions that minimize eye contact with passersby are desirable. In the Dome and Anaconda studies, it was found that using a solid panel across the strip of glass at the level where eye contact is made, a smaller glass strip next to the entry door, or a glass panel at the top of a solid panel would help to eliminate this effect.

People do not always suffer passively from the lack of privacy, however. In the Procter and Gamble and Petro-Canada studies, workers reported that they used informal, nonverbal cues to induce a person who shared the office to leave the room. In the ARCO and Dome studies, workers described postures and furniture arrangements they employed to signal their desire for privacy. In the Senate study, many workers said they worked late, after everyone left, or went somewhere else to work. In both the ARCO and Senate studies, some workers reported that conflict may result if the desire for privacy is not clearly stated physically, nonverbally, or verbally. These workers became annoyed with the other people, feared alienating others by asking them to leave once they were there, and felt some anxiety about being unable to complete their work as a result.

To summarize, the designed environment implicitly and subtly affects our interaction with others as well as our ability not to interact with them when that is desirable. To optimize a work environment so that it complements the objectives of the organization, the designed environment must respond to the social processes inherent in the group life of people working together. The designer needs to identify and design for the company culture as well as for the building in which the office is situated. And in responding to these requirements, the designer must consider unintended effects on the culture and social processes produced by a particular design solution. Some of these effects are counterintuitive, such as heightening a person's susceptibility to acoustical distractions in certain situations by providing him or her with greater visual privacy, and may not be immediately obvious.

THE ORGANIZATION AND THE
DESIGNED ENVIRONMENT

Organization variables such as the social climate, corporate culture, size of the organizational units, morale, and the particular industry the company is in are likely to affect or to be affected by the designed environment of the office. One of the reasons chief executives cite for building new office buildings or for creating new office environments is the need to establish a new image or a more dynamic corporate ethos. This dynamic relationship between the social organization and the physical environment, although investigated in factories and mines in sociotechnical literature (Emory and Trist 1975), has not been adequately investigated in office research.

One variable, designated as *corporate culture,* has received a good deal of attention recently. Corporate culture refers to the shared values, beliefs, and ideals of a particular corporation. It is its overriding set of norms: what is important to the company, what the company stands for, and the management style. One study (Peters and Waterman 1982) that compared very successful companies to other less successful ones found that the corporate culture most reliably differentiated the successful ones from the others.

In the TRW study, the client specifically requested an analysis of its corporate culture. The aim was to describe the culture, to determine the design implications for the site master plan, the building, and its interiors, and to recommend criteria and design concepts that responded to the findings. The work was also to develop employee related programs and to suggest how the culture might be changing. The analysis, based on many in-depth interviews and extensive participant observation, identified important recurring themes, significant values, and dynamic characteristics of the company's culture, including the importance and dignity of the person, the emphasis on communication and collaborative decisionmaking, and the professionalism, competence, and openness of the personnel. The organization is a multinational, high-technology conglomerate well known for its people-oriented philosophy as well as for its leadership in its industries.

The study made many design recommendations. Layouts were developed around work group clusters to facilitate group identity, cohesion, and involvement. Common-use areas were created in strategic places to facilitate contact and informal communication across work groups and departments. Individuals were afforded a great deal of control over their environment and its use. Users at all levels chose products for their workspace from many alternatives. Orientation programs, full-scale office mock-ups, special research studies and frequent "all-hands" meetings kept all of the users involved and informed.

The study for the new Senate Office Building in Washington, D.C., examined the influence of the new office furniture systems and the ambient environment on the social climate. The offices of five senators and two committees were selected for the research. Each office consisted of five to six rooms in which three to seven people worked. Each of the offices was studied by various design, management, and behavioral specialists both before and after systematic environmental modifications were made to the rooms.

Interviews with all the respondents after they had worked in the new environment and had used the new furniture systems suggested that the new workplace had a subtle influence on the climate. In one office suite, most of the respondents reported that they detected greater cohesiveness and a sense of belonging to their work group. They attributed this to the newness of the environment, to its positive effect on morale, and to reduced perceptions of crowding. They now had their own defined area (it was less defined before the introduction of work stations) and at the same time could hear and see those with whom they worked. They also reported that they got on each others' nerves less often. These subtle changes had the overall effect of enhancing the social climate of the office.

In summary, the organization and its culture has (or should have) a significant impact on the office building and its interior environment. The floor size, core-to-window dimensions, core configuration, the types of building and interior systems utilized, amenities, common-use spaces, as well as other building characteristics should all respond to the organization and its needs. The organization, whether tenant or owner, should not have to squeeze its business operations into a space that does not suit its requirements or that interferes with its activities. The building and its interior environment also help to create a certain image and ambience, which subtly influence the social climate and the sense that workers have about themselves, their work, and the company.

TECHNOLOGY AND THE DESIGNED ENVIRONMENT

With the introduction of new office technology, the character, quality, and possibilities of work are changing. Computer-mediated work is more mental than physical. Workers think and interact with information through a machine interface. Mental operations, like concept development, abstract reasoning, and complex problem solving, are becoming the office functions of the future.

Although individuals who use computers extensively generally report positive experiences and feelings about the technology, some types of problems with new office technology (see below) have been reported. Other factors, such as the type of work and its organization (National Institute for Occupational Safety and Health 1981), the design of the surrounding environment, and the furniture and fixtures used, have been implicated as the causes of these problems rather than the technology itself.

Much of the research has focused on physical problems associated with the prolonged use of VDTs. These problems have included stress, general fatigue, muscle tension, headaches, eyestrain and upper shoulder and back aches. Interviews with professionals who use VDTs extensively and with computer programmers at Dome and Amoco suggest that the type of work, the furniture, and the type of lighting in the space play a significant role in producing these conditions. These respondents reported that they occasionally developed these problems when they did not get up and get away periodically, when they worked intensely for long periods of time in one posture, or when they used a keyboard positioned on top of a standard-height desk. Rest periods, an appropriate chair, and a movable keyboard eliminated these problems.

These same professionals suggested that poor lighting was their biggest problem with the office setting. Glare from too many fixtures, glare from poor placement of the CRT vis-à-vis the overhead lighting, and inadequate contrast levels were the most frequently reported problems. Many improvised cardboard shades that they taped like a visor to the top of the screen to eliminate light shining on the screen. Several respondents at Dome also reported image flicker when the CRT was placed near a neon task light. New lighting fixtures and solutions are beginning to address these problems more effectively.

VDT workers report that they need less task privacy for functional reasons. They say they frequently enjoy working with others nearby because then they can ask questions about their work or just socialize for a while. This offsets the tedium and boredom of the work. These workers nonetheless reported a need for psychological privacy at times. They wanted a more private space, a safe haven, a secure place in which to settle and be alone. They also reported a greater need to get out of the office to go outside and spoke about the fresh air and out-of-doors as helping to overcome a sense of being closed in. At least one company (TRW) has actively developed its new headquarters building with some of these considerations in mind. It designed an atrium with a character very different from that of the office environment, planned the atrium and the outdoor areas for socializing, and carefully thought through the environmental conditions needed to offset some of the effects of technology.

Other studies have reported that office automation can lead to less risk-taking behavior and a loss of authority and expertise (Zuboff 1981). Automation can also change normal social patterns that have developed in the office with unintended consequences for the organization and its culture. This was one of the concerns at TRW; they have endeavored, through the use of clustered layouts that group people into groups, an atrium that encourages meeting and interaction, and employee involvement programs to encourage social interaction and communication.

In summary, the introduction of electronic technology into the office is already changing the character of the office as well as the kind of environment that people need. It is becoming increasingly more important for designers to consider mental functions along with the physical functions of work. Social interaction and a sense of belonging to a company will need to be built into the environment. The new office will need to be more intimate, comfortable, sensual, casual, personal, soft, and informal. Quality, symbolic meaning, drama, excitement, and a sense of the natural will need to be evoked. In the office of the future, the "human logic" will become more important than the "technologic."

THE DESIGNED ENVIRONMENT

The physical environment itself is important to office workers. A recent national survey indicates that workers give improved working conditions credit for having improved the quality of working life over the past ten years (Harris 1978). The same survey showed a majority of office workers recognize that their satisfaction with their office surroundings affects their job performance a great deal and feel that doing their job well, in turn, is central to both job satisfaction and getting the things they most want out of life (Harris 1978).

In the Anaconda study, workers were asked to rate the importance of their satisfaction with their personal workspace. Of these, 75% rated it as very important, whereas the other 25% rated it as of average importance. These findings confirm results of the Harris national survey (1978). Harris found that the way their personal workspaces look and work for them is important to 94%, and very important to close to half of all office workers surveyed.

How the personal workspace is designed has a significant relationship to a person's satisfaction with his or her personal workspace. In the

ARCO, Senate, Anaconda, and Dome studies, a person was less likely to be satisfied with his or her space if the space did not have clearly defined boundaries, if the person sat in the open near an entranceway or machine area, if the space was perceived as crowded, or if the personal space was too small. Overall, however, individuals did not overgeneralize from a particular design problem to a general dissatisfaction with their workspace. Specific design problems did annoy the users, and they chose to correct them whenever possible.

People tend to arrange their personal workspace in similar ways. In most of the studies to date, it has been observed that in corporate environments the majority of individuals in private offices tend to place their desks so that these divide the room into three zones: a personal work area behind the desk, a visitor area in front, and a circulation/ display area connecting the two. In this configuration, they face the door to show their availability to others. They report that this position allows them to control the space visually, to work in a territory defined by their furniture, and to control interaction by inviting others into their space. Those few individuals who arranged their desks against the wall did so for three major reasons: (1) because they wanted to minimize visual distraction; (2) because the space was too small to allow them to arrange all their pieces in another way; or (3) because the furniture did not allow other arrangements. Most would place work tables behind the desk against the wall. Workers reported carrying out detailed work tasks at these work tables because they were less likely to be disturbed by others when working there.

In many available work stations, the space is configured such that work surfaces are attached to the perimeter partitions. Users sit in the center, with two or three work surfaces around them. The partitions are about 30 inches in front of them and the stations provide minimal space within them. Also, there are no barriers between the entranceway and worker. This causes problems. In the Dome and Senate studies, respondents reported that they wanted more enclosure of the space and that they experienced a loss of control over their personal environment, even though they had greater availability to others. Most reported the need to get away from their work space, to look out across the space, or gaze out a window to get a sense of vista and openness.

Workers have also reported preferences for certain furniture configurations, one of which is C-shaped. This provides three separate work surfaces: a private surface at the rear of the personal area; a semipublic surface at the front for meetings, communicating, and general correspondence; and a surface in between for the telephone and supplies. Although professionals are usually provided with this arrangement, senior secretaries who report a need for a secondary surface are not. A lack of adequate work surfaces is associated with feeling crowded and not having enough space. In the Senate study, spaces characterized as disorganized, with many objects in them, were more likely to be described as crowded.

The fit between work tasks and the kind of furniture used in an office is also important. Although wood furniture is usually perceived as richer, earth science professionals report that it does not provide a good writing or cutting surface. They place a sheet of glass on top to make it work for them. Most users do not like built-in furniture as much as furniture that can be rearranged. They want to be able to set up their space to fit the way they work rather than work to fit the space (left-handed individuals are especially sensitive to this). Some furniture does not properly accommodate office equipment, severely restricting how equipment can be used and forcing the worker to assume awkward positions in order to accomplish work tasks.

Although the physical environment is important to users, nonphysical and nondesign factors play a significant role in user acceptance and how people feel about their personal workspace. Two of these, personalization and participation, are especially important.

Personalization, making the space more of one's own by introducing personal items into the workspace, was observed in all the companies studied. The type and amount of personalization differed, however, by job type and sex. Financial personnel, administrators, and engineers personalized their space the least. Geologists, secretaries, and marketing personnel personalized their space the most. Women were more likely to personalize the space aesthetically (with plants, posters, and personal items), whereas men tended to display personal achievements or family attachments. Managers and executives typically displayed personal items (art, furniture, photos) that enhanced their status.

At Anaconda, the company restricted personalization of the new environment to minimize damage and visual disorganization. Earth-science professionals, secretaries, and computer-science personnel (the individuals who personalize their space the most) described the environment as sterile, impersonal, and cold. Those groups who personalized the least, however, were most likely to describe it as pleasant, comfortable, and attractive.

Active user participation in the design process has been generally regarded as an important step for meeting user needs and ensuring greater user acceptance. One study (Harris 1978) has indicated that many office workers feel that having a greater say in office planning would effectively increase both their satisfaction with their office surroundings and their productivity. The same survey revealed that few office workers are aware of the role architects and interior designers play in the design of the office environment. Many design professionals also felt that the communication they had with the users of the offices they plan was not adequate.

In the Senate study, the research and design team interacted a great deal with the final users of the office; yet, less than 20% of the users responded that they had participated in the design process to a great extent. Additional interviews suggested that without feedback, the workers were not able to see how any information they provided at the beginning was utilized in the design concept, nor were they aware of any trade-offs that had to be made. Unaware of this ongoing process, they tended to be negative about some design features because they did not get what they had requested. Users, although they appreciated new office systems, did not like to feel that their personal workspace was imposed upon them without their involvement and consultation.

The kind of physical environment in which people work is important to them. That environment affects their performance and work life directly by the kind of working conditions it creates, indirectly by influencing psychosocial and organizational processes, and symbolically by its meaning to them. This office environment, as it is used and lived in, becomes animated with memories and meaningful experiences. With time it becomes a familiar place and an extension of self.

In creating that environment, a product to be used so intimately by its occupants, designers must involve users in the process—not to take over and design the environment, but to inform and enrich the process. User research can help, but of more importance are the opportunities for facilitating communication and information exchange between users and designers during various parts of the design process.

CONCLUSIONS

Several conclusions emerging from this summary of studies have design implications for both the product (the particular environmental solution) and the process (the manner in which the problem is conceptualized, solved, and communicated to the user).

First, there is a close interdependency between the physical, designed environment and the five other subsystems that make up the office system. The designer is not just providing furniture. He or she is creating conditions that can hinder, support, or enhance the user's behavior and experience. In the process, the designer is intervening in a social system.

Second, not every office problem needs to be solved by a "design" solution. People can change, too. They are part of the problem, and they need to be part of any solution. Design approaches that emphasize user participation, openness, and communication between user and designer are essential if worker acceptance is to be gained. Imposed solutions are resisted and workers build up resentment against the environment, the designers, and the company because of the treatment they have received.

Third, more attention must be paid to the educational aspects of design. The studies here suggest that users will accept new design concepts if they understand how a particular solution was arrived at and how to utilize the new system effectively.

Fourth, user needs are not user wants, nor are they based only upon a worker's functional requirements. User needs represent deeper, psychological strivings of the working person trying to achieve a satisfying and meaningful work life. These needs should be understood and addressed in the creation of new office environments.

Fifth, design solutions must provide more opportunity for the individual to personalize the individual workspace. Workers need to be able to adapt the physical environment to fit their own requirements, to control its use and regulate its ambient conditions, and to create personal spaces that enhance the well-being of its users.

More attention should be paid to the "human logic" as well as the "technologic" in designing the office of the future. The psychological dimension of office design becomes increasingly important as the office becomes more mechanized and places more demands upon the person's mental and physical resources. The human dimension (high touch) is intimately connected with and impacted by the more complex physical and technical environment (high tech). If we fail to address the human logic in our planning of the office of the future, if we fail to see that "design" changes social systems as well as physical ones, and if the final users of our design are not involved in the changes and the planning, then we will re-create the same kinds of psychological and social problems that are associated with automating the factory. The new office should support and enhance its chief strategic resource—the brainpower of its users.

Providing this kind of functional workplace, a workplace for mental functions, requires an interdisciplinary approach to the design of the office environment. Planning for the office of the future will require greater knowledge of people, the work that they do, the technology they use to do it, their social and communication patterns, and the organization within which they work. Design solutions, responding to this challenge, could become more human, creative, and dynamic than ever before.

REFERENCES

Altman, I. 1975. *The environment and social behavior.* Monterey, CA: Brooks/Cole.
Building Programs International. 1980. Unpublished study, New York.
Business Week. 1981. The speedup in automation. (August 3): 55–61.
Caplan, R. 1971. Organizational stress and individual strain: A social-psychological study of risk. Ph.D. dissertation. University of Michigan, Ann Arbor.
Festinger, L., S. Schachter, and K. Back. 1950. *Social Pressures in Informal Groups.* New York: Harper & Row.
Golan, M. B., and F. C. Justa. 1976. The meaning of privacy for supervisors in an office setting. *Proceedings of the Environmental Design Research Association (EDRA) VII conference.*
Goodrich, R. 1976. Post design evaluation of Centre Square project. Philadelphia: Atlantic Richfield Co.
Goodrich, R. 1979. How people perceive their office environment. New York: Citibank.
Goodrich, R. 1982. Seven office evaluations: A review. *Environment and Behavior* 14 (3): 353–378.
Hall, E. T. 1966. *The hidden dimension.* Garden City, NY: Doubleday.
Louis Harris and Associates. 1978. *The Steelcase national study of office environments: Do they work?* Grand Rapids, MI: Steelcase Inc.
Josefowitz, N. 1980. Management men and women: Closed vs. open doors. *Harvard Business Review* 58(5): 56–62.
Laufer, R. S., H. Proshansky, and M. Wolf. 1974. Some analytic dimensions of privacy. *Proceedings of the Third International Conference in Architectural Psychology,* Lund, Sweden.
Moleski, W., and R. Goodrich. 1972. The analysis of behavioral requirements in office settings. In N. Mitchell (Ed.), *Proceedings of the Environmental Design Research Association (EDRA) III Conference.* Los Angeles: University of California at Los Angeles.
National Institute for Occupational Safety and Health. 1981. *Select research reports on health issues in video display terminal operations.* Cincinnati, OH: U.S. Department of Health and Human Services.
Newman, O. 1972. *Defensible space.* New York: Macmillan.
Peters, T., and R. Waterman. 1982. *In search of excellence.* New York: Harper & Row.
Scheflen, A. 1972. *Body language and the social order.* Englewood Cliffs, NJ: Prentice-Hall.
Scheflen, A. 1976. *Human territories: How we behave in space-time.* Englewood Cliffs, NJ: Prentice-Hall.
Sommer, R. 1969. *Personal space.* Englewood Cliffs, NJ: Prentice-Hall.

SECTION III

BEHAVIORAL ISSUES

In this section, research results for specific aspects of work environments are presented, including the open-office concept, privacy and communication, status support, lighting, and office automation. Implications for the planning and design of office settings are discussed.

Hedge presents a comparative study of local government offices under open-plan and traditional enclosed office conditions. The results indicate that a variety of ambient environmental problems were present in these offices. A clear relationship between job characteristics and attitudes toward the office was demonstrated. Employees who enjoyed performing managerial and technical tasks reacted more unfavorably to office conditions than did clerical staff, who generally viewed their work as undemanding. Loss of privacy and increased disturbances were consistently at the source of these negative reactions, and the interrelationship of these problems also emerged from factor analysis of the data. Although the office did create a favorable social climate, this did not offset employees' negative reactions to work conditions; rather, it appeared to exacerbate the problems. Consequently, no evidence was found to support the claim for improved productivity in open-plan arrangements. The author recommends increased user control and environmental diversity in response to the changing and divergent needs of office workers.

The chapter by Sundstrom explores the concept of privacy. The author describes two empirical studies of the relationship of the physical environment of the office to privacy, and the relationship of privacy to employees' satisfaction. Results indicate that to the extent that privacy in the office depends upon the physical environment, privacy is most consistently provided by enclosure of the workspace by walls or partitions. Results also suggest that workers with different jobs may perceive privacy differently, and that particular jobs may create different needs for privacy and different criteria for judgments regarding privacy. Sundstrom concludes that although privacy may contribute to a worker's satisfaction with the workspace, the level of privacy and the specific types of privacy associated with maximum satisfaction probably vary with the job.

The symbolic qualities of workspaces and offices are addressed by Konar and Sundstrom. In particular, the environmental characteristics that demarcate status are identified; the extent to which these characteristics are related to a sense of status support and the association of status support with workspace and job satisfaction are discussed. Results indicate that status support, a product of consistent status demarcation, is associated with environmental satisfaction and, to a lesser extent, job satisfaction. Status demarcation may clarify roles within an organization and establish status-relevant behavior norms. By providing a context for organizational interaction, effective status demarcation serves to increase the predictability of behavior and the ease of communication. However, status incongruency (inconsistent or inappropriate status demarcation) may have significant adverse effects for the individual and the organization. Office designers must be aware of these indicators and responsive to their effects on individuals and organizations.

Ellis presents a review of three case studies of lighting in offices. Lighting systems of various configurations (task/ambient, indirect up-lighting, and conventional overhead) and luminaire types (metal halide discharge, high-pressure sodium discharge) are compared. Results indicate that workers prefer lighting schemes with multiple-source, directional lighting as compared to uniform lighting. Thus, higher levels of satisfaction are associated with the task/ambient and indirect uplighting schemes than with overhead direct illumination. Negative responses to the high-pressure sodium lamp are discussed. This work emphasizes the importance of user involvement in the planning and design processes to promote acceptance of innovative or nontraditional lighting schemes.

In the chapter by Kleeman, major technological changes that are affecting the office, its ways of operation, and the behavior of office workers are surveyed. Research here and in Europe has shown the need for ergonomic design of the computer terminal work station—especially the need for fully adjustable furniture. The emerging technologies of video disc storage, micrographics, optical wire, robotics, networks, and video teleconferencing will continue to generate changes in space planning, equipment, and office workers' skills. In view of the continuing reduction in costs of computing and information transmission, these technologies are also speeding the dispersal of the office to homes and other spaces smaller than typical central city office buildings. Increasingly, office workers express dissatisfaction with present office conditions and a desire to affect the design of their own workspaces. Several successful participatory design projects demonstrate that this process can generate satisfaction with the office environment and respond to the needs of office workers in a setting undergoing significant change.

Open versus Enclosed Workspaces: The Impact of Design on Employee Reactions to Their Offices

ALAN HEDGE
Applied Psychology Division
University of Aston
Birmingham, United Kingdom

In the late 1950s, Walter Schnelle headed a team of design consultants, working in the Hamburg suburb of Quickborn (the Quickborner Team). Together they developed the then revolutionary *Bürolandschaft* (office landscape) approach to office design, which advocated replacing internal walls, partitions, and grid systems of furniture, typical of conventional, cellular layouts, with movable screens, furniture clusters, and planters arranged to optimize interpersonal communication and work flow. It was, and still is, claimed that *Bürolandschaft* creates flexible space, allowing layout to be more sensitive to changes in organizational size and structure; that the absence of internal physical barriers inevitably facilitates communication between individuals, groups, and even whole departments sharing floors; that this improves morale and productivity; and, above all, that there is a saving of around 20% of the costs of creating and maintaining office space (Starbuck 1976).

Given these supposed advantages, many organizations have and are continuing to opt for office landscaping or one of its subsequent variants, such as open plan. The popularity of *Bürolandschaft* is well illustrated by noting that the first landscaped office in West Germany was adopted by a company in Mannheim only in 1960, whereas by 1977 around 90% of white-collar staff were working in this type of accommodation (Kraemer, Sieverts, and Partners 1977). A similar pattern of rapid adoption of this

* Alan Hedge, "Open versus Enclosed Workspaces: The Impact of Design on Employee Reactions to Their Offices," *Environment and Behavior,* vol. 14, no. 5 (September 1982), pp. 522–36. Copyright © 1982 by Sage Publications. Reprinted by permission.

kind of approach to office planning can also be found in most Western countries.

However, in spite of the initial impressive claims and the enthusiastic support for *Bürolandschaft* by many architects and space-planning consultants (Boje 1971; Jaeger 1969; Kraemer et al. 1977; Palmer and Lewis 1977; Pile 1977, 1978), surveys of user reactions to landscaped offices and other variants, for example, open plan, have almost invariably highlighted numerous serious problems with the resulting office conditions. Those problems most frequently experienced are well documented in many studies (for extensive selected bibliographies of these see Starbuck 1976 and Cakin 1981), and there is a remarkable consensus on these across offices (Wineman 1982). Typical among the problems are complaints of loss of privacy (both visually and conversationally), high incidence of both visual and aural distractions, frequent interruptions by other employees, and problems with the ambient conditions (Brookes 1972, 1978; Brookes and Kaplan 1972; Dick, Compart, Reinartz, Schnadt, and Tossing 1981; Harris and Associates 1980; Duffy and Ellis 1980; Hedge 1980, 1982; Johnson 1970; Kraemer et al. 1977; Marans and Spreckelmeyer 1982; Meyer and Wenk 1975; Nemecek and Grandjean 1973; Sundstrom, Burt, and Kemp 1980; Sundstrom, Herbert, and Brown 1982; Sundstrom, Town, Crown, Forman, and McGee 1982).

Recent evidence suggests that in addition to problems with privacy and disturbances many staff members in air-conditioned open-plan offices also suffer a higher incidence of eye, nose, and throat irritations than do those working in unconditioned conventional offices, even when there appears to be no physical evidence that levels of any of the known indoor pollutants exceed current health standards (Hedge 1984a, 1984b; Turiel, Hollowell, Miksch, Rudy, and Young 1983). In fact, so strong are the feelings against open-plan offices in many countries that this approach has now been abandoned in the Netherlands and, based on the results of a five-year research program, Dick and associates (1981) have called for its abandonment in West Germany.[1] However, in spite of the controversy, many organizations in the U.K. and the U.S.A. remain staunchly committed to the concept of open-plan offices.

Nevertheless, in spite of the impressive body of research, it is important to note that not all employees in open-plan offices necessarily suffer problems with their working conditions; even among those who do, complaints often are not directed at the same problems, nor do individuals suffer these to the same severity. Indeed, a wide variety of factors have, to date, been shown to mediate between actual office conditions and employees' reported experiences of these: for example, work-related factors (job type, complexity, satisfaction) can influence employee reactions to privacy, distractions, and other problems with the office environment

(Hedge 1980, 1982; Johnson 1970; Sundstrom, Burt, and Kemp 1980; Sundstrom, Town, Brown, Forman, and McGee 1982). These studies have found that the reactions of those involved in supervisory, managerial, or complex technical jobs to working conditions in open-plan offices are typically less favorable than those of other staff members.

Unfortunately, one problem with trying to evaluate the efficacy of open-plan offices is that analysis has all too often been applied in an indiscriminate fashion across different kinds of buildings, employees, and, indeed, organizations.[2] Duffy (1974a, 1974b) has developed a basic office type taxonomy, as shown in figure 8-1, in which he emphasizes that open plan is not a panacea, but rather that it is crucially important in designing the most suitable office layout to match office conditions to a wide variety of organizational variables (organizational structure, management style, work type, and so on). However, more extensive replication of this study across a broader range of organizations than those examined by Duffy, incorporating information on user requirements and reactions, might profitably result in a more accurate taxonomy of office types, one that could be of immediate benefit to space planners.

To explore further the problems of open plan in a systematic way, this chapter describes two case studies of user evaluations of their offices. Both these case studies were conducted in local government offices and they examine the relationships between employee characteristics and attitudes to various aspects of office conditions, health, and work. Also, as recommended by Marans and Spreckelmeyer (1982), where possible, objective environmental measures were taken and used as corroborative evidence. The first case study is of the open-plan offices of a metropolitan county council, and details of this survey have been published (Hedge

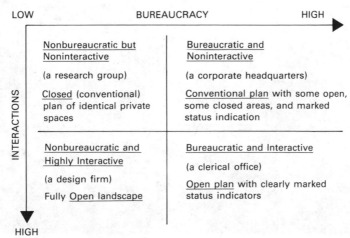

8-1. Taxonomy of office types (Duffy 1974a, 1974b)

1980, 1982). The second case study compares the reactions of staff to working in either the conventional or open-plan offices of a metropolitan district council. Such comparative research is particularly important because previous work has shown that marked changes occur in employees' attitudes to their offices when they move from conventional to open plan (Brookes 1972, 1978; Brookes and Kaplan 1972). Scandinavian research has found evidence of higher levels of physiological and psychological stress in employees after making such a move (Singer 1980) and higher levels of satisfaction have been found among those in conventional private offices compared with those in open-plan or pool offices where problems of visual and conversational privacy were very pronounced (Marans and Spreckelmeyer 1982).

CASE STUDY 1

The Offices

This building had originally been used as a warehouse and it was converted into office accommodation for the local authority in 1972. The building comprises five floors of offices and a basement containing staff dining facilities and a social area (fig. 8-2). Each floor of the building approximates an L shape, as shown in figure 8-3, and the result is that a high proportion of staff members sit in peripheral positions. This plan

8-2. The offices surveyed in Case Study 1

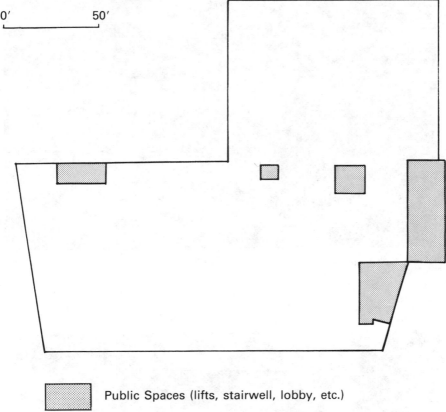

0'　　　　　50'

■ Public Spaces (lifts, stairwell, lobby, etc.)

8-3. Floor plan of the office building surveyed in Case Study 1

is followed on all floors except the ground (first) floor, where office staff occupy only the short arm of the L. The total floor area of open-plan accommodation is some 130,000 square feet (approximately 12,000 square meters). On all floors of the office building, there is a widespread use of screening to create smaller work areas. The offices also contain a small number of planters (a rather feeble attempt at office landscaping), and yet staff strongly express their liking for even this modest greenery (figs. 8-4 and 8-5).

Method

The Survey Questionnaire

Following discussions with representatives of the staff and a review of the literature on attitudes to open-plan offices, a self-completion questionnaire was constructed and piloted. The final form of this questionnaire

8-4. A typical open-plan area on the third floor

8-5. A typical open-plan area on the fourth floor

comprised 96 statements of attitudes to various aspects of the office, and the staff was asked to rate the degree of agreement or disagreement with each of these statements on a 5-point rating scale. In addition, 16 questions about each employee's spatial position in the office, 2 questions on the employee's personal details, and 3 open-ended questions about the employee's likes and dislikes in the office were included. These questions provided useful information for qualifying the earlier answers. The statements included in the first part of the questionnaire were initially classified under the headings shown in Table 8-1, although the actual order in which they were presented was randomized.

Distribution and Sample

The final survey was conducted in early summer. All the questionnaires were internally distributed and collected. They were given only to those staff members working in the open-plan offices and this excluded, among others, chief officers, the chief executive, computer staff, and typing pool staff. A total of 896 questionnaires were distributed and 649 of these were returned, a response rate of 72.4%. Of this sample, 70% of respondents were men and 30% were women (this generally reflected the pattern of employment in the authority).

Results

The results provided extensive information on user reactions to the office accommodation, and although much of it was specific to this office

Table 8-1. General Categories of Attitude Statements Used in the Evaluation Questionnaires

Category Groups	General Categories
Physical Factors	1. Ambient environment
	2. Office layout
	3. Office furnishings
	4. Disturbances/distractions
Psychosocial Factors	5. Health
	6. Privacy
	7. Social environment
	8. Proprietary attitudes
Work	9. Job characteristics
General	10. General opinions of office

building; those data of more general interest are described in the following sections.

The Ambient Environment

As Marans and Spreckelmeyer (1982) point out, in any user survey it is desirable to assess how closely expressed attitudes correspond with actual physical conditions and behavior in the accommodation being studied. Fortunately, measures of temperature, relative humidity, and lighting had been regularly recorded in these offices for a 12-month period prior to the survey; comparisons of attitudinal and environmental measures were therefore made and, in general, a high correspondence between these was found.

Reactions to the ambient conditions are summarized in Table 8-2. These results show that even though the ambient environment was supposedly being maintained around an "optimum" level in physical terms, adverse reactions to this were still quite pronounced.

Temperature. For the previous 12 months, the air temperature on each floor of the building had varied only between 20°C and 23°C in the daytime, and yet there were marked differences in opinion on the thermal conditions. It was found that 48% (311) of staff members complained that the offices were "too hot" and 21% (136) found them to be "too cold." There was a significant negative correlation[3] between responses to these two questions ($r = -.69$, $n = 640$, $p < 0.001$). Many variables appeared to influence staff reactions. For example, a majority of the

Table 8-2. Employee Reactions to the Ambient Environment in the Offices

Ambient Conditions	% Agreement	(Frequency)
TEMPERATURE		
Office too hot	48	(311)
Office too cold	21	(136)
VENTILATION		
Desire to open window	77	(499)
Office too stuffy	61	(397)
Object to others' smoking	50	(323)
LIGHTING		
Prefer more daylight	76	(493)
Lighting too bright	33	(207)
ELECTROSTATIC		
Frequently get static electricity shocks in the office	50	(325)

staff on floors 2, 3, and 4 felt that the office was "too hot": 76% (102), 68% (95), 54% (87), respectively. On the other hand, those on the ground (first) and top (fifth) floors found it "too cold": 46% (23) and 59% (93), respectively. The differing response patterns may be explained by at least three factors. First, the nature of the work on the ground floor (administration) resulted in employees' being more sedentary than else-where in the building. Second, subsequent examination of the air-con-ditioning system showed that four times as many air changes per hour were occurring on the top floor than on any other floor. Finally, there appeared to be a sex difference in perceived comfort levels, with a greater proportion of female employees reporting that office conditions were "too cold" (31%) compared with male employees (17%). This difference was even more pronounced on the ground and top floors: ground floor, 64% (14) women and 31% (8) men; top floor, 80% (30) women and 49% (60) men. This finding is in keeping with that reported by Boje (1971), who gives the comfortable temperature range for men as 20°C to 21°C, and for women, 23°C to 24°C. Other recent surveys have also confirmed this difference (Harris and Associates 1980; Hardy 1982). However, lab-oratory-based experimental work has thus far failed to demonstrate sex differences in levels of perceived thermal comfort (Rohles 1971); and although field studies of thermal comfort do show some sex effects, these appear to be age dependent (Grivel and Barth 1980). Unfortunately, it is not clear whether the present findings are indicative of basic sex differences in thermal comfort levels, or whether they simply indicate differences that are a function of, for example, clothing, since the male employees tend to wear heavier, warmer clothes than the female employees do. It also seems that between the ages of 30 and 50, men become increasingly tolerant to thermal discomfort, whereas women of the same age do not (Hardy 1982). Regardless of the source of the difference, the fact remains that it created problems with regulation of the air-conditioning because even though the temperature could be adjusted for fairly small areas of the office (approximately 400-square-foot units), a satisfactory level was seldom found whenever both men and women shared adjacent workspaces.

Ventilation. Of the 77% of staff members who reported a desire to be able to open a window, 72% of these also agreed that the office was "too stuffy," and this reaction was strongest on floors 2, 3, and 4. This appears to be consistent with the findings on temperature, since these floors were also rated as being "too hot." Indeed, there was a significant correlation between opinions on temperature and stuffiness: $r = .59$, $n = 642$, $p < 0.001$. One reason for the apparent inadequacy of the ventilation system was that 37% (70) of those sitting near a ventilation unit (these being arranged around the office periphery) either covered the air outlet or reversed the direction of the outlet vanes to direct air away from the center of the office in order to reduce drafts in their immediate vicinity. Subsequent discussions with staff members near these units also revealed that they frequently used them as temporary storage surfaces for books, reports, papers, and so on because of a general lack of suitable paper storage facilities. So the ventilation problems in this office may be attributable largely to inappropriate staff behavior rather than simply to an inadequate air-conditioning system.

Lighting.   Opinions on lighting varied considerably, although a sizable proportion of the staff felt that the lighting was "too bright" on the first three floors. Subjective and objective assessments of this are compared in Table 8-3.

The high level of illumination on the fifth floor is attributable to the fact that skylights take up a substantial area of the ceiling; yet this is the floor with the least number of employees reporting that the lighting is "too bright." This strongly suggests that employees' reactions to brightness were a product of factors other than just the actual level of illumination. For example, the work of the staff on the first three floors is primarily clerical and administrative. These floors were awaiting the replacement of the existing fluorescent tubes. Because of the design of the recessed lighting fixtures and the ceiling surface, there may also have been greater problems with reflected glare on these floors (figures 8-3 and 8-4 illustrate the problems of ceiling reflections).

Finally, even though 47% of the staff members worked near a window, there was still a marked preference for more daylight in the office (76% agree). This preference varied considerably with the employee's location in the office: 88% (213) of those not seated near a window, 82% (84) of those near a window but with an obstructed view, and 54% (106) of

Table 8-3.   A Comparison of Employee Reactions to the Office Lighting Compared with Actual Levels of Illumination

	LIGHTING TOO BRIGHT		AVERAGE ILLUMINATION (LUX)*	
Floor	*% Agreement*	*(Frequency)*	*Center Office*	*Office Periphery*
1st (ground)	47	(23)	680	2500
2nd	40	(53)	680	2500
3rd	53	(73)	680	2500
4th	25	(40)	680	2500
5th (top)	11	(18)	12050	–

*Average noon readings over a working week in early summer

8-6. The work area on the fifth floor beneath the skylights

those near a window and with a clear view said that they would like more daylight in the office. This finding is consistent with the results of a study reported by Wells (1965), which showed that a majority of office staff surveyed preferred working by daylight and also that staff in central office positions greatly overestimate the amount of daylight available to them.

Electrostatic. Somewhat surprising is the finding that 50% of staff members reported receiving frequent static electricity shocks. Several factors appear to have contributed to this problem: for example, the widespread presence of artificial fabrics in office furnishings (carpet tiles, chairs, and so on had not had any antistatic treatment) and in clothes; and the generally low relative humidity (this averaged only 22% for the past 12 months compared with Boje's (1971) recommendation of 40 to 50%). As a result, the office air was also almost entirely depleted of negative air ions (<200 cc^{-1}). Several recent studies have shown that a relationship may exist between artificially enhanced concentrations of negative air ions and improved psychomotor performance (Hawkins and Barker 1978), and reduced incidence of headaches, nausea, dizziness, and subjective discomfort (Hawkins 1981a, b). To date, however, much of the research into air ionization effects on people has produced conflicting results (Hedge and Eleftherakis 1982) and more work on these possible effects is needed.

Privacy and Disturbances

Studies of open-plan offices have typically found frequent staff complaints of both high levels of distractions and disturbances and low levels of visual and conversational privacy. The results of this study further support this with staff reports of "too many disturbances and distractions" (Table 8-4) and a general "lack of privacy" (Table 8-5). These views are also significantly correlated ($r = .53$, $n = 644$, $p < 0.001$). It appears almost inevitable that the creation of an environment in which there is greater openness and accessibility between staff members will also produce a variety of disturbance problems for those employees; it is notable that for the present offices, the major problems arise from the behavior of staff rather than from office machinery noise. (The authority had, however, taken steps to remove most noisy office machinery from the main body of the office.) Thus, one possibility for reducing levels of distractions involves changing staff behavior in addition to modifying the environment. Also, it has been suggested that employees will quickly learn to adapt to the higher levels of disturbances in open plan (Boje 1971), and some evidence in support of this was found with 54% of staff members reporting adaptation to frequent interruptions. No evidence was found, however, to suggest that such adaptation either improves with length of employment (up to five years) or is dependent on previous experience of different office types, although it does appear to be influenced by the employee's job (see Job Characteristics).

The strength of staff complaints about a general lack of privacy is to some degree dependent on an employee's previous experience of office accommodation, with 74% (361) of those who had only or at some time

Table 8-4. Employee Reactions to the Disturbances in the Offices

Disturbance	*% Agreement*	*(Frequency)*
GENERAL		
Too many disturbances and distractions	74	(476)
Frequently interrupted by trivial matters	61	(394)
SPECIFIC SOURCES		
Other staff talking	55	(358)
Staff holding meetings nearby	50	(326)
Telephones	45	(293)
Office machines	34	(220)
EFFECTS ON JOB PERFORMANCE		
Much more difficult to concentrate	68	(439)
Telephone conversations more difficult	57	(367)
Decision making more difficult	49	(312)

Table 8-5. Employee Reactions to the Levels of Privacy in the Offices

Privacy	*% Agreement*	*(Frequency)*
GENERAL		
Distinct lack of privacy	71	(455)
Screens improve privacy	73	(474)
Would like a door to close on others	51	(331)
Often feel overlooked	48	(310)
CONSEQUENCES		
Easy to overhear private conversations	84	(504)
Difficult to deal with confidential matters	71	(462)

worked in a small office agreeing that the open-plan office creates a marked lack of privacy, whereas only 57% (92) of those employees who had worked only in large or open-plan offices shared this view. Overall, 72% (366) of staff members with varied previous office experience said they most enjoyed working in a small office.

Finally, the openness and accessibility created by open plan does create a cohesive social environment (89% report that they "get on well with colleagues" and 70% say that they "socialize with other staff in office hours"), and for many employees, this carries over into their leisure time (41% "socialize with others after office hours").

Job Characteristics

One of the supposed benefits of open plan is an improvement in productivity. However, other than for clerical or administrative jobs, arriving at a satisfactory definition of productivity in a local government context (and, indeed, in many other white-collar sectors) is currently an extremely difficult if not impossible task (Fleming 1977). Similarly, it was not practicable to attempt a very lengthy classification of the enormous variety of jobs within the local authority. Consequently, employees were asked what kinds of skills (clerical, technical, managerial, other) they felt were essential to their particular jobs. Employees were allowed to indicate one or any combination of these. On the assumption that the first three categories reflect increasingly complex skills, single or combination responses were subsequently categorized under the same four headings: for example managerial and technical was categorized as managerial. However, for the most part employees indicated only one skill category. This gave the following profile of the office workforce: 44% (286) managerial, 30% (194) technical, 20% (128) clerical, and 6% (36) other. This information was then used to qualify employees' responses to characteristics of their work and to office conditions (Table 8-6).

Table 8-6. Relationship between Employees' Job Descriptions and Reactions to Work and the Office

Job Characteristics	% AGREEMENT (FREQUENCY)					
	Managerial		Technical		Clerical	
WORK						
Really enjoy my work	63	(179)	63	(119)	39	(50)
Frequently get bored at work	1	(39)	5	(39)	53	(69)
Work needs deep thought and concentration	83	(232)	56	(106)	22	(27)
Job requires a small office	42	(119)	18	(35)	21	(27)
OFFICE CONDITIONS						
Difficult to concentrate with so many people around	79	(227)	60	(116)	53	(68)
Lack of privacy	77	(221)	64	(122)	64	(82)
Difficult to deal with confidential matters	84	(241)	64	(123)	55	(71)
Like to have a door to close on others	65	(183)	38	(72)	43	(55)
Decision making more difficult	62	(175)	50	(80)	30	(38)
Grown used to interruptions	51	(145)	53	(101)	64	(83)
Office conditions prevent effective working	73	(206)	56	(107)	49	(61)
Generally satisfied with present office conditions	30	(87)	47	(90)	46	(59)

Those employees whose jobs demanded only clerical skills voiced higher levels of boredom and lower levels of enjoyment with their work than did those using managerial or technical skills. Similarly, the managerial staff expressed a strong need for conditions conducive to thinking and concentration and they showed a preference for small offices. What is more, managerial staff members were also the most sensitive to the problems of disturbances and lack of privacy; they reported that office conditions prevented rather than facilitated effective working. These adverse views were also significantly negatively correlated with expressed general satisfaction with office working conditions ($r = -.57$, $n = 634$, $p < 0.001$).

Health

Many members of the staff reported problems of ill-health that seem to be related to office conditions (Table 8-7). Of particular concern were complaints of frequent headaches, sore eyes, and upper-respiratory-tract irritation (sore throats, colds, and so on). There were significant correlations between the incidence of sore eyes and reported deterioration in eyesight

Table 8-7. Employee Responses to Questions on Health

Health	% Agreement	(Frequency)
Frequently get sore eyes	50	(325)
Eyesight deteriorated since working in office	40	(259)
Frequent headaches	39	(254)
Frequent sore throats, colds, coughs	40	(252)
Often feel tense at work	36	(230)

($r = .54$, $n = 645$, $p < 0.001$); headaches ($r = .54$, $n = 645$, $p < 0.001$); and sore throats, coughs, and colds ($r = .43$, $n = 630$, $p < 0.001$). Also, complaints of sore eyes were correlated with complaints of dazzle from the fluorescent lights ($r = .46$, $n = 634$, $p < 0.001$). Finally, over one-third of the staff said that they frequently felt tense at work, and there was a significant negative correlation between this and general satisfaction with office working conditions ($r = -.42$, $n = 640$, $p < 0.001$). This suggests that those most dissatisfied with their working conditions also may be suffering from work-related stress.

Factor Analysis of Attitudes to the Office Conditions

The data from the first part of the questionnaire (96 statements) were analyzed using factor analysis (Principal Components Analysis with VARIMAX rotation). Due to limitations of core size, seven statements had to be dropped from the analysis, and these were selected on the basis of neutrality and limited general importance. Application of Kaiser's criterion to the outcome of this analysis (Child 1970) revealed eight group factors, which together accounted for 75% common factor variance (Table 8-8). The first group factor to emerge was one of *disturbances and privacy*, which clearly shows the interrelationship of these two concepts and highlights their joint role underlying the adverse reactions to open-plan offices found among many employees. The second factor, *health*, represents a combination of somatic symptoms, such as frequent headaches or respiratory ailments, with ambient conditions, such as problems of glare or poor ventilation, and this suggests an important relationship between physical environmental parameters and personal well-being at work.

Problems with the *thermal conditions* (temperature and air movement) appeared as a separate factor (III) independent of other aspects of the ambient environment, the staff generally finding offices too warm and inadequately ventilated. Factor IV, *workspace*, relates to employees' views on the office equipment and the facilities available to allow them to organize their own workspaces as desired. Feelings of inadequate and inappropriate workspace appear to be quite separate from other opinions

Table 8-8. Summary of the Group Factors from Factor Analysis of the Attitude Ratings for Staff in the Open-plan Offices in Case Study 1

Factor	Eigenvalue	% Common Factor Variance	Sample of High Loading Statements**	Factor Loading	Mean***	SD
I. Disturbances and Privacy (37 statements)*	16.52	37.6	Difficult to concentrate on work	.80	2.20	1.02
			Too many disturbances and distractions	.79	2.07	.92
			Need quieter conditions for complicated work	.75	1.99	.95
			Distinct lack of privacy	.70	2.10	.90
			Office conditions prevent effective working	.69	2.33	1.05
			Like a door to close on others	.65	2.52	1.14
II. Health (11 statements)*	5.51	12.5	Frequently get sore eyes	.77	2.63	1.22
			Eyesight deteriorated since started working in office	.58	2.75	1.01
			Lights too dazzling	.50	2.66	1.35
			Office too stuffy	.39	2.28	1.10
III. Thermal Conditions (5 statements)*	2.75	6.3	Office too cold	.84	3.49	1.24
			Office too hot	-.82	2.72	1.33

IV.	Workspace (7 statements)*	2.19	Work area too cramped	.69	2.65	1.11
			Adequate storage space	−.48	3.52	1.15
V.	Decor (5 statements)*	1.79	Office colors are pleasant	−.71	3.16	.92
			Office needs to be brightened up	.64	2.60	.91
VI.	Job Characteristics (3 statements)*	1.59	Work is simple and demands little concentration	.67	4.21	.91
			Work requires deep thought and concentration	−.66	2.32	.94
			Frequently bored by work	.59	3.36	1.17
			Really enjoy work	−.46	2.46	.91
VII.	Furnishings (3 statements)*	1.41	Office furniture is comfortable	.80	2.58	.90
			Office furniture is satisfactory	.66	2.73	1.05
			Office carpet is satisfactory	.42	2.51	.88
VIII.	Routes (3 statements)*	1.15	Main corridors not properly used	.62	2.94	1.11
			Corridors well defined	−.57	2.94	1.04
			Staff frequently shortcut through work area	.46	3.16	1.06

*Significant loadings
**In summarized form
***5-point scale from 1 (strongly agree) to 5 (strongly disagree)

on office layout. Factor V, *decor*, emerged as independent of other aesthetic dimensions. This shows generally adverse opinions on color scheme because the use of color was very limited in these offices; indeed, many employees voiced a strong preference for a greater variety of pleasant colors to brighten the office. A *job characteristics* factor (VI) comprised only those statements specifically concerned with the requirements of employees' jobs, showing that, overall, staff members found their work complex, demanding, and interesting. Factor VII, *furnishings*, describes general satisfaction with both office furniture and carpets, and furniture comfort. Finally, factor VIII, *routes*, reflected feelings of inadequate provision of well-defined corridors around the office, which resulted in problems of people wandering through what staff members felt were their private work areas.

CASE STUDY 2

The Offices

As with the previous study, the employees surveyed worked for a local authority in either the traditional small group or private offices of a Victorian Town Hall building or in the open-plan offices of a modern Civic Offices building completed for occupation in 1976 (fig. 8-7). The staff in the treasurer's department work mainly on the top two floors of the three-floor Town Hall; whereas those in the other departments work mainly on the top three floors of the four-floor Civic Offices. Both buildings are connected by an enclosed overhead corridor (fig. 8-8). Offices in the Town Hall follow a conventional cellular arrangement along a central corridor and are not air-conditioned; whereas the Civic Offices are predominantly open plan and are air-conditioned (figs. 8-9, 8-10). For the top three floors, the Civic Offices are arranged in a quadrangle around a central atrium. Only chief officers have their own private rooms in this building.

Method

The Survey Questionnaire

Based on the previous study and on discussions with union officials, safety officers, architects, and staff representatives, a questionnaire was constructed and piloted. In its revised form, this comprised 50 statements of attitudes to a wide range of office issues, which were answered using a 5-point rating scale from "strongly agree" to "strongly disagree." A

8-7. The open-plan office building surveyed in Case Study 2

8-8. The conventional offices of the Victorian Town Hall and the linking overhead walkway

8-9. A typical open-plan area in the Civic Offices. This area was the one with the highest incidence of health problems

8-10. The open-plan area on the fifth floor of the Civic Offices redesigned by space-planning consultants

further 11 questions gathered other information from employees on their personal details, job characteristics, spatial position in the office, previous work experience, and likes and dislikes about the offices.

Distribution and Sample

The final survey was conducted in early spring, 1982. All questionnaires were internally distributed and collected by staff representatives. Of 800 questionnaires distributed to those working permanently in either the open-plan or conventional offices, 359 completed questionnaires were returned by those in open-plan and 59 by those in the conventional offices, a total response rate of 52.3%. Of the respondents in the sample, 53% were men and 47% were women, and this mirrors the employment profile for the authority.

Results

The Ambient Environment

Heating and ventilation. Markedly different heating and ventilation systems service the two buildings. The Civic Offices, designed as a low-energy-consumption open-plan accommodation, are fully air-conditioned and possess a good heat envelope (only 24% of the wall area comprises sealed, double-glazed, solar-reflecting glass). Waste heat from lighting and from occupants is reclaimed and so only a low output system for background heating is provided. Throughout the year of the survey, the air temperature had been recorded at 21°C ± 3°C.

Air is delivered into the Civic Offices via a constant velocity, variable volume system comprising four air-handling plants. Delivery is controlled locally by thermostats, each of which regulate the output from eight ceiling diffusers by the movement of a mechanical damper. Almost all the thermostats in the building are set for 21°C, and most of these are sealed to prevent employee tampering. Air is extracted from the offices via the lighting system to collect the maximum amount of heat. Depending on external conditions, between four and ten air changes per hour are delivered and between 25 and 100% of this can be fresh air. All air is electrostatically filtered (removing 90% particles at 0.6 μ and 100% at 4 μ) and humidified at the source (between 30 and 55% relative humidity).

In contrast, the conventional offices of the Town Hall are heated by steam-fed radiators with no thermostatic controls and the building is not air-conditioned. Ventilation control is achieved by openable windows.

User reactions to their ambient working conditions in each of the offices are summarized in Table 8-9. Comparisons between the two offices showed no significant differences in responses to statements on ambient

Table 8-9. Comparison of Employees' Views on the Ambient Conditions in the Open-Plan and Conventional Offices

	OPEN PLAN		CONVENTIONAL				
Ambient Conditions	*% Agree*	*(Freq.)*	*% Agree*	*(Freq.)*	*t*	*df*	*p*
HEATING							
Often too warm	40	(141)	43	(25)	1.80	416	ns
Usually too cold	33	(113)	19	(11)	−2.70	410	0.01
VENTILATION							
Well ventilated	15	(55)	29	(17)	3.72	414	0.001
Often too drafty	38	(135)	17	(10)	−3.30	413	0.001

temperature. Overall, around 40% of the staff sampled in each building agreed that their office was often "too warm."

These reactions varied significantly by floor in the open-plan offices (χ^2 = 10.66, df = 3, p < 0.02), where proportionally more complaints were made by those on the lower floors (Table 8-10), and a similar although nonsignificant trend was shown by those in the conventional offices. Responses to the statement that the office was "usually too cold" were significantly negatively correlated with those to the office's being "often too warm" in both the open-plan (r = −0.57, n = 354, p < 0.001) and conventional offices (r = −0.35, n = 59, p < 0.003).

There were significant differences between the two office buildings in staff responses to statements on ventilation (Table 8-9). Overall, fewer staff members in the open-plan offices felt that these were well ventilated and more complained that these were "often too drafty." Responses to ventilation varied significantly by floor in these offices χ^2 = 14.07, df = 3, p < 0.001), with fewest staff members complaining of poor ventilation on the top floor (Table 8-11); however even here, over two-thirds of the staff felt that the ventilation system was inadequate.

The analysis of responses to ventilation by floor in the conventional offices was nonsignificant. Finally, there were no significant correlations

Table 8-10. Comparison of Employee Agreement That "The Office Is Often Too Warm" by Floor between the Two Buildings

	OPEN PLAN		CONVENTIONAL	
Floor	*% Agree*	*(Frequency)*	*% Agree*	*(Frequency)*
1st (ground)	67	(12)	68	(8)
2nd	48	(16)	48	(14)
3rd	40	(66)	30	(3)
4th (top)	32	(47)	−	

Table 8-11. Comparison of Employee Disagreement That "The Office is Well Ventilated" by Floor between the Two Buildings

	OPEN PLAN		CONVENTIONAL	
Floor	*% Disagree*	*(Frequency)*	*% Disagree*	*(Frequency)*
1st (ground)	78	(14)	83	(10)
2nd	70	(23)	49	(18)
3rd	82	(133)	30	(3)
4th (top)	67	(98)	–	

between complaints about ventilation and complaints about drafts in either building. This suggests that the reported ventilation problems resulted from employees' feeling that there was too little rather than too much air movement in the offices; however, no independent data on air flow were collected.

Lighting. In both office buildings, the primary lighting system comprises ceiling-mounted "cool white" fluorescent luminaires, which were supposedly replaced on a regular, systematic maintenance schedule (although, in practice, this was less than perfect). For certain staff members, this lighting is supplemented by desk-top incandescent lamps. The general level of illumination was supposed to be 600 lux (56 footcandles). Actual measures, however, showed that in certain areas of the open-plan offices, the levels were as low as 350 lux (33 footcandles), and this situation was exacerbated by frequent moving of desks by the staff from their "ideal" position in the planned layout for the lighting system. By way of contrast, in addition to the fluorescent lighting, the smaller, conventional offices typically had larger windows, higher ceilings, and more direct task lighting, and these afforded less scope for rearranging the layout of desks. Also, significantly more staff members sat close to a window in these conventional offices (54%) than in the open-plan offices (41%: $\chi^2 = 13.19$, $df = 3$, $p < 0.01$).

Overall reactions to lighting were significantly less favorable in the open-plan offices (Table 8-12). Employees' opinions on the adequacy of lighting did not correlate with their position in the office relative to a window and this may be because of the limited window area in the Civic Offices and the use of dark tinted glass. However, responses did vary significantly by floor in these offices ($\chi^2 = 26.92$, $df = 3$, $p < 0.001$), with more staff complaints of poor lighting on the second and third floors (70% and 75%, respectively) than on either the ground (first) or top (fourth) floors (44% and 54%, respectively).

Also, there were many more complaints of glare problems in the open-

Table 8-12. Comparison of Employees' Reactions to Office Lighting

	OPEN PLAN		CONVENTIONAL				
Lighting	*% Agree*	*(Freq.)*	*% Agree*	*(Freq.)*	*t*	*df*	*p*
Lighting is good	23	(80)	49	(29)	−6.39	413	0.001
Frequent glare problems	55	(198)	21	(12)	−5.97	414	0.001

plan offices than there were in the conventional offices (Table 8-12). In both types of accommodation, complaints about glare were weakly correlated with desk position in the layout relative to a window (open plan, $r = .13$, $n = 352$, $p < 0.01$; conventional, $r = .28$, $n = 57$, $p < 0.025$), such that those closest to the windows appear to experience fewest glare problems. This may be one reason staff members in both the open-plan (70%) and conventional offices (58%) express a strong desire for a view through a window, which similarly correlated with complaints about glare in both buildings (open plan, $r = .19$ $n = 352$, $p < 0.01$; conventional, $r = .26$, $n = 58$, $p < 0.025$). Problems of glare, however, were most strongly correlated with negative opinions of lighting in the open-plan offices ($r = -.53$, $n = 356$, $p < 0.001$), whereas this was not true of the conventional offices, where no significant relationship was found.

Privacy and Disturbances

Responses to questions on privacy and disturbances in the two offices are summarized in Table 8-13. No significant correlations were found between an employee's job type and responses to these questions; consequently, only aggregated data are presented in this table. More staff members in the open-plan offices complained of a "lack of privacy" and of "too many disturbances and distractions." Indeed, these views were significantly correlated for both offices (open plan, $r = .41$, $n = 354$, $p < 0.001$; conventional, $r = .45$, $n = 59$, $p < 0.001$). Similarly, more staff members in the open-plan offices agreed that the office was "too noisy," and, again, this was significantly correlated with views on disturbances and distractions in both samples of employees (open plan, $r = .52$, $n = 353$, $p < 0.001$; conventional, $r = .54$, $n = 59$, $p < 0.001$). In both offices, staff members felt that "other people's talking" contributed significantly to the overall noisiness of the office (open plan, $r = .65$, $n = 349$, $p < 0.001$; conventional, $r = .76$, $n = 57$, $p < 0.001$); however, noise from the ringing of telephones only contributed to the noise problem in the open-plan offices ($r = .44$, $n = 353$, $p < 0.001$). No significant differences between the two offices were found in levels of perceived personal accessibility, frequency of contact with or trivial interruptions

Table 8-13. Employees' Reactions to Privacy and Disturbances in the Two Offices

Reactions	OPEN PLAN		CONVENTIONAL		*t*	*df*	*p*
	% Agree	*(Freq.)*	*% Agree*	*(Freq.)*			
PRIVACY							
Too accessible to others	38	(133)	28	(17)	−1.11	411	ns
Too frequently in contact with others	26	(93)	17	(10)	− .94	409	ns
Would like a door to close on others	58	(205)	45	(24)	−1.46	408	ns
Distinct lack of privacy	73	(262)	47	(18)	−3.94	416	0.001
DISTURBANCES							
GENERAL							
Too frequently interrupted by trivial matters	49	(173)	37	(22)	−1.74	413	ns
Too many disturbances and distractions	69	(249)	51	(30)	−2.03	416	0.05
Office too noisy	51	(182)	30	(18)	−3.05	414	0.01
Learned to ignore distractions	47	(166)	41	(24)	1.07	412	ns
SPECIFIC SOURCES							
Other staff talking	49	(174)	35	(20)	−1.79	409	ns
Telephones	38	(136)	17	(10)	−3.67	414	0.001

by others, or desire for control of a door; also, no evidence was found to suggest that the staff in the open-plan offices have more successfully learned to ignore their highly distracting environment than their counterparts in conventional offices have. Similarly, no significant differences were found in the frequency of social contacts with others in the two offices (frequent social contacts: open plan, 34%; conventional, 37%). Given that both offices created comparable social environments, this does not confirm the supposed facilitation of social cohesiveness often attributed to open plan. Moreover, the general lack of privacy felt by the staff in open plan appears to directly reflect a loss of both visual and conversational privacy, plus a high level of distractions, rather than merely being the product of an increased frequency of interpersonal contacts.

Job Characteristics

As was mentioned for the previous study, it is not easy to classify employees' jobs in Local Government accurately without developing a lengthy and cumbersome taxonomy. In the previous survey, jobs were classified as managerial, technical, clerical, or other on the basis of employee self-reports, so this approach was further refined for this survey. Here, all employees were asked to indicate what percentage of their job demanded managerial, professional/technical, clerical, or other types of skills, and based upon these data, jobs were then classified into four corresponding categories. A person's job was included in a particular category provided that it predominantly demanded one type of skill: e.g., when more than 50% of the job required managerial skills, this was classified as a managerial job. When this 50% criterion could not be satisfied, jobs were placed in an "other" category, and these were removed from subsequent analyses. The resulting employment profiles of the staff in the samples from the two offices are shown in Table 8-14, and, overall, these two profiles are very similar. It is worth noting that the resulting proportion of managerial jobs is smaller than in the previous survey and this may be because jobs were being classified in a more stringent way. However, the fact that the present survey was conducted for a Borough Authority whereas the previous one examined a County Authority will also have influenced this: Staff members at the former are more concerned with day-to-day operational activities whereas those at the latter are more involved with strategic planning and other nonoperational roles, and these role differences markedly influence staffing grades.

As in Case Study 1, attitudes to work characteristics and office conditions were separated for those in each of the three main job categories in each office, and these are summarized in Table 8-15.

There was no systematic pattern of strong correlations between job type and attitudes toward work and conditions for either office. Also, there were no differences between overall staff opinions on job satisfaction in either, although several significant differences between staff views on their working conditions in the two offices were found (Table 8-15). Of those in the open-plan offices, 61% compared with 41% of those in conventional accommodation, felt that the office layout was not optimal

Table 8-14. Classification of Jobs in the Samples of Employees in the Two Offices

Job Type	OPEN PLAN		CONVENTIONAL	
	%	(Frequency)	%	(Frequency)
Managerial	18	(64)	9	(5)
Professional/Technical	47	(167)	54	(32)
Clerical	31	(108)	32	(19)
Other	4	(15)	5	(3)

Table 8-15. Relationship Between Employees' Job Description and Reactions to Work and Conditions in the Two Offices

OPEN PLAN

Work Characteristics	Managerial		Professional/ Technical		Clerical		Total		CONVENTIONAL Managerial		Professional/ Technical		Clerical		Total				
	% Agree	(Freq.)	% Agree	(Freq.)	% Agree	(Freq.)	% Agree	(Freq.)	% Agree	(Freq.)	% Agree	(Freq.)	% Agree	(Freq.)	% Agree	(Freq.)	t	df	p
JOB SATISFACTION																			
Really enjoy my work	73	(47)	58	(96)	38	(40)	59	(192)	80	(4)	63	(20)	42	(8)	53	(32)	− .15	413	ns
Frequently get bored at work	5	(3)	11	(18)	24	(26)	15	(53)	0		6	(2)	21	(4)	12	(7)	0.83	415	ns
Job requires a small office	40	(25)	23	(38)	18	(19)	28	(91)	25	(1)	28	(9)	26	(5)	26	(15)	− .37	409	ns
Very satisfied with job	68	(43)	47	(77)	30	(32)	45	(162)	60	(3)	47	(15)	37	(7)	43	(25)	− .67	399	ns
OFFICE CONDITIONS																			
Layout ideal for my work	18	(11)	18	(30)	7	(8)	15	(54)	40	(2)	6	(2)	16	(3)	15	(9)	2.82	414	0.01
Conditions help me do a good job	9	(6)	9	(15)	8	(9)	10	(33)	80	(4)	16	(5)	0		16	(9)	4.48	416	0.001
Conditions help improve personal productivity	8	(5)	6	(10)	4	(4)	7	(21)	40	(2)	6	(2)	5	(1)	9	(5)	3.13	413	0.01
Disturbances from others talking impair decision making	52	(32)	48	(80)	16	(17)	39	(137)	50	(2)	34	(11)	32	(6)	33	(19)	−1.03	405	ns
Conditions hinder concentration on work	58	(37)	57	(96)	39	(42)	52	(186)	20	(1)	37	(12)	26	(5)	30	(18)	−3.72	413	0.001
Generally satisfied with working conditions	36	(23)	30	(50)	19	(21)	28	(100)	80	(4)	47	(15)	63	(12)	54	(32)	6.04	415	0.001

for their work. Clearly, the flexibility of layout in open plan was not being appropriately utilized in these Civic Offices. Also, 63% of those in open plan compared with only 33% of those in conventional offices complained that office conditions did not help them do a good job, and this general pattern was found for complaints that conditions hindered concentration on work (52% open plan; 30% conventional) and personal productivity at work (70% open plan; 49% conventional). Similar percentages of both groups of staff, however, agreed that disturbances impair their decision making. Finally, 42% of the staff in open plan expressed dissatisfaction with their conditions, compared with only 18% of those in the conventional offices.

Health

Some of the most disturbing differences found between the staffs in the two offices concerned their self-reports of ill-health (Table 8-16). Significantly more staff members in open plan complained of frequent headaches, eye irritation, and sore throats, coughs, and colds at work. Subsequent analysis of these data showed that 49% (70) of the open-plan sufferers found their offices to be too warm and 91% (128) complained of inadequate ventilation. Furthermore, 42% (69) of those in open plan suffering frequent sore throats, coughs, and colds also complained of frequent headaches and eye irritation. This suggests that a sizable number of employees were consistently suffering multiple problems of ill-health associated with their working conditions. It is interesting that many of those staff members who experienced the most severe problems were

Table 8-16. Responses of Employees to Health Problems in the Two Offices

Health	OPEN PLAN		CONVENTIONAL		t	df	p
	% Agree	(Freq.)	% Agree	(Freq.)			
Frequently get headaches at work	39	(142)	16	(9)	−4.41	415	0.001
Frequently suffer eye irritation	45	(162)	17	(10)	−4.81	414	0.001
Often get sore throats, coughs, colds at work	46	(166)	24	(14)	−3.01	414	0.01
Often feel tense at work	38	(136)	33	(19)	−1.92	414	ns

located in the same quadrant of the open-plan offices (each quadrant being served by a separate air-conditioning plant), and, consequently, a more detailed study of ambient conditions was undertaken for this area. This study, in summary, showed that there was no difference either in the recorded air temperature in this area and in other parts of the open-plan offices (average 20°C over a one-month period) or in relative humidity levels (average 50%). Lighting levels in this area, however, tended to be lower than those elsewhere (around 350 to 450 lux compared with 600 lux in other areas). Also, although no differences in negative ion concentrations could be detected (average 200 cc^{-1}), the air in this region of the offices actually contained five times the concentration of positive ions detectable elsewhere (average 1000 cc^{-1}), and there is recent evidence that for certain types of people, short-term exposure to high levels of positive ions results in detrimental effects on performance and mood (Charry and Hawkinshire 1981). Conversely, it seems that exposure to high concentrations of negative ions over long time periods may lead to reduced frequency and severity of headaches in office staff (Hawkins 1981a; 1981b) although these results have not been subsequently replicated (Hawkins and Morris 1984). Thus, the possibility remains that these conditions, perhaps in concert with the poorer lighting, may have been instrumental in increasing the incidence of ill-health in office workers in this area, but this clearly warrants further study.

Finally, there was a trend for proportionally more employees in the open-plan offices than the conventional offices to complain of feelings of tension at work, but this just failed significance.

Factor Analysis of Attitudes to the Office Conditions

Because of the relatively small size of the sample of employees in the conventional offices compared with the number of variables, it was felt unwise to submit these data to factor analysis (Child 1970). However, the attitude data for staff in the open-plan offices were analyzed using factor analysis (Principal Components Analysis with VARIMAX rotation), with the same criteria being employed as previously described. The results of this analysis showed that six group factors together accounted for 76% common factor variance (Table 8-17).

The first two factors to emerge were identical with those found in the previous study. A *disturbances and privacy* factor accounted for the largest percentage of common factor variance. Statements describing problems of disturbances loaded more highly on this factor than did those describing losses of privacy, but, again, these are clearly seen as interrelated by the employees. The second factor was one of *health*, and this includes both statements describing somatic symptoms, such as eye

Table 8-17. Summary of the Group Factors from Factor Analysis of the Attitude Ratings for Staff in the Open-Plan Offices in Case Study 2

Factor	Eigenvalue	% Common Factor Variance	Sample of High Loading Statement**	Factor Loading	Mean***	SD
I. Disturbances and Privacy (12 statements)*	8.47	33.5	Too much noise from others talking	.80	2.57	1.01
			Difficult to concentrate on work	.79	2.54	1.05
			Office too noisy	.77	2.51	1.03
			Disturbances impair decision making	.72	2.76	1.02
			Too many disturbances and distractions	.66	2.16	1.11
			Distinct lack of privacy	.50	2.02	1.07
II. Health (7 statements)*	3.80	15.1	Frequent eye irritation	.66	2.83	1.26
			Frequent glare problems	.65	2.54	1.22
			Frequent headaches at work	.62	3.06	1.28
			Office lighting good	−.58	3.69	1.16
			Frequent sore throats, coughs, or colds at work	.57	2.80	1.23

		Eigenvalue	% Variance	Statement	Loading	Mean	SD
III.	Job Satisfaction (4 statements)*	2.34	9.3				
				Very satisfied with job	.87	2.80	1.02
				Really enjoy work	.80	2.58	.98
				Frequently bored with work	-.75	3.52	1.12
IV.	Office Conditions (5 statements)*	2.00	7.9				
				Conditions help me to do a good job	.66	3.78	.94
				Conditions improve personal productivity at work	.61	3.84	.86
				Satisfied with office conditions	.42	3.26	1.06
V.	Workspace (3 statements)*	1.50	5.9				
				Workspace too cramped	-.72	2.80	1.20
				Ample space for papers, files, books, etc.	.65	3.38	1.22
				Office layout ideal for work	.50	3.63	1.02
VI.	Decor (4 statements)*	1.12	4.4				
				Office colors are pleasant	.75	3.56	.96
				Office needs to brightened up	-.69	2.24	.97
				Furnishings look attractive	.48	3.84	.90

*Significant loadings
**In summarized form
***5-point scale from 1 (strongly agree) to 5 (strongly disagree)

irritation, headaches, and respiratory ailments, and problems with ambient conditions, such as poor lighting or frequent glare. A *job satisfaction* factor (III) appeared which was independent of employees' views about other aspects of their work and conditions in the office and which shows the general satisfaction of staff members with their jobs. Factor IV, termed *office conditions*, shows widespread disagreement with statements on beneficial office conditions and personal productivity at work. Finally, *workspace* (factor V) and *decor* (factor VI) show unfavorable employee reactions to their office area and the layout of their workspaces, the general layout of the offices, and the attractiveness of the color scheme and furnishings in the offices.

CONCLUSIONS FROM THE CASE STUDIES

The results of the two user surveys show both a high degree of consistency in employees' attitudes to working in the two open-plan offices as well as many differences between these and the attitudes held by the staff working in conventional offices. As expected from the results of the previous studies of user reactions to office conditions described in the introduction, those working in open plan complained of a substantial loss of both visual and conversational privacy. What is more, the second study clearly demonstrated that this is not felt as strongly by those working alone or in small groups in the conventional offices. It is interesting that there were no differences between staff in the two offices in terms of their perceived accessibility, frequency of interpersonal contacts, and frequency of trivial interruptions. This may reflect the fact that many of the conventional offices were actually occupied by several employees (five or less), and it may also account for the quite high proportion (almost half) who still complained of a loss of privacy. Associated with these privacy problems, more complaints of disturbances, distractions, and general noisiness were voiced by those in open plan. Here telephone noise appears to be a potent source of annoyance (indeed, in the first study some employees had learned to cope with this by hiding telephones in drawers, wastebaskets, and so on), and if one accepts these results, then the installation of quieter telephone systems could immediately help with reducing the disturbance problems in these open-plan offices.

No differences were found between aggregated data on employees' attitudes to their work in the different offices; indeed, at this level, the staff sampled appeared to enjoy their work and to be generally satisfied with it. Classification of responses by job skills, however, showed that managerial staff members were typically those most satisfied with the nature of their work but least satisfied with their working conditions, whereas the reverse was true for clerical workers. Furthermore, the attitudes of the staff in open plan to their working conditions were significantly more negative than those of the staff in the conventional offices. While proponents of open plan have often recognized the almost inevitable occurrence of these problems, claims that open plan creates a more cohesive social environment that mitigates the otherwise adverse conditions have frequently been advanced. It is certainly true that those in the open-plan offices of the present surveys found that this facilitated a sociable work environment; however, the second survey showed that these views may not in fact differ from those of staff members working in small groups in conventional offices. Given this situation, any argument advocating a compensatory effect of sociability in open plan must be treated with some degree of skepticism.

No evidence for any improvement in self-reported productivity was found among those working in open plan; in fact, a reverse relationship emerged, with those in conventional offices reporting higher productivity. It may be that at the organizational level, there are apparent increases in productivity with open plan if space-saving costs are included in any productivity equation; however, at the personal level, such evidence still remains to be convincingly demonstrated.

One particularly disturbing result to emerge from the present work is the difference between the reported incidence of health problems in employees in air-conditioned open-plan offices compared with those in unconditioned conventional offices. Staff in open-plan offices consistently reported significantly more headaches, eye problems (soreness, itching, and so on) and coughs, colds, and sore throats, and this finding is in keeping with that of Dick and associates (1981) and Turiel and associates (1983). In spite of the fact that the Turiel group took comprehensive records of indoor air quality (temperature, relative humidity, air flow, odor, microbial burden, particulate mass, carbon monoxide and dioxide levels, nitrogen dioxide levels, and 28 organic compounds), they failed to find any single cause for the higher incidence of health complaints among employees in air-conditioned open-plan offices.

Similarly, in the second case study reported in this chapter, measures of temperature, humidity, air ion levels, and lighting levels failed to show large differences between those in the open-plan and conventional offices. A subsequent, more detailed analysis, however, has revealed that the highest incidence of health problems is in an area where the relative concentration of positive ions is high, and, as previously mentioned, certain types of sensitive individuals show adverse emotional and performance changes when exposed to very high concentrations of positive ions for short periods of time (Charry and Hawkinshire 1981). The possibility that for such people there may also be some kind of cumulative effect such that prolonged exposure to somewhat lower levels of positive ions (although still the dominant ion polarity) results in a deterioration in health remains to be investigated. In addition to this possibility, the incidence of eye complaints correlated with negative reactions to the fluorescent lighting in the offices and the incidence of headaches correlated with this and with perceived inadequate office ventilation.

It is interesting that recent studies of other local authority offices have produced evidence that suggests these health problems need not be a necessary product of open plan per se, but rather that they appear to be related to the use of air-conditioning for ventilation and to inadequate daylight penetration into the offices (Hedge 1984a, 1984b). Given this growing body of work on the incidence of ill-health in office workers, further systematic research of the health problems briefly discussed in this chapter and their effects on productivity is urgently needed.

Finally, given the wide diversity of issues that have been described, it is clear that the future development of a closer liaison among designers, behavioral researchers, and other professionals involved in the operational management of offices must be encouraged if any comprehensive and systematic approach to resolving those problems currently facing many office staff is to succeed.

BEYOND OFFICE SURVEYS

All the issues discussed in this chapter have been based on the results taken from user surveys, but, in conclusion, it is worthwhile to point out that such an approach suffers many inherent weaknesses. At best, a user survey, if well designed, can accurately reflect the office conditions as perceived by employees at a specific time and, therefore, can constitute a useful starting point for remedial action; at worst, it may produce a highly distorted image. Consequently, several problematic points need to be borne in mind when considering the wider implications of the results presented. First, it was not possible to control sampling of employees in the surveys and, therefore, those who made returns constituted a self-selected group. It may be that in some ways their views differed from those of employees who did not return the questionnaire, thereby biasing the results; unfortunately, no data are available to clarify this situation. Also, there were problems with the questionnaires used because they did not contain definitions of standards. Thus words like *productivity*, *privacy*, and so on may have been interpreted differently by different staff members. Similarly, although some objective measures of ambient conditions were taken to corroborate answers to questions on these standards in the survey, no such measures were taken either for other quantifiable variables, such as noise, space, and health, or for less tangible concepts, such as productivity and satisfaction. Even though many questions were phrased in terms of frequency of occurrence, again no objective criterion for this was advanced. Finally, at a general level, different respondents may well have interpreted attitude statements in different ways. In spite of these limitations, however, the high level of agreement between the results from the two studies and between these and the findings of many of the other studies cited strongly suggests that such work has validity and is highlighting important issues.

Overall, the greatest limitation with this type of user survey is perhaps that the results afford few firm recommendations for action in terms directly useful to office space planning. Although many significant differences in user reactions to conventional and open-plan offices have been shown, questions such as which is "better" are not particularly meaningful, and knowing what the problems are with each type of office does not necessarily reveal the solutions to these at either a global or a specific situational level. However, maybe we should not expect too much from survey studies, and perhaps the real value of the results they produce lies in the way in which these can help question the prevailing philosophy underlying office design. At present, much office space planning is devoted to meeting standards for space, temperature, lighting, and so on, and it tends to deal with problems of workspace design to satisfy organizational rather than individual requirements. From this stance, standards are seen as criteria rather than guidelines for good design. Unfortunately, and albeit with the best of intentions for creating optimal working conditions, such an approach strives for, or at least frequently produces, environmental uniformity: uniform temperature, uniform lighting levels, uniform colors, uniform furniture. The people who work in these settings, however, are usually far from uniform and have differing wants, needs, and goals; and user surveys highlight this variety of environmental requirements by emphasizing the diversity of attitudes to and problems experienced with working conditions such that defining standards becomes an almost impossible task.

In keeping with Wineman (1982), perhaps we may find the solution to this dilemma by noting other work in environmental psychology, which shows that people often have a strong desire to control their immediate environment, that they place different demands on it, and that these demands may change over time. In private or small group offices such intimate control over work, workspace, and ambient conditions is typically easier to exercise than it is in larger open-plan offices, and without doubt this is central to the aversion of many employees to open plan. Consequently, unless we are to opt for simple solutions to the dilemmas of open planning, such as abandoning this approach to office design altogether, future research might profitably investigate alternative ways of humanizing offices. The development of better ways of involving employees in the design of their workspaces and in giving them greater control over these and their working conditions will be a good avenue of exploration for all concerned with the future planning of effective and productive offices.

NOTES

1. To date, there is no complete English translation of this work but from that currently available there do seem to be serious methodological problems of sampling and of questionnaire design that limit the general validity of the conclusions drawn from the research data.
2. From the inception of *Bürolandschaft*, Walter Schnelle recognized that this could be successful only for large, square areas rather than other office developments (personal communication with a Quickborner client).
3. All correlations presented are Pearson product-moment correlation coefficients and all significance levels are one-tailed. Kendall's Tau correlation coefficients were also calculated to check for any bias due to tied ratings and these closely followed the pattern for Pearson coefficients.

References

Boje, A. 1971. *Open plan offices*, London: Business Books Ltd.

Brookes, M. H. 1972. Changes in employee attitudes and work practices in office landscape. In W. J. Mitchell (Ed.) *Environmental design: Research and practice*. Proceedings of the Environmental Design Research Association EDRA3/AR8 Conference, University of California at Los Angeles.

Brookes, M. H. 1978. Changes in employee attitudes and work practices in an office landscape. In A. Friedmann, C. Zimring, and E. Zube (Eds.), *Environmental design evaluation*. London: Plenum Press, pp. 35–45.

Brookes, M. H., and A. Kaplan. 1972. The office environment: Space planning and affective behaviour. *Human Factors* 14:373–391.

Cakin, S. 1981. *A selected bibliography on office environments*. Technische Hogeschool Delft. Afdeling der Bouwkunde. Centrum voor Architectuuronderzoek. Delft, The Netherlands.

Charry, J. M., and V. F. R. W. Hawkinshire. 1981. Effects of atmospheric electricity on some substrates of disordered social behavior. *Journal of Personality and Social Psychology* 41:185–197.

Child, D. 1970. *The essentials of factor analysis*. New York: Holt, Rinehart, & Winston.

Dick, C., I. Kompart, G. Reinartz, H. Schnadt, and N. Tossing. 1981. *Auswirkungen der Tatigkeit in Grossraumburos auf die Gesundheit der Beschaftigten. Pt. II*. West Germany: Der Bunderminister für Arbeit und Sozialordnung.

Duffy, F. 1974a. Office design and organizations: 1. Theoretical basis. *Environment and Planning B* 1:105–118.

Duffy, F. 1974b. Office design and organizations: 2. The testing of a hypothetical model. *Environment and Planning B* 1:217–235.

Duffy, F., and P. Ellis. 1980. Lost office landscapes. *Management Today* (May): 47, 50, 52.

Fleming, A. M. 1977. White collar productivity. Strathclyde, U.K.:Strathclyde Business School.

Grivel, F., and M. Barth. 1980. Thermal comfort in office spaces: Predictions and observations. In E. de Oliveira Fernandes et al. (Eds.), *Building energy management: Conventional and solar approaches*. London: Pergamon Press, pp. 681–693.

Hardy, A. C. 1982. An investigation into the relative importance of design and performance on the acceptability of the environment within open plan office buildings. Proceedings of the Commission Internationale de L'Eclairage Workshop. Capenhurst, U.K.

Hawkins, L. H. 1981a. Air ionisation and office health. *Building Services and Environmental Engineer* (April).

Hawkins, L. H. 1981b. The influence of air ions, temperature and humidity on subjective well-being and comfort. *Journal of Environmental Psychology* 1:279–292.

Hawkins, L. H., and T. Barker. 1978. Air ions and human performance. *Ergonomics* 21:273–278.

Hawkins, L. H., and L. Morris. 1984. Air ions and sick building syndrome. In B. Berglund, T. Lindvall, and J. Sundell (Eds.), *Indoor air: Sensory and hyperactivity reactions to sick buildings*, Vol. 3, *Proceedings of the 3rd International Conference on Indoor Air Quality and Climate*. Stockholm, Sweden: Swedish Council for Building Research, pp. 197–200.

Hedge, A. 1980. Office design: User reactions to open plan. In R. Thorne and S. Arden (Eds.), *People and the man-made environment: Building, urban and landscape design related to human behaviour*. University of Sydney, pp. 57–68.

Hedge, A. 1982. The open-plan office: A systematic investigation of employee reactions to their work environment. *Environment and Behavior* 14:579–542.

Hedge, A. 1984. Ill health among office workers: An examination of the relationship between office design and employee well-being. In E. Grandjean (Ed.), *Ergonomics and health in modern offices*. London: Taylor and Francis, pp. 46–51.

Hedge, A. 1984a. Evidence of a relationship between office design and self-report of ill health among office workers in the U.K. *Journal of Architectural and Planning Research* 1(3):163–174.

Hedge, A., and E. Eleftherakis. 1982. Air ionization: An evaluation of its physiological and psychological effects. *Annals of Occupational Hygiene* 24:409–419.

Jaeger, D. 1969. Office landscape: A systems concept. In N. Polites (Ed.), *Improving office environment*. IL: The Business Press, pp. 12–33.

Johnson, K. E. 1970. The office environment people prefer. *American Institute of Architects Journal* 53:56–58.

Kraemer, Sieverts and Partners. 1977. *Open-plan offices: New ideas, experience, and improvements*. (English translation by J. L. Ritchie.) New York: McGraw-Hill.

Louis Harris and Associates, Inc. 1980. *The Steelcase National Study of office environments No. II: Comfort and productivity in the office of the 80s*. Grand Rapids, MI: Steelcase, Inc.

Marans, R. W., and K. E. Spreckelmeyer. 1982. Evaluating open and conventional office design. *Environment and Behavior* 14:333–351.

Meyer, G., and S. Wenk. 1975. Das Grossraumbüro: Ein contra aus der sicht der darin arbeitenden. *Der Architekt* 24:473–474.

Nemecek, J., and E. Grandjean. 1973. Results of an ergonomic investigation of large space offices. *Human Factors* 15:111–124.

Palmer, A. E., and J. Lewis. 1977. *Planning the office landscape.* New York: McGraw-Hill.

Pile, J. F. 1977. The open office: Does it work? *Progressive Architecture* (June):68–81.

Pile, J. F. 1978. *Open-office planning: A handbook for interior designers and architects.* London: Architectural Press.

Rohles, F. J. 1971. Thermal sensations of sedentary man in moderate temperatures. *Human Factors* 13:553–560.

Singer, G. 1980. Physiological costs of the work environment. In H. L. Bartley (Ed.), *Stress at work.* La Trobe University, Department of Psychology, Melbourne, Symposium Series 1, pp. 17–22.

Soyka, F., and A. Edmonds. 1977. *The ion effect.* New York: Bantam Books.

Starbuck, J. C. 1976. Open-plan offices (office landscaping): A chronological bibliography of magazine articles in English. *Council of Planning Librarians, Exchange Bibliography* 1119:1–6.

Sundstrom, E., R. E. Burt, and D. Kamp. 1980. Privacy at work: Architectural correlates of job satisfaction and job performance. *Academy of Management Journal* 23:101–117.

Sundstrom, E., R. K. Herbert, and D. W. Brown. 1982. Privacy and communication in an open-plan office: A case study. *Environment and Behavior* 14:379–392.

Sundstrom, E., J. P. Town, D. W. Brown, A. Forman, and C. McGee. 1982. Physical enclosure, type of job and privacy in the office. *Environment and Behavior* 14:543–559.

Turiel, I., C. D. Hollowell, R. R. Miksch, J. V. Rudy, and R. A. Young. 1983. The effects of reduced ventilation on indoor air quality in an office building. *Atmospheric Environment* 17:51–64.

Wells, B. W. P. 1965. Subjective responses to the lighting installation in a modern office building and their design implications. *Building Science* 1:57–68.

Wineman, J. D. 1982. Office design and evaluation: An overview. *Environment and Behavior* 14:271–298.

Privacy in the Office

ERIC SUNDSTROM
Department of Psychology
University of Tennessee
Knoxville, Tennessee

This chapter discusses the concept of privacy and describes two empirical studies[1] of the connection of the physical environment in the office with privacy and the connection of privacy with employees' satisfaction. Both studies point to the importance of the individual's job.

The Concept of Privacy

The term *privacy* usually refers to a psychological state that accompanies a satisfactory retreat from, or regulation of, social interaction. However, definitions vary. A few focus on the deliberate withdrawal by an individual or group from contact with other people (e.g., Bates 1964). Many approaches emphasize either control over social interaction or autonomy of action. For example, Westin (1970) defined privacy as the ability of individuals or groups to control the communication of information about themselves to others. Marshall (1970) proposed a broader definition: control over access to the self. Beardsley (1971) defined privacy in terms of autonomy of action and selective disclosure of information about oneself. Kelvin (1973) argued that privacy involves a restriction of knowledge about an individual's actions by others, which provides a "positive limitation of the power of others" (p. 260). Other definitions have also

* Eric Sundstrom, "Privacy in the Office," *Environment and Behavior*, vol. 14, no. 3 (May 1982), pp. 382–89. Copyright © 1982 by Sage Publications. Reprinted by permission.

been proposed (see reviews by Altman 1976; Margulis 1977; Pennock and Chapman 1971).

One of the most widely accepted definitions of privacy comes from Altman's (1975) theory: "selective control of access to the self or one's group" by other people (p. 18). Altman proposed a general theory on the regulation of social interaction, or *privacy-regulation*. The theory suggests that people attempt to optimize social contact, including both incoming stimulation and outgoing information. When individuals or groups experience too much or too little social interaction, they use privacy-regulation mechanisms to withdraw from interaction or seek it out. Privacy exists when these efforts succeed.

An empirical study has suggested that privacy in the office involves the ability to control access to one's self or group, particularly the ability to limit others' access to one's workspace. Justa and Golan (1977) questioned 40 business executives who worked in offices and asked them to describe situations involving privacy in the office. Many participants listed more than one situation; the most frequently mentioned was being able to work without distraction (60%). Others included controlling access to information (35%); freedom to do what they want (35%); controlling access to space (35%); and being alone (25%).

Conventional definitions of privacy in the office include speech privacy and visual privacy. *Speech privacy* refers to a person's ability to converse without being understood outside the room (Cavanaugh, Farrell, Hirtle, and Watters 1966). (The term *conversational privacy* is synonymous. The related term *acoustic privacy* includes speech privacy plus isolation from intruding sounds.) *Visual privacy* generally refers to the ability to work without unwanted surveillance and sometimes includes isolation from visual distraction, such as the sight of other people working or passing by.

For the present chapter, privacy is defined as the ability of individuals or groups to satisfactorily regulate their accessibility to others. This definition encompasses the conventional meanings of privacy in the office along with most of the situations mentioned in the empirical study by Justa and Golan (1977).

Privacy and the Physical Environment

Privacy apparently depends to some extent upon physical seclusion, which is available in varying degrees in the office. Archea (1977) suggested that people obtain privacy by positioning themselves within areas surrounded by walls, partitions, doors, and other barriers to unwanted surveillance. Office workers spend much of their time at assigned workspaces where privacy may depend on these physical enclosures.

Although physical enclosure of workspaces may aid privacy, some office designers regard physical enclosure as detrimental to communication. On the other hand, open offices that place co-workers close to one another without intervening barriers are thought to encourage face-to-face communication (e.g., Pile 1978).

Research evidence generally suggests an association between physical enclosure of workspaces and privacy, but the connection between physical environments and communication is less clear-cut. The evidence comes from two sources: studies of open-plan offices, and field research on the physical enclosure of offices.

Studies of Open-Plan Offices

Open-plan offices evolved from the German *Bürolandschaft*, loosely translated as "office landscape," which began to appear in the United States in the 1960s. In their pure form, these offices differed from conventional arrangements in that they contained no private offices and few floor-to-ceiling walls. Workers of all ranks occupied large, open areas where they were separated from each other mainly by low partitions or office furniture. The premise was that the open office made workers accessible to each other, which in turn was thought to promote communication. This was further aided by locating people adjacent to co-workers with whom they needed to communicate. In the United States, the German plan evolved in several variations that contained partly enclosed workspaces defined by interlocking partitions of varying heights (Pile 1978; Sundstrom 1984).

Research on the open-plan office has consisted primarily of attitude surveys (e.g., Louis Harris 1978, 1980) and postoccupancy evaluations that assess employees' responses to a new office environment. Some postoccupancy evaluations have incorporated *retrospective surveys*, in which employees recall earlier work environments and make comparisons with current ones. Results of retrospective surveys conducted among people who occupied open offices consistently indicated a decline in privacy and an increase in noise and interruption (Boje 1971; Hundert and Greenfield 1969; Kraemer, Sieverts, and Partners 1977; Nemecek and Grandjean 1973; Sloan, undated). Results suggested an improvement in some types of communication, such as interdepartmental contact, and deterioration of other types, especially confidential conversation.

A second group of postoccupancy evaluations incorporated a stronger research approach, with surveys both before and after relocation. Results generally showed a decrease in privacy (Boyce 1974; Brookes 1972a; also Brookes 1972b; Brookes and Kaplan 1972; Hanson 1978; Oldham and Brass 1979; Riland and Falk 1972; Zeitlin 1969). The before-and-after studies gave mixed results on communication, with improvements in some types but not others.

The research on open offices suggests that, on average, privacy decreases when office employees move into open offices. Unfortunately, these studies provide only a very generalized picture of the relationship between privacy and physical enclosure of workspaces, because none assessed the degree of enclosure of individual workspaces.

Field Research on Enclosure and Privacy in the Office

A series of field studies assessed the enclosure of individual workspaces and found enclosure to be correlated with privacy. In the first of three studies, Sundstrom, Burt, and Kamp (1980) questioned 85 administrators, who indicated how many of the four sides of their workspaces were covered by high partitions or walls, and whether or not they had a door they could close. Both the number of enclosed sides and the presence of a door were correlated with ratings of privacy. The second study focused on 30 clerical workers and incorporated direct observations of their workspaces. Ratings of privacy were inversely correlated with the number of people in the same room (i.e., those not separated by walls to the ceiling). The third study involved 98 office workers who held a variety of jobs, including clerical, technical, and managerial. Direct observations of individual workspaces provided data on the number of sides of the workspace enclosed by walls or partitions at least 6 feet high (workspaces had a maximum of four sides). The distance between workspaces, the number of co-workers in the vicinity, and other environmental variables were also measured. Employees' ratings of the privacy of their workspaces were consistently correlated with the number of walls or high partitions around the workspace, regardless of job-type, and inversely related to the number of people in the immediate vicinity.

In all three studies, the environmental variable most strongly correlated with privacy was the index of physical enclosure based on the number of sides of the workspace enclosed by a wall or high partition. These results support the hypothesis that privacy in the office depends to some extent upon physical enclosure.

Privacy and Satisfaction

One measure of the impact of privacy on office workers is its relationship with their satisfaction, which includes two concepts: (1) *Satisfaction with the workspace* (or the physical environment) refers to an individual's subjective evaluation of the office environment; (2) *job satisfaction* has traditionally referred to the subjective evaluation of the job as a whole, including not only the physical environment, but also other aspects of the job, such as supervision and pay (Landy and Trumbo 1976). For privacy to contribute significantly to job satisfaction, it must be relatively potent in comparison with the many other factors that contribute to job satisfaction.

In theory, privacy should gain importance as an individual's job becomes more complex, for at least three reasons. First, people doing complex tasks may be subject to distraction or overload from social stimulation, and privacy allows limitation of social contact to an optimal level. Second, surveillance creates arousal (Geen and Gange 1977), which according to the arousal hypothesis may be detrimental to performance as the complexity of the task increases. Third, people doing simple or routine tasks may find them monotonous and may seek social contact rather than try to limit it. All this suggests that for office workers with professional-technical or managerial jobs, whose duties are relatively complex, privacy should be correlated with satisfaction.

The studies by Sundstrom, Burt, and Kamp (1980) found privacy correlated with satisfaction in all jobs, including clerical. In the study of 85 administrators, privacy was strongly correlated with satisfaction with the workspace (but this study did not assess job satisfaction). The study of 30 clerical workers found a strong correlation of privacy and job satisfaction (but this study had no measure of satisfaction with the environment). The third study found privacy significantly correlated with both satisfaction with the workspace and job satisfaction, regardless of the job. There were, however, some suggestive differences among jobs, which prompted the follow-up study described next.

STUDY 1

This study (Sundstrom, Town, Brown, Forman, and McGee 1982) investigated the correlates of privacy as a function of different job types. The general hypotheses were: (1) privacy is associated with features of workspaces that allow the occupants to limit their visual or auditory commerce with others; and (2) the importance of privacy increases with the complexity of the job, because people with complex jobs are relatively sensitive to distraction by noise and visual disturbance; (for those with managerial jobs, enclosure also allows confidential conversation, an important facet of privacy for managers).

Studying the differences among jobs in the correlates of privacy is complicated by several factors. One problem is the tendency of people with complex jobs to have relatively high ranks in the organization, and the tendency of people with high ranks to obtain greater privacy by virtue of their status. Also, employees with routine jobs may be placed in relatively unenclosed workspaces to allow easy supervision. The resulting association among job complexity, rank, and physical enclosure makes certain combinations of jobs and workspaces relatively rare (e.g., secretaries in private offices). Further, an enclosed workspace may contribute to satisfaction through its association with rank (Konar, Sundstrom, Brady, Mandel, and Rice 1982).

The present study involved a sample of office workers in homogenous job groups in which rank and job duties were similar, but work environments were varied. Three job categories with varying degrees of job complexity were selected: *secretaries*, whose jobs were fairly routine; *bookkeepers* and *accountants*, whose work was more detailed; and *office managers* and *administrators*, whose work included complex individual tasks and supervision. Specific predictions were: (1) For all jobs, privacy is associated with physical enclosure and physical separation from other people; (2) privacy and physical enclosure are associated with satisfaction with the workspace and with job satisfaction; and (3) the association of privacy and satisfaction is strongest among office managers and administrators and weakest among secretaries.

Method

Data came from a questionnaire completed by 154 office employees, and from physical measurement of their workspaces. Two data-sets were combined for analysis: data from 80 employees, collected specifically for this study, and data from 74 employees from study 3 of Sundstrom, Burt, and Kamp (1980), which gave a sufficiently large group of employees to conduct the desired analyses.

Participants and Setting

All participants were nonacademic employees of the University of Tennessee, selected specifically for their job titles, including 88 secretaries, 44 bookkeepers and accountants, and 22 office managers and administrators. With only a few exceptions, those with the same job worked in buildings scattered throughout the campus. In some cases, two or three of the secretaries worked in the same room, but this happened with fewer than half.

Questionnaire

Volunteers agreed to have their workspaces measured and completed a questionnaire at their workspaces. The questionnaire consisted mostly of questions that called for ratings on 7-step scales on the physical environment. Some questions were combined into indexes, as shown in Table 9-1.

Physical Measurements

Before delivering the questionnaire, researchers visited each workspace and made measurements with a rolling tape-measure. Relevant variables appear in Table 9-2.

Table 9-1. Variables Based on Questionnaire Items

Variable	Questionnaire Item(s)[a] and Scoring
Job Complexity (α = .58)	". . . how does your job seem to you?" Simple (1) vs. Complex (7) Boring (1) vs. Exciting (7)
Job Satisfaction	"All things considered, how satisfied are you with your job?" Very Dissatisfied (1) vs. Very Satisfied (7)
Satisfaction with Workplace	"All in all, how satisfied are you with your personal work area?" Very Dissatisfied (1) vs. Very Satisfied (7)
Privacy	"Rate your personal work area . . . ." Not Private (1) vs. Private (7)
Proximity Crowding Noise	Too Close to Co-workers (1) vs. Too Far from Co-workers (7) Not Crowded (1) vs. Crowded (7) Quiet (1) vs. Noisy (7)
Distraction	"During your last normal workday, how often were you distracted from your work. . . ." Almost Constantly (1) vs. Hardly Ever (7)
Pleasant Place (α = .85)	"Please indicate how your personal work area seems:" Uncomfortable (1) vs. Comfortable (7) Drab (1) vs. Colorful (7) Boring (1) vs. Interesting (7) Unattractive (1) vs. Attractive (7)

a. Questionnaire items appeared in a different order, with adjectives in different positions, arranged so that the favorable adjective was on the left as often as on the right.

Table 9-2. Variables Based on Physical Measurements of Workspaces

Variable	Feature of Workspace and Scoring
Enclosed Sides	Number of walls, panels, or partitions at least 6' high around work surface and chair, with no thoroughfare or workspace intervening (scored 0, 1, 2, 3, or 4)
Workspaces in Room	A "room" had structural walls to the ceiling; the number of workspaces in the room included the participant's own workspace (scored 1, 2, 3 . . .)
Private Office	Participant's workspace occupies entire room with door (yes or no)
Distance to Nearest Workspace	Distance in feet, from chair-center to chair-center to nearest adjacent workspace, if the room had two or more workspaces
Workspaces Visible	Number of co-workers visible from participant's primary work position, with door open, if any (scored 0, 1, 2 . . .)
Workspaces Within 25'	Number of co-workers' workspaces within walking distance of 25' (0, 1, 2 . . .)
Floorspace	Floorspace of room or of participant's share of a room as divided by boundaries formed by median distances between work surfaces, in square feet.
Distance to Common Entrance	A "common entrance" to the building or office area served people other than the participant (distance in feet)
Visible to Supervisor	From supervisor's primary work position to participant's primary work position, with doors open, if any (yes or no)

Results

Most secretaries shared an office (only 25% had private offices); about half the bookkeepers and accountants (45%) and most managers and administrators (82%) had their own offices. Table 9-3 shows selected physical variables for the three groups. The secretaries had the least physical separation from co-workers, and the office managers and administrators the most.

The three job-groups differed in their responses to the questionnaire, as shown in a discriminant function analysis of the variables from the questionnaire, which indicated that the jobs differed on privacy, job complexity, "pleasant place," and distraction ($F = 7.16$; $df = 4,278$; $p < .001$). As predicted, the jobs differed on ratings of complexity (univariate $F = 12.23$; $df = 2,144$; $p < .001$). Office managers and administrators gave highest ratings ($\bar{X} = 5.6$), followed by bookkeepers and

Table 9-3. Physical Features of Workspaces of Participants in Three Job Types

	AVERAGE VALUE		
Physical Variable	*Secretaries*	*Bookkeepers & Accountants*	*Office Managers & Administrators*
Enclosed Sides	2.1	2.8	3.5
Workspaces in Room	3.5	3.6	1.4
Floorspace	107.5 sq. ft.	105.7 sq. ft.	122.6 sq. ft.
Distance to Common Entrance	33.4 sq. ft.	29.0 sq. ft.	29.8 sq. ft.
Visible to Supervisor	74%	21%	9%

accountants (X = 5.3); secretaries gave the lowest ratings ($\bar{X}$ = 4.5). (Newman-Keuls tests showed the secretaries' ratings were lower.) These differences supported the assumption that office managers' and administrators' jobs were the most complex, and secretaries', the least.

The job-groups differed on privacy (F = 9.76; df = 2,153; $p < .001$). Office managers and administrators reported the most privacy ($\bar{X}$ = 4.8); bookkeepers gave intermediate ratings ($\bar{X}$ = 3.3); secretaries gave lowest ratings ($\bar{X}$ = 2.7). (Newman-Keuls tests showed that the office managers and administrators gave higher ratings than the others.) This finding agrees with the differences in physical enclosure that favored the office managers and administrators.

Physical Correlates of Privacy

Correlations for all participants combined showed ratings of privacy to be strongly and positively correlated with the number of sides of the workspace enclosed by walls or partitions (r = .61; $p < .001$). Figure 9-1 shows a regular increase in privacy with each enclosed side.

When the three job-groups were considered separately, only one physical feature was correlated with privacy in all groups: the number of enclosed sides. Having a private office was also correlated with privacy but was essentially the same as having four enclosed sides plus a door. For all jobs, privacy was higher among those who had private offices, but ratings differed among job-groups as shown in Figure 9-2. A multiple regression analysis was conducted with private office, job type, and the interaction of job type and private office as predictors of privacy (with the interaction entered first; see Kerlinger and Pedhauser 1973). The analysis yielded a significant regression equation (F = 22.18; df = 4,149, $p < .001$). (Using

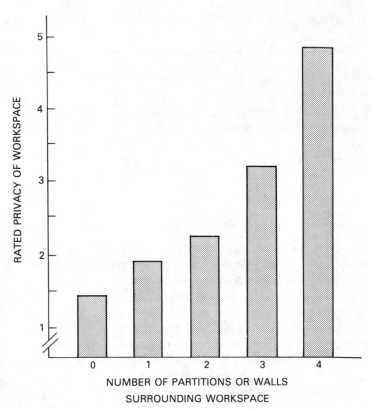

9-1. Ratings among 154 office employees of the privacy of workspaces as a function of the number of sides of the workspace enclosed by a wall or partition at least 6 feet tall

the formula of Theil, 1971, the adjusted R^2 was .37.) Having a private office was the strongest predictor of privacy (adjusted $R^2 = .31$); the interaction was also significant (adjusted $R^2 = .04$). The interaction suggested that among occupants of private offices, office managers and administrators gave higher ratings of privacy than bookkeepers and accountants, who gave higher ratings than secretaries.

Table 9-4 shows the significant physical correlates of privacy for the three job-groups. For secretaries, the only correlates of privacy were the number of enclosed sides of the workspace and the number of workspaces in the room. For bookkeepers and accountants, correlates of privacy included the number of enclosed sides, having few co-workers visible, having few co-workers within 25 feet, and not being visible to the supervisor. For office managers and administrators, correlates included

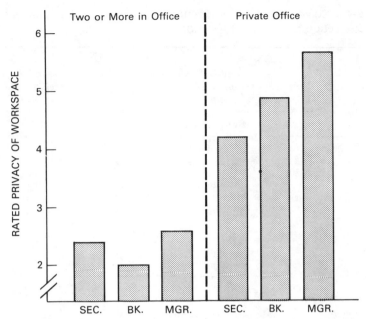

9-2. Average ratings of privacy of workspaces by 88 secretaries, 44 bookkeepers, and 22 office managers who worked two or more to an office or in private offices

the number of enclosed sides, floorspace, few co-workers within 25 feet, and not being visible to the supervisor.

Satisfaction with the Workspace

For all participants combined, the only significant physical correlates of satisfaction with the workspace were the number of enclosed sides ($r = .32$); and for those in nonprivate offices, the distance to the nearest neighboring workspace ($r = .20$). When the job-groups were considered separately, a different set of correlates emerged for each, as shown in Table 9-4. For secretaries, physical correlates of satisfaction with the workspace included the number of enclosed sides, floorspace, and the distance from a common entrance. Subjective predictors included "pleasant place" and items related to crowding and privacy. Results of multiple linear regression analysis (summarized in Table 9-5) showed that physical features accounted for 13% of the variance in satisfaction with the workspace; subjective correlates accounted for 40%.

Among bookkeepers and accountants, physical correlates of satisfaction with the workspace included distance from the nearest neighbor (in non-

Table 9-4. Correlates of Privacy, Satisfaction with the Workspace, and
Job Satisfaction in Three Job Groups

Physical Correlates of Privacy		Physical and Subjective Correlates of Satisfaction with the Workspace		Physical and Subjective Correlates of Job Satisfaction	
SECRETARIES (n = 88)					
Enclosed sides	.52	Enclosed sides	.25		
Workspaces in room	−.26	Distance/entrance	.18		
		"Pleasant place"	.55	Job complexity	.46
		Privacy	.45	Satisfaction/workspace	.24
		Crowding	−.39	"Pleasant place"	.27
		Distraction	−.36	Privacy	.21
		Noise	−.35		
		Proximity	−.32		
		Job Complexity	.19		
BOOKKEEPERS AND ACCOUNTANTS (n = 44)					
Enclosed sides	.61	Distance/neighbor[a]	.48		
Co-workers/25'	−.40	Enclosed sides	.36		
Co-workers visible	−.34	Floorspace	.28		
Visible to supervisor	−.26	Co-workers visible	−.25		
		"Pleasant place"	.61	Satisfaction/workspace	.38
		Privacy	.57	Noise	−.40
		Proximity	−.55	"Pleasant place"	.36
		Distraction	−.43	Distraction	−.27
		Crowding	−.40		
		Noise	−.33		
OFFICE MANAGERS AND ADMINISTRATORS (n = 22)					
Enclosed sides	.57	Visible to supervisor	−.58	Visible to supervisor	−.63
Co-workers/25'	−.48	Floorspace	.45		
Floorspace	.45	Co-workers/25'	−.42		
Visible to supervisor	−.39	Co-workers visible	−.34		
		Proximity	−.61	Job complexity	.70
		Job complexity	.49	Satisfaction/workspace	.59
		Distraction	−.48	Distraction	−.51
		"Pleasant place"	.40	Proximity	−.36
		Crowding	−.36		

Note: Only significant correlations are listed ($p < .05$, two-tailed).
a. Only for participants not in private offices.

Table 9-5. Summary of Multiple Linear Regression Analyses of
Satisfaction with Workspace and Job Satisfaction in Three Job Groups

Criterion Variable	Type of Predictors	Significant Predictors	F for Regression	df[a]	Adj. R²
SECRETARIES (n = 88)					
Satisfaction with Workspace	Physical	Enclosed sides Distance/entrance Floorspace	5.0-	3,77	.13
	Subjective	"Pleasant place" Privacy Crowding	18.7**	3,78	.40
Job Satisfaction	Physical	–	–	–	–
	Subjective	Job Complexity Distraction	13.1**	2,79	.23
BOOKKEEPERS & ACCOUNTANTS (n = 44)					
Satisfaction with Workspace	Physical	Enclosed sides Floorspace	5.1*	2,40	.16
	Subjective	"Pleasant place" Privacy	30.5**	2,38	.60
Job Satisfaction	Physical	–	–	–	–
	Subjective[b]	Distraction	6.7*	1,39	.12
OFFICE MANAGERS & ADMINISTRATORS (n = 22)					
Satisfaction with Workspace	Physical	Visible to supervisor Floorspace	8.4**	2,19	.41
	Subjective	Job complexity "Pleasant place"	4.8*	2,19	.27
Job Satisfaction	Physical	Visible to supervisor	13.1**	1,20	.37
	Subjective[b]	Job complexity Distraction Privacy	9.2**	3,18	.54

Note: R^2 values for the subset of predictors in each of the reduced models reported were representative of those obtained using the entire set of predictor variables (Aitkin 1974).
a. Totals vary due to missing values.
b. Excluding satisfaction with the workspace.
*$p < .05$
**$p < .01$

private offices), the number of enclosed sides, and the amount of floorspace. Subjective correlates included "pleasant place" and five items related to privacy. Physical correlates accounted for 16% of the variance in satisfaction with the workspace; subjective correlates accounted for 60%.

Among office managers and administrators, physical correlates did not include the number of enclosed sides (probably because of restricted variability—a majority of the people in this job group had private offices). The strongest correlate of satisfaction with the workspace was not being visible to the supervisor; other correlates included floorspace, co-workers within 25 feet, and co-workers visible. Physical predictors accounted for 41% of the variance in satisfaction with the workspace. Of the subjective correlates, job complexity and "pleasant place" were significant predictors in the regression analysis, accounting for 27% of the variance.

Job Satisfaction

For all participants combined, the strongest correlates of job satisfaction were job complexity ($r = .41$) and satisfaction with the workspace ($r = .35$); others included "pleasant place" ($r = .34$) and privacy ($r = .21$).

When the job-groups were considered separately, only satisfaction with the workspace was correlated with job satisfaction in all three groups. Among secretaries, there were no physical correlates of job satisfaction; subjective predictors accounted for 23% of the variance in job satisfaction. Among bookkeepers and accountants, there were no physical correlates of job satisfaction; the one subjective predictor, distraction, accounted for 15% of the variance. Among office managers and administrators, the only physical correlate of job satisfaction was not being visible to the supervisor, which accounted for 37% of the variance. Subjective predictors accounted for 54% of the variance in job satisfaction.

Discussion

Results clearly supported the hypothesis that physical enclosure of the workspace is associated with privacy. The number of enclosed sides of the workspace was the principal correlate of privacy. Furthermore, the most private workspace was the fully enclosed office. Other physical features were sometimes related to privacy, but not consistently so.

The second hypothesis—that privacy is more important for satisfaction with the workspace and for job satisfaction with increasingly complex job duties—was not supported. Instead, the results suggested that people with different jobs may have perceived privacy differently.

The job-groups differed on physical enclosure, as expected: secretaries had least and managers had most. But in the workspaces with equivalent enclosure—private offices—the job-groups showed differential ratings of privacy, with lowest ratings by secretaries. This could reflect social norms. Secretaries have low ranks, and co-workers or visitors may feel free to walk unannounced into their workspaces. However, they may knock respectfully at the entrance of the workspaces of managers. (Managers also sometimes have receptionists, although practically none in the present study did.) Perhaps a private office is more private when occupied by a manager than when occupied by a secretary.

Differences among job-groups concerning the correlates of privacy suggest that the jobs created different priorities. Everyone apparently saw privacy in terms of the number of sides of their workspace enclosed by walls or partitions. Secretaries, who had the least enclosure, paid attention to the number of people in the room, and some of the strongest subjective correlates of satisfaction with the workspace were privacy and crowding.

Bookkeepers and accountants had more enclosure, and their perceptions of privacy apparently focused on the number of co-workers in their vicinity. Distraction and noise were important enough to emerge as correlates of job satisfaction.

Office managers and administrators, with the greatest degree of enclosure, apparently saw privacy in terms of visibility to the supervisor, floorspace, and the number of co-workers in the vicinity. Not being visible to the supervisor emerged as a strong correlate of job satisfaction. Another study implies that this may reflect a desire for *job-autonomy* (Szilagyi and Holland 1980).

One explanation for the differences among job groups is based on the idea that different jobs create different needs for privacy. Among those whose environments give little control over access by others, the most basic need for privacy is to optimize social contact and avoid crowding (e.g., Altman 1975). For those with greater enclosure—and in many organizations that means a higher rank and a more complex job—basic control over social contact may be provided. The next need may concern mental concentration and the avoidance of distraction, interruption, and noise, which may be salient among professional and technical employees, such as bookkeepers. For those with supervisory responsibilities—who may have still more enclosure—neither crowding nor concentration pose problems, but a third category of needs may become salient: autonomy and conversational privacy. Visual barriers and a buffer zone of floorspace may help meet these needs.

Jobs may create different needs for privacy. If so, however, the details remain to be specified. One possibility is that job complexity adds new needs for privacy. A second possibility is that jobs create *unique* needs for privacy that do not exist in other work. For instance, privacy for mental concentration may be important only in professional-technical jobs.

If jobs do create different needs for privacy, and if the needs for privacy operate by either of the dynamics suggested, then perceptions of privacy may vary with the kinds of privacy needed for the job. For instance, a secretary who has less physical enclosure than an office manager could actually experience greater privacy—because the secretary's workspace satisfies minimal needs for control over social contact whereas the office manager's does not give enough separation from the supervisor.

In summary, the findings of Study 1 suggest that physical enclosure by walls or partitions is strongly associated with privacy in the office. However, people in different jobs may perceive privacy differently, perhaps partly because of different needs for privacy created by their jobs, including gross control over social contact, control over distraction and interruption, autonomy from supervision, and conversational privacy.

STUDY 2

This study (Sundstrom, Herbert, and Brown 1982) addressed the relationship between physical enclosure and privacy in a group of employees who left a conventional office and relocated to an open-plan office. The general hypothesis held that privacy depends on physical enclosure of individual workspaces and on the individual's job.

Setting

A group of employees of a large corporation about to move to a new office building presented an unusual opportunity to study privacy. Employees at four job levels had different types of workspaces with greater enclosure at higher levels, but the workspaces were practically identical within job levels. Each employee was given about the same amount of floorspace after changing offices he or she had before. The amount of enclosure changed at each job level, but the new workspaces were identical within job levels. As a result, privacy could be assessed within job levels before and after a change in physical enclosure, while conditions otherwise remained virtually constant.

Before relocation, secretarial employees (job level 1) worked at unenclosed desks in small, open-office areas. People at the next job level (2), staff specialists, were located in double offices (10' × 15') with doors. The two highest levels (3 and 4) were managerial employees located in their own walled offices.

Relocation involved moving to a smaller building a few miles away. The new building lacked internal walls, except at the core, and workspaces were separated by movable partitions. Secretarial employees (job level 1) had workspaces near major pathways; the workspaces were bounded on one or two sides by 48-inch panels. Employees at job level 2 moved to individual workspaces with about the same amount of floorspace as before, bounded on four sides by 60-inch panels but with no doors. Those at job level 3 also retained the same amount of floorspace as before, and had individual, doorless enclosures of 60-inch panels adjacent to window-walls. Employees at job level 4 had individual enclosures surrounded by 78-inch partitions, which were arranged to limit the visibility through the doorless entrances. Relocation meant giving up convenient access to the corporate dining room, library, gymnasium, and underground parking. Also, secretarial support for many level 2 and 3 employees increased. However, the organization remained virtually unchanged.

Hypotheses

Predictions for the study were based on the idea that needs for privacy increase with job level, because of increasing needs for concentration and confidential conversation. Before relocation, satisfaction with privacy was expected to be highest among managerial (level 3 and 4) employees, who had walled offices, and least among secretarial employees in open areas. After relocation, those in secretarial jobs (level 1) gained some enclosure and were expected to be slightly more satisfied with their privacy. Those at job level 2, who left double offices for doorless enclosures, traded one type of enclosure (double offices with doors) for another (individual spaces) and were expected to show little change. Those at job levels 3 and 4 were expected to be less satisfied with their privacy as they left walled offices for doorless enclosures. Also, the study allowed a test of the idea that satisfaction with communications increased with the greater accessibility of an open-plan office.

Method

A total of 70 employees completed a questionnaire before and after relocating. (Out of about 130 employees invited to participate, a total of 115 returned questionnaires before moving; a total of 108 returned questionnaires after moving, including 70 who completed the first questionnaire.) Representative workspaces were subjected to acoustical measurements.

Characteristics of workspaces before and after relocation are summarized in Table 9-6.

Questionnaire

Participants filled out the questionnaire six months before relocation and six weeks afterward. It included 32 statements about the office environment, calling for a response on either a 5-step scale that ranged from "strongly agree" (1) to "strongly disagree" (5) or an adjective-pair with five steps. An index of satisfaction with privacy consisted of the average of the responses to five items (shown in Table 9-2). An index of satisfaction with communications was also a composite of five items. Other indexes were also calculated, along with a measure of internal consistency, coefficient alpha, as shown in Table 9-7.

Acoustical Measurements

The principal acoustical measure was the Articulation Index (AI), which reflects the proportion of speech that can be understood with speaker and listener in different positions, such as on opposite sides of a wall. The higher the index, the more the listener can understand, and the less "speech privacy" the speaker has (Cavanaugh et al. 1962). For this study,

Table 9-6. Work Environments by Job Level before and after Relocation

Job level	n	Workspace Before Relocation	Workspace After Relocation
1	9	Unenclosed desk in suite with others	Open area with one or two 48″ partitions
2	33	Walled, double office with door	Individual enclosure with 60″ partitions on four sides; no door
3	23	Walled office with door	Individual enclosure with 60″ partitions and window wall; no door
4	5	Walled office with door	Individual enclosure with 78″ partitions and window wall; no door; restricted visibility through entrance

Table 9-7. Questionnaire Items and Indexes

Index	Coefficient Alpha[a]	Items[b]
Satisfaction with Privacy	.94	I can have a conference without distracting others. I have sufficient privacy in my work area. I can have confidential conversations easily. I can work uninterrupted for long periods. I have enough personal privacy in my work area.
Communications	.76	I can communicate effectively with others. It is easy to contact associates with whom I deal regularly. My office area enhances required communication. I have easy access to those providing clerical support for me. I have easy access to other groups that I deal with frequently.
Noise	.90	The noise in my office is not distracting. I can work effectively with the constant level of office sounds around me.
Workspace Utility	.94	Pleasant-Unpleasant[c] Adequate-Inadequate[c] Useful-Useless[c] Satisfying-Dissatisfying[c] Productive-Unproductive[c]

a. Based on pretest data.
b. Responses were on 5-step "agree-disagree" scale except as noted.
c. Rating of "physical environment in your work area" on 5-step scale.

AI was assessed with test equipment. Using peak voice levels (normal voice plus 12 dB) defined in the standard method of the American National Standard Institute, and correcting for measured noise reduction between source and receiver, AI was calculated from the sum of weighted signal-to-noise ratios in the 15 one-third octave bands between 200 and 5000 hertz. (The signal-to-noise ratio is the difference between the peak voice at the listener position and the background noise level.) The test equipment consisted of an artificial source (speaker) and receiver (listener). The source simulated a person talking; the receiver monitored the sound in adjoining workspaces. The source consisted of a pink noise generator, a 10-watt amplifier, and a voice coverage loudspeaker.

Acoustical measurements were made at representative workspaces before and after relocation for job levels 2, 3, and 4. At each job level, a single work station was tested, except that in the open office for job level 2, two floor plans were tested, and at job level 3, three were tested. The voice-source was placed in the same position as the employee's chair, facing the desk squarely, with the center of the speaker 44 inches above the floor. The receiver was placed in each adjoining workspace, also 44 inches above the floor.

Results

Questionnaire Data

A 2-factor multivariate analysis of variance was applied to the variables based on the questionnaire; job level (1, 2, 3, and 4) was a between-subjects variable, and before versus after relocation was a within-subjects variable. Results of the multivariate test indicated significant differences as a function of relocation ($F = 6.2$; $df = 5, 52, p < .001$) and job level ($F = 3.67$; $df = 15, 182; p < .001$). Univariate analysis indicated differences in satisfaction with privacy by job level ($F = 4.6$; $df = 3, 66; p < .01$) and relocation ($F = 5.26$; $df = 1, 64; p < .05$). Means, shown in figure 9-3, only partly agreed with predictions. Before relocation, managers (levels 3 and 4) were relatively satisfied with the privacy afforded by their walled offices. After relocation, satisfaction with privacy declined, primarily among managers.

To further analyze the impact of relocation on privacy, the index of satisfaction with privacy was broken into components: *personal privacy* ("I have sufficient privacy in my work area" and "I have enough personal privacy in my work area"); *speech privacy* ("I can have confidential conversations easily"); *interruptions* ("I can work uninterrupted for long periods"); and *auditory isolation* ("I can have a conference without disturbing others"). Univariate ANOVAs revealed differences only in speech privacy, which varied by job level ($F = 4.76$; $df = 3, 70; p < .01$) and relocation ($F = 6.80$; $df = 1,66; p < .05$). Apparently the relocation brought a decline in the ability to hold confidential conversations, especially among managers. (Speech privacy showed a strong, positive part-whole correlation with the privacy index: $r = .84; p < .01$.) There were no differences in satisfaction with communication.

Correlation coefficients were calculated among the four variables based on the questionnaire before and after relocation. All were significant, as shown in Table 9-8. Surprisingly, satisfaction with communication was *directly* associated with satisfaction with privacy.

Acoustical Measurements

The average "worst case" AIs for job levels 2, 3, and 4 (worst case refers to the AI for the neighboring position from which the most speech could be heard through the partitions with normal voice) are given below.

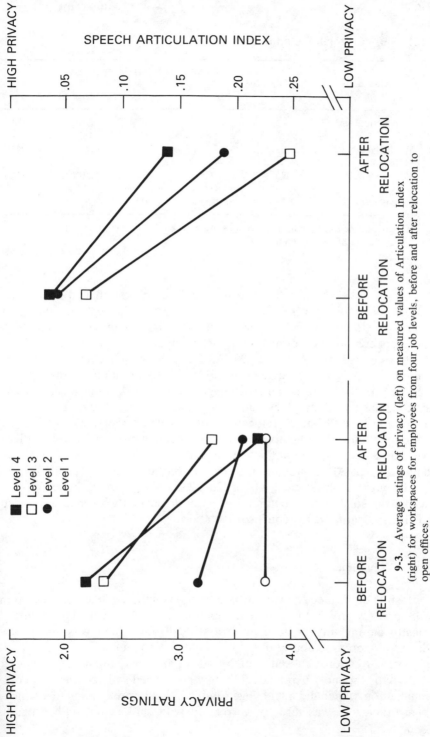

9-3. Average ratings of privacy (left) on measured values of Articulation Index (right) for workspaces for employees from four job levels, before and after relocation to open offices.

Table 9-8. Correlations among Variables[a]

		VARIABLE (NUMBER)				
Variable		*1*	*2*	*3*	*4*	*5*
1.	Satisfaction with Privacy	–	.68**	.40**	– .76**	.38**
2.	Workspace Utility	.83**	–	.50**	– .74**	.34**
3.	Communications	.46**	.53**	–	– .50**	.47**
4.	Noise	– .76**	– .83**	– .43**	–	– .38**
5.	Locatability	.21*	.29**	.38**	– .21*	–

a. Figures in the upper right-hand triangle are before relocations; those in the lower left-hand triangle are after relocation.

$*p < .05$
$**p < .01$

For job level 2, the shared offices before relocation had very good acoustical privacy with doors closed, with a worst case AI of .04. (This figure overlooks the other person in the same room, who could hear most speech in the room.) With doors open, the worst case AI for positions outside the office was .23. After relocation, job level 2 workspaces varied. In workspaces adjacent to job level 3 workstations, the AI was only .14; in the more common arrangements next to other level 2 work-spaces, the two floor plans had worst case AIs of .22 and .24.

For job level 3 before relocation, offices had a worst case AI of .07 with doors closed, indicating good acoustical isolation. Job level 4 offices were also acoustically well isolated, with the worst case AI at .04 with doors closed. After relocation, three different desk arrangements for job level 3 yielded worst case AIs of .22, .23, and .27, which indicated less acoustical isolation than before. The AI in the level 4 workspace advanced to .14, indicating less acoustical isolation.

Discussion

Results confirmed the earlier finding of a general decline in satisfaction with privacy after relocation to an open-plan office. The decline occurred mostly among former occupants of walled offices and was apparently due to a decreased ability to hold confidential conversations in the open-plan office. Acoustical data confirmed the decrease in speech privacy.

Perhaps the most paradoxical finding concerned satisfaction with com-munication, which did not change significantly after relocation to an open-plan office and was directly correlated with satisfaction with privacy.

This suggests that participants were more satisfied with their communications in workspaces they rated as most private. Perhaps the ability to hold confidential conversations contributed to satisfaction with communications in workspaces rated as private. The open-plan office, with its greater physical accessibility and planned layout, may have made communication easier in some ways, but perhaps made it more difficult by not allowing everyone the speech privacy they needed.

In summary, the results indicated a clear parallel between physical enclosure of workspaces and satisfaction with privacy. The most important component of privacy was the ability to hold confidential conversations, which apparently declined in managerial employees after relocation to an open-plan office.

Conclusions

A review of literature on privacy in the office, along with two empirical studies, suggests the following conclusions: First, to the extent that privacy in the office depends upon the physical environment, privacy is most consistently provided by enclosure of the workspace by walls or partitions. Workers obtain greatest privacy in individual offices with walls to the ceiling and doors.

Second, people with different jobs may perceive privacy differently. For instance, in one study described here, clerical workers in walled offices reported lower privacy than did managers in offices with equivalent enclosure.

Third, jobs may create different needs for privacy, which in turn may be associated with different criteria for judgments regarding privacy. For instance, managers and administrators were particularly sensitive to conversational privacy, in Study 2, perhaps because of a need for confidential conversation inherent in their jobs.

Finally, although privacy may contribute to an individual's satisfaction with the workspace, the level of privacy and the specific types of privacy associated with maximum satisfaction probably vary with the job.

NOTE

1. The two studies discussed in this chapter were first described in separate articles in *Environment & Behavior*'s 1982 issues on office design, edited by Jean Wineman: Sundstrom, E., Herbert, R. K., and Brown, D., "Privacy and Communication in an Open Plan Office: A Case Study," *Environment and Behavior,* 1982, *14*(3), 379–392; and Sundstrom, E., Town, J., Brown, D., Forman, A., and McGee, C., "Physical Enclosure, Type of Job, and Privacy in the Office," *Environment and Behavior,*

1982, *14*(5), 543–559. Both articles are copyright by Sage Publications, Beverly Hills, California. Condensed versions and associated tables and figures are reproduced here with permission.

REFERENCES

Altman, I. 1975. *The environment and social behavior.* Monterey, CA: Brooks/Cole.

Altman, I. 1976. Privacy: A conceptual analysis. *Environment and Behavior* 8:7–29.

Altman, I. 1977. Privacy regulation: Culturally universal or culturally specific? *Journal of Social Issues* 33(3):66–84.

Aitken, M. A. 1974. Simultaneous inference and the choice of variable subsets in multiple regression. *Technometrics* 16:221–227.

Archea, J. 1977. The place of architectural factors in behavioral theories of privacy. *Journal of Social Issues* 33(3):116–136.

Bates, A. 1964. Privacy: A useful concept? *Social Forces* 42:432.

Beardsley, E. L. 1971. Privacy: Autonomy and selective disclosure. In J. R. Pennock and J. W. Chapman (Eds.), *Privacy.* New York: Atherton Press.

Boje, A. 1971. *Open-plan offices.* London: Business Books, Ltd. (German edition published in 1968.)

BOSTI (Buffalo Organization for Social and Technological Innovation, Inc.) MONSANTO Central Information Service. Unpublished report, December, 1977.

Boyce, P. R. 1974. Users' assessments of a landscaped office. *Journal of Architectural Research* 3(3):44–62.

Brookes, M. J. 1972a. Office landscape: Does it work? *Applied Ergonomics* 3(4):224–236. (Apparently reports the same data as Brookes 1972b and Brookes and Kaplan 1972.)

Brookes, M. J. 1972b. Changes in employee attitudes and work practices in an office landscape. In W. J. Mitchell (Ed.), *Environmental design: Research and practice.* Proceedings of EDRA3/AR8 Conference at U.C.L.A., January. (Same data as Brookes and Kaplan 1972.)

Brookes, M. J., and A. Kaplan. 1972. The office environment: Space planning and affective behavior. *Human Factors* 14(5):373–391.

Cavanaugh, W. J., W. R. Farrell, P. W. Hirtle, and B. G. Watters. 1962. Speech privacy in buildings. *Journal of the Acoustical Society of America* 34(4):475–492.

Geen, R. G. and J. J. Gange. 1977. Drive theory of social facilitation: Twelve years of theory and research. *Psychological Bulletin* 84(6):1267–1288.

Hanson, A. 1978. Effects of a move to an open landscape office. *Dissertation Abstracts International* 39(6):3046-B.

Hundert, A. J., and N. Greenfield. 1969. Physical space and organizational behavior: A study of an office landscape. *Proceedings, 77th Annual Convention, A.P.A.,* pp. 601–602.

Ives, R. S., and R. Ferdinands. 1974. Working in a landscaped office. *Personnel Practice Bulletin* 30(2):126–141.

Justa, F. C., and M. B. Golan. 1977. Office design: Is privacy still a problem? *Journal of Architectural Research* 6(2):5–12.

Kelvin, P. 1973. A social-psychological examination of privacy. *British Journal of Social and Clinical Psychology* 12:248–261.

Kerlinger, F. N., and E. J. Pedhazur. 1973. *Multiple regression in behavioral research.* New York: Holt, Rinehart, & Winston.

Konar, E., E. Sundstrom, C. Brady, D. Mandel, and R. Rice. 1982. Status markers in the office. *Environment and Behavior* 14(5):561–580.

Kraemer, Sieverts & Partners. 1977. *Open plan offices: New ideas, experience and improvements.* London: McGraw-Hill (German edition copyright 1975 by Verlag Moderne Industrie.)

Landy, F., and D. Trumbo. 1976. *Psychology of work behavior.* Homewood, IL: The Dorsey Press.

Louis Harris and Associates, Inc. 1978. *The Steelcase national study of office environments: Do they work?* Grand Rapids, MI: Steelcase, Inc.

Louis Harris and Associates, Inc. 1980. *The Steelcase national study of office environments No. II: Comfort and productivity in the office of the 80's.* Grand Rapids, MI: Steelcase, Inc.

Margulis, S. T. 1977. Conceptions of privacy: Current status and next steps. *Journal of Social Issues* 33(3):5–21.

Marshall, N. 1970. Environmental components of orientations toward privacy. In J. Archea and C. Eastman (Eds.), *EDRA TWO: Proceedings of the Second Annual Environmental Design Research Association Conference,* October 1970. Stroudsburg, PA: Dowden, Hutchinson and Ross.

Nemecek, J., and E. Grandjean. 1973. Results of an ergonomic investigation of large-space offices. *Human Factors* 15(2):111–124.

Oldham, G. R., and D. J. Brass. 1979. Employee reactions to an open plan office: A naturally occurring quasi-experiment. *Administrative Science Quarterly* 24:26–283.

Pennock, J. R., and J. W. Chapman. 1971. *Privacy.* New York: Atherton Press.

Pile, J. F. 1978. *Open office planning.* New York: Whitney Library of Design.

Riland, L. W., and J. Z. Falk. 1972. *Employee reactions to office landscape environment.* Technical report, Psychological Research & Services, Personnel Relations Department, Eastman Kodak Company, April 1972.

Sloan, S. Undated. *FAA tenant GSA Landlord Maslov love participation satisfaction offices personal space work production social needs designers users product process.* Spokane, WA: People Space Architecture Co.

Sundstrom, E. 1984. Physical environment and social behavior. In K. Deaux and L. Wrightsman (Eds.), *Social psychology in the eighties,* 4th ed. Monterey, CA: Brooks/ Cole.

Sundstrom, E., R. Burt, and D. Kamp. 1980. Privacy at work: Architectural correlates of job satisfaction and job performance. *Academy of Management Journal* 23(1):101–117.

Sundstrom, E., J. Town, D. Brown, A. Forman, and C. McGee. 1982. Physical enclosure, type of job, and privacy in the office. *Environment and Behavior* 14(5):543–559.

Sundstrom, E., R. K. Herbert, and D. Brown. Privacy and communication in an open plan office: A case study. *Environment and Behavior* 14(3):379–392.

Szilagyi, A., and W. Holland. 1980. Changes in social density: Relationships with functional interaction and perceptions of job characteristics, role stress, and work satisfaction. *Journal of Applied Psychology* 65(1):28–33.

Theil, H. 1971. *Principles of econometrics.* New York: John Wiley & Sons.

Westin, A. 1970. *Privacy and freedom.* New York: Atheneum Publishers.

Wolgers, B. 1973. Study of office environment: Attributes to office landscapes and open-plan offices. *Build International* 6:143–146.

Zeitlin, L. R. 1969. *A comparison of employee attitudes toward the conventional office and the landscaped office.* Technical Report, Port Authority of New York, April 1969.

Status Demarcation and Office Design

ELLEN KONAR
Buffalo Organization for Social and Technological Innovation (BOSTI)
Buffalo, New York

ERIC SUNDSTROM
Department of Psychology
University of Tennessee at Knoxville
Knoxville, Tennessee

The functional qualities of offices and workspaces have always figured prominently in office design. The symbolic qualities of those workspaces and offices have typically received far less attention in this context. Despite this relative lack of attention in the design process, offices and workspaces consistently and effectively perform at least one symbolic role, the demarcation of status. Any observer can note what professional organizational observers have long recognized: A person's status in an organization is indicated by the nature of his or her workspace/office (e.g., Behling and Schreisheim 1976; Duffy 1969; Halloran 1978; Steele 1973).

In this chapter the process of using the physical setting as a sign of the status or rank of an individual in an organization is referred to as *status demarcation*. Although it seems to be a well-entrenched, pervasive, and well-recognized facet of workspaces and offices, status demarcation is a subject of controversy among behavioral scientists, managers, and office designers. It is a topic much discussed and little understood (Steele 1973); speculations regarding status demarcation and its impact on people and work proliferate, but little empirical evidence exists on the subject.

This chapter examines the controversies in status demarcation in light of the available evidence. After defining a few basic terms, we address the pervasiveness of status demarcation, then briefly review some of the common status markers identified in the earlier, largely anecdotal literature. Recognizing the controversial nature of status markers, we briefly review the broad arguments pro and con. We then examine the impact of status demarcation through an examination of both the underlying processes and research evidence. Finally, we consider the implications of the foregoing for office design.

DEFINITIONS

The term *status* refers to the value placed on an individual in comparison to other individuals (see Davis 1977). In an organization, the status of an individual tends to coincide with his or her formal rank in that organization; the higher the rank, the higher the status. Yet status can be an index of rank on any scale of value. Duffy (1969) has suggested that although authority is perhaps the most obvious scale of value in an organization, there are at least two other dimensions on which status may be determined: In addition to formal rank or authority, an individual's status may be determined by the importance of the job she or he does in the technical structure (technical value) and/or his or her value in the sentiments of other organizational members (social value).

The term *status demarcation* refers to the process of symbolically indicating a person's position in the organizational hierarchy by the nature of his or her possessions or facilities. Historically, the analysis of status demarcation has been viewed as an analysis of *status symbols*. It has therefore been limited to a discussion of those objects or arrangements that, because of their visibility, rarity, and association with high-ranking individuals, have themselves come to indicate high status (Blumberg 1974). This conception of the phenomenon overlooks the process of status communication and does not acknowledge the tendency to use physical objects to indicate the entire range of status levels, rather than just the highest ranks. We broaden the discussion to include all aspects of status demarcation, using the term *status marker* instead of the more narrowly conceived status symbol to refer to any physical object or arrangement that connotes status, regardless of level (Konar, Sundstrom, Brady, Mandel, and Rice 1982).

PERVASIVENESS OF STATUS DEMARCATION

Historically, status demarcation has been a pervasive aspect of work environments, especially the office. Government organizations have mandated status demarcation through the use of standards that entitle individuals of a given rank a restricted range of options in such things as the amount of space, furniture (quantity, materials), and so on. Status demarcation seems no less pervasive among private sector corporations, whether by mandate or otherwise (Duffy 1969; Duffy, Cave, and Worthington, 1976; Langdon 1966; Manning 1965; Pile 1978; Steele 1973).

Recently, however, indications of waning interest and regard for this long-standing practice have begun to surface, leading some to question the future of the practice. Blumberg (1974), for instance, argues that the decline and fall of the status symbol is imminent. Originators of the German "office landscape" approach to office design (predecessor of the now common open-office plan) actively encouraged the removal of status markers from the workplace. Kanter (1983) has recently noted a relative absence of status markers in some "high technology" firms. For example, Union Carbide boldly built its new headquarters in Danbury, Connecticut, with all offices the same size, presumably to diminish status demarcation (Bennett 1983).

Although it is too early to determine the fate of egalitarian tendencies in office design, Duffy (1969) argues that moves toward egalitarian work environments are temporary and inevitably will give way to status demarcation in some form. Duffy observes that although German office landscape designs often remove traditional status markers, closer study reveals that other devices, such as corner locations and strategic interposing of secretaries, are often used to achieve the same ends. "The director's work station, even on the open plan, is certain to be far larger, far more carefully protected and far grander than the typist's" (p. 10).

A recent study of the office environments of organizations and government agencies that had recently moved into open-plan office arrangements found that individuals (especially supervisors) on average thought their new environments were *more* reflective of their status than before (BOSTI 1981). A clear majority of the individuals surveyed (almost 70%) believed that workspaces in their organization reflected the status or rank of the workspace occupants. That the majority experienced and were aware of such practices says much regarding the prevalence and salience of the practice in the United States today and little to substantiate Blumberg's prediction of the decline and fall of the status symbol.

Although status demarcation in the work environment is relatively pervasive, variations in level and prominence occur. Most observers who have noted such variations attribute them to differences among organizations, particularly the degree to which the organization emphasizes a hierarchy of authority. The nature of the relationship between degree of hierarchical structure in the organization and the level or salience of status demarcation, however, is far from clear.

Steele (1973) suggests that the amount of emphasis on status symbols is inversely related to the extent to which people receive direct, concrete feedback about their standing and performance in the organization. He implies that status demarcation develops by default as the way in which an individual's standing in the system is communicated to others. He speculates that symbolic status indicators will be particularly salient in organizations that "have large groups of people without formal differentiation in positional level" (p. 54).

On the other hand, the degree of environmental status demarcation may be positively related to the general level of status demarcation/differentiation in the organization. Highly bureaucratic organizations with strong differentiations by rank, such as the military and the civil service, mandate very strict adherence to inclusive "guidelines" regarding status markers in work environments. The pervasiveness of status demarcation in traditionally very hierarchically oriented industries such as banking likewise seem to support this position. Kanter's (1983) observation regarding the relative absence of traditional status markers among the typically flatter structures of the newer high-technology companies may be seen as further evidence. It would appear that the authority orientation of a company is often reflected rather than complemented by environmental status demarcation.

COMMON STATUS MARKERS

As indicated previously, a status marker can be any characteristic that, through its relative scarcity and value and long-term association with individuals of a given status range, comes to indicate that status. Although seemingly infinite in variety, status markers in the office appear to cluster into several distinct categories. Duffy (1969) identified four basic types: allocation of space, quantity and quality of furnishings, relative location, and degree of screening. On the basis of a factor analysis of user responses to a questionnaire, Konar and associates (1982) derived a similar set of five categories: the nature of the furnishings, location, size of workspace, control over access, and personalization. The increasing prevalence of high technology in the office may create a sixth category, which could be called extra amenities and facilities. (The nature of one's high-tech facilities may be the newest status marker; see Buss 1982).

Furnishings

The nature of even the most basic office furnishings can serve to demarcate the status of the workspace occupant. Desks, chairs, storage cabinets, and other furniture come in a wide variety of materials, sizes, and styles, and much of the variation is status relevant. Size typically varies directly with status: The higher the status, the larger the chair and/or desk. The status properties of materials are based on economics. Woods, more expensive than metals (broadly speaking), are more likely to appear in the offices of high-status individuals. Thus a large teak desk with a high-backed leather chair clearly indicates very high status. In stark contrast, a small metal desk with an armless chair signals low status (Duffy 1969).

The allocation of more and more varied furniture to high-ranking executives may serve some useful purposes. For instance, a high-ranking executive probably needs more seating and additional workspaces for meeting and doing work with others. Yet, the degree of variation in workspace characteristics, which coincides so well with rank, seems to far exceed the extent of differences mandated by the characteristics of individuals or functional requirements of the tasks they perform. In fact, the environmental differences are often in direct contradiction to the work demands: A secretary handling the paperwork of four managers probably has less workspace surface area and storage capacity than any of the managers she or he serves, but needs them more to do the job.

Other workspace furnishings also vary systematically with status. Those most commonly identified include: the size, number, and materials of desk ornaments (ashtrays, pen sets, letter openers), waste baskets, clothes racks or stands, draperies, phones (Smith 1970), and the presence and quality of luxury items such as rugs, paintings, credenzas, cocktail cabinets, coffee tables, and couches (Cartwright 1962; Davis 1977; Mortensen 1963).

Even if materials or styles change with the times and fads, the size and general expense of the item relative to others serving the same functions will indicate status. The less functional an item, the higher the status it connotes. At present, it would appear that furnishings associated with homes rather than work (e.g., coffee tables, couches) tend to indicate high status. These objects, being less essential to conducting office work, comfortable and quite expensive, are good candidates for markers of high status.

Although newness might seem to connote high status, and in many cases it does, old (at least when considered antique), as Packard (1959) has noted, is often indicative of truly high status. Thus a genuine antique (scarce and unusual) indicates higher status than the more available modern glass and brass.

Both the general level of resources in an organization and the current availability of a specific commodity can affect the level of status at which a particular marker becomes prevalent because this alters the local value and scarcity. In a time of industrial or general economic tightening, or as the value of the commodity increases through supply and demand, what once was a marker of second-level management can come to indicate third-level management. When the demand for office space increases, the size requirements for offices for a given job level often drop. On the other hand, as organizational resources increase, as the availability of the commodity increases, or if the commodity becomes more essential to work, something previously the purview of second-level managers might become common among first-level managers. For example, when ergonomic chairs were introduced, they were given to senior managers. Now, some organizations have given such chairs to professionals and secretaries. In evaluating the status properties of furnishings, one should evaluate within rather than across organizations. A good sense of contextual factors will always be helpful.

Location

The location of a workspace can also suggest the status of its occupant. Some locations are considered intrinsically desirable. Others seem to derive their status properties from their nearness to other things of value, for instance a boss. A corner office seems to have intrinsic value in its remoteness from traffic and its multiple vantage points of the outside world. Elevation is also a status-relevant aspect of location, possibly because of the view characteristics. In multistory office buildings, lower-status individuals are usually located closer to ground level than are their higher-status counterparts.

Other aspects of location are more variable, depending on their as-sociation with other things of value. For instance, one status marker is the rank of the individuals nearby. Much as in housing, neighbors benefit or suffer from each others' status. If executives of similar rank are located near one another, an individual of lower rank who is located nearby may benefit. Although there are often minor aberrations—the workspace of the chief executive officer's secretary is typically closer to the chief's workspace than is the second in command—these deviations mandated by function are clearly in the minority.

Differentiation of workspaces through location seems especially important where there is little variability in the intrinsic value of other workspace characteristics. The workroom layout in the Hawthorn studies reportedly involved the use of location to indicate status in relatively nonobvious ways. Workers with the lowest-status jobs were reportedly relegated to the "back of the room," away from the door. As people acquired higher status, they moved toward the door (Roethlisberger and Dickson 1939); but in other instances, the opposite pattern has been noted (Steele 1973).

Privacy

The degree of privacy or control over access afforded individuals by their workspaces also serves as a status marker. The higher the status of the individual, the more private his or her workspace and the greater his or her control over access to the workspace (Konar et al. 1982; Sundstrom, Burt, and Kamp 1980). Private offices provide high status because they give their occupants a great deal of control over their passive accessibility by others: By closing a door, the private office occupant visibly discourages intrusions, (although even a private office does little to reduce intrusions by a persevering coworker). However, as private offices become less prevalent and open-plan offices more common, accessibility will increasingly be limited to partial enclosure of workspaces. The degree of enclosure (the number of sides of a workspace and the height of the enclosures) will no doubt function as a status marker. In fact, Sundstrom and associates (1982) found managers in more highly enclosed workspaces than other employees. Degree of enclosure, and the control over accessibility it affords, provides relatively costly (therefore scarce) but also very desirable freedom from disturbance and other types of unwanted access.

Size

The size or amount of floorspace in the workspace is another attribute that varies systematically with status. The U.S. General Services Administration, the British government, the Canadian government, as well as a host of private corporations have published space standards that dictate workspace sizes for each rank or employee level (Duffy et al. 1976; Pile 1978). The space allocated a given individual, including those at the very top and the very bottom of the hierarchy, is restricted within a fairly narrow range on the basis of rank. Even organizations without explicit standards, however, have guidelines for space allocation based on status or job level (BOSTI 1981; Langdon 1966; Manning 1965; Steele 1973).

Personalization

The opportunity to personalize a workspace may be one of the more subtle types of status markers. The freedom to add one's own personal artifacts (pictures, ashtrays, plants, and so on) tends to be restricted to relatively high-status individuals. Although freedom of this type is not costly and can easily be provided to all, common practice in large offices is to restrict lower-status individuals from engaging in such practices. For example, secretaries are often asked to refrain from posting photographs and other personal items that are commonplace in executive offices. These artifacts may signal to others something about the degree to which the individual can influence his or her own lifespace and their use is therefore limited to reflect organizational realities (Steele 1973).

Extra Equipment and Facilities

The entry of high-technology products into the office, varying in desirability, scarcity, and value, has made this category more prominent than it has been in the past. But it is not new. In previous years, for example, the intercom and electronic calculator were often provided only to high-status organizational members (in addition to lower-level employees with specific needs). More elaborate, scarce, and desirable high-technology management aids have since entered the private offices of senior management; these include video systems, videophones, and audio-visual systems. Now sophisticated microcomputers offering electronic mail, decision support systems, color graphics capabilities, and calendar systems are surfacing. Other types of facilities, such as personal gyms, are also being made available to the elite.

Empirical Support

The status-marking properties of these office characteristics have received a great deal of testimonial support. A recent empirical study of six organizations (three public, three private) in which 529 office workers were about to be moved to new office facilities actually tests these assertions (Konar et al. 1982). The data provide support for the general notion that these various workspace characteristics correspond to the status of the occupants. As indicated in Table 10-1, the workspaces of supervisory personnel (high-status individuals) were significantly less accessible, were larger, had a greater number and higher quality of furnishings, and provided greater capacity for personalization. A secondary analysis showed that among government workers, where finer distinctions of rank were available, rank (G.S. grade and step) was significantly and linearly associated with measures of quality and quantity of furnishings and control over accessibility.

The same study found that the presence of such markers was linked to perceptions of status support, particularly among high-status workers

Table 10-1. Status Markers in Supervisory and Nonsupervisory Personnel Workspaces

Status Markers	AVERAGE SCORE		Univariate F	Multivariate F
	Supervisors (n = 138)	Nonsupervisors (n = 391)		
CONTROL OVER ACCESS				18.82**
No. of people in room	16.69	26.26	7.05*	
Private office	45%	13%	62.35**	
Have door	49%	15%	70.18**	
No. of people can see you	2.01	2.92	38.26**	
Screening capabilities	1.35	−.55	62.61**	
SPACE				7.22**
Neighbor too close	2.65	3.25	16.88**	
Can work across surface	3.31	2.73	12.59**	
Bump when stretch	1.37	1.42	1.00	
FURNISHINGS				7.08**
Desk size	3.27	2.71	12.59**	
No. of chairs	2.86	2.15	10.14**	
No. of work surfaces	1.82	1.57	22.72**	
Quality of furnishings	2.37	2.32	.22	
Storage capacity	5.30	4.62	7.40**	
CAPACITY FOR PERSONALIZATION	3.53	2.88	18.03**	

*p < .01, Wilks
**p < .001, Wilks
Source: Konar, Sundstrom, Brady, Mandel, and Rice 1982

(supervisors). As indicated in Table 10-2, the status support characteristics that provided increased control over access, particularly, were more critical to the supervisors' perceptions of status support than to those of nonsupervisors.

In summary, common status markers appear to fall into six categories, including furnishings, location, control over access/privacy, size, personalization, and special facilities and equipment. In general, the more rare and valuable the commodity or privilege in the environment or organization, the higher the status the individual must have to receive it and, therefore, the higher the status it comes to indicate. The more common and less valuable a commodity or privilege, the lower the status of the individuals who have it and the lower the status it indicates. In the office, the things that tend to be rare and valuable are those that, although visually or otherwise appealing, are too costly to distribute to all (or even most) employees. Thus space or privacy barriers, windows, large work surfaces, and anything made of expensive materials are allocated

Table 10-2. Relationships between Status Markers and Status Support

| Status Markers | CORRELATIONS WITH STATUS SUPPORT | | | |
	Total Sample (n = 331)	Supervisors (n = 100)	Nonsupervisors (n = 231)	Difference Z
CONTROL OVER ACCESS				
Private office	.25***	.41***	.14**	2.50*
Door	.24***	.44***	.08	3.27**
No. of people can see you	−.10	−.35***	.02	2.88**
Screening capabilities	.25***	.51***	.07	4.11***
People in room	−.06	−.05	−.07	n.s.
SPACE				
Neighbor too close	−.37***	−.53***	−.27***	2.61**
Work across surface	.31***	.35***	.27***	n.s.
Bump when stretch	−.20***	−.15	−.21***	n.s.
FURNISHINGS				
Desk size	.39***	.58***	.30***	2.95**
No. of chairs	.18***	.34***	.08	2.28*
No. of work surfaces	.12*	.18	.07	n.s.
Storage capacity	.36***	.43***	.34***	n.s.
Quality	−.27***	.26**	.26***	n.s.
CAPACITY FOR PERSONALIZATION	.37***	.53***	.28***	2.52*
MULTIPLE CORRELATION (R)	.51***	.72***	.48***	−

*p < .05, two-tailed test
**p < .01, two-tailed tests
***p < .001, two-tailed test
Source: Konar, Sundstrom, Brady, Mandel, and Rice 1982

in direct proportion to rank and/or status. The absence of high-status markers results in a "bare bones" environment that is interpreted as indicative of low status. Fluctuations in determinants of value or organizational resources can cause fluctuations in the allocation patterns and, eventually, the perceived status associated with a given commodity.

THE CONTROVERSY OVER STATUS DEMARCATION

The reactions of observers to status demarcation in organizations vary from contempt to fascination (Duffy 1969) and can be seen to reflect one of three basic views. At one extreme is the first view: The practice of determining office and workspace characteristics on the basis of status is deplorable and reflects a potentially harmful preoccupation with external appearance rather than functional reality (Mortensen 1963; Packard 1959;

Peck 1980). A second view suggests that the practice is essentially harmless (albeit sometimes costly) (Buss 1982; Smith 1970). A third perspective evident in the literature is a conditional positive, which argues that status demarcation is a potentially useful strategy to inform and make salient the organizational hierarchy and the positions of the individuals within it. Like any other organizational strategy, it must be evaluated on the basis of impact, both intended and unintended. (Few, if any, seem to take an unconditional positive view of the practice.)

The most negative position (the first view) interprets such practices to be the result of the ego needs of those at the top who seek and even demand benefit from symbols of their own success. The practice is seen as ill-intended and detrimental to others in the organization and/or the organizations themselves. According to Mortensen (1963), "Status symbols seem to have been designed deliberately to keep the top and lower echelons of the firm apart; thus neither category will find out that the other consists of reasonable human beings. Special entrances and lifts, separate secluded dining rooms and gardens and a special segregated staff that serves the executive floor all combine to imbue top management with an aura of hushed reverence. Surrounded by the rituals of the status hierarchy, management remains aloof and is bewildered by the fact that the employees regard such reasonable human beings as themselves almost as ogres" (p. 33). The same writer referred to the unusual individual who "breaks down stupid status barriers" and is "not bound by the tyrannical limits of petty prestige values that dominate the establishment" (p. 33).

Similarly, Peck (1980) has denounced both the goals and consequences of what he terms "indiscriminate use of status symbols" that serve to "hide the anxieties and insecurities" of management. He suggests that reliance on artificial status props tends to "create ill will and may destroy the cooperation, loyalty, creativity and initiative of others." (p. 76)

Packard, a less strident critic, seems to oppose the status hierarchy more than the markings of it. Yet he implies that there is an additional negative impact of the markings in that they function as disincentives to actual achievement. Markers of status (achievement) may get mistaken for the status they typically accompany so that individuals begin to strive for, and be reinforced by, the symbols rather than the achievement they indicate. A high-potential employee could presumably be encouraged to strive for a fancy office rather than for real achievement and increased responsibilities. Being content with the new office could cause him or her to forget about the position and opportunities it once represented.

A broader concern is that status markers can further impede status mobility. If only those with the markers of previous success are allowed to play critical organizational roles, the opportunities of those without such markers will be limited. In the social arena, where one can more easily purchase status symbols with the successes of others (ancestors), this may be an even more common problem than in organizations, where status markers are not easily attained without individual achievement.

The second view considers status demarcation part of a good-natured game. Status markers, from this perspective, are little more than tokens that make the competitive sport more fun and contribute to the pleasure/ satisfaction of generally deserving individuals. Somewhat characteristic of such a perspective is the view of Buss (1982) in a recent *Harvard Business Review* article, "Making It Electronically." In it Buss describes the delight of a hypothetical success, "Richard Forrest." Just promoted to executive vice president of a large corporation, he finds himself within reach of the top of the corporate electronic tree: His firm is providing a dish antenna with sending and receiving equipment for his suburban Connecticut home. Forest has "the look of a man who knows he has made it." Musing and smiling, he thinks of the series of electronic wizardry that accompanied his climb to the top over the years. There appear to be no personal or societal costs to his rewards, nor, on the other hand is there any function or purpose to the rewards he receives.

Smith (1970), quoting another observer, summarizes this perspective, noting that "it's unhealthy to deny the fact that you deserve these little pleasures. Life would be very gray without them" (p. 97).

A third reaction to status demarcation is one that focuses on its purposes and outcomes, both personal and organizational. This view, described in *Iron Age* (1969), suggests that status demarcation may contribute to the communication of information about organizational structure, and that, even after taking some potential problems with functional needs versus symbolic allocations into consideration, the organization may find such communication aids useful and practical. Although this perspective is not the most common, it was taken as an approach to this chapter because it allowed for an examination of both the potential costs and benefits of status demarcation. Such an examination follows.

THE IMPACT OF STATUS DEMARCATION

Status demarcation is a complex issue, but its role in organizations seems to hinge on its role in two larger organizational arenas or systems: employee compensation and organizational structure. We argue that (1) as a system that dictates commodities and privileges be made on the basis of assessments of individual value or contribution, status demarcation is part and parcel of the organizational compensation system; and (2) by creating an environment that derives from and reflects the organizational structure and hierarchy and indicates each person's position in it, status demarcation furthers the goals and the impact of the organizational hierarchy (both positive and negative). The role of status demarcation as a component in each of these systems and the impact of the practice are discussed in detail below.

Compensation Value

When an individual's status is altered in any appreciable sense (as in a formal promotion or demotion), the practice of status demarcation calls for commensurate changes in the environment. Promotions are accompanied by workspace enhancements or a relocation to a superior workspace. Rare is a promotion that will not result in environmental changes as diverse as a move from a windowless office to an office with a window, a move to a larger office, or even the privilege of requesting artwork. Demotions, when they are made explicit, can result in the withdrawal of special features (a fancy phone system, a special credenza, or a piece of art) or a move to a less desirable office.

(Sometimes, the system appears to have gone awry. An individual who has performed poorly is "promoted" and given a new office with the "trappings of success." Yet just as the promotion may not be a real promotion in the sense of increased responsibilities, the status markers may not really communicate achievement. The new office may be bigger, but located in a particularly undesirable location, e.g., away from the action.)

The appeal of status symbols, and therefore their value as rewards, is generally high. Although the key to the executive washroom does not have much appeal today, other traditional markers, such as high-backed office chairs, still have wide appeal, making them rewards not unlike other types of compensation (for example, raises, bonuses). With the more recent scarcity of privacy and privacy barriers, enclosure and the resultant privacy have become much-sought-after status markers. In the BOSTI (1981) study, fully 68% of the sample preferred to work in a private office (only 11% of these actually did after a move to open-plan.)

The greater the appeal of a status marker, the greater its reward value. Like rewards, status demarcation can affect satisfaction and motivation, positively or negatively.

One important aspect of any part of a compensation system is the perception of equity that it promotes or diminishes. (For a broader discussion on the effects of compensation, see Lawler 1981). Equity theory, developed by Adams (1965), holds that satisfaction is maximized when the ratio of an individual's inputs to his or her outputs is equivalent to those of a "comparison other," the person to whom one compares oneself. Broadly speaking, status markers can be considered an output—something the individual receives. Things such as expertise, effort, and actual accomplishments are considered inputs. Applying the theory in a general way, we propose that if one's status markers are similar to those of others who provide similar inputs, greater than those of others with lesser inputs, and less than those whose inputs are greater, the situation is perceived as equitable. If one perceives that someone with a similar level of input has higher-level status markers or that someone of lower input has similar-level status markers, the situation is perceived as inequitable. (The situation in which one is overrewarded is also thought to result in perceptions of inequity, although research is inconclusive.)

Perceptions of equity are critical to job satisfaction. A high-performing, hard-working person who finds himself or herself in a workspace not visibly different from that of a seemingly less capable or motivated person is likely to be dissatisfied with his or her workspace and, possibly, with his or her job. The correspondence of one's workspace with one's sense of status we call *perceived status support*. Based on equity theory, status support is therefore predicted to be positively correlated with job and work environment satisfaction.

The study by Konar and associates (1982) tested the relationship of status support to environmental and job satisfaction. Status support, measured by a question that asked to what extent the individual thought his or her workspace accurately reflects his or her status in the organization was found to be positively correlated with workspace satisfaction. As Table 10-3 indicates, this relationship between status support and environmental satisfaction was found among supervisors and nonsupervisors alike, in both the private and public sectors. Correlations with job satisfaction were weaker and significant only for supervisors in the public sector; they were nearly significant for supervisors in the private sector. Thus it appears that appropriate status demarcation, in which the individual perceives his or her environment as accurately reflecting his or her status may be a positive factor in an office worker's satisfaction.

Compensation has been known to affect organizational behavior as well as affective reactions. Status demarcation, as a part of the compensation system, should have consequences for organizational behaviors such as motivation. On the basis of expectancy theory (Vroom 1964), which was developed to address motivation in organization, we argue that appropriate status demarcation can heighten motivation, whereas inadequacies in the system can have equally negative ramifications.

Table 10.3. Relationship of Environmental Status Support with Workspace Satisfaction and Job Satisfaction

Type of Satisfaction/ Type of Organization	CORRELATIONS WITH STATUS SUPPORT		Difference Z
	Supervisors	*Nonsupervisors*	
WORKSPACE SATISFACTION			
Private Sector	.53**	.34**	1.71, $p < .04$[a]
	($n = 73$)	($n = 208$)	
Government	.52**	.33**	1.55, $p < .06$[a]
	($n = 61$)	($n = 162$)	
JOB SATISFACTION			
Private Sector	.16 ($p < .09$)	.00	n.s.
	($n = 72$)	($n = 201$)	
Government	.31*	.08	1.6, $p < .06$[a]
	($n = 58$)	($n = 159$)	

$*p < .01$, one-tailed test
$**p < .001$, one-tailed test
a. one-tailed test
Source: Konar, Sundstrom, Brady, Mandel, and Rice 1982

Broadly, expectancy theory suggests that motivation is affected by two cognitive factors: (1) the perception of the likelihood that effort will result in achievement or success; and (2) the perception of the instrumentality of achievement in obtaining valuable rewards. The theory maintains that motivation is a multiplicative function of the two factors, the first called *expectancy* (of achievement) and the second, *instrumentality* (of achievement for obtaining desired outcomes).

To evaluate the impact of status demarcation on motivation we need to consider the extent to which such a system affects one's expectancy for success and the instrumentality of that success. We found no empirical evidence relevant to these hypotheses; however we can consider the likely scenarios in order to develop hypotheses regarding the impact of a status demarcation system. First, status markers provide visible, highly salient reminders of one's own previous achievements and those of others. As such, they are likely to increase the individual's expectancy for future success. Second, as demonstrations of something desirable allocated on the basis of achievement, they attest to the instrumentality of achievement. Thus the perceptions of instrumentality should increase. On the other hand, to the extent that status markers are misallocated, or denied to deserving individuals, both instrumentality and expectancy will be negatively affected and motivation and performance reduced.

Status and Organizational Structure

As a visible, concrete, and salient indicator of the hierarchical structure of an organization and an individual's position within it, status demarcation furthers the goals and consequences of the structure itself. As Duffy (1969) suggests, the status hierarchy is a rank ordering of organizational members, based largely on authority level. Such a hierarchy is largely consonant with the broader organizational hierarchy, at least within functions. (The functions themselves may be loosely ordered and thus form a hierarchy within a hierarchy, a factor we will consider later.)

Such organizational and status hierarchies (1) define each individual's position relative to that of others, both for that individual and for those with whom she or he deals; (2) suggest behavioral norms that set limits on appropriate behavior with that individual. We will consider the role of status demarcation for each of these functions.

Knowing, and keeping in mind, one's own and other's standing and authority is critical to effective functioning in organizations. Salient reminders such as status markers assist in this effort (see, for example, Barnard 1946). Moving into a private office for the first time will likely serve as a reminder of one's new level of authority and responsibility. Seeing an individual in a small, poorly furnished space can remind one of that person's limited responsibility and authority. Visitors can thereby quickly assess with whom they are dealing and can appropriately evaluate responses relative to level of authority or lack thereof.

Knowing where an individual (including oneself) stands in the organizational hierarchy can be useful to newcomers and even oldtimers. It is important because this knowledge creates certain expectations and limits on patterns of interaction among organization members and even between individuals of different organizations. Status-relevant norms are evoked, almost magically, in heavily demarcated environments. For example, awe, compliance, and respect are cued by offices larger or more ornately furnished than one's own. Smaller or less handsomely appointed spaces cue more aggressive, commanding behavior from a visitor.

Although such behavioral norms tend to make things run smoothly, they can reduce the likelihood of potentially important behavior. Norms that dictate respect and compliance also mitigate against collaboration, conflict, and, perhaps, creativity. To the extent that status markers make authority more salient than collaborative needs of the task at hand, status demarcation may be detrimental to the work at hand and the organization itself.

Few tests of the impact of status demarcation on such factors have been conducted, although several older studies and a recent unpublished study are suggestive. Whyte, in his classic study of street-corner gangs (cited in Secord and Backman 1964), noted that gang members' bowling scores were consistent with their status in the group, but only when they were bowling with the group. Strong norms regarding acceptable conduct and performance may have made it difficult for low-status individuals to outperform their superiors in the presence of those individuals. Extrapolating to the context of an organization, we can infer that the stronger the status cues, the less likely the occurrence of nondeferential behavior of the subordinate in a context in which the status differential is salient, even when such nondeference would result in a better project or product.

Konar and Daniel (1982) found that status markers defined status and had an impact on behavior in a laboratory environment. Individuals of unknown status were assumed to have status consistent with the level of their status markers. The researchers also found that compliance was greatest when the requestor had both high status and high-level status markers. The results provide empirical support of the power of status markers to define status and evoke status-appropriate behavior.

To the extent that status and status demarcation clarify who is who and what behavior is appropriate, behavior becomes more predictable and communication clearer. Consistent with this proposition is the recent finding by BOSTI (1981) wherein people who perceived their status support as having improved during a move (their new workspace more accurately reflected their status) found their ease of communication improved.

In summary, status demarcation can have powerful effects on people and organizations. Research findings suggest that status support, the result of consistent status demarcation, is associated with environmental satisfaction and (although to a lesser extent) job satisfaction. Status demarcation helps us to know who we and other organizational members are in the organizational context. It is likely to evoke status-relevant behavioral norms, increasing the likelihood of certain types of behavior (that is, authority-consistent behaviors such as compliance) but may minimize important others (collaboration, conflict, and so on). By providing a context for organizational interaction, status demarcation serves to increase the predictability of behavior and can increase the ease of communication.

Errors in Status Demarcation

In contexts in which status demarcation is pervasive (and, again, the BOSTI data indicate this is typically the case), when workers have status markers that are inconsistent with their status and when their workspaces under- or overrepresents them in relation to superiors or subordinates, the result is "status incongruency" (Secord and Backman 1964). This situation can be the result of deliberate action or just inattention. An employee can sometimes have special access to valued commodities that are not typically made available to others at the same rank, perhaps as a function of seniority or personal relationships. The resultant status incongruency may be perceived by others as inequitable and could cause psychological distress (Adams 1965).

Underrepresentation of status may be even more distressing and have higher organizational costs. As a result of severely limited resources or a lapse following a status change (e.g., promotion, demotion), an individual may have the status markers more appropriate for his or her subordinates than for peers. Such instances, particularly among managers, may result in difficulties in exercising rightful authority, which, in turn, could diminish the individual's effectiveness.

IMPLICATIONS FOR OFFICE DESIGN

Our analysis strongly suggests that issues of status and status demarcation should not be ignored in thoughtful office design. The practice of status demarcation in workplaces, and the office in particular, has a long, if not entirely glorious, history. For this reason alone, there are strong expectations among organizational members regarding their workspace, particularly in relation to the workspaces of others. Simply acting as if such considerations did not exist will not make them go away.

Status demarcation can be emphasized or minimized through environmental design, but decisions in this regard should not be in the hands of office designers. Instead, organizational decision makers must develop a general policy and work with the designer to implement it. Designers who purposely or inadvertently upset a system of status markers or who introduce new ones without the participation of those involved are likely to generate chaos for themselves and the organization.

It may be difficult to address the issue of status demarcation directly. Many still think of status as a dirty word, the desire for status markers evidence of self-aggrandizement. Managers may be reluctant to ask for the trappings they feel they deserve without emphasizing functional purposes ("I need a large ashtray because visitors smoke a lot") for fear of seeming undemocratic or elitist. Even when most members of the organization admit that some differences "make sense," they may disagree on the level and the methods of implementation.

It may be easiest and most effective to derive general standards by developing model workspaces for each level, on the basis of a consensus of a team of individuals from that level and one level above and one below. One may be able to arrive at reasonable standards, with recognition of the symbolic and functional value of the characteristics being determined. In this manner, the most desirable, and perhaps useful, status markers for each level can be identified. It avoids a not uncommon tendency for individuals to try to obtain gratuitous extras (e.g., fancy wastebaskets and desk accessories) to provide the desired status support rather than more useful "extras" like soundproof barriers.

The design process can be a technique for solidifying well-developed organizational norms or a mechanism for change. A consensus among participants may mandate a continued moderate status demarcation and support, a return to a previous (higher or lower) level, or an attempt to alter previous practices in line with new notions of authority and collaboration by reducing or increasing the variance in workspaces associated with status or rank.

In new headquarters for Union Carbide (Bennett 1983), for example, a decision was made to diminish status demarcation radically. All managers were provided offices of equal size. The results of this decision are not yet clear. Yet building standard-size offices does seem to have one rather pragmatic effect. This system is flexible enough to respond to changes in an organizational structure that alter the number of individuals at a given level or even the number of levels. When Union Carbide reorganizes and adds a vice president, it does not have to knock down walls to provide one more executive office of a size equivalent to the others. This example illustrates a more general consideration. Flexible or portable markers may be desirable in that they allow the environment to quickly respond to changes in organizational structure. Ideally, status markers would facilitate marking even minor alterations in the status hierarchy without costly alterations.

Status demarcation can also be a tool in organizational change efforts. An organization actively trying to alter its status hierarchy can look to status markers to introduce and communicate new organizational policy or understanding. Recognizing that a certain important function typically receives too little recognition and support to attract or maintain high-power individuals, an organization can attempt to improve the status of this function, and the individuals in it, through changes in status markers.

For example, the typically sparse and minimal workspaces of high-level engineers can be enhanced to improve the status of an engineering function. Together with enhanced functional responsibility and other types of recognition (e.g., titles and pay) and opportunities, status markers could communicate a higher level of status for technical contribution and negate the common belief that engineers must become managers to make important contributions. Workspace enhancements, visible to all, would provide other employees with evidence and salient cues to this organizational change, increasing the recognition and the authority of these individuals in their organizations.

To summarize, status demarcation is a pervasive factor in the office. Contrary to some recent forecasts, there appears to be little evidence of a decline in status marking in offices, even in open-plan arrangements. By allocating a diverse set of status markers, organizations provide visible signs of their own recognition for individual achievement and a graphic system of communicating to others the organizational structure and the individual's roles within it. Office designers must recognize and be responsive to the factors underlying the need for the practice and to its effects on individuals and organizations. Working with organizational decision markers, they can heighten, maintain, enhance, or just fine tune a status demarcation system to maximize effective individual and organization performance and the quality of work life among an organization's members.

REFERENCES

Adams, J. 1965. Inequity in social exchange. In L. Berkowitz (Ed.), *Advances in experimental social psychology*, vol. 2. New York: Academic Press.
Barnard, C. I. 1946. Functional pathology of status systems in formal organizations. In W. F. Whyte (Ed.), *Industry and society*. New York: McGraw-Hill.
Behling, O., and C. Schreisheim. 1976. *Organizational behavior*. Boston: Allyn and Bacon.
Bennett, R. A. 1983. New look in space. *New York Times* (July 13): Section C1.
Bird, C. 1968. Women in business: The invisible bar. *Personnel* 3:29–35.
Blumberg, P. 1974. The decline and fall of the status symbol: Some thoughts on status in a post-industrial society. *Social Problems* 21:480–498.
BOSTI, 1981. *The impact of office environment on productivity and quality of working life*. Technical Report. Buffalo, N.Y.: BOSTI.
Buss, M. 1982. Making it electronically. *Harvard Business Review* 1:89–90.
Cartwright, P. A. 1962. What's in a name plate. *Personnel Administration* 25:21–23.
Davis, K. 1977. *Human behavior at work*. New York: McGraw-Hill.
Duffy, F. 1969. Role and status in the office. *Architectural Association Quarterly* 1:4–13.
Duffy, F., C. Cave, and J. Worthington. 1976. *Planning office space*. London: Architectural Press.
Halloran, J. 1978. *Applied human relations: An organizational approach*. Englewood Cliffs, NJ: Prentice-Hall.
Iron Age. 1969. Status symbols have a definite value. 203:23.
Kanter, R. M. 1983. Woman managers: Moving up in a high tech society. In Jennie Farley (Ed.), *The woman in management*, Ithaca, N.Y.: ILR Press.
Konar, E., and R. Daniel. 1982. The effect of status and environmental status demarcation on compliance. Unpublished technical report, University of Western Ontario.

Konar, E., E. Sundstrom, C. Brady, D. Mandel, and R. Rice. 1982. Status demarcation in the office. *Environment and Behavior* 14:561–580.

Langdon, F. J. 1966. *Modern offices: A user survey.* National Building Research Paper No. 41. London: HMSO.

Lawler, E. E. 1981. *Pay and organizational development.* Reading, MA., Addison-Wesley.

Lippert, F. G. 1966. Responsibilities of a supervisor. *Supervision* 4:13–14.

Manning, P. (Ed.). 1965. *Office design: A study of environment.* Liverpool, England: University of Liverpool.

Mortensen, V. 1963. Are status symbols inevitable? *Personnel Administration* 26:31–34.

Packard, V. 1959. *The status seekers.* New York: David McKay Co.

Peck, W. 1980. Administrative reflections: Management at ease. *Administrative Management* 41:76.

Pile, J. F. 1978. *Open office planning.* New York: Whitney Library of Design.

Preston, P. 1974. What does your office say about you. *Supervisory Management* 19:28–34.

Roethlisberger, F. J., and W. J. Dickson. 1939. *Management and the worker.* Cambridge: Harvard University.

Secord, P. and C. Backman. 1964. *Social psychology.* New York: McGraw-Hill.

Smith, J. 1970. Status symbols are changing too. *Dun's Review.* 9:52–97.

Steele, F. I. 1973. *Physical settings and organizational development.* Reading, MA: Addison-Wesley.

Sundstrom, E., R. E. Burt, and D. Kamp. 1980. Privacy at work: Architectural correlates of job satisfaction and job performance. *Academy of Management Journal* 23:101–117.

Sundstrom, E., J. Town, D. Brown, A. Forman, and C. McGee. 1982. Physical enclosure, type of job and privacy in the office. *Environment and Behavior* 14:379–392.

Vroom, V. 1964. *Work and motivation.* New York: John Wiley & Sons.

Functional, Aesthetic, and Symbolic Aspects of Office Lighting

---

PETER ELLIS
Building Use Studies Ltd.
London, United Kingdom

A number of surveys of office workers have shown that lighting of the workplace is one of the most important factors contributing to their comfort and satisfaction. A Louis Harris poll (1978) commissioned by the Steelcase Furniture Company found that 85% of those questioned believed that good lighting was the number one factor in comfort at the workplace. The majority were satisfied with the lighting they had, and the high priority given to it appeared relatively independent of the office workers' particular circumstances.

Nevertheless, in my experience, general standards of office lighting, both in the United States and in Europe, are frequently poor. The convention of the last 20 years or so has been to provide overhead fluorescent lighting at uniformly high levels of illumination throughout the office. If badly designed, such lighting may create glare, with consequent headache and eyestrain; it is aesthetically uninteresting if not downright unpleasant; and it is wasteful of energy because it produces more light than is needed. One of the consequences of the energy crisis has been the realization both by lighting designers and users that lower levels of nonuniform lighting have potential benefits instrumentally, aesthetically, and in energy savings.

225

LIGHTING'S IMPACT ON THE INDIVIDUAL

Studies of the different ways in which lighting makes its impact on the individual user show that these can be divided broadly into functional and aesthetic factors. *Functional* factors refer to those characteristics of the lighting that affect conditions of adequate illumination of the work task and avoidance of user discomfort. *Aesthetic* factors refer to nonfunctional characteristics that nevertheless appear significant to users' general evaluations of lighting.

The main functional factors found by the studies may be summarized as follows (Boyce 1981)[1]:

1. *Illuminance.* This refers to the quantity of the light that reaches a surface. It may be measured either on the horizontal surface, or as spherical or cylindrical illuminance, which allows assessment of the illuminance of three-dimensional objects. Clearly if the illuminance is inadequate, task visibility will be affected. Excessive illuminance may cause discomfort.
2. *Uniformity of illuminance.* This refers to the extent to which a whole surface or object is illuminated evenly. A high degree of nonuniformity on flat surfaces will affect task visibility and comfort.
3. *Glare.* Distinction is made between disability glare, which impairs vision through direct dazzle from a light source, and discomfort glare, which arises from excessive contrast between bright and dim surfaces. Glare is the most frequent cause of eyestrain and headaches.
4. *Veiling reflection.* This is a particular kind of glare in which the part of the task that needs to be seen is actually veiled by reflection from the task surface. Veiling reflections are common when glossy surfaces are illuminated by bright point sources from acute angles. These reflections directly affect task visibility.
5. *Color properties.* The frequencies of light emitted by a source in relation to the whole color spectrum will affect how clearly the eye can distinguish different colors of objects illuminated by the source. The color properties of the source are not generally a major instrumental factor, however, except in the case of tasks involving fine color discrimination.
6. *Luminance ratio of work surface to surroundings.* Luminance refers to the apparent brightness of a surface and is a product of the illuminance (light falling on the surface) and the surface reflectance. Discomfort may be caused if the luminance ratio is excessive.

Aesthetic factors that do not instrumentally affect task visibility or user comfort include the following:

1. *Color appearance.* Apart from its instrumental value, the color appearance of light emitted by a source has aesthetic significance. However, the major determinant of the color appearance of an office is the interior design, and the light source plays a relatively minor role except in extreme cases (Boyce 1981, 317).
2. *General room appearance.* The principal way in which a lighting scheme can affect the appearance of a room, apart from color properties, is in the way the general distribution of light creates contrasts between bright and dim areas (room contrast). Room contrast becomes more critical when nonuniform lighting is being used. Some studies have shown that a modicum of room contrast is found pleasing and interesting by users, but that excessive contrasts can create gloomy and therefore aesthetically unacceptable interiors (Hawkes, Loe, and Rowlands 1977).

MODELS OF MAN-ENVIRONMENT RELATIONS

Most studies that have incorporated user assessments of office lighting have involved a simulation of real office conditions: The users were unconnected to the organization of the office in question, including the design management process whereby the lighting conditions being assessed were brought about. In contrast, the case studies that are reported in this chapter involved situations in real organizations where a novel lighting scheme had been introduced, with some element of worker involvement in the assessment.

The theoretical assumption that often underlies simulation studies is that the organizational context and the design management process are not relevant to the measurement of user responses. This implies a particular theoretical model for man-environment relations, one that assumes human reactions to environments are fixed and unchanging. It is a mechanistic model and takes for granted the idea that the "performance" of human beings can be measured and generalized in the same way that the performance of physical components of the environment can. The inadequacy of this model for man-environment relations has become increasingly clear in the research of the last 20 years. Expectations that social science can build a body of knowledge about human performance for use by the design professions have largely failed to materialize. It seems that human reactions are variable and inconsistent; few rules or generalities are to be found. In particular, it is apparent that people's reactions to environmental stimuli are affected by their perception of the social situations in which they find themselves.

An alternative theoretical model for man-environment relations, one that is better able to take these findings into account, is symbolic interactionism. In this model, physical environment is viewed not as an independent variable that evokes human responses, but as a medium for symbolic communication in the course of social interaction. The model is based largely on the work of G. H. Mead.[2] Its basis is that individuals and groups of individuals engage in symbolic transactions or interactions with each other in the course of pursuing their day-to-day goals and objectives. A variety of media, both verbal and nonverbal, may be used in such social communication, and the physical environment is an important nonverbal medium of communication. As such, it acquires symbolic value, in addition to its purely functional significance, because of the role it plays in social interaction. The sociologist H. J. Gans (1978) has expressed the basic idea underlying the interactionist model very clearly:

Between the physical environment and empirically observed human behavior, there exists a social system and a set of cultural norms which define and evaluate portions of the physical environment relevant to the lives of the people involved and structures the way people will use (and react to) this environment in their daily lives (p. 5).

The implication of the interactionist model for studies of user assessments of lighting is that in addition to the functional and aesthetic significance of lighting to users, it is also significant symbolically. Users' assessments of their lighting are likely to be influenced by their understanding of the management process whereby the lighting scheme came about. Studies that ignore this organizational context are unlikely to produce results generalizable to other situations. The symbolic aspect of lighting is likely to be of particular significance when novel forms of lighting, such as those in this chapter, are considered.

People often feel threatened by new technology and are suspicious of its origins and possible effects. This makes them more likely to question the design management process and to seek some involvement in that process. Such feelings will influence the way they react to and use the lighting. Design researchers cannot afford to ignore this organizational context: first, it provides a key to understanding the reasons behind users' expressions and feelings; and second, through an understanding of the organizational context, researchers may be able to influence it in order to increase the probability that the design will be accepted and effectively used. The functional, aesthetic, and symbolic aspects of office lighting all interact with each other. The following case studies aim to illustrate the nature of those interactions.

CASE STUDY 1

Task Lighting for Engineering Draftsmen

Background

This study was commissioned by a firm of architects designing a new office building for a client in the north of England. The building was to be occupied by 1,800 draftsmen from the client's Engineering Design Division. The design team was investigating the feasibility of a lighting scheme that would show a substantial reduction in running costs over a conventional overhead scheme, which can often consume 50% of the energy input to a typical medium-depth office building. Low-energy lighting would, besides reducing energy consumed as light, also reduce the cost of the mechanical ventilation plant needed to remove the heat generated by lighting. It was understood that there were several ways of achieving these desired savings in energy used for lighting: (1) by selecting energy-saving luminaires; (2) by maximizing natural light, e.g., larger windows and less deep office spaces; and (3) by moving light sources closer than normal to the surfaces to be illuminated (i.e., by task lighting).

The problem was to reconcile low energy with the lighting conditions needed for very exacting drawing work. It was decided that there was insufficient knowledge available about task lighting to allow a scheme that met these criteria to be designed with any confidence. The solution was to mount a trial in order to test a variety of forms of task lighting in an experimental installation, allowing the prospective users themselves to try out and assess the schemes, as well as to subject them to a rigorous technical assessment. Another reason for conducting a user trial was that it was known a strongly conservative attitude toward lighting prevailed among the user group. It was hoped that their participation in the trial would foster a more flexible and open-minded attitude to novel forms of lighting.

Types of Lighting Tested

The trial was designed to test the performance of three major lighting options open to the design team. Scheme A (fig. 11-1) was devised to test task lights mounted on or directly above drawing boards or desks. The aim was to achieve 350 lux ambient light from ceiling-mounted luminaires, and to raise this to 750 lux on drawing boards and 500 lux on desks by task lights mounted on furniture. Scheme B (fig. 11-2) was installed to investigate the concept of *localized* lighting: that is, luminaires,

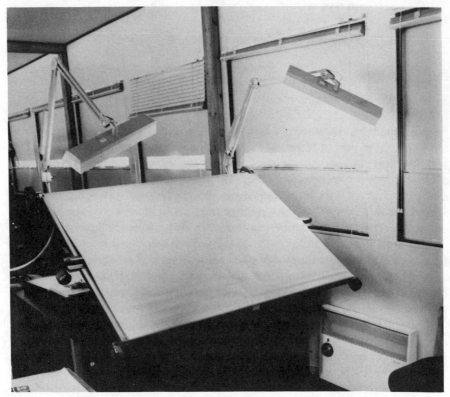

11-1. Scheme A was devised to test task lights mounted on or directly above drawing boards or desks.

suspended above work stations, that provide both ambient illumination and direct light on the work surface to the same levels specified for Scheme A. Scheme C (fig. 11-3) was a conventional overhead system providing uniform light of up to 1,000 lux on the horizontal plane. It was the lighting type the user group experienced in most of their existing drawing offices and was included in the trial as a control condition. The expected figures for energy consumption of the three schemes were: Scheme A, 10 watts per square meter; Scheme B, 20 watts per square meter; and Scheme C, 30 watts per square meter.

Method

The Trial Installation

A large room in one of the client's existing offices was set aside for the trial. Work stations for 32 draftsmen were laid out in eight cruciform

11-2. Scheme B investigated localized lighting. Luminaires were suspended above workstations to provide both task and ambient light.

blocks of four. Eight work stations for professional and technical officers who worked at desks were also provided. The drawing boards and desks in half the room were fitted with furniture-mounted task lights (Scheme A); those in the other half were given suspended localized lights (Scheme B). The existing installations in an adjoining room constituted Scheme C.

Users taking part in the trial were drawn from different parts of the Engineering Design Division and spent a total of three weeks working in the experimental room. They were divided into two groups, each of which spent half the time working under Scheme A and the other half working under Scheme B.

User Assessments

Users' assessments of the lighting were obtained through small group discussions. Five groups were formed, four of draftsmen and one of

11-3. Scheme C was a conventional overhead arrangement providing uniform ambient light.

professional and technical officers. Each group met with researchers on three occasions. On the first, they described and discussed the lighting in buildings they had worked in previously and their first reactions to the trial lighting schemes. On the second and third occasions, they discussed their experiences of either Scheme A or Scheme B, whichever they were currently using.

Each discussion, or small group meeting, lasted about one hour and was divided into two phases:

1. the main phase of open discussion during which the researchers encouraged the users to express their opinions freely, and noted down the criteria employed by users in making judgments and evaluations; and

2. a more formal summing-up phase during which each user was asked to use a 5-point evaluative scale to rate the lighting scheme under discussion on each of the criteria established during phase 1.

Technical Measurements

A variety of technical measurements of the lighting schemes were made. These included planar illuminance, cylindrical illuminance, daylight factor, discomfort glare, and contrast rendering factor.

Results

User Assessments

Both schemes were strongly criticized on a number of criteria, which evidently became more critical once light fittings were brought down from the ceiling closer to the task surface. The range of criteria spontaneously generated in group discussions was highly consistent from one group to another and also with criteria that have emerged from other studies discussed in the beginning of this chapter (Boyce 1981; McKennan et al. 1980).

Table 11-1 shows the full framework of ideas that emerged from user discussions. Concepts could be divided into four categories represented by the four columns. Generally, users started off by talking about their experience and its subjective consequences; further questioning and probing was often needed in order to elicit the responsible objective features of the lighting and to infer the likely objective consequences.

In discussion of subjective consequences, it was possible to separate those aspects of the lighting that were important aesthetically from those that had functional significance. The most important aesthetic features were the degree of contrast in the room and the color appearance. Both these were reported to exert significant effects on users' mood and general state of mind, which in turn, it was reported, affected their attitudes to their work and the amount of time they found reason to be absent from the office.

Other reported features of the lighting had primarily functional significance, affecting users' physical comfort, convenience, and ability to perform their work:

1. *Uniformity across work surface.* For the board-mounted lights, the illuminance range across drawing surfaces was very large, in one case 9:1. Performance of suspended lights was better, with a maximum ratio of about 4:1. This factor was critical for the large-scale drawing tasks, and was compounded by difficulties of mechanical adjustment.
2. *Illuminance and discomfort glare.* The effects of the general illuminance of the work surface in contrast to surrounding surfaces was distinguished by users from the illuminance required for perceptual clarity of the task. Many of the board-mounted fittings created strong contrast, resulting in discomfort glare.

Table 11-1. Framework of Ideas from User Assessment of Task Lighting in Case Study 1

Objective Light Characteristics	Reported Experience	Subjective Consequence	Likely Objective Consequence
Position of light relative to board (distance, angle)	Degree of heat from source Degree of glare on board, flicker/nonflicker Degree of dazzle from source	Degree of physical comfort	Place of work, amount of absenteeism and staff turnover
Intensity of source, type of source (point, linear), and distribution from source	Degree of uniformity on board Degree of shadow on board Presence of veiling reflections Degree of room contrast	Convenience for drawing task Mood: cheering/oppressive	Need for adjustment of task lights Need for supplementary ambient lighting
Color Appearance	Warm/cold; soft/harsh	Mood: cheering/oppressive	Pace of work, etc.
Maintenance	Degree of brightness, amount of flicker or discoloration	Physical comfort	Pace of work, etc.
Switch control	Convenience of location		
Mechanical adjustability	Degree of ease and stability in adjustment	Convenience, safety	Pace of work, etc., safety

3. *Disability glare.* When task lights are mounted near eye level and not fitted with adequate shades or diffusers, disability glare, referred to by users as "dazzle," is bound to occur. Most of the suspended fittings had good diffusers and did not give rise to this problem.

4. *Veiling reflections.* Board-mounted lights also caused problems of glare reflected off shiny work surfaces by light sources set at acute angles to the line of vision. This, again, is largely a problem of adequate diffusion from the source.

5. *Shadows on work surface.* Light sources set at an angle to the work surface cause shadows to be cast on it by instruments and the hands that hold these. This causes particular difficulty for accurate figure drawing.

The symbolic significance of the lighting was evident in the change of attitude that took place among users over the course of the consultations. At the first meetings, many of the users of Schemes A and B displayed strongly conservative feelings about lighting, expressing skepticism and in some cases hostility toward the innovative departures from conventional overhead lighting. But by the time of the third meeting, which was held two weeks later, most of these prejudices were much reduced: in general, users displayed an open-mindedness toward new forms of lighting, which paved the way for the acceptance of a low-energy scheme.

It might be thought that these prejudices were dispelled by users' experiences of the good qualities of Schemes A and B. But while they were more ready to take an open-minded attitude, users were, in fact, extremely critical of both trial schemes, particularly of Scheme A, to the extent that none of the trial installations was judged adequate to meet the task requirements. The researchers' conclusion was that it was primarily the participative design process that fostered the change in user attitudes, as indeed had been hypothesized. This conclusion supports the general thesis that people's attitudes to features of physical environment are not fixed or immutable, but governed to some extent by social situations and circumstances and therefore amenable to change. What was of particular interest in this study was that even though, in general, there was a positive change in attitude to low-energy lighting, there was a simultaneous negative attitude to the trial schemes.

Technical Assessments

In general, technical assessments tended to confirm the user assessments. In Scheme A, the illuminance range across drawing boards was very large and in one case exceeded a ratio of 9:1, with parts of the task surface receiving very low illuminance. Both discomfort glare (referred to by users as dazzle) and reflected glare (veiling reflections) were measured on many work surfaces. Mechanical adjustability of the board-mounted lamps was in several cases below normally accepted standards. Contrasts between ambient and task levels of light, particularly in Scheme B, exceeded the ratio of 3:1, which other studies have suggested is the maximum acceptable by users (Hawkes et al. 1977).

Outcome of the Trials

As a result of the low evaluations made of both Schemes A and B by user and technical assessments, the designers decided to reject all the tested installations and to search for an alternative low-energy solution. The development of this alternative and the further trials that followed are discussed in the next section.

CASE STUDY 2

Uplighting for Engineering Draftsmen

Background

The difficulties experienced with localized, suspended, and furniture-mounted task lights in meeting the lighting requirements of engineering draftsmen (Case Study 1) led the designers to consider an entirely different form of lighting: indirect lighting.

Uplighting is an odd technique whereby task surfaces are illuminated indirectly by light reflected off the ceiling and walls. It has recently been reintroduced as a result of technical developments in high-pressure discharge lamps. These lamps give high efficiency and long life combined with a color appearance increasingly similar to that of conventional fluorescent lighting.

By adopting the principle of nonuniform task-ambient lighting, it is possible to achieve substantial reductions in energy consumption. One American case study reports a consumption figure well below 10 watts per square meter (Bulleit and Fairbanks 1980), although precise illuminance levels yielded by this installation were not reported. In other cases reported in the U. K., a consumption of 13 watts per square meter was achieved by an uplighter installation that alone provided 300 lux ambient and 500 lux task illuminance on desks grouped adjacent to the uplighters; and also by a combined uplighter and desk-mounted luminaire scheme that gave 2 to 300 lux ambient and 750 lux task illuminance (Bedocs and Page 1980; Lemmons and Robinson 1979).

Although little systematic research was available to assess the value of uplighting in meeting the demanding requirements of engineering draftsmen, discussions with manufacturers supported the designers' notion that reflected indirect light should be better at overcoming problems of lack of uniformity and glare than were the nonuniform direct schemes previously tried.

Method

The Installation

A trial uplighter installation was set up in the client organization's existing offices for feasibility testing. The trial area was occupied over the study period of four weeks by 12 staff members from the client organization, 8 of whom worked mainly at drawing boards, the others at desks. Some, but not all, of these users had taken part in the previous trials. Two alternative schemes were installed for the user trials. The

11-4. The uplighting trial area simulated a section of the future office building. Uplighter mountings were fitted alternately with metal halide and highpressure sodium discharge lamps.

first consisted of four 250-watt metal halide discharge lamps, and the second of the same number of 250-watt high-pressure sodium discharge lamps, each in free-standing luminaires. The trial area was constructed to simulate a small section of the future office building and incorporated a circulation area lit with a strip of fluorescent lamps (fig. 11-4). Both schemes were designed to provide 750 lux on drawing boards at angles up to 30° from the horizontal and 500 lux on desks, at an energy consumption of less than 20 watts per square meter. In this case no additional task lights were provided.

Assessments

As in the previous trial, technical and user assessments of the experimental lighting were integrated. The user assessments were conducted in two ways: first, through participant observation by one researcher who spent a total of three days working in the experimental area alongside staff users; second, through group discussions held at key points of the trial, identically to the previous trials.

Results

Functional Factors

Both technical measurements and user assessments supported the hypothesis that a well-designed uplighting scheme can give a superior performance to conventional overhead direct lighting or to the nonuniform schemes tested in the previous trial, in terms of freedom from glare, veiling reflections, and shadow. It was able to cast uniform light across large work surfaces and at the same time achieve better energy targets.

Measures of illuminance showed that designed levels of 750 lux on the horizontal and inclined plane were reached. At some drawing boards, this level was maintained at drawing board angles of considerably more than 30° to the horizontal. One of the advantages of indirect lighting is the multidirectional illumination of tasks. Clearly good design can take advantage of this feature.

Users of both desks and drawing boards were satisfied with illuminance levels. There was no demand for additional task lighting, although this was in part a result of a local situation in which it had never been supplied. Some desk users were experiencing levels of over 500 lux and found these to be too high. This led to a recommendation that board and desk use should not, when possible, be spatially mixed because the lighting requirements of each were quite distinct.

Aesthetic Factors

Technical assessment indicated some distortion in color rendition by the sodium lamps, but not to an unacceptable degree by normal standards. This would cause problems only where accurate color judgments were called for.

The main criticism was of a general feeling of dimness associated with the yellowish appearance of the sodium light; universally, users stated a preference for the whiter metal halide lamps. Not only was the sodium color said to reduce the clarity of the task, but it was also criticized on aesthetic grounds for conflicting with the color of daylight, which was unanimously preferred. The color of the metal halide source was thought to blend well with daylight.

Walls and ceilings had high luminance and this clearly contributed to the efficient reflection of light. A matte paint finish on the low bulkhead ceiling was found preferable by users to an eggshell finish because the former reduced ceiling luminance to some extent. Users were somewhat critical of the lack of visual interest in the room. This was attributed partly to the uniform white decor in the trial area, and partly to the flattening effect and reduced shading caused by multidirectional light. It was concluded that there was ample scope for creating visual interest through skillful use of color and contrast in decoration and choice of furniture.

Symbolic Factors

There is no doubt that the carefully designed uplighting schemes installed for this project demonstrated objective qualities that exceeded both designers' and users' expectations. Functionally and aesthetically, the schemes proved their ability to meet the engineering draftsmen's exacting requirements, as well as meeting the requirement of low energy consumption. But symbolic factors were also important. In view of the conservative attitudes expressed at the beginning in Case Study 1, it is unlikely that the users would have been receptive to the qualities of a novel form of lighting unless they had been involved in its introduction. The consultations that took place in the first trial paved the way for an open-minded attitude toward the second trial. Even though only a small sample of users was involved, and participants varied somewhat from one trial to the other, the effects of this user involvement penetrated quite deeply into the whole user organization. This was evidenced particularly by the number of interested visitors to the trial area during the second trials. The researchers had asked the company management to allow anybody who was interested to visit and had used display boards to communicate verbally and graphically the nature of the trial. After the formal trial was over, the installations and the display boards were retained as a demonstration of some of the proposed features of the new office building, and interested users continued to visit for several weeks afterwards.

CASE STUDY 3

Uplighting for a Design Partnership

The Installation

Indirect lighting had been installed for trial purposes on two floors of the London offices of a large design consultancy, occupied mainly by architects and engineers. For comparison, a different type of uplighting had been fitted on each floor. The author's firm was commissioned to conduct user evaluations of both schemes.

Lighting on the second floor, which accommodated some 30 workspaces, consisted of fifteen 250-watt mercury halide "Kolorarc" discharge lamps and had been installed for about one year at the time of the user evaluation study. The third floor, with 27 workspaces, was fitted with fifteen 250-watt high-pressure sodium discharge lamps about six months before the study and had since had four extra fittings with similar lamps installed. Both schemes were designed to give average illuminances of around 500 lux on the horizontal work surface. Individual desk-mounted lights were made available where needed. The specified energy performance for the uplighting on each floor was 19 watts per square meter.

The great majority of users from both floors first filled in individual questionnaires to assess various aspects of the lighting quality in their workspaces; they then attended one of a number of small group meetings held with the researchers, at which a structured discussion of issues that users regarded as relevant to evaluating the lighting was conducted.

Results

"It is a tremendous relief to be away from a harsh overhead fluorescent and its incessant flicker which, over the years, I have found damaging to the eyes and exhausting to body and mind." Although not all endorsements of the uplighting were as wholehearted as this one by a draftsman working on the second floor, the main conclusion drawn from the study was that both types of uplighting offered distinct advantages over conventional overhead lighting, particularly for drawing-board users.

As found in Case Study 2, uplighting seemed to be free of the defects often associated with direct lighting. These include: glare, both reflected from bright surfaces and direct from light sources; veiling reflections from work surfaces; shadows on the work surface cast by hand or instrument; and uneven light across a large work surface.

The use of uplighting stimulated lively and mixed views during the group discussions on whether such a system reduced flexibility in workplace layout. To the extent that uplighters require the maintenance of a fixed relationship between each installation and one or more workplaces, they are bound to constrain layout. Users on one floor had discovered this when they moved several work stations beyond a certain distance away from the luminaires. Good design followed by careful space management are both critical for the successful operation of this type of low-energy uplighting scheme.

Although uplighting had these advantages for users, the study concluded that there were also a number of reservations to be made about the trial installations and about the suitability of uplighting for this kind of office work. The first of these concerned the quality of light emitted by the sodium source. Consistent with the findings of several previous studies, users distinguished between the illuminance or "brightness" on a task surface and the clarity with which the task could be perceived. While perceptual clarity from the mercury halide source was not adversely criticized, perceptual clarity afforded by the sodium source at similar illuminance levels consistently was. There was some evidence that this perceived lack of clarity derived from the color-rendering properties of the sodium source. Some users pointed to specific difficulties of color matching or distinguishing color negatives; others attributed lack of clarity to dimness or low illuminance. Although illuminance was equivalent on both floors, evidence from previous studies suggests that in situations of poor color rendition, a higher level of illuminance is required before the lighting is judged satisfactory by users (Boyce 1981, 321–324). The color-rendering (CR) index of the sodium source was similar to that of the mercury halide—about 70—but color rendition has other dimensions than those measured in the CR index, and the precise sodium lamp characteristics that affect visual clarity merit further investigation.

Aesthetic Factors

Consistent with the findings of Case Study 1 and other studies cited (Hawkes et al. 1977), a modicum of contrast in illuminance levels between one surface and another was found to be both pleasing and interesting. With a provision of 500 lux on horizontal work surfaces, the rooms were generally bright, and the gentle modulation of light caused by the distribution of luminaires was generally valued. On one floor, however, excessive contrast was caused by several dark spots in locations where it had been found difficult to place the furniture-mounted luminaires. This revealed very clearly the importance of employing a range of uplighting fittings suited to varying furniture requirements.

As in Case Study 2, both sodium and metal halide lamp types were on trial, and there was an opportunity to compare user reactions to them. In this case, however, the users had worked with a particular type for several months. Intriguingly the user assessments of color appearance differed from those in Case Study 2. A culture of "brand" loyalty appeared to have grown up around the color on each floor. Users on the second floor who worked under the metal halide lamps described them as bright and businesslike, and referred disparagingly to the third-floor sodium color as "gloomy," and like a "boutique" or "disco." Third-floor users, on the other hand, valued their sodium light for its "warmth" and "homeyness," and criticized the second-floor lamps as giving a "cold and clinical" feeling to the room.

Symbolic Factors

The divergence of attitudes between these two subcultures illustrates very clearly the way in which the aesthetic and the symbolic aspects of lighting can become mixed. It shows how difficult it is for the researcher to establish any constant aesthetic preferences, since these are always subject to influence by social and cultural factors, whether the reference is to national culture or to local subcultures.

As in the other cases studied, this case also showed the importance of lighting's symbolic aspects through the process of user involvement. In the individual questionnaires that users completed before the group discussion sessions, a number of users, particularly from the third floor, were extremely critical of their lighting. During the course of consultation, however, it became apparent that this criticism was mainly directed against the way in which the experimental lighting had been introduced: without sufficient consultation of users by management. Assessments of the lighting itself became more favorable (although users were still critical, as indicated above) once users, in the course of discussion, were able to separate out their feelings about the management from their feelings about the lighting.

GENERAL DISCUSSION OF RESULTS

Novel Forms of Office Lighting

Technological advances and the rising price of energy have caused rapid changes in office equipment in recent years, not least in lighting.

Novel forms of office lighting, such as task, task-ambient, and indirect uplighting, are being introduced on the assumption that they can provide objectively satisfying lighting conditions, as well as meet the requirements of reduced energy consumption. The aim of the case studies in this chapter is to illustrate that the success of these novel forms of lighting depends not just on these objective, functional characteristics, but also on lighting users' attitudes toward them. These attitudes are colored by users' perceptions of the lighting's general aesthetic qualities and also by the symbolic role the lighting plays in organizational life, in particular whether users are involved in its introduction—the design management process. The instrumental, aesthetic, and symbolic aspects of lighting all interact with each other. Accurate predictions of the success or failure of particular lighting forms cannot be made unless all three aspects are considered. Social research used to assess the impact of novel lighting forms must be based on a methodology that allows study of interactions among the three aspects. The nature of the various interactions will now be discussed in turn in light of the case studies.

The Functional and the Aesthetic

In the beginning of this chapter, a number of studies were cited showing the way in which users' evaluations of a lighting scheme appeared to be affected by their evaluation of the general overall appearance (McKennan et al. 1980, Hawkes et al. 1977). This interaction can be critical in the case of low-energy, nonuniform lighting schemes because of the close association between the distribution of light around the office and the general appearance of the room. With a uniform scheme, adequate illumination of the task surface also implies good illumination of the room. But the most tempting route for the lighting designer to lowered energy consumption is to concentrate illumination where it is needed and to reduce it where it is not needed. The case studies reported indicate that there is scope for a greatly improved lighting aesthetic along this route: Conventional uniform schemes tend to be criticized as oppressive, uninteresting, and often uncomfortable. But there is also scope for creating lighting environments which are gloomy and depressing. Such reductions in aesthetic quality color the user's assessment of the lighting's objective capability in illuminating the task.

The objectivist might argue that this interaction between functional and aesthetic aspects of lighting in the users' evaluations is irrelevant. What matters is the objective lighting quality: Whether it is appreciated or not is a management problem. But the fact is that office managers find themselves dealing on the one hand with an increasingly articulate body of users and, on the other, with increasingly expensive office technology that, if misused, maladapted, or rejected, can quickly become a wasted resource whatever its objective qualities. In this situation the onus is on the lighting designer to take into consideration the management implications of his or her designs and to give as much weight to the subjective consequences of the lighting as to its objective characteristics.

The importance of room contrast resulting from nonuniform distribution of light was evident in all three cases studied. Another factor, significant in the two uplighting studies, was the effect of color appearance. Objectively, both types of high-intensity discharge lamp used in these studies (the metal halide and the sodium) had the same color-rendering index: approximately 70. Yet under conditions of equal illuminance, in both uplighting studies, users reported that with the sodium light there was some loss of "perceptual clarity." This may be attributed partly to an objective cause, as previously discussed. At the same time, there was also a link between assessments of perceptual clarity and color appearance. In Case Study 3, particularly, those users who were most critical of the appearance of the sodium lighting were also critical of its clarity. Again, to dismiss such subjective criticisms as being without objective foundation is hazardous, because a user who believes that the lighting clarity is inadequate, for whatever reason, is likely to experience and to report the consequences of that inadequacy (e.g., headaches or eyestrain) and to behave accordingly (e.g., by absenteeism). Good design management must understand the importance of the aesthetic in interaction with the functional in users' consciousness.

The Functional and the Symbolic

Evidence of the organizational and individual benefits of user participation in decisions affecting their work was discussed in the beginning of this chapter. The cases studied give specific support to this thesis in the context of attitudes toward lighting. In Case Studies 1 and 3, situations that existed within the organizations concerned were unfavorable to the fair assessment or acceptance by users of novel lighting forms. In Case Study 1, a large group of engineering draftsmen was convinced that the demands of their work could be met only by the high-intensity uniform overhead lighting to which they were accustomed. Initial skepticism about any nonuniform scheme, and particularly task illumination, clearly colored the users' first reactions to the schemes on trial. The effect of participating in the user assessments was to loosen these prejudices and to allow distinction to emerge between users' feelings about novel lighting forms in general, and their more neutral assessments of the objective characteristics of the schemes on trial. Precisely how the group meeting technique can effect this "objectivization" is discussed below.

In Case Study 3 the initial prejudices of the user groups resulted from feelings of noninvolvement in the design management process whereby the trial uplighting schemes had been introduced. The way these feelings colored users' assessments of the lighting was clear from the questionnaire responses made in advance of the small group meetings. Again, the effect of involvement in the group discussions was to allow articulation of attitudes toward the organization as distinct from assessments of the lighting, generating a neutrality from which fair and reasonable judgments could be derived.

The Aesthetic and the Symbolic

It is the basic thesis of this chapter that generalities about user needs and preferences from the physical environment are difficult to establish because of the inevitable intrusion of elements of the social situation into users' judgments. In no aspect of environment is this more true than in the aesthetic. For years, architects have pleaded with social scientists to give them information about people's aesthetic preferences (Heath 1974). And consistently, social scientists have failed to deliver anything but the most diffuse generalities. But it is only from a highly mechanistic model of relations between man and environment that consistent and universal aesthetic preferences would be expected. When the physical environment is thought of as one medium for symbolic communication in the course of social transactions, then it follows that aesthetic preferences are likely to be colored by the part the physical environment plays in the lives of those involved.

The attempt to isolate aesthetic judgments from their social context by studying them in the laboratory has been shown a misguided endeavor, since laboratories have their own social contexts, which are frequently ignored by academic researchers. An alternative strategy, favored in the present thesis, is to rely upon the common sense of users themselves (a much undervalued resource in conventional psychology) to distinguish between social and environmental influences upon their judgments. This is not to imply that a set of universal objective aesthetic preferences is to be found; rather, that the origin of aesthetic judgments in the prevailing social context can be understood through use of appropriate methodology, allowing better and more useful information to be fed back to the designer.

In Case Studies 1 and 2, the most significant aesthetic aspect of the trial lighting was room contrast. The significance of this factor is well established, and evidence that a particular degree of contrast may be generally preferred has been reported (Hawkes et al. 1977). But it was clear in Case Study 1 that perception of room contrast was closely related to subjective experiences of mood, feelings of cheerfulness or oppression, which in turn were linked with general attitudes toward work and the organization. A strong prejudice in favor of uniform high-intensity lighting meant that any departure from uniformity would be prone to adverse comment. The existence of a "culture of expectation," which colors individual reactions to novel events, is one manifestation of the interaction between the aesthetic and the symbolic.

The influence of culture, or of subcultures within an organization, was even more evident in Case Study 3, where the prime aesthetic aspect of the lighting was color appearance. Subcultures grew up around the different colors of the uplighters on the two floors where trial schemes were installed. "Brand loyalty" appeared to be the main characteristic of aesthetic judgments, with no clear preference emerging among users as a whole for one color or the other. This finding appears to support the idea of physical environment as a medium for symbolic communication. In the organizational context, it seems that the lighting color was being used in support of group loyalty and cohesion. Regardless of objective characteristics, in-group cultures branded their own color as "good" and the other as "bad."

It is important that such organizational processes should be understood by researchers. The next section considers methodology that allows them to tap in to organizational culture, and indeed to influence it.

Appropriate Research Methodology

It is difficult, if not impossible, for the researcher using questionnaires to take account of or to understand the organizational context that influences its members' responses to aspects of the physical environment. The symbolic aspects of environment and the way these interact with functional or aesthetic factors can be adequately explored only through direct communication with members of the organization. The researcher who accepts this then has a choice between individual interviews or group discussions. There are a number of reasons a group technique is likely to be more useful and appropriate to the kind of research situation described in this chapter.

The environmental designer is not normally in a position to cater to the varying individual needs of different members of a work organization. He or she is obliged to design for the group and so needs an aggregated response from users. It is possible to aggregate responses from interviews with individual users, but the expression of individual views and opinions in a group situation gives them a value and a validity, both to the researcher and to the user, that they lack outside the group setting. In the course of discussion, individual opinions are modified by the responses of others, and, generally, there emerges some kind of group opinion, one that varies from the one held by many of the individual members, but to which they are prepared or persuaded to subscribe.

This does not mean that a group discussion will always arrive at a complete consensus: That depends on the size of the group and the issues involved and may not necessarily be a good thing if it buries conflicting interests. But the group situation does allow the airing of different views, which, through a process of negotiation in public, can deliver the researcher/designer with a useful aggregated opinion. Furthermore, user involvement in group discussion generates a commitment to any resulting decisions, one that is unlikely to come from interviewing individuals separately.

A full discussion of the dynamics of group consultation is beyond the scope of this chapter. It is, however, a research methodology that should be used with caution, because it is capable of creating situations in which people express strong feelings, which they would normally restrain, about each other and about the organization.

Certainly it is useful and productive for the design researcher to bring together individuals who share the same environment to talk about it. This leads to the second advantage of the group meeting technique: the way in which it allows control over the validity and reliability of individual responses. Much criticism of "subjective" research techniques, that is, taking account of what people have to say, centers on the researcher's difficulty in knowing whether the subject is telling the truth; or indeed whether the subject is *conscious* of the truth.

The group meeting deals with this criticism in three ways. First, public expression of views and opinions makes it difficult for an individual to consciously distort reality. Extreme views tend to be challenged by other members of the group and subsequently modified. Errors of fact are generally corrected, and accounts delivered in the group are generally more reliable than purely individual ones are.

Second, group discussion helps individuals to separate out their attitudes toward different aspects of environment, leading to greater objectivity of response. The cases reported illustrated this well. Users whose assessments of objective characteristics of their lighting were colored by their feelings about the organization were able to separate these elements in the course of discussion. The expression of an extreme view would be challenged by other members of the group; subsequent self-examination would generally reveal the reason for it. The common sense and intellectual ability of a discussion group (regardless of job grade or education level) is a great resource to the researcher in disentangling the interactions between functional, aesthetic, and symbolic aspects of environment in users' responses.

Third is the issue of how, in the realm of attitudes, truth is to be defined. A symbolic interactionist perspective implies that an action, whether verbal or behavioral, is "complete" only when it is publicly expressed. Its meaning and relevance are derived from a shared understanding of its part in social interaction. In the same way that elements of environment such as lighting acquire symbolic meaning through the part they play in organizational life, so individual attitudes and opinions acquire meaning and relevance when expressed in the group setting.

This has important implications not just for understanding an organizational context, but also in considering organizational change. It means that the researcher who uses group discussion techniques is inevitably involved in organizational change, however minor. During the course of a group meeting, new ideas emerge and are made public. Perceptions and opinions change, and these changes are carried over into the rest of the organization. In group discussions, the researcher is tapping into the organization's culture and various subcultures. As was seen in Case Study 3, subcultures may pick on aspects of environment, such as lighting color, to express or reinforce themselves. Since this symbolic function of environmental design affects users' reactions to it and, consequently, the success or failure of the design, the design researcher's ability not only to understand but also to influence organizational culture is important.

Whether such influence becomes manipulative or not is an ethical problem that social researchers invariably have to face. Certainly, researchers using group techniques have scope for organizational change in varying degrees, depending on the situation; the important thing is for them to be aware of this potential.

SUMMARY AND CONCLUSION

The cases studied have illustrated the distinct nature of functional, aesthetic, and symbolic aspects of office lighting in its impact on the user, and the way that the three aspects interact. Functionally, they showed that certain forms of nonuniform low-energy lighting, particularly uplighting, can provide satisfactory, indeed good-quality, light conditions at dramatically reduced levels of energy consumption. Another form of low-energy lighting, furniture-mounted task lighting, created problems of glare and lack of uniformity, which rendered it unsatisfactory to the demanding needs of engineering draftsman. Therefore, however effective low-energy lighting may be functionally, the success or failure of its application has been shown to depend on other factors.

This chapter urges design researchers aiming to assess the impact of office lighting, and design managers wishing to influence the success of particular applications, to take account of the interaction in users' responses to functional, aesthetic, and symbolic aspects of lighting. The aesthetic factor likely to be critical in the case of nonuniform lighting is the effect of contrast between bright and dim areas on the general appearance of the office. The critical symbolic factor in the case of any radical innovation such as low-energy lighting is the extent to which users are involved in the design planning and management process.

A particular research method, the small group meeting technique, was used in the cases studied and is advocated as appropriate both for studying the interaction between different aspects of user response to lighting, and for allowing the design researcher to intervene in the "cultural life" of the organization, in which physical components of the office environment such as lighting frequently play a significant part.

NOTES

1. Boyce (1981) provides a good discussion on criteria for user satisfaction. See, in particular, pp. 289–321 on lighting.
2. For a recent discussion of Mead's work, see Farr (1978), 503–525.
3. The author would like to thank Dr. Peter Boyce of the Electricity Council Research Centre for his help in preparing this chapter.

REFERENCES

Bedocs, L., and R. K. Page. 1980. Some low energy office task lighting systems. Paper presented at Chartered Institute of Building Services National Lighting Conference, London, U.K., March 1980.

Boyce, P. R. 1981. *Human factors in lighting*. London: Applied Science.

Bulleit, D., and K. Fairbanks. 1980. An ambient/task high intensity source office lighting system. *Lighting Design and Application* (June): 41.

Farr, R. M. 1978. On the varieties of social psychology: An essay on the relationships between psychology and the other social sciences. *Social Science Information* 17(4/5), 503–525.

Gans, H. J. 1968. *People and plans: Essays on urban problems and solutions*. New York: Basic Books.

Hawkes, D. J., D. L. Loe, and E. Rowlands. 1977. A note towards the understanding of lighting quality. Report to the Illuminating Engineering Research Institute, New York. Project No. 96-71.

Heath, T. F. 1974. Should we tell the children about aesthetics, or should we let them find out in the street. In D. Canter and T. Lee (Eds.), *Psychology and the built environment*. London: Architectural Press.

Lemons, T. M., and A. V. Robinson. 1979. Exploring indirect lighting. *Lighting Design and Application*. (December): 37.

Louis Harris and Associates. 1978. *The Steelcase national study of office environment: Do they work*? Grand Rapids, MI: Steelcase, Inc.

McKennan, G. T., C. M. Parry, and M. Tilic. 1980. An investigation of task lighting installations. Paper presented at the Chartered Institute of Building Services National Lighting Conference, London, U.K., March 1980.

The Office of the Future

WALTER B. KLEEMAN, JR.
Union Graduate School
Cincinnati, Ohio

The office has come a long way from its known beginnings in religious shelters: money changers conducted business in the Temple at Jerusalem some 2,000 years ago; medieval cathedrals bustled with business activity (they were usually the only protected public open spaces); and many office buildings built as late as 1904, such as Frank Lloyd Wright's Larkin Building, preserved the cathedral floor plan. Offices were in the streets, too, when indoor space became overloaded: "During the South Sea Bubble of 1720, for example, Change Alley was more like a fair crowded with people, than a mart of exchange, as were all the avenues leading to it; and there was a little hump-backed man, who, seeing this mania, made his fortune by lending his back, as a desk to make transfers on, to those who could not afford time to run to the coffee houses" (Mullin 1976, 16).

As of January 1981, the white collar part of America's work force had become a majority at 53% of the total (Towers, Perrin, Foster, and Crosby 1982, 10D), and the office had become a highly organized interior space. By the turn of this century, that 53% will have become more than 70%, and the changes inside that highly organized interior space will be

* Walter B. Kleeman, Jr., "The Office of the Future," *Environment and Behavior,* vol. 14, no. 5 (September 1982), pp. 595–609. Copyright © 1982 by Sage Publications. Reprinted by permission.

considerable (Falluchi 1982, 39). Another measure of the significance of the office work force is that "in 1980, 60% of the $1.3 trillion paid out for wages, salaries and benefits in the U. S. went to office workers" (Uttal 1982, 196). Abelson (1982, 752) adds: "Two-thirds of the work force [in the U.S.] is concerned with information handling."

Today a growing share of information handling in the office is accomplished with the aid of computers and other electronic devices. So the first questions about the future of the office must be: Is the office as we know it obsolete? Are its artifacts obsolete? The chances are that both are. Why? The reasons concern technical changes in the office and modifications in human behavior resulting from these technical changes. Consider the computer as a factor in technical changes in the office. According to Roger Martin (1981),

A Video Display Terminal (VDT) is installed in an office somewhere in this country every 13 minutes. . . . There's one VDT for every twenty office desks right now [October 1981], and by 1990, there will be one for every three desks. . . . The number of desks will be increasing, too. . . . This part of the labor force [office workers] is growing at the rate of 2% annually and already numbers nearly 50 million people. . . . Right now there are approximately 1.2 million large business computers in this country. By 1985 the figure will be 5.4 million or 1 for every 42 people.

Skerritt (1982, 42) pointed out that "IBM expects to have one terminal for every two employees by 1986." Martin (1981) quotes Stanford University economist Edward Steinmuller: "If airline technology had changed as rapidly as computer technology, the Concorde would be carrying half a million passengers at 20 million miles per hour . . . for less than a penny per passenger."

There are many problems arising from the use of computers in the office and the literature dealing with them is growing. In addition to the works cited below, substantial portions of the *Human Factors Journal* (Bhise and Rinalducci 1981, 385–438, 515–586) are devoted to the health effects of CRT viewing. Job stress, radiation, visual fatigue, and other industrial hygiene issues are identified as health concerns. Cakir, Hart, and Stewart (1980) have provided an important comprehensive study of the computer terminal workplace done in England and Germany. This work discusses the emerging technologies of flat panel display devices: plasma panels, vacuum fluorescence, electroluminescence, light-emitting diodes, and liquid crystals, as well as their potential health effects. (In the summer of 1983, IBM began widely marketing an electroluminescent flat screen.) Grandjean and Vigliani (1980) held an international workshop on the Ergonomic Aspects of Visual Display Terminals in Milan that dealt with similar health topics from the European as well as the American point of view; a trade union examination of VDTs is included in the proceedings.

Fatigue is also an issue. Mauro (1981, 29) reports that "for example, Volkswagen requires a minimum rest period of 15 minutes per hour for all workers who interact with a VDT for extended periods." Makower (1981, 104) states that "in Germany agreements have been reached between banks and bank tellers for the following breaks: 10 minutes after 60 minutes of "feeding" the computer and 10 minutes after 50 minutes of reading from the screen." He also quotes a NIOSH (National Institute of Safety and Health) recommendation that "there should be mandatory work-rest breaks of at least 15 minutes every two hours for workers under high visual demands (p. 106)."

In another context, W. J. Smith (1981, 370) underscores the "at best, minimal training" that some "unskilled, untrained users receive"; this is an important factor because training might forestall some of the fatigue problems, especially better training to show the operator how the furniture may be adjusted for greater comfort. In any event, the recovery value of the breaks is undisputed, although exact times allowed for them varies, and much research remains to be accomplished in this area.

COMPUTER TERMINAL FURNITURE DESIGN

A number of studies suggest that the design of the computer terminal workplace may be at least partially responsible for the long list of health concerns voiced by video display terminal (VDT) operators: headaches (perhaps from visual overload and fatigue); excess electromagnetic radiation; photosensitive epileptic episodes; muscle, joint, and tendon pain (especially in the neck, back, and wrist); irritability; depression; anxiety; blurred vision; burning and irritated eyes; eye strain; and glare discomfort.

Need for Adjustability

Stewart (1980, 233–240), in analyzing 17 different designs for computer terminal workplaces, found that 27% of them had no chair adjustability and that for 95%, it was poor:

The majority of the chairs had some adjustability but it was usually difficult to use. Typically it involved getting off the chair and exerting considerable force on a knurled knob. As a consequence, these chairs were seldom adjusted. Only one type of workplace had a gas-lift chair action and these were fully exploited by the users (p. 236).

12-1. Chair suitable for use by a computer terminal operator. It has push-button controls underneath the seat to control seat height, back angle, and back height, and it allows the full 120° tilt necessary for the relaxed posture preferred by the majority of terminal operators. (Courtesy Comfort, Inc.)

Stewart also found that 94% of the workplaces he examined had no adjustability in the other work station furniture—particularly the work surface heights and inclinations on desks and tables.

A study of terminal operators conducted by Miller and Suther (1981, 492–496) indicated that many adopt postures similar to those associated with driving a car; the results of their study may change the needed ranges of adjustments for chairs and work surfaces and it reinforces Hünting, Läubli, and Grandjean's (1981) recommendation that a terminal operator's chair have a back at least 50 cm (20 in.) high above the seat and have adjustable seat height and adjustable inclination (the angle between the seat and back of the chair) to accommodate the relaxed posture observed in their studies. The ranges for these adjustments remain tentative awaiting further research in this area.

In a subsequent study, Grandjean (1980) confirmed these findings, saying, "The great majority of VDT operators adopt a very special seating posture; they lean the trunk backwards with angles of 105 degrees to 120 degrees.'' Grandjean, Hünting, and Piderman (1983) say further, "VDT operators exhibit a good instinct when they prefer a backward leaned trunk posture and ignore the recommended upright trunk position (p. 173)'' and cite the Swedish and Japanese studies of Nachemson and Elfstrom (1970), Andersson and Ortengren (1974), and Yamaguchi and Ishinada (1972), which show that reduced muscle activity and reduced intervertebral disc pressure are associated with the more relaxed posture.

Grandjean, Nishiyama, Hünting, and Piderman (1982) found fewer physical complaints when adjustable work surfaces were used than when "imposed" or nonadjustable work surfaces were employed, saying, for instance, "the range of preferred keyboard heights lies between 71 cm (28 in.) and 84 cm (33 in.). If the subjects can choose the heights inside of this frame, the complaints are reduced to a minimum but, as soon as a uniform level of 74 cm (29.1 in.) is imposed, the complaints increase" (p. 299).

Grandjean and associates (1982) above found in their final evaluation of the adjustable work station that 66% of the keyboard operators they studied preferred a keyboard with hand support; 78% found that the hand support did not hinder their work on the keyboard; 97% felt that a height-adjustable keyboard table was useful; 97% felt that a height-adjustable

12-2. A portable, movable terminal table for users who must share a single terminal. Keyboard and screen surfaces are adjustable separately, using gas cylinders. (Courtesy Knoll International)

screen was useful; and 97% felt that the screen distance should be adjustable. As Grandjean and associates (1982) state:

From all these considerations and from our results, two conclusions become obvious: (1) Adjustable VDT work stations enable the assessment of preferred settings and of relaxed postures in the back-shoulder-arm-hand area; (2) No recommended single uniform dimension falls into the frame of all individual ranges of tolerable limits; that is, no single figure can suit everybody. Adjustable work stations are therefore suitable (p. 304).

Hünting and associates (1981) set forth these recommendations for the design of terminal workplaces:

There should be separate vertical adjustments for the keyboard, display screen and documents. Keyboard surfaces should be close to the table top. Keyboards should be movable. It is important to provide space to support forearms and hands; this is especially important for conversational terminals. Seats should have high backrests and adjustable inclination. Good readability of terminal characters and documents is necessary to allow visual distances of 40–80 cm (15.75–31.5 in.). A work organization is required that permits a reduction of the repetitive character of the work and a greater diversity of movement (p. 943).

Most of the authors above agree that the computer terminal workplace should be free of veiling reflectances (glare). This can be accomplished by using window-shading devices, "matte finishes of reflective surfaces, baffles beneath ceiling lights, VDT glare screens and hoods (Waters 1983, 74)," making the terminal platform tiltable and providing the operator with adjustable task lighting.

Anthropometric Considerations

Evidence for the adjustment needs shown above may be found in NASA's Reference Publication 1024, *Anthropometric Source Book* (Webb Associates 1978). Several ranges of specific anthropometric measurements are cited later in this section. The extremes available for each dimension are used (1st and 99th percentiles where available, and 5th and 95th percentiles where the 1st and 99th are not available). Using these extremes is not the traditional method that designers have employed; some designers use dimensions from only 5th percentile to 95th and some use 10th to 90th.

The NASA material comes from studies of a wide variety of races and nations around the world: the United States, Czechoslovakia, Holland,

12-3. One type of adjustable VDT work station. Here the distance between screen and keyboard is fixed because both move up and down together. (Courtesy Spec' Built)

West Germany, England, Sweden, Australia, Japan, Turkey, Greece, Italy, France, Bantu (Africa), Canada, New Zealand, Chile, Panama, Columbia, Ecuador, Bolivia, Peru, Venezuela, South Africa, Thailand, Vietnam, Korea, and Iran. Every one of these is represented in the United States, which has the most diverse ethnic and racial mix of any country in the world and unless the extremes are used, many of our largest and smallest people cannot be comfortably accommodated by designs for furniture and interiors.

There are drawbacks to the NASA material, even though it is the best available. Some of the samples are small and many of them are not recent; therefore, it is quite possible that some of the extents of difference shown below might be even larger. There is evidence, for instance, from U.S. Air Force anthropometric studies that American body dimensions are changing; we are becoming a group of larger people (Kleeman 1983, 108). There may be recent differences in other lands and races as well.

Here, then, are the measurements and their ranges from NASA Reference Publication 1024, Volume 2 (Webb Associates 1978):

Measurement #32, Acromion to Dactylion Length: 26.1 in. (66.2 cm) to 33.1 in. (84.0 cm). This is essentially a measurement of the length of the human arm. Extent of difference: 7 in. (17.8 cm).

Measurement #80, Arm Reach from Wall: 27.9 in. (70.8 cm) to 38.5 in. (97.9 cm). Extent of difference: 10.6 in. (27.1 cm).

Measurement #194, Buttock-Knee Length: 18.2 in. (46.3 cm) to 26.9 in. (68.3 cm). Extent of difference: 8.7 in. (22 cm).

Measurement #200, Buttock-Popliteal Length: 14.8 in. (37.7 cm) to 22.8 in. (57.9 cm). Extent of difference: 8 in. (20.2 cm).

Measurement #312, Elbow Rest Height: 6 in. (15.4 cm) to 12.6 in. (32 cm). Extent of difference: 6.6 in. (16.6 cm).

Measurement #330, Eye Height, Sitting: 25.9 in. (65.7 cm) to 34.9 in. (88.7 cm). Extent of difference: 9 in. (23 cm).

Measurement #381, Forearm-Hand Length: 14.7 in. (37.4 cm) to 21.2 in. (53.8 cm). Extent of difference: 6.5 in. (16.4 cm).

Measurement #529, Knee Height, Sitting: 16.6 in. (42.2 cm) to 24.6 in. (62.4 cm). Extent of difference: 8 in. (20.2 cm).

Measurement #572, Maximum Reach from Wall: 30.5 in (77.4 cm) to 43.1 in. (109.5 cm). Extent of difference: 12.6 in. (32.1 cm).

Measurement #612, Midshoulder Height, Sitting: 20.6 in. (52.3 cm) to 28 in. (71.1 cm). Extent of difference: 7.4 in. (18.8 cm).

Measurement #666, Patella Top Height: 15.2 in. (38.6 cm) to 24 in. (61.1 cm). Extent of difference: 8.8 in. (22.5 cm).

Measurement #678, Popliteal Height: 13.3 in. (33.4 cm) to 20.3 in. (51.4 cm). Extent of difference: 7 in. (18 cm).

Measurement #758, Sitting Height: 29.6 in. (75.2 cm) to 39.7 in. (100.8 cm). Extent of difference: 10.1 in. (25.6 cm).

Measurement #867, Thumb-Tip Reach: 24.5 in. (62.2 cm) to 37.3 in. (94.6 cm). Extent of difference: 12.8 in. (32.4 cm).

Focusing on the differences in the body measurements above gives some indications of the extent of adjustability required for computer terminal operators' comfort and health; however, body measurements alone do not provide a definitive solution to the problem of adjustability; a number of other factors are involved. An example is the influence of the relaxed posture found by Miller and Suther (1981), and Grandjean and associates (1982) as described above. Some of these influencing factors are yet unknown and much research remains to be accomplished in this area.

The work of Kroemer and Robinette (1968), as analyzed by Kleeman (1983, 93), indicates that a range of seat height adjustability of from 13.3 inches (33.4 cm) to 20.3 inches (51.4 cm) might be needed; however

12-4. A fully adjustable VDT work station. Keyboard and screen surfaces adjust up and down separately, and each can be tilted. Height-adjustable auxiliary surfaces in either a triangular or a rectangular form can be attached to either side. (Courtesy Steelcase, Inc.)

Damon, Stoudt, and McFarland (1966) present evidence for a needed adjustability range of 9.5 inches (24.1 cm). This would relate to the extents of difference for popliteal height, 7 inches (17.8 cm); patella top height, 8.8 inches (22.6 cm); and knee height sitting, 8 inches (20.2 cm). However, the relaxed posture described above might call for lower seat and keyboard heights as well as a higher screen height.

To obtain indications for the range of keyboard height adjustment we might look at the ranges above together with elbow rest height where the extent of difference is 6 inches (16.6 cm). Kroemer and associates (1968), as analyzed by Kleeman (1983, 113), suggest typing heights from

12-5. Even in olden times, an adjustable document holder with adjustable lighting was needed. (Courtesy Hickory Chair Company)

20.5 inches (52.1 cm) to 26.5 inches (67.3 cm); however, their work was directed at ordinary typists' tasks and was done before the computer became so pervasive in the office.

One manufacturer of computer terminal furniture offers 22 inches (55.9 cm) to 32 inches (81.8 cm) for keyboard height adjustment; this is probably close to what is needed for sit-down work. Another manufacturer's adjustment system allows keyboard surface heights from 26 inches (66 cm) to 42 inches (106.8 cm), which, while its lower limit is a bit too high, does allow a stand-up position as well as a sit-down one.

For the needed adjustment of the screen, it might be useful in setting the range to take the following extents of difference into consideration: for eye height, sitting, 9 inches (23 cm); midshoulder height, 7.4 inches

(18.8 cm); and sitting height, 10.1 inches (25.5 cm). Each of these manufacturers offers the same range of adjustment for the screen as for the keyboard; the 26-inch to 42-inch range probably is better for the relaxed postures discussed above.

The cathode ray tube (CRT) surface needs to be tiltable. Grandjean and associates (1982) found a preferred range of from 82° to 104° for the horizontal surface. They also found the satisfactory range of head inclinations to be from 34° to 65° which might affect the needed height adjustment for the CRT.

The keyboard surface must also have the capability of moving toward or away from the user. This adjustment range would be affected by the extents of difference for acromion to dactylion length, 7 inches (17.8 cm); arm reach from the wall, 10.6 inches (27.1 cm); forearm-hand length, 6.5 inches (16.4 cm); maximum reach from the wall, 12.6 inches (32.1 cm); and thumb-tip reach, 12.8 inches (32.5 cm). One manufacturer cited above offers a 10-inch (25.4 cm) range for this adjustment, which, based on present knowledge, seems adequate.

Current Trends

To mitigate fatigue and the various physical discomforts and ills listed above, furniture specifically designed for computer terminal users has appeared on the market, both here and in Europe. Facit says that its first adjustable terminal work surface appeared in 1975 in Sweden and NKR in the same country was not far behind. In March 1981, International Business Machines Corporation (IBM) introduced its own line of height-adjustable terminal work surfaces and height-adjustable chairs in the United States. This line includes a height-adjustable desk as called for by Kleeman (1983, 114–115, 117). Since that time more than four dozen furniture makers in the United States have launched lines of computer terminal furniture competitive to those of IBM.

Various kinds of furniture have also appeared to make terminal sharing easier; this may consist of a revolving lazy susan embedded in the work surface or it may take the form of 120° work stations that allow three workers to share one terminal. Portable terminal tables, also height-adjustable using gas cylinders and with heavy casters, are on the market, too. When more than one operator uses the same chair, it may need gas cylinder adjusting devices for quick and easy changes. As Driscoll, Marzeki, and Wilson (1982) put it, "it may be 'hot-seated,' scheduled for use by different workers at different times of day. . . . Such chairs must be sophisticated in their adjustability" (p. 8).

Productivity

Evidence is beginning to appear indicating that use of the adjustable furniture described above and use of flexible, changeable furnishings increase the productivity of office workers.

Springer (1982) conducted a study of productivity in the offices of a major insurance company, comparing the work of those employees using adjustable computer furniture with the work of employees using conventional, nonadjustable office furniture:

Improvements in performance were observed for each of the alternative work station designs when compared to the present company standard. The NKR and IBM work stations resulted in a 15% improvement in data entry performance and a 10% improvement in dialog transactions.

Employees showed a strong preference for the NKR, IBM and Gutmann work stations on the basis of comfort, ease of adjustment, space and adequacy with which job needs were met [all three used gas-cylinder adjusting chairs].

Characteristics of work stations with the greatest importance to employees were comfort, ability to adjust the furniture themselves and height adjustment in the writing surface, the terminal screen surface and the keyboard surface. Seating characteristics included seat height adjustment, back height adjustment, ability to turn while seated and back tilt adjustment (p. 5).

The abstract of a study by Dainoff, Fraser, and Taylor (1982) at the National Institute for Occupational Safety and Health states:

An experimental simulation of a VDT entry task was conducted during five three-hour sessions in which subjects worked under ergonomic conditions alternating between good and poor features as defined by adjustments of working and seating surfaces, lighting and glare. Performance measures were taken during each session and a battery of psychophysical/physiological measures and subjective complaints were taken before and after each work session. Preliminary results indicated a 24.5% improvement in performance as well as a decrease in musculoskeletal complaints attributed to good ergonomic design characteristics (p. 144).

IBM and Wrightline work stations were used as well as ergonomically designed lighting and glare reduction equipment to produce the total result.

Human Factors/Industrial Design, Inc. (Brookes and Mitchell 1982) conducted a productivity research project sponsored by Westinghouse Open Office System Furnishings at Blue Cross/Blue Shield of Michigan. Productivity measures were taken in a standard bull pen office where the desks were laid out in long rows with no screens or partitions between them. These employees were then moved to an office fitted out with Westinghouse screens and component furniture. The results, as reported by Westinghouse, were that "compared to the estimated national average of 0.4 percent growth in white collar productivity, the Blue Cross/Blue Shield workers showed an average 5.5 percent increase. . . . improvement value per employee [was] $979 [per] year . . . [the] payback on office furnishings [was] 23 months" (Brookes and Mitchell 1982, 3).

Further evidence (though much of it is anecdotal) of increased productivity comes from *White Collar Productivity: The National Challenge*, a series of studies sponsored by Steelcase, Inc. and conducted by the American Productivity Center (Steelcase 1983). The following is a summary of their findings.

1. Bethlehem Steel's automation of its offices produced the following estimated improvements: Increased output, 20%; more timely delivery, 80%; credibility of offices improved, 20%; work force morale improved, 20%; task difficulty reduced, 20%; communication facilitated, 50%; office space more effectively used, 25%; response time reduced, 80%; errors reduced, 5%; and quality of service enhanced, 50%.

2. Blue Cross/Blue Shield of Virginia started a comprehensive study of its offices in 1973 and has been automating and redesigning workflow since then. Claims processed per labor hour rose from 1.6 in 1973 to 4.22 in 1982, an increase of 164%. Measured another way, by claims processed per employee (full-time equivalent), this measure showed a rise from 2,857 to 7,563 over the same time period, yielding an almost identical percentage increase.

3. "Continental Insurance is based in Piscataway, NJ. With 40 branches around the country, its total staff in early 1980 was 7,000. By the end of 1982, this figure dropped to about 5,500 in 36 branch offices. This [more than] 20% staff reduction resulted largely from attrition and an early retirement program. However, partially due to a large-scale productivity measurement effort which tracked branch office activity, service actually improved 12.5% in the same time period. . . . From the end of 1981 through 1982, productivity [work load compared to staffing] rose 18.4% . . . and branch expenses dropped about 5%."

4. Federal-Mogul made microcomputers and software packages available to departments wishing to try them for six months. "No plant has exercised its option to return the equipment. . . . Several . . . plants use spread sheets to execute complex equations used in manufacturing. In these cases, they have replaced Fortran programs, formerly run

via timesharing [on a mainframe], [with the minicomputers] *paying back* on the $3,500 systems in *four months*."

5. First Bank of Edina, Minnesota, was reorganized, training programs were revitalized, and "the physical facility was made more comfortable . . . [with] new carpeting, contemporary office furniture and improved air quality control. . . . The work stations are comprised of modular units with partitions which enhance employee privacy and reduce noise and distractions. . . . An independent bank staffing analysis revealed that overall efficiency improved from 77.8% in May 1980 to 93% in November 1982." During this same time period the number of employees dropped from 146 to 126.

6. According to Honeywell, "introduction of technology into an office may be furthered by exposing the appropriate personalities. Management . . . observed that their electronic systems were more readily accepted in offices where extroverted, 'social' personnel used the systems first. Apparently such persons were more likely to discuss the technology over lunch, seek out new uses for the system and encourage their colleagues to overcome basic fears. Where more reserved, introverted persons were the initial users, interest and development of applications were slow to evolve. . . . Finally, the branch managers experienced a favorable employee response to the open landscape concept. While some employees were potentially confronted with less privacy and more distraction, the majority responded favorably due to more professional appearing surroundings and greater personal space than was possible with conventional designs."

7. London Life, London, Ontario, extensively polled its employees before refurbishing and automating their offices. "The polls indicated inadequate facilities and equipment were the most serious obstacles to productivity improvement." The designer selected to do the job asked two key questions of each employee: "(1) What do you need to do your job? (2) Who do you need to be close to?" It was found that "Productivity improvements have been accomplished through participative planning. As a result little apprehension is expressed by employees, an accomplishment for a company that has undergone a major organizational change and staff reduction [2,100, to 1,500] during the same period. . . . Top management recently announced a corporate productivity increase of 10.6% last year [1982]. Currently there are 84 different productivity measures. . . . In fact, productivity has risen at London Life from 5% to 10% annually over the last five years."

8. Memorial Hospital Southwest in Houston installed computerized

record management and word-processing equipment and upgraded office procedures in its radiology department with the following results: "(1) The number of radiology reports transcribed increased from a baseline of 70 per month per typist to between 95 to 121 per month per typist. (2) The average number of overtime hours decreased from 25.12 hours to 4.50 hours per pay period. (3) The distribution of x-ray reports to patient floors became more time effective, improving from a 7 PM distribution baseline to 5:50 PM."

9. "The corporate culture at Polaroid has been a decisive factor in the shaping of office automation efforts and policy. Autonomous initiative of individuals and business units is highly valued." This corporate climate became very helpful during a necessary staff reduction from more than 18,000 persons in 1978 to about 14,000 by 1982. One example of savings in hard dollars occurred in the Polaroid Materials Laboratory. Before word-processing equipment was introduced, the laboratory had two professionals at $30,000 each per year and six typists at $16,667 each per year for a total cost of $160,000. After word-processing equipment was installed, three professionals at $30,000 each handled the work load that had formerly required eight persons, at a total annual cost of $90,000; the annual cost savings was $70,000.

10. The Southern Company is the second largest utility company in the United States and the largest investor-owned one. In 1979 its Southern Company Services subsidiary started a program to increase productivity in its Engineering Division. "To provide visibility, the 'Engineering, Productivity and Information Center' (EPIC) was created. EPIC, a conference room with walls covered by graphic representations of engineering productivity measures, was built specifically for this purpose. Currently 97 charts representing 193 indicators are in use. . . . Employees now strive to improve their measures and many units within Engineering are posting charts in their own office areas. A competitive spirit has developed as the EPIC concept is utilized, in microcosm, throughout the organization." One example of the results is that "savings of 3 to 1 have been realized over manual drafting methods with automated drafting equipment. At present, Engineering has five complete automated drafting systems operating on three shifts producing 30% to 35% of their drawings."

Although it is not apparent in some of the brief excerpts above, a main theme running through all of these Steelcase-American Productivity Center case histories is: *Get full cooperation and participation from all employees. Find out what they need. Involve them in the productivity process.*

Since most of the studies excerpted above covered a period when this country was in a recession, it is not surprising that several of them involve significant reductions in staff. However, considering the large amounts of savings reported and that the pace of office automation is still increasing, the question arises: How many of those people who lost their jobs are going to get them back even in a period when economic activity is increasing?

THE CHANGING OFFICE TECHNOLOGY

Any estimates of adjustability ranges needed must be tentative for another reason: The computers themselves are changing. Technical changes and new models are introduced almost daily; computer technology is anything but static, and the changes will keep on coming. This underlines the growing need for adjustable, flexible, and changeable interior furnishings so that interiors can be easily rearranged and altered to accommodate these continuing advances. For example, field reports say that the advent of flat wire cable under movable carpet tiles has solved many electrical and telephone change problems.

Smaller and Less Expensive

The value of flexible, movable furnishings will increase as the tempo of technical change in computers continues. For instance, computers are getting smaller and less expensive with continuing improvements in the technologies of the semiconductor, microchip, and microprocessor.

Eastman Kodak (1982, 13) sees the future possibility of "molecule-size electronic devices" and Chace (1983) reports that

a small number of computer scientists are engrossed in trying to prove that someday it will be possible to create an organic computer or "biochip," an incredibly small package of computer circuits assembled from molecules. They hope that their research in molecular electronics will result in a new generation of computers that is many times smaller, faster and cheaper than today's state-of-the-art machines assembled from silicon micro-circuits. The work so far is purely theoretical (p. 1).

There is also renewed interest in piezoelectric materials for computers; mechanisms using them can turn pressure into electricity or electricity into pressure (Shaffer, 1981a, 29). Surface Acoustic Wave (SAW) devices form a new technology being used now because, according to Shaffer (1981b, 27), "for their size, weight and power needs they are thousands of times faster than the electronic computer circuits that do the same work."

Although computers have become small enough and efficient enough that a small business computer can be housed in what looks like a simply designed single-pedestal desk (available now on the American market), there are other results of the continuing miniaturization: It is now possible for firms with large computers to provide their executives with small, personal computers. An advertisement in the *Wall Street Journal* (1981a, 5) for Apple computers shows a "big eight" CPA firm with not only a very large computer for the firm's use, but also Apple computers for its partners.

There may be barriers, however, to the use of such secondary systems. Haavind (1981) sees corporate politics and empire building as preventing their use in some corporations; he notes "the difficulty in breaking through the empires that have grown up around multi-million-dollar data-processing facilities in large organizations (p. 30)." Brancatelli (1981) points out that until voice-activated or touch-activated computers become widespread, "managers and professionals will be asked to operate their work stations by typing messages on a keyboard. Unfortunately, 'keyboarding' is a skill that is still too close to the typing tasks managers have traditionally delegated to secretaries" (p. 87). Will managers and executives "lower" themselves and learn to type? It may be that executives will be more likely to "type" as computers become more "user-friendly" and accept English language commands rather than computer language ones.

There are some who are doing it now. Uttal (1982, 196) tells of companies where the chief executive officer puts a terminal in his office and uses it; then the practice spreads down through the company. He cites as examples Lincoln National Life, Merrill Lynch, Northwest Industries, and Schering-Plough and quotes a Schering-Plough spokesman as saying, "We're putting in electronic mail and we're driving it from the top down. People have an incentive to use the system if the boss may have left them a message" (p. 196).

New Mail Methods

Several devices now on the market, known as Voice Mail or Electronic Mail equipment, contribute strongly to the paperless office. Services provided by one such system, Outvoice (Voice & Data Systems, Inc. 1981, 1–2) include: Message Deposit, Message Retrieval (from any phone), Message Transfer, Mass Calling, Future Calling, and Personal Greeting. As Brancatelli states (1981, 95), "from any phone" above means that "remote dictation and transcribing" is now possible "from anywhere in the world." Electronic mail is already international; Spinrad (1982, 812) tells of receiving an electronic communication from Vienna directly to his office in Palo Alto, California: "it was simply . . . waiting for me one morning in my electronic mail."

Inman (1983, 16) reported that MCI Communications Corporation is offering a new service where its customers can send letters within the United States using their own personal computers and MCI's telephone lines; MCI Mail charges $2 for the first 7,500-character block sent within its own system. Meanwhile, Western Union (1983, 16) is advertising "Reach anyone with your small computer," touting its EasyLink services that link a personal computer with "more than 1.5 million businesses in 154 countries" who have Telex service from Western Union.

Another innovation that increases the understandability of international communications is the development of a much faster method of generating ideographic languages (Chinese, Japanese) electronically for Telex messages (*Wall Street Journal* 1980, 1).

One factor that points up the growing significance of these advances in communication technology is the continuing deterioration of the U.S. Postal Service. It is no longer a completely reliable means of communication, thus giving impetus to other means of transmitting information. The *Wall Street Journal* (1982a, 1) reported that "about 6% to 9% of the mail in recent tests never reached its destination at all, the Direct Mail Marketing Association says."

Video Disc Storage

Advances in computer and information technology are continuing. Brancatelli (1981, 95) says that although video disc systems are thought of as home entertainment devices, a laser-optical type of video disc for information storage will find much use in the office because it increases the amount of information that can be stored and greatly improves access to that information. Anderson (1982) reports that a video disc-based storage facility called Megadoc, made by Phillips, can store 3,465,000 pages of information, including printed matter, motion pictures, and graphics. According to *High Technology* (1982, 46), "strips of optical recording material can be embossed in plastic. . . . A 1.25 cm. by 7.5 cm. strip . . . could hold 1.2 million bits of data while a magnetic strip the same size holds only 1700 bits." The magnetic strips on credit cards are approximately 1.25 cm by 7.5 cm.

Micrographics

According to Gupta (1982), "micrographics aids filing, storage and retrieval of large amounts of information. Micrographic systems range from simple step and repeat cameras and viewers to sophisticated centers that include cameras, computer output microfiche and processors for cross-referencing, archival storage, supplemented by intelligent viewing systems. Present day systems can replace 250 filing cabinets in one-eighth the space and retrieve the desired information in 8 seconds. Further, they can be linked to intelligent copiers and terminals connecting executives. A recent example is the Eastman Kodak IMT-150 that merges computer and micrographics technology to retrieve records from microimage files (p. 233)." Micrographics is being widely used in conjunction with large mainframe computers.

Optical Wire

Information transmission wiring is also improving; American Telephone & Telegraph Company (AT&T) is a leader in the use of glass fibers (optical wire that carries light waves) for voice, data, and television transmissions. In an advertisement, AT&T (1983, 7) states that it has in service "250,000 miles of fiber in 60 lightwave communications routes" and that "a single light-guide cable can carry 240,000 telephone calls at once."

This technology, which is immune to electromagnetic interference, is also known as *guided wave optics* and promises to cut costs and reduce space needs for transmission lines.

Networks

Also noted is the increasing use of the millimeter bands of radio waves as well as cordless telephones and cordless printers, together with another phenomenon that could revolutionize much of the office world—networks. Now that computers can talk to one another without human intervention, Xerox Corporation, backed by Digital Equipment and Intel corporations, is promoting its network, called Ethernet. This network is "essentially a coaxial cable that would be installed in walls and conduits much as standard electrical and telephone lines are installed. Machines designed to fit the system could simply be plugged in," according to Tannenbaum and Bulkeley (1981, 10). These machines are electronic office files and printers as well as other types of machines. Kleiner (1980, 534–536) describes several personal and expert computer networks that are already in place. According to Driscoll and associates (1982), "the network is the vehicle. All the powers of modern technology are made available to the work force through it. The machines become what the user wants them to be, and the implementing mechanism is the telecommunications network" (p. 70).

One of the problems with networks has been that computers and other electronic office devices made by one manufacturer cannot communicate with those made by another manufacturer. However, it was announced in the *Wall Street Journal* (1982c, 6), that a new AT&T subsidiary will offer "Advanced Communications Service over which dissimilar computers will be able to 'talk' to one another." This system is called Unix and General Electric has announced a system, called GEnet, for the same purpose, (*Wall Street Journal* 1982f, 16). Also, the giant of the computer industry, IBM, announced a nationwide information network in the same newspaper (1982, 6), and Bulkeley and White (1982, 29) have stated that IBM will go after the local network business with new methods of joining office machines together. IBM is one of the few computer makers who manufacture almost all of the various electronic devices that are joined together in a network.

CAD, CAE, and CAM

Building on the networks discussed above will be three technologies already in place: Computer Aided Design (CAD), Computer Aided Engineering (CAE), and Computer Aided Manufacturing (CAM).

At the National Exposition of Contract Furnishings (NEOCON) in Chicago in June 1982, Steelcase, Inc., the world's volume leader in office furniture manufacturing, in combination with Intergraph, an established firm in the growing field of CAD, had an operating on-line CAD system in their showroom. This system is derived from a full-capability interactive graphics system packaged for the interior design and architectural professions; the Steelcase-Intergraph package is aimed at the office designer. Another office furniture maker, Herman Miller, also has such a system.

What this system produces on the screen, in its memory, and on paper comes from its software packages: architectural production drawings, engineering production drawings, 3-D solid modeling, and space planning/ facility management programs. The 3-D modeling turns out to be a rather crude (at this stage of the art) but provides an accurate rendering of an interior space and its furnishings. It is probably less misleading and certainly faster and less expensive than conventional renderings, especially for firms doing a high volume of sometimes repetitive office design. It can save quite a bit of designer drudgery.

However, the increased productivity afforded by CAD, CAE, and CAM in the manufacturing process should be mentioned. According to Hughes Aircraft Company (1982), "through intimate teamwork between engineering and manufacturing functions and ever-increasing use of computers, electronics firms are boosting productivity even as their products grow more technically advanced. Computer-aided design and manufacturing routinely offer productivity improvements on the order of 4-to-1 and sometimes as high as 10-to-1'' (p. 14).

Robots

CAD, CAE, and CAM are already, and in the future will increasingly be, connected to robots that will accomplish the physical actions needed in the office and on the manufacturing floor. There is a somewhat eerie report in *Fortune* (1982, 11) that describes Seiuemon Inaba, president of Fujitsu Fanuc, a Japanese world leader in robotics and numerical controls, watching "the company's robots at work making robots" on a TV screen in his office. *Fortune* (1982, 11) also announced that General Motors has teamed with Fujitsu Fanuc in a joint venture, GMFanuc Robotics Corporation, to manufacture industrial robots in a suburb of Detroit. However, most of the robots around the world are so-called dumb robots; they do what they are programmed for, automatically, and they have been very useful doing jobs that are repetitive, boring, and sometimes dangerous, especially in the auto industry.

An example of a robot that started out "dumb" and is getting smarter is the Bell & Howell Mailmobile® (Bell & Howell 1982, 30). This mail delivery vehicle is self-propelled and follows an invisible chemical path applied to the floor; it stops at designated points automatically. To change the stopping points, the path is erased and a new path applied. With the addition of more advanced microprocessors and "intelligent" capabilities, the Mailmobile® can "interface with elevators to serve multiple floors and perform varying stopping sequences."

The development of artificial intelligence (AI) is well under way. *Business Week* (1982, 66) says that "computers are starting to reason, make judgments and learn. By 2000 they will be radically altering society." A recent event is an augury of how robots will spread to affect every facet of human life. Chace (1982, 10) describes the introduction of a programmable IBM robot that can be hooked up to the IBM personal computer for programming and use, the 7535 Manufacturing System. This robot can also understand and respond to some short English-language commands. Anderson (1982) asserts that "a new generation of computerized and sensory robots with 'feel, think and see' capabilities is coming" (p. 5).

Advances in Optical Character Recognition (OCR) foreshadow the development of what Anderson (1982) calls "white collar robots." An example is Gupta's (1982, 221) report that "the accuracy of OCRs has . . . increased significantly (one error per million scanned characters)." Hughes (*Science* 1982, 1165) has developed an integrated optic chip and

Hughey (1982, 27) says that "optical fibers are beginning to appear in new sensing devices, from gyroscopes to thermometers, that may be cheaper, more reliable, and, in many cases, more sensitive than existing equipment." Some of these can be used in OCRs. An OCR now on the market, made by Kurzweil Computer Products, a Xerox company, "optically scans any typeface, then converts it into spoken English so that the blind can hear. But the machine can also convert text into computerized data—no speech is necessary—which is an obvious savings of time and salary in word-processing" (Hollerith 1982, 11). This can mean that a "white collar robot" can do much paper work automatically, unseen by human eyes and untouched by human hands; the robot with OCR capability reads the document, an order, for instance, and transmits the order to numerically controlled machines in the factory for manufacture and shipment. Branscomb (1982, 757) predicts that "by the mid-1980's recognition of optically scanned hand-printed information should be possible in a range of applications."

Anderson (1982) believes that, as a conservative estimate, by 1988 more than 10 million of these "white collar robots" or advanced work stations will occupy places in the office. He also says that "today the average company has one (advanced) work station for every 24 employees; by 1985 there will be one for every 10 workers. Some companies, such as IBM, will have one for every 3.4 employees" (p. 5).

Combinations of Devices

Also important in the office automation process are the combinations and transmutations of office devices. Duffy and Pye (1979) have said that the real significance of computers, semiconductors, chips, and microprocessors and the communication that they make possible comes from the fact that "what were once separate devices . . . typewriter, telephone, filing, copier and computer . . . have now become . . . not only linked but inseparable" (p. 673). For instance, the file can be in the computer and there is the definite possibility that the office bookshelf will be in a computer memory (Gallese 1981, 25).

An ad for Digital Equipment Corporation (1982) shows a VDT and a keyboard as "the same old desk in a whole new form," with labels pointing to various parts of the keyboard as "Waste-Basket, In-Basket, Calendar, Telephone Directory, Bulletin Board, Distribution Lists, Master List, Things To Do Lists and File Folders." According to Spinrad (1982), "already it is cheaper to store reference files magnetically than on paper"

(p. 809). (Now that the waste basket can be electronic erasure, designers will not have to worry about its shape, color, style, and size.)

However, there are even more graphic examples of linked devices. Perhaps the most obvious one is Northern Telecom's (1982) Displayphone; this device was advertised in the *Wall Street Journal* as an "advanced business telephone and computer (p. 27)." According to the ad, this office appliance can store a small telephone directory and automatically dial a selected number from it, access in-house or outside data banks, and display information from them on its screen, all using the hands-off telephone; the user can also send and receive electronic mail through it. In addition, it contains an electronic clock and timer for long-distance calls and other purposes. Another ad in the *Wall Street Journal* advertises the Burroughs Corporation (1982) OFIS℗ file, an electronic storage and retrieval system with a 30,000-page memory. A competitor advertises a "fastidious electronic janitor who makes his rounds and empties waste from your electronic wastebaskets."

The Paperless Office and Cost Reductions

Toffler (1981) tells of an experimental paperless office set up by Micronet, Inc., in Washington, D. C. He quotes Micronet president Larry Stockett as saying, "there are no misfiles; marketing, sales, accounting and research data are always up to the minute; information is reproduced and distributed at hundreds of thousands of pages per hour for a fraction of a cent per page; and . . . information is converted back and forth from print to digital to photographic media at will" (p. 188–189).

One of the factors that makes the communications and computer revolution possible is the tremendous reduction in computer function costs. Toffler (1981, 187) estimates that these costs are down "100,000 fold" in the past 13 years. From another point of view, Branscomb (1982) asserts that "the price of small, general-purpose computers of comparable power . . . in dollars per instruction executed per second, has been dropping at an annual compound rate of about 25 per cent per year since the early 1950's. The average rate of improvement for the largest general-purpose computers has been about 15 per cent per year—less steep than for comparable small machines because the large computers offer added function as well as more computing power" (p. 755). Duffy (1982, 11) describes the process another way: "The first post-war Volkswagen Beetles and the first viable valve computer are contemporaneous. And yet, if the car had developed at the rate of the computer, today's Beetle would travel at 600 mph, do 30,000 miles to the gallon, travel for 10,000 years between services and cost 50 pence."

Video Teleconferencing

The text above has concentrated on the transmission of voices and data. However, in many offices and conference areas there will be one more CRT—for video teleconferencing. Faces, voices, and data can be televised now and Brancatelli (1981) reports that an "electronic blackboard that allows images to be drawn on a special display" (p. 95) is in development by a number of companies. Lowndes (1981, 333) lists 14 American companies either now providing video teleconferencing or planning to do so in the near future. He also lists (1981, 322–332) 11 companies now manufacturing earth stations that can be used to transmit and receive video and audio signals to and from satellites used for this purpose.

One example of this is the Picturephone. In 1982 AT&T inaugurated this nationwide service (*Wall Street Journal* 1982d, 29), which would be available at telephone company offices; customers could also have AT&T install video teleconference rooms in their own offices for an initial fee of $117,500 plus an $11,760 equipment rental fee per month on a two-year lease. The private room charge between New York and Washington is $600 per hour; between New York and Los Angeles it is $1,640 per hour. The public room charges for the same cities are $1,340 and $2,380 per hour, respectively.

Lowndes (1981, 329) has stated that the airlines may experience less business travel as video teleconferencing increases and as the cost comes down. A typical round trip regular coach fare between New York and Los Angeles or between New York and San Francisco was $700 for one person in August 1982. As hotel bills, meals, and entertainment, together with the cost of executive travel time, are added to airline fares and multiplied by the number of individuals traveling to a meeting, a Picturephone conference or other forms of video teleconferencing look better and better to corporate treasurers. According to Morris (1983, 25), it is estimated that 3,800 participants in a teleconference arranged by the Bank Administration Institute to tell bank managers how to set up the new market-rate bank accounts saved the conferees $2 million in expenses for travel, lodging, and food.

In addition, *Aviation Week & Space Technology* (1981a, 101) tells of the definite possibility that video teleconferencing costs will be reduced by satellite time-sharing. Shaffer (1982, 15) predicts that overall satellite transmission costs will continue to fall because of a wide variety of technical developments already accomplished or near introduction. Branscomb (1982) flatly states that "communications satellites offer a channel cost that is falling at 40 per cent a year as demand rises. The information inside a computer runs at millions of characters per second, but can be accessed at only a few thousand characters per second over telephone lines. The satellite allows computers to communicate at the same speed at which they operate. Satellites are also making it possible to combine data-processing applications with digital voice communications, office applications, such as facsimile, and video applications, such as teleconferencing" (p. 759).

In 1981, *Aviation Week & Space Technology* (AW&ST) announced that Crocker National Bank was planning video teleconferencing using Satellite Business System's four earth stations (AW&ST 1981, 16). According to Crocker, it might save as much as 20% of its travel costs this way. AW&ST (1981c, 26) also reported that GTE Satellite Corporation had awarded a contract to RCA for the construction of three satellites that together can "handle 30,000 simultaneous telephone calls or 300 two-way video conferences." Atlantic Richfield is planning a $15 million satellite network to link its contiguous American locations with Anchorage and Prudhoe Bay; Federal Express Corporation has awarded a $16 million contract for a private satellite communications network; and Arthur Andersen & Co., IBM, Texas Instruments, Exxon, Procter and Gamble, Texaco, Montgomery Ward, and Aetna Life & Casualty Co. are experimenting with video teleconferencing by satellite (Lowndes 1981, 327).

What effects may we expect from the increased use of this medium? According to Desmond Smith (1981), "within a decade or so, the requisite equipment will be standard in all major corporate headquarters. And in the not too distant future, it should be a common feature in homes, making a trip to the office unnecessary for many executives" (p. 27). This means that more office areas will be dedicated and equipped for video teleconferencing. It also means that executives will spend less time traveling. As another example of what can be done with the medium, the *Wall Street Journal* (1981b, 31) reported on 32-city video teleconferences used as seminars by lawyers, doctors, and nurses. The lecturers did not have to travel to 32 cities and each listener attended in his or her city of residence at the same time.

Evidently video teleconferencing is widespread. In April 1982, *Frequent Flyer* magazine (p. 14), published by the Official Airline Guides, polled its readers on several issues. One question read, "Have you ever participated in a meeting via teleconference?" Of the 6,200 who returned questionnaires, 39.3% said yes. This is almost 2 of every 5, and these readers are frequent flyers.

There may be still another reason for the increase in use of this medium. Birrell and White (1982), in a study of video teleconferencing and its participants, stated: "The findings from this project which are reported here show that video teleconferences are in general more task oriented and are especially useful for the more competitive tasks. . . . We can, however, claim that rather than necessarily always being a poor substitute, teleconferences do have some clear advantages over face-to-face meetings in terms of the discussions themselves and not simply in terms of their cost" (p. 319).

Intercontinental Hotels and Comsat General corporations announced in the *Wall Street Journal* (1982b, 14) that they would offer the first international televised conference service to the public beginning December 1982. This service can also transmit documents rapidly in both directions and costs between $1,500 and $2,000 per hour; here in its international application video teleconferencing can save much time and money. This joint venture has plans to expand from the announced New York–London link to other cities and countries. Hilton International (1982, 6) advertised a similar international and national service. In addition, Anderson (1982) sees video teleconferencing used for "intrafacility and interfacility" communication, especially for large companies.

The Office Can Be Anywhere

A computer keyboard and two VDTs—one for data transmission and receiving and the other for video teleconferencing—can connect the operator to the information world. With the costs of communication coming down, a job or an office can be anywhere; as Toffler (1981) points out, in making the decision of location, "the key question is: When will the cost of installing and operating telecommunications equipment fall below the . . . cost of commuting? While gasoline and other transport costs . . . are soaring everywhere, the price of telecommunications is shrinking spectacularly. At some point the curves must cross" (p. 200–201). The means now exist for geographic dispersion of offices with excellent coordination of activities.

Desmond Smith (1982, 32) cites two examples. Motivated by an opportunity to cut labor costs, Citicorp has moved its credit card operations, and thousands of jobs, to Sioux Falls, South Dakota, from New York City. Satellite Data Corporation (SDC), Smith's other example, is moving much of its work to various places in the Caribbean, where "average pay for Caribbean data entry personnel [is] running $1.50 an hour (it is as much as $9 an hour in New York.)" SDC is using satellites to transmit data to and from New York, of course. It is also looking at India. According to George Simpson, president of SDC, "it's an ideal place. . . . Their day shift is our night shift and the biggest part of the market is in doing stuff overnight for people. India has a sophisticated labor force, and they have an enormous amount of underemployment—you get Ph.D.s doing clerical work over there" (as quoted by Desmond Smith 1982, 32).

The Office Goes Aloft

Some private aircraft with sophisticated communications equipment already serve as offices and 10 airlines, including at least 7 major trunks, are installing Airfones, a device that allows passengers to make phone calls in flight (Weber 1982, 2–B). Bulkeley (1982, 12) tells about a pocket computer terminal on the market that can be plugged into a telephone. United Airlines is working with Airfone, Inc. and Western Union to make it possible to use portable terminals in flight; there is even a possibility that airlines may carry rentable portable terminals aboard.

The Office Moves

So, the research department no longer needs to be located next door to the advertising department; it can be hundreds or even thousands of miles away. Does the marketing department have to be next to the production control department? Not necessarily, not now. Why bother with the traditional office building in the future?

One central fact is that the growing concentration of offices in buildings and of office buildings in cities is increasing the inconvenience of getting to and from the office, as well as increasing the difficulty of living near the office. These problems do not make the lives of those who work in offices happy ones and they make the problems of recruiting competent people for office jobs more difficult. To attract competent workers, offices may have to move out of the crowded, unattractive cities. That may be the first step. The next step could be home and office combinations for many jobs for which the requisite communications equipment is available now.

Toffler (1981, 194–207) calls home the "electronic cottage" for a variety of reasons. Some of the activities that are carried on in homes now, even though most homes are not well equipped to handle them, include filling out various tax forms and preparing family budgets, tasks that are at least a bit more complicated than some of those that are performed in offices. *Time* magazine (1982, 54) predicted that there would be more than 5 million home computers by the end of 1983. That, however, may be just the tip of a growing iceberg; International Telephone and Telegraph Corporation (1982, 20) predicted that with the advent of "digital" television,

278   BEHAVIORAL ISSUES

which replaces about 350 parts in a typical television set with 8 semi-conductor chips, the home TV set will also become a computer.

A 1981 article in the *Wall Street Journal* (1981c, 25) stated that "the developers of a new condominium in New York City are offering buyers more than the usual assortment of appliances. As a standard feature, each apartment will include a computer terminal." Also, each condominium in a newly restored loft building in TriBeCa, likewise in New York City on West Broadway, will also be equipped with a computer terminal, as well as cable TV, according to McKeon (1981, 50); the terminals in both buildings will be hooked up to data banks. Further, Guenther (1982, 25) says: "Colonnade 57, a New York condominium offers buyers home computers featuring airline schedules, stock quotes and other services."

The beginnings of a trend that moves work out of the office and into the home is already apparent. Vicker (1981, 46) reports that Data General Corporation "has about 25 terminals that can be taken out by . . . people when they prefer to work at home." He also states that Digital Equipment Corporation has several hundred employees who work at home and that "the term 'telecommuting' has been coined to denote the electronic connection between home and office." Vicker (1981, 46) also describes experiments in this same vein now going on involving a bank, another computer company, and a management consulting firm.

A computerized community is being created in Ridgewood, New Jersey, under the auspices of AT&T and CBS, Inc. (Rothfeder 1982, 1–2). A total of 200 houses there are being wired for computers of two types: one is a free-standing machine and the other attaches to an existing TV set, using the TV screen as the screen for the computer. Services offered in this experiment, called Videotex, include news reports from CBS and the *Record of Hackensack*, banking services, household hints, and national and local advertising (with the ability to buy items through the computer).

The entrance of the computer into the home has resulted in the establishment of a few new securities trading firms that are run from the homes of the owners (Carrington 1981, 25). At least one architect in New York City, Peter Wheelwright, has his office and home in a spacious loft and "now has a booming business designing space for individuals who live and work in one location" (Pettus 1982, 33). Because the computer and improving communications make the office in the home possible, more handicapped people who cannot easily travel to the office will find it possible to work in their homes. Another major advantage is that people who work at home will not occupy expensive space in office buildings.

Incidentally, in that home-away-from-home, the motel or hotel room, computer terminals utilizing the ubiquitous in-room TV set as a screen began appearing in early 1983, offering electronic mail, airline reservations, stock market quotations, the purchase of flowers and gifts, lists of real estate agents, and many other services (*Hotel & Resort Industry* 1982, 102, 104).

The movement of the computer and office work performed with it into the home offers greater freedom of work location and Duffy and Pye (1979, 672) suggest that another change may be in the making: They say that we "may be moving from an *employment* economy, in which most of us sell our time in blocks of eight hours, five days a week, to a *contractual* economy, in which services rather than hours are sold."

Further, they see offices as smaller units that can occupy a wide variety of spaces, not necessarily in the central city core. Duffy and Pye (1979) see a future "demand for many small units of space, of high but varying quality. Dispersed old warehouses [and] old houses [are] office buildings no architect ever thinks of . . . Georgian houses, commerical palaces of the 20's . . . living rooms, the whole fabric of city and town" (p. 672). These smaller offices may therefore be put in redesigned older buildings.

THE CALUS STUDY

The Centre for Advanced Land Use Studies (CALUS) has issued a research report entitled *Property and Information Technology* (CALUS 1983). Although this study was done from a real estate point of view, it does cover both British and American opinions and presents information useful in determining the office of the future.

The following are some excerpts from the CALUS research report:

Too many commentators have fallen into the trap of viewing Information Technology in isolation from broader economic, sociological and cultural factors. When IT is placed in a wider perspective it can be seen that the "office of the future" (at least during the 1980's and 1990's) will certainly not be very futuristic and, it will be argued, may very well not be an office at all (p. 22).

Changes in the structure of the economy have resulted in a breaking down of the traditional distinction between office and non-office activities and a growing demand for more flexible buildings which are interchangeable between office, assembly, research and other activities. Examples of such buildings are rare in Britain but plentiful in the United States (p. 24).

[From an electronics firm] Automation has not led to any lay-offs but it has reduced the increase in staff requirements to handle a growing level of business (p. 28).

[From a respondent in the financial sector] We have been able to substantially expand our business without having to obtain more accommodation for head office and processing functions, as a direct result of information technology (p. 28).

All indicators in the U.K. and elsewhere, particularly in the U.S.A., suggest the development of microprocessors has been accompanied by a strong, steady growth in space per person and total space required. There is no indication at present that this process will be reversed (p. 30).

Between 1966 and 1976 there was a 45% increase in the amount of office space in England and Wales but the number of office staff only rose by 13%. The difference is due to the increased level of floorspace allocated to each office employee (p. 32).

In America . . . the level of floorspace per employee is increasing in gross terms, but the amount of private space (net allocation) is declining. More space is being used for machines and the sizes of people-space are being reduced, except for meeting rooms and training spaces (p. 33).

Work stations with word processors may require up to 75% more space than those incorporating electric typewriters (p. 39).

Office equipment gives off heat. A word processor may have heat loading as high as 400 watts, ten times that of an electric typewriter. A high performance photocopier may produce forty times as much heat as an office worker (p. 39).

Some U.S. organizations change the configuration of work stations up to ten times per year in response to changes in the structure of their work.

Information Technology extends the range of buildings that are suitable for housing office activities. It is feasible that the office of the future will not be housed in purpose-built office buildings but in converted warehouses or even operate from individuals' own homes. It is more likely that an increasing amount of office activities will be undertaken from a new form of property outside of the existing definition of an office but constituting a complete production facility which is interchangeable between office and non-office use (p. 46).

Interior designers and architects take notice.

INDUSTRIAL DEMOCRACY

There are factors in operation other than the communications revolution that may change the office.

Two Books

The rise of industrial democracy in offices may get some stimulation from two books, one published in England and one here in the United States. Both were published in 1981, and their titles as well as their chapter headings tell part of their stories. Both books are also trade union documents—giving reasons office workers should join unions.

The British is the *Office Workers Survival Handbook: A Guide to Fighting Health Hazards in the Office* by Marianne Craig. The chapter headings read like a catalog of complaints: "Stress," "Noise," "Sitting, Standing and Strains," "Dangerous Substances," "Injury and Fires," and "Microelectronics: What Computers Are Doing to Office Work and Office Workers."

In the introduction, Craig (1981) says, "This book emphasizes repeatedly that you have a *right* to a safe and healthy job. But more than that, you have a right to work in a stress-free job, where there is flexibility and where you have control over what you are doing. You have a right to work in comfort with good facilities such as canteens, rest rooms and nurseries. In an age when we sent men to the moon, there is no reason why the basic rights should not be ours" (p. 7). She ends the introduction with, "Office work is dangerous to your health, but where you can trace the cause of ill-health and organise against it, it can be prevented" (p. 8).

Distributed by the Trade Union Book Service in London, Craig's book is well researched. Duffy (1981b) calls it a "brilliant polemic" and says, "What should concern architects most is the long catalog of deficiencies in the physical environment of the office. . . . Craig's clear and cleverly directed book is as valuable as most architectural guidance on office design. More significantly, it is evidence of an expanding and increasingly active and demanding client body. We architects will have to learn how to design not for but *with* these multiple and often fractious client bodies. It will be an interesting test for which neither our old professional arrogance nor some still hypothetical humility has prepared us" (p. 495).

The American book is *Office Hazards: How Your Job Can Make You Sick* by Joel Makower (1981). Its provocative chapter headings include: "There's Something in the Air," "Design Neglect," "More Than Meets the Eye," "Stressed to Kill," "Terminal Illnesses," "The Slow Burn," "Danger: Office Zone," and "The Future of the Office of the Future."

The introduction to *Office Hazards* is by Karen Nussbaum, president of Working Women, an affiliate of the Service Employees International Union. In it she says: "The health of office workers is threatened daily by the machines we use, the chemicals in common office products, by the design of our offices and by the very structure of our work" (p. x). District 925 (Working Women) won its first election in February 1982 at an Equitable Life Assurance Society office in Syracuse, New York (Lublin 1982, 1). Makower (1981), in a press release accompanying the issuance of the book, suggests: "The nature of the problem is such that the individual hazards in offices are rather small, seemingly trivial things. An uncomfortable chair may not seem like a major calamity; neither does stuffy air or a few ringing telephones. But put an office worker in a bad chair in a noisy, stuffy office, require that worker to perform a dead-end job for low pay on a video display terminal with a dirty screen made worse by the harsh glare from fluorescent lights; add a dash of pressure—a ruthless supervisor, for example, or economic or family problems—and you've got a potentially explosive situation."

Two Major Studies of Office Workers

These books can be viewed along with the background information from two surveys of office workers in the United States, one completed and the other ongoing. The completed study was performed for Steelcase, Inc. (1980), the world's largest office furniture manufacturer; it surveyed 1,004 office workers and 203 executives.

The following are some of the findings included in this report:

1. Of the office workers surveyed, 91% "feel that it is very or somewhat important for them to have a say in . . . decisions about getting whatever they need to feel comfortable in their jobs. . . . Fewer office workers now have a voice in . . . office decisions than would like to" (p. v).
2. The highest-ranking factors in office workers' comfort are (a) good lighting; (b) a comfortable chair; and (c) the opportunity to stretch and move around during the day (p. iv).
3. A total of "56% of the office workers surveyed have experienced problems with back strain or tired back, and 64% of these relate it to their work. Twenty eight percent say that an uncomfortable chair contributed to their discomfort . . . 58% of these office workers believe a *choice* in chairs would give them more comfort and make them more productive" (p. vi).
4. Of the office workers surveyed, the majority stated they did not have the following: "(a) the right temperature; (b) sufficient quiet; and (c) ability to change their office furniture as their jobs change" (p. iii).

5. Of the office workers surveyed, 47% said that they did not have "a place to work when [they needed] to concentrate without distractions" (p. v).

6. A total of "70% of office workers have complained about the comfort of their offices and 80% of those who complained say the discomforts inhibited their job performance" (p. iii).

7. According to the executives, fans, heaters, and other appliances were used by 58% of the workers in an effort to make offices more comfortable (p. v).

8. Office workers prefer windows that can be opened over central heating and air conditioning systems where they do not (p. iv).

9. Eyestrain on the job was attributed to lighting by 26% of the office workers (p. v).

10. "Office workers feel that they have little or no say in obtaining: (a) the most comfortable working temperature; (b) lighting; (c) a place to relax; (d) the type of office chair they have" (p. iii).

The second, ongoing survey is being done by BOSTI, Inc. (The Buffalo Organization for Social and Technical Innovation), which is surveying 10,000 office workers. The following interim findings were presented in a speech by Michael Brill, President (1980):

1. "Some of the principal issues being explored by BOSTI include: interaction, privacy, difficult pathfinding, flexibility, personalization, status, noise, lighting, colors, spaces, materials, job satisfaction, and productivity."

2. "BOSTI is planning to ask 364 (mostly objective) questions of each worker and a typical question will ask 'Does something happen? How frequently? How does it affect you?'"

3. "On the privacy issue, while 90% of the workers want fewer people than they now have in their workspace, two-thirds of them do not want private offices; 44% want from one to seven total workers in their workspace and only 22% want to work in offices with eight or more people in them."

4. "The privacy issue was underscored further by the finding that 98% of the workers surveyed so far can hear people talking, 97% can hear phones ringing, and 94% can hear typewriters—all clearly. These figures are staggering because they include people in private offices."

5. "Of the workers surveyed, 43% are bothered by glare or shadows."

6. "Windows do not affect light quality."

7. "People who need the best lighting, those with demanding visual

tasks, have the worst lighting, while those who need it least, the managers, have the best lighting."

8. "The desire to change one's own office space increases with rank to reflect status."

9. "Of the workers surveyed, 81% so far are not allowed to participate in design decisions, 79% of them want to participate in them, and 72% are dissatisfied because they are not allowed to participate in them."

It seems quite clear from the results of these two studies that many office workers in the United States want to participate in design decisions concerning their immediate environments in the office, although they do not have that opportunity. These two studies and the books cited above (Craig 1981; Makower 1981) also show that many office workers are dissatisfied with their immediate working environments.

One way of attacking these problems might be to use the participatory design process where the office workers themselves tell the designer what they want and need.

Participatory Design

Although it is far from a trend in the United States, Duffy and Pye (1979, 670–671) see industrial democracy as the wave of the future and call Centraal Beheer the turning point in Europe. Centraal Beheer is an insurance company office building in Apeldoorn, Holland, designed by architect Herman Hertzberger to be unfinished when it was occupied, inviting the users to finish it with their own decorations and personalizations, thus participating in the design. Duffy and Pye (1979, 671) see what is happening in Europe as a change in "social management" style, with the regimentation of the prevailing "open plan" being overtaken by "industrial democracy" and office workers' freedom of choice in decorating their own workplaces.

Industrial democracy has become part of the law in Sweden (Kleeman 1983, 14). Workers, whether in offices or on a production line, must be consulted on the design of their working environment before planning permission is given for a new building or before changes are made in existing buildings. W. J. Smith (1981, 370) points out that West Germany is passing "the most extensive laws in the form of Safety Regulations which specify, in detail, design requirements of visual display units." Smith also adds that similar specifications have been or are on the current agendas of the Netherlands, Norway, and Austria.

Participatory design worked well in the design of the Northwest Regional Offices of the Federal Aviation Administration, where more than 350 office workers told designers what they wanted and needed—and got the necessary design and artifacts (Kleeman 1983, 293–317). Concerning the participatory design process there, Harris (1977) said: "When a radical design group consulted Seattle white-collar workers about office furniture and layout for a new Federal Aviation Administration building, morale and satisfaction soared. Compared with FAA workers in a fancier building in Los Angeles, Sommer reports, the Seattle Workers were significantly happier, more pleased with everything—from their jobs to the air conditioning system" (p. 54). (However, although every worker was offered a chance to participate in the design of his or her own space in Seattle and each worker there was interviewed by the design team, only 2% of the Los Angeles work force said that they had participated actively in the design process.)

There is other evidence that participatory design works. Ellis and Duffy (1982, 33) report a successful project for a warehouse for Unipart, the parts division of British Leyland, the auto maker; the entire work force was brought into the design process, from top management down to shop floor workers. Frequently, the designers were mediators where different opinions existed.

Nightingale (1981) concluded that "significant worker control over decision making does lead to positive outcomes, and this relationship is found when the nature of the work is controlled. In other words, attitudes can be improved even in organizations in which major task design is impossible. Apparently, uninspiring work can be tolerated if employees have the right to exercise influence over other areas of their work lives" (p. 291). He based his statement on the results of a thorough survey of 1,000 employees in 20 matched industrial organizations in Canada. Ten organizations were formally participatory and ten were of conventional hierarchical design.

Cave (1981, 957) reports that "a study ending in March 1981 by the British Institute of Management (BIM) of 300 of its subscriber companies with more than 1,000 employees, concluded that consultation and employee participation had vastly increased in recent years. In all, 82% of the respondents had employee councils or committees; 77% claimed to use these committees for consultation. The next step, however," Cave continued, "of 'joint decision-taking' is clearly a long way off and treated with suspicion. No respondent interpreted joint decision-taking as board level participation" (p. 45).

In an earlier study of office environments, Steelcase, Inc. (1978) said:

There is, in effect, a collision course indicated here—too little consultation with office workers affected by change, too much avoidance of the privacy issue by office decision-makers, too little understanding by office workers of the reasons office decision-makers feel the open plan office has important advantages over a conventional plan office and too little dialogue between office workers and office decision-makers about potential drawbacks.

Increased employee participation in the office planning process would clearly go a long way toward alleviating the intensity of the collision. Unfortunately, unless employees come to feel truly involved in the decisions that most affect their office environment, this aspect of democracy in the workplace might become another "hot issue" over the next ten years rather than a tool for solving a communications problem, with the stake being productivity in the workplace (p. vii).

Several large corporations in the United States are experimenting with Japanese "quality circles" (worker participation in decisions concerning production work) and, recently, these circles have spread to offices here. According to Main (1982, 62–63), the construction group at Westinghouse Electric Corporation in Pittsburgh has a successful office quality circle in their information and communications center. Main (1982) comments: "Lately its quality circle has been discussing how to train bosses to dictate more efficiently—they should organize better and not mumble" (p. 63). Also, Tannenbaum (1983, 1) reports that quality circles are spreading to banks and other service concerns. Citibank has 15 of them in New York; Republic Bank in Houston has increased from 5 last year to 13 this year and will increase to 18 soon; and RCA's Hertz unit in Oklahoma City has made some car-reservation procedures more efficient.

Analyzing a 1982 study by the National Academy of Engineering, Norman (1982) said: "The study concludes, if the U.S. [auto] industry is ever going to recover its competitive position, it must change the way it does business. In particular, it must start bringing workers into decision-making and create an environment where innovation is encouraged. . . . Japanese companies, it says, have been able to change and innovate more rapidly and have managed to maintain an excellent system of quality control. In comparison, the American industry tends to be more rigid, labor-management relations are more hierarchical and adversarial, and there has been less scope for innovation" (p. 518).

This situation would seem to offer opportunities for designers to use the participatory design process in the design and planning of offices. Using this process would not alleviate all the problems and symptoms found above, but it might at least identify some of them more clearly and even help solve a few of them. As Duffy (1981, 955) observed:

"Never have offices been so central to society; we would do well to take their design seriously."

With the use of flexible, adjustable, and changeable interior furnishings together with participatory design, designers should be able to fully explore the potential for a successful fit between people and the office environment as changes continue to occur in the future.

The largest office furniture manufacturer in the world, Steelcase, Inc., has, in effect, clearly expressed its belief in the necessity of participatory design by releasing to its dealers a quite comprehensive series of seven questionnaires that allow the individual office worker to participate in the design of his or her own work station. After the questionnaires are completed the dealer sends them to Steelcase for analysis on Steelcase's computer; then the printout is sent back to the dealer so that it can be used in the design of individual workplaces and for the office as a whole.

Although Herman Miller and several large space-planning firms have such questionnaires and computer programs for years, when the largest office furniture manufacturer in the world goes into the questionnaire business, clearly this means that participatory office design has arrived.

NOTE

1. The author wishes to express his appreciation to Francis Duffy, Peter Ellis, H. T. E. Hertzberg, and Wanda Smith for their help in preparing this chapter.

REFERENCES

Abelson, P. H. 1982. The revolution in computers and electronics. *Science* 215 (4534):752.

Anderson, H. 1982. *Yankee Ingenuity* 6:5.

Andersson, B. J. G., and R. Ortengren. 1974. Lumbar disc pressure and myoelectric back muscle activity. *Scan. J. Rehabilitative Med.* 3:115–121.

AT&T. 1983. Advertisement. *High Technology* (7 October).

Aviation Week & Space Technology. 1981a. Time sharing to cut teleconferencing. 114:101.

Aviation Week & Space Technology. 1981b. Crocker National Bank is considering teleconferencing. 114:15.

Aviation Week & Space Technology. 1981c. GTE satellite awards spacecraft contract. 115:26.

Bell & Howell. 1982. Advertisement in *Facilities Design & Management.* 1:30.

Bhise, V. D., and E. J. Rinalducci (Eds.) 1981. CRT Viewing I. *Human Factors* 23:515–586.

Bhise, V. D., and E. J. Rinalducci (Eds.) 1981a. CRT Viewing II. *Human Factors* 23:385–438.

Birrell, J. A., and P. N. White. 1982. Using technical intervention to behavioral advantage. *Behavioral and Information Technology*. 1:305–320.

Brancatelli, J. 1981. Office of the future: The people factor. *EXTRA* (The Continental Airlines Flight Magazine) 3:81–98.

Branscomb, L. M. 1982. Electronics and computers: An overview. *Sceince* 215: 755–760.

Brill, M. 1980. Productivity: How to define it and achieve it in the office. Presentation at National Exposition of Contract Furnishing (NEOCON), June, Chicago, The Merchandise Mart.

Brookes, M. J., and P. P. Mitchell. 1982. A study of white collar productivity and open office system furnishings. Brochure published by Westinghouse Open Office Systems.

Bulkeley, W. M. 1982. Pocket terminal said to speed access to large data banks is unveiled. *Wall Street Journal* (February 25):12.

Bulkeley, W. M. and J. A. White. 1982. IBM prepares a new approach to office-machine networks. *Wall Street Journal* (March 26):29.

Burroughs Corporation. 1982. OFIS™ file. The search is over. Advertisement in *Wall Street Journal*. (May 13):22.

Business Week. 1982. Artificial intelligence: The second computer age begins. (March 8):66.

Cakir, A., D. J. Hart, and T. F. M. Stewart. 1980. *Visual display terminals: A manual covering ergonomics, work space design, task organization, health and safety*. New York: John Wiley & Sons.

CALUS. 1983. *Property and information technology: The future for the office market*. Whiteknights, England: College of Estate Management.

Carrington, T. 1981. Computer linkups let traders start up securities firms at home. *Wall Street Journal* (December 9):25.

Cave, C. 1981. Changing roles. *The Architect's Journal* 174:45.

Chace, S. 1983. Tomorrow's computer may replace itself, some visionaries think. *Wall Street Journal*. (January 6):1.

Chace, S., and J. A. White. 1982. IBM enters computer services market with a nationwide information network. *Wall Street Journal* (February 3).

Craig, M. 1981. *Office workers' survival handbook: A guide to fighting health hazards in the office*. London: BSSRS Publications.

Dainoff, M. J., L. Fraser, and B. J. Taylor. 1982. Visual, musculoskeletal, and performance differences between good and poor VDT workstations: Preliminary findings. *Proceedings of the Human Factors Society 26th Annual Meeting*. Santa Monica: Human Factors Society.

Damon, A., H. W. Stoudt, and R. A. McFarland. 1966. *The human body in equipment design*. Cambridge, MA: Harvard University Press.

Digital Equipment Corporation. 1982. Introducing the same old desk in a whole new form. Advertisement in *Wall Street Journal* (January 8):23.

Driscoll, P., J. Marzeki, and F. Wilson. 1982. Architecture and the information revolution. *AIA Journal* 71:70.

Duffy, F. 1981a. Changing offices. *The Architect's Journal* 174:45.

Duffy, F. 1981b. Nine to five. *The Architect's Journal* 174:495.

Duffy, F. 1982. The architect and information technology. *The Architect's Journal* 175 (34):11.

Duffy, F., and R. Pye. 1979. Offices, the future landscape: Paper factory or room with a view. *The Architect's Journal* 170:669–675.

Eastman Kodak Company. 1982. Advertisement. *High Technology* 1(2): 13.

Ellis, P., and F. Duffy. 1982. Building for better labour relations. *Management Today* (July).

Falluchi, A. 1982. There's too much at stake to ignore tomorrow's office. *Facilities Design and Management* (June):39.

Fortune. 1982. Robot ally GM's Japanese partner. (July 28):11.

Frequent Flyer. 1982. Part 2 OAG Pocket Flight Guide. (September):14.

Gallese, L. R. 1981. Publishers try adapting print to video uses. *Wall Street Journal* (November 2):25.

Grandjean, E. 1980. *Fitting the task to the man*, 3rd ed. London and Philadelphia: Taylor & Francis.

Grandjean, E., and E. Vigliani. 1980. *Ergonomic aspects of visual display terminals.* London: Taylor & Francis.

Grandjean, R., K. Nishiyama, W. Hunting, and M. Piderman. 1982. A laboratory study on preferred and imposed setting of a VDT workstation. *Behavior & Information Technology* 3:289–304.

Grandjean, E., W. Hunting, and M. Piderman. 1983. A field study of preferred settings of an adjustable VDT workstation and their effects on body postures and subjective feelings. *Human Factors Journal* 25(2):161–175.

Guenther, R. 1982. Houston Zoning? . . . Pursuing Mingles . . . Partnership Sales. *Wall Street Journal* (July 28):25.

Gupta, A. 1982. An overview of contemporary office automation technology. *Behavior and Information Technology* 1(3):217–236.

Haavind, R. C. 1982. Breaking down corporate empires. *High Technology* 1(1):30.

Harris, G. T. 1977. Psychology of the New York work space. *New York* 10 (44):51–54.

High Technology. 1981. Optical storage on cards. 2(3):46.

Hilton International. 1982. Advertisement. *Wall Street Journal* (October 29):6.

Hilton, J. 1981. Face to camera at an actual teleconference. *Wall Street Journal* (July 13):23.

Hellerith, R. Jr. Design influencing dual market products for the handicapped. *Industrial Design* 28(2):11.

Hotel and Resort Industry (magazine). 1982. 5(12):102–103.

Hughes Aircraft Company. 1982. Advertisement. *Wall Street Journal.* (September 24):14.

Hughey, A. 1982. Optical fibers could produce better and less costly sensors. *Wall Street Journal* (June 4):27.

Hünting, W., T. Laubli, and E. Grandjean. Postural and visual loads at VDT workplaces I. Constrained postures. *Ergonomics* 24(12):917–932.

Inman, V. 1983. MCI unveils service using its phone lines for electronic mail. *Wall Street Journal* (September 28):16.

International Business Machines Corporation. 1982. Advertisement. *Wall Street Journal* (March 25):6.

International Telephone and Telegraph Corporation. 1982. Advertisement. *Wall Street Journal* (December 15):20.

Kleeman, W. B., Jr. 1983. *The challenge of interior design.* New York: Van Nostrand Reinhold.

Kleiner, A. 1980. Life on the computer frontier. In S. Brand (Ed.), *The next whole earth catalog.* Sausalito, CA: Point.

Kroemer, K., H. Eberhard, and J. C. Robinette. 1968. *Ergonomics in the design of office furniture: A review of the European literature.* Report AMRL-TR-68–80. Wright-Patterson Air Force Base, Aerospace Medical Research Laboratories, July.

Lowndes, J. C. 1981. Teleconferencing systems expected to reduce costs. *Aviation Week & Space Technology* 114(23):323–333.

Lublin, J. S. 1982. Labor letter. *Wall Street Journal* (February 16):1.

Main, J. 1982. Work won't be the same again. *Fortune* (June 28):63.

Makower, J. 1981. *Office hazards: how your job can make you sick.* New York: Tilden Press.

Martin, R. 1981. Speech given at *New Directions and Issues for Interior Design Practice and Education in the '80s* symposium, at the University of Cincinnati, October, 1981.

Mauro. 1981. Human factors study crucial for future office. *Industrial Design* 28(2):29.

McKeon, N. 1981. Wired for the future. *New York* 14(34):50.

Miller, I., and T. W. Suther. 1981. Preferred height and angle settings of CRT and keyboard for a display station input task. *Proceedings of the 25th Annual (1981) Human Factors Society Meeting.* Human Factors Society, Santa Monica, 492–496.

Morris, B. 1983. Hotels start luring video conferences. *Wall Street Journal* (February 25):25.

Mullin, S. 1976. Some notes on an activity. In F. Duffy, C. Cave, and J. Worthington (Eds.), *Planning office space.* London: The Architectural Press.

Nachemson, A., and G. Elfstrom. 1970. Intravital pressure measurements in lumbar discs. *Scan. J. Rehabilitation* Med. Suppl. 1.

Nightingale, D. V. 1981. Work, formal participation, and employee outcomes. *Sociology of Work and Occupations* 8(3):277–291.

Norman, C. 1982. Tokyo's edge over Detroit. *Science* 217(4559).

Northern Telecom. 1982. Advertisement. *Wall Street Journal* (April 12):27.

Pesmen, C. 1982. The missing link. *Frequent Flyer* (August):47.

Pettus, T. 1982. Computerized community being built. *The New York Times* (New Jersey Edition) (August 8):1 ff.

Science. 1982. Hughes Science/Scope advertisement. 215(4537):1165.

Shaffer, R. A. 1981a. Fresh promise is seen in link between electricity and pressure. *Wall Street Journal* (November 13):29.

Shaffer, R. A. 1981b. Acoustic wave devices bring big microelectronics changes. *Wall Street Journal* (November 20):27.

Shaffer, R. A. Satellite transmission of data may take off. *Wall Street Journal* (July 2):15.

Skerritt, J. 1982. Banking: Containing the costs. *The Architect's Journal* 174(34):42.

Smith, D. 1981. Info city. *New York* 14(6):24–29.

Smith, D. 1982. The city's coming white-collar crisis. *New York* 15(38):32.

Smith, W. J. 1981. Sociopolitical impact on human factors. *Proceedings of the 25th Human Factors Society Annual Meeting.* Santa Monica: Human Factors Society.

Spinrad, R. J. 1982. Office automation. *Science* 215(4534).

Springer, T. J. 1982. Visual display terminal workstations: A comparable evaluation of alternatives. Bloomington, IL: State Farm Mutual Automobile Insurance Company.

Stewart, T. F. M. 1980. Practical experiences in solving VDT ergonomics problems. In E. Grandjean and E. Vigliani (Eds.), *Ergonomic aspects of visual display terminals.* London and Philadelphia: Taylor & Francis.

Steelcase, Inc. 1978. *The Steelcase national study of office environments: Do they work?* (Conducted by Louis Harris and Associates, Inc.). Grand Rapids, MI.

Steelcase, Inc. *The Steelcase national study of office environments, No. II: Comfort and productivity in the office of the '80s.* (Conducted by Louis Harris & Associates, Inc.) Grand Rapids, MI.

Steelcase, Inc. 1983. *White collar productivity: The national challenge.* Written by the American Productivity Center, Houston, TX, and sponsored by Steelcase, Inc. Grand Rapids, MI.

Tannenbaum, J. A. 1983. Quality circles spread to banks and other service concerns. *Wall Street Journal* (February 3):1.

Tannenbaum, J. A., and W. M. Bulkeley. 1981. Device makers dream of electronic offices, but obstacles remain. *Wall Street Journal* (March 13):1.

Time, Inc. 1982. Price war in small computers. (September 20):54.

Toffler, A. 1981. *The Third Wave*. New York: Bantam Books, Inc.

Towers, Perrin, Foster, and Crosby. 1982. Special report prepared for A.B. Dick Co. *Printing Impressions* (February):100–101.

Uttal, B. 1982. What's detaining the office of the future? *Fortune* (May 3):196.

Wicker, R. 1981. Computer terminals allow more people to work at home instead of commuting. *Wall Street Journal* (August 4):46.

Voice & Data Systems, Inc. 1981. Outvoice the electronic message system. Descriptive specification sheet. Chicago.

Wall Street Journal. 1980. Business Bulletin (December 8):1.

Wall Street Journal. 1981a. Toche Ross adds Apples. (November 24):5.

Wall Street Journal. 1981b. The latest in seminars: A TV hookup. (October 15):31.

Wall Street Journal. 1981c. Developers offer that something extra. (September 16):25.

Wall Street Journal. 1982a. Mail deliveries get even slower. (March 4):1.

Wall Street Journal. 1982b. Business conferences via global television to begin in December. (March 31):14.

Wall Street Journal. 1982c. AT&T unit selling unregulated services gets FCC approval and may begin in July. (June 11):6.

Wall Street Journal. 1982d. AT&T starts its picturephone service (July 9):29.

Wall Street Journal. 1982e. AT&T seeks bids for fiber optics produced in the U.S. (July 20):10.

Wall Street Journal: 1982f. GE develops system to hook together computer products. (March 31):16.

Waters, C. R. 1983. Just when you thought it was safe to go back to the office. *INC.* (January):74.

Webb Associates, (Ed.) 1978. Anthropometry source book, Vols. I, II, and III. NASA Reference Publication 1024. Washington, D. .C. July 1978.

Weber, J. 1982. Comic promoting for continental. *Rocky Mountain News* (February 2):2–8.

Western Electric. 1983. Advertisement. *High Technology* (3 November):14.

Western Union. 1983. Advertisement: Reach anyone with your small computer. *Wall Street Journal.* (September 23):16.

Yamaguchi, Y., and Y. Ishnada. 1972. Sitting posture: An electromyographic study on healthy and notalgic people. J. Jap. Orthop. Assoc. (46):51–56.

CONCLUSION

Current Issues
and Future Directions

Jean D. Wineman
College of Architecture
Georgia Institute of Technology
Atlanta, Georgia

The work in this volume has much to say about the planning, design, and management of the workplace. In these concluding remarks, I would like to emphasize a number of points that seem to be of broad significance, to consider in some depth three topics that are of particular concern to the field—lighting, air quality, and open-office planning—and to provide recommendations for office design.

Much of the research on behavioral aspects of office design focuses on worker satisfaction, and satisfaction as an indicator of work performance. The initial chapter of this volume raises questions about this relationship. However, it can be concluded that, irrespective of the strength of its relationship to performance, worker satisfaction with the workplace is important to the well-being of office workers and to the health of the organization. The work of Marans and Spreckelmeyer (this volume) demonstrates the close relationship between satisfaction with the immediate workspace and satisfaction with the work environment in general. Satisfaction with any one aspect of daily life has broad implications for other life realms. Thus, satisfaction with office space can have a positive influence on perceptions of the job, the organization, and other life satisfactions. A more satisfied outlook has direct implications for such productivity measures as tardiness, absenteeism, and turnover.

Aspects of the physical design of office settings are not usually the major concerns of office workers. If asked to identify those items that contribute most to their satisfaction and performance, more typical responses relate to job characteristics, organizational effectiveness, rewards, and so forth. Although it is all too often overlooked, the design of the workspace and its organizational context have direct effects on use patterns and the support of work tasks. An appropriate fit between the physical setting and the work process, at both the individual and the organizational level, provides intrinsic rewards (satisfaction with engaging in and accomplishing work tasks) and extrinsic rewards (physical setting rewards for performance) that motivate future performance. Another role of environmental factors is their indirect influence on worker satisfaction and performance mediated by worker attitudes and perceptions (as described by the models of Marans and Spreckelmeyer, this volume, and Ferguson and Weisman, this volume).

Give the potentially powerful influence of facilities improvements on the total lifecycle costs of an office building (see Introduction), these are areas of research that deserve greater attention. A comprehensive understanding of worker satisfaction and performance in office settings requires exploration of a complex set of interacting subsystems, including physical environmental factors, job characteristics, organizational factors, sociocultural characteristics, and past experience of workers.

METHODOLOGICAL LIMITATIONS

Relatively little field research has been conducted on behavioral responses to office settings, and the work that does exist is composed primarily of isolated case studies that often lack comprehensiveness. As suggested by Ferguson and Weisman (this volume) there is a need to move away from the single case study to demonstrate results across settings (across organizations, job types, and design features), thereby improving the generalizability of research results and furthering the theoretical understanding of the field. The efforts initiated by Marans and Spreckelmeyer (this volume) and Ferguson and Weisman (this volume) to build a theoretical understanding of the interacting subsystems contributing to office worker satisfaction and performance should be extended.

The research that has been presented in this volume suggests that perhaps too little attention has been given to the importance of job type and organizational characteristics. A worker's job type defines a position within the organizational hierarchy (status), a set of work tasks and potential rewards, perceptions of choice, control, and participation in organizational decision making. These factors clearly influence environmental satisfaction and worker performance. Similarly, organizational characteristics such as work tasks, modes of work, hierarchical arrangement, and reward systems have been shown to affect satisfaction and performance. A better understanding is needed of the influential characteristics of these factors and how they interact within the context of the office system.

It is also imperative that more detailed operational definitions be developed for the variables being investigated. As Hedge (this volume) points out, many of the concepts under study, such as noise, space, health, privacy, satisfaction, and productivity, are open to differing interpretations. For example, the physical qualities of the "open" office should be defined in order to avoid confusion with the "bull pen" type of office with no partitions whatsoever. The operational definition should include factors such as those defined by Sundstrom, Burt, and Kamp (1980) and Ferguson and Weisman (this volume), including number of enclosed sides, partition height, presence or absence of a door, visibility of others from seating position, visual exposure to others, and number of employees sharing the space. Without such definition, the ability to corroborate results across settings and to apply results in design are severely restricted.

CURRENT CONCERNS

As described by Kleeman (this volume), the office environment is undergoing rapid change due to technological advances. In the future, the work experience as we know it may be radically altered. The introduction of new technologies and an increased concern for energy efficiency, growth, and change have added and will continue to add new dimensions to the set of interacting subsystems that constitute the work environment. In responding to these new forces, office designers and management personnel have increasingly focused on three issues of office design that have reappeared as concerns throughout this volume: lighting, air quality, and open-office planning. Current research and directions for future efforts will be explored for each of these issues in the following sections.

LIGHTING

Lighting is a factor with which most office workers express satisfaction (Elder, Turner, and Rubin 1979; Elder and Tibbott 1981; Farrenkopf and Roth 1980; Goodrich 1979; Louis Harris and Associates 1980; Kraemer, Sieverts & Partners 1977). However, lighting is also an area with some of the greatest potential for cost savings in energy usage. Lighting systems are often the major sources of energy use in an office setting as well as the major contributors to cooling load. Because of the heat produced by lighting systems, more energy is typically consumed in cooling than in heating office buildings, even for buildings in the northern United States. With today's critical need for energy conservation, exploration of alternative lighting systems and their influence on user satisfaction and productivity is a top priority.

Artificial Sources

Much of the past research on lighting has been conducted in laboratory settings, so care must be exercised in applying results to the real world. Laboratory research (Spencer, Flynn, Hendrick, and Martyniuk 1979; Hawkes, Loe, and Rowlands 1979) on people's subjective responses to lighting design indicates that people found settings with more than one type of lighting and light source more interesting than those in which there was repetitive use of a luminaire or illumination from a single source. They preferred a complex variety of focused, directional light sources. Subjects also preferred higher overall light levels. Laboratory studies conducted for tasks involving critical visual discrimination (Barnaby 1980; Hughes and McNelis 1978) indicate that productivity and accuracy increase with higher illumination levels.

Some office setting research has been conducted recently on worker responses to alternatives to standard overhead fluorescent lighting. Ellis (this volume) conducted a comparative study of worker satisfaction with overhead direct lighting systems, a combination of task/ambient lighting, and an indirect uplighting system. Results of this study and several others indicated that, similar to the results obtained in laboratory settings, workers preferred lighting schemes with multiple-source, directional light as compared to uniform lighting. Thus, higher levels of satisfaction appear with the task/ambient and indirect uplighting schemes than with direct overhead illumination.

Research has also been conducted into the effects of variation in the spectral quality of lighting. Recent research has suggested that full-spectrum lighting (lighting with a spectral distribution similar to natural daylight) may increase visual acuity, reduce overall fatigue, and improve work performance (Hughes 1981; Maas, Jayson, and Kleiber 1974).

The optimum amount of the ultraviolet spectrum included in artificial light sources is a question requiring further research. Exposure to ultraviolet radiation has been found to influence the formation of vitamin D and the ability of the body to absorb calcium (Wurtman 1975). Preliminary research also indicates that exposure to small amounts of ultraviolet radiation may contribute to lower rates of illness due to colds. Similar findings have led to the specification of full-spectrum lighting for schools and work environments in the USSR (Hughes 1980, 1981). However, cautions are clearly in order here: There are serious health consequences of overexposure to ultraviolet radiation and air quality considerations have been indicated by preliminary research findings on interactions between air pollutants and ultraviolet radiation (see discussion of air quality in this chapter).

High-pressure sodium lamps, which, because of their low energy consumption, are being considered for office installations produce a yellower spectrum of light than the more common fluorescent lamps do. The impact of color rendition on worker satisfaction is controversial. The work of Williams (1975) indicated general acceptance by workers; whereas in a number of recent studies (Elder and Tibbott 1981; Flynn 1977; Wineman 1981), high-pressure sodium lighting was found to be considerably less acceptable than fluorescent sources. Aston and Bellchambers (1969) suggested that if a light source is perceived as giving poor color rendition, people require higher levels of light to reach a given level of satisfaction. To date, the research on high-pressure sodium lighting is quite limited, however, and further study is required to draw definitive conclusions.

In the area of lighting where people have very strong expectations based on past experience, care must be exercised to involve them in change processes and increase their awareness of the potential benefits of change (this may equally apply to innovations in space planning such as open-office systems). The importance of this involvement on user acceptance is clear from the work of Davis and Szigeti (this volume) and Ellis (this volume).

Natural Lighting and View

Research studies have repeatedly indicated that natural lighting and views to the outside are important to office workers (Boyce 1974; Elder and Tibbott 1981; Farrenkopf and Roth 1980; Goodrich 1979; Louis Harris and Associates 1978; Wineman 1978). Natural light appears to be important to workers, independent of its contribution to task visibility (Goodrich 1979; Wineman 1978). It is unclear, however, what qualities of natural light and view are most desired and/or to what extent these preferences are independent of the status value associated with offices located on an exterior window wall. Goodrich (1979) suggests that "such things as the color, the temperature, the variation of natural light, its soft texture and its ambience are important but neglected factors in lighting" (p. 9).

Natural lighting does not contribute significantly to illumination levels at distances from windows greater than twice the height of the windows above the floor (Crouch 1978). However, research by Wells (1965) indicates that workers who are located much farther into the space than light travels perceive they are receiving some amount of natural light. Because of the high positive value associated with natural light, workers' evaluations of the overall quality of their lighting are more positive in these cases.

The characteristics that contribute to the desirability of views outside are not well understood. It is of some importance to workers to be in contact with the time of day, weather conditions, and other aspects of the outside world (Elder and Tibbott 1981); and distant views provide eye muscle relaxation and visual relief. Both factors may also be functional in reducing perceptions of crowding (Evans 1979a; 1979b).

The ability to control drafts, heat gain, and glare are important aspects of window design and treatment (Wheeler 1969). Luminance of the sky as viewed through clear glass may range from between 10 and 100 times the optimal luminance required by typical office tasks. Crouch (1978) suggested that luminance that is higher for viewing than it is for the task severely reduces immediate scanning sensitivity and, thus, task performance for certain tasks. Natural lighting that is controlled, however, and that approaches the work surface at wide angles with the vertical is effective in overcoming veiling reflections (the reflected image of the light source) and provides high visibility (Crouch 1978).

Consideration should be given to the interaction between natural and artificial lighting. Both sources of illumination should be controllable so that as work tasks or conditions of natural lighting vary, lighting levels appropriate to the task may be achieved.

AIR QUALITY

Air quality in the office environment is of increasing concern among workers. Hardy (1974) and Wheeler (1969) found that good air circulation and the right workspace temperature are among the most important factors to office workers' comfort, yet these are factors with which many workers are dissatisfied (Louis Harris and Associates 1980). Recently, energy-savings efforts have been made to reduce the leakage of exterior air into the interiors of office buildings. According to a report by the National Research Council Committee on Indoor Pollutants (1981), however, these efforts to achieve tightly sealed buildings, coupled with energy-conserving reductions in ventilation rates, could aggravate problems of indoor air quality.

If the supply of exterior air in inadequate, the percentage of oxygen in the interior air declines. This perceived "freshness" of air is of concern to many office workers (Louis Harris and Associates 1980; Parsons 1976). Poor air quality has resulted in health effects ranging from fatigue, headaches, and irritation of the eyes, ears, and throat, to nausea, colds, bronchitis, and long-term respiratory diseases such as lung cancer (Working Women 1981).

Sources of air contaminants in offices include vapors from office products or construction materials, fumes from office machines, outdoor pollutants drawn inside the building, and asbestos fibers from insulation or decorative materials. Twenty possible airborne irritants have been identified as potential contributions to office workers' health complaints (Stellman 1977; Working Women 1981). Among some of the more common irritants are formaldehyde, asbestos fiber, tobacco smoke, carbon monoxide, microorganisms, and allergens. Some of the negative impacts associated with air pollution include lowered arousal, decreased performance on vigilance tasks, and decrements in short-term memory (Evans and Jacobs 1982). There is increasing evidence that concentrations of pollutants previously not thought to be harmful may have significant effects on mental and physical health (Mehrabian and Russell 1974).

Potentially harmful sources of office air pollution include:

1. *Ozone.* Exposure to low concentrations acts as a depressant and causes drowsiness. Prolonged exposure can cause permanent lung damage (United States Department of Health, Education, and Welfare 1973). The National Institute of Occupational Safety and Health (NIOSH) recommends that unnecessary exposure to even small concentrations be avoided. Photocopying machines and electric typewriters emit ozone. A recent study found that, without adequate ventilation, making 83 photocopies over a two-hour period could cause a health risk (Working Women 1981).
2. *Methanol or methyl alcohol.* Some duplicators contain methanol or methyl alcohol. Chronic exposure can irritate the mucous membranes of the eyes, nose, and throat; low concentrations may result in headaches, giddiness, insomnia, and blurred vision (Working Women 1981).
3. *Other hazardous materials.* A number of harmful chemicals are contained in commonly used office supplies. Nitropyrene is found in some photocopying toners and is a suspected mutagen and carcinogen. Trinitrofluorenore (TNF) is found in large IBM printers and copiers. Trichloroethylene (TCE) and tetrachloroethylene are found in liquid eraser products (Working Women 1981).

Recent research demonstrates a higher incidence of complaints of eye, nose, and throat irritation among occupants of air-conditioned open-plan offices than among occupants of unconditioned conventional offices (Hedge 1983; Turiel, Hollowell, Miksch, Rudy, and Young 1983). This was found to be true even when tests indicated that no known indoor pollutants exceeded current health standards. Similar results are reported by Hedge (this volume). It was found, however, that the highest levels of health complaints were from individuals occupying office locations where the relative concentration of positive ions was high, a factor that has been associated with adverse emotional and performance changes. Other potential factors associated with reported health complaints were the presence of fluorescent lighting and perceptions of inadequate ventilation. Hedge suggests that these results may not be due to the open-plan per se but to the use of air conditioning for ventilation and to inadequate daylight penetration into offices.

Another study that suggests a potentially significant interaction between air quality and lighting was conducted by Sterling and Sterling (1981) in Vancouver, British Columbia. The study was initiated at the request of office building tenants, primarily clerical workers and lawyers, who had moved from an older office building with operable windows to a recently remodeled, sealed, mechanically ventilated office building. Soon after the move, incidences of absenteeism and health complaints of eye irritation, headaches, nausea, and drowsiness increased. The research team, studying both lighting and air quality, found that the most dramatic reductions in eye irritations occurred when both the lighting and the ventilation were changed. These results led them to hypothesize that the ultraviolet radiation from lighting was interacting with air pollutants to create a "photo chemical smog," the cause of eye irritation.

The factors responsible for health complaints related to air quality are not well understood. Numerous "health hazard evaluations" have been requested from NIOSH in response to outbreaks of health complaints. (Scientists have developed the term *tight building syndrome* to classify general outbreaks due to unspecified air quality conditions.) Needed is further research into the role of such factors as indoor pollutants, ventilation, ion content, natural lighting, and the spectral characteristics of artificial light sources.

OPEN-OFFICE PLANNING

A major area of controversy in office planning and design concerns the effectiveness of open-office systems. Although open-office planning remains the predominant design approach in new office construction in the United States today, this approach to office design has been abandoned in the Netherlands, and researchers involved in a five-year research program have called for its abandonment in West Germany (Hedge, this volume).

The use of the open plan and the concept of the office landscape evolved in response to technological advances in office building design and the need for greater flexibility and compatibility of office systems. In the 1920s and 1930s, office buildings were designed as tall, narrow structures to maximize natural lighting and ventilation. With the introduction of air conditioning and uniform lighting systems following World War II, wider buildings with large uninterrupted floor spaces became the norm.

In the 1940s and 1950s, a few pioneering office designers began to search for new designs that would better meet the needs of the organization and the workers of that organization. Their problem-solving approach focused on the concepts of total flexibility, interchangeable modular parts, and systems thinking (Shoshkes 1976). Early examples of the application of this approach are Skidmore, Owings & Merrill's Union Carbide headquarters building of 1959 and Design for Business's building for Time Incorporated, also constructed at that time.

The office landscape, or *Bürolandschaft*, was developed in 1959 by the Quickborner Team, a German planning and management consulting firm. Originally, this company specialized in materials, furnishings, and equipment for offices. The office landscape concept grew out of their recognition of the incompatibility of these existing products and was an attempt to develop a flexible, compatible office system that would facilitate communications and paper flow. They felt the open office layout could best meet these goals. The office landscape was first utilized as a planning concept for the Bertelsmann Publishing Company in Gütersloh, West Germany. In the early 1960s, the concept was applied in other European cities, and by the 1970s it was being applied worldwide (Palmer and Lewis 1977).

Today open planning is used for a number of reasons. It provides flexibility for organizations that often experience the need for rearrangement to facilitate work group organization and work flow, and to maximize space utilization. It is cost-effective; furnishings have a shorter expected life than building components do and can be amortized over a shorter period of time. It is more energy efficient to heat and cool one large space (with low partitions) than a series of subdivided spaces. In those office buildings with large floor areas, open planning allows more workers access to outside views than conventional office designs do.

Proponents of open-plan systems suggest that, because of efficient storage capabilities and the integrated design of furnishing components, more workers can be accommodated within a given area than with conventional office design. They also argue that open planning increases interaction and communication among workers and therefore positively influences productivity.

To obtain a better understanding of the effectiveness of using an open office system, it is useful to explore its behavioral implications.

Visual Access to Windows

A number of research studies indicate the importance of natural lighting and outside views to environmental satisfaction in offices (Boyce 1974; Elder and Tibbott 1981; Farrenkopf and Roth 1980; Goodrich 1979; Louis Harris and Associates 1978; Wineman 1978). As mentioned previously, the desire for natural lighting appears to be relatively independent of its contribution to task visibility (Goodrich 1979; Wineman 1978).

Although the amount of natural light reaching open-plan office spaces some distance from the window wall may be minimal, workers tend to overestimate the amount of natural light that reaches their work surface (Wells 1965). Thus, open-office planning is one of the ways to maximize the positive effects of natural lighting on workers' evaluations of lighting quality.

Interaction and Communication

Oldham and Brass (1979) suggest that, based on a social relations model, if opportunities for physical contact are increased, one would expect to increase interaction among workers and enhance the conditions for improved task performance. They argue, therefore, that open-office planning should provide increased opportunities for performance feedback, friendship formation, and the resolution of interpersonal conflicts, and thus enhance worker motivation and job performance. In fact, a number of research studies have shown that open-office planning improves ease of communication and opportunities for interaction (Hundert and Greenfield 1969; Ives and Ferdinands 1974; Brookes and Kaplan 1972; Allen and Gerstberger 1973). However, as Oldham and Brass suggest, the relationship to improved communication is less clear. In their own work, Oldham and Brass (1979) found a decrease in motivation and work satisfaction with a move from conventional to open-plan offices. Perceptions of task identity, supervisor feedback, friendship opportunities, and job significance decreased.

As a result of this work, Oldham and Brass developed an alternative model (using a sociotechnical approach) that stresses the importance of physical boundaries. This approach suggests that boundaries such as walls or partitions create private defensible space and improve task identity and perceptions of job significance. Given the assumption that lasting friendship relations require the opportunity for personal conversations and the sharing of information in private, the model predicts that increased physical contact will result in increased friendship formation only if the opportunity exists for privacy.

Previous studies (Sundstrom, Herbert, and Brown 1982) have shown an increase in some types of interpersonal communication, such as interdepartmental contact and supervision, with a move to open-office systems; whereas other types of communication decrease, especially confidential conversations. Sundstrom and his associates found that satisfaction with communications and satisfaction with privacy were directly related. They propose that the open plan provides easier physical access to colleagues and thus makes communication easier; but at the same time the lack of speech privacy means confidential conversations are more difficult.

Visual and Acoustical Privacy

A recent study was conducted of Blue Shield offices in Michigan (American Productivity Center 1983) in which 122 clerical workers were involved in a move from a bull pen space (without any walls or partitions) to an open-plan office space (with less than full-height partitions). Productivity ratings (daily logs of time spent on jobs), already in use at Blue Cross/Blue Shield, were evaluated to assess productivity change. Results indicated a significant increase in both satisfaction with the workplace and productivity after installation of the open-office furnishing system.

This study demonstrates, as have many others, the importance of some delineation of personal space to worker satisfaction and productivity. However, the workers were clerical employees moving from open-pool arrangements to open-plan offices. Results indicated that the workers were more satisfied with the privacy of their workspaces than they had been previously, but satisfaction with privacy was still not high. The question remains whether open planning provides sufficient privacy to increase productivity for workers in other job categories and/or for those who have moved from other office space arrangements (such as conventional offices).

In fact, results from previous evaluations have shown significant decreases in visual and acoustical privacy in moves from office space types other than the open-pool arrangement to open-office systems (Hundert and Greenfield 1969; Kraemer, Sieverts & Partners 1977; Nemecek and Grandjean 1973; Sundstrom et al. 1982). Generally, these studies show an increase in noise and interruptions, although the results are varied.

Research suggests that a lack of privacy may in fact improve performance for certain job tasks. A person may be motivated to work more effectively if he or she sees others who are working or who are rewarded for increased productivity. Eye contact with either a supervisor or colleague can also function as a motivating factor (Parsons 1976). Similarly, the presence of some level of sound helps maintain arousal and masks unpredictable sounds (Holahan 1982). This work suggests that a balance should be achieved between task and environment. A moderately arousing setting is expected to be beneficial to boring or monotonous tasks, whereas a nonarousing setting is expected to be more appropriate for moderately complex tasks.

Sundstrom and his associates (1980) tested the hypothesis that for routine tasks, social contact could provide a source of stimulation and function as a facilitator of job performance. In contrast to this hypothesis, research results indicated that even for jobs involving routine tasks, workers preferred private spaces to more accessible workspaces; and, in fact, job performance was found to be higher in the more private spaces. The researchers suggest that people may prefer private workspaces because of their symbolic status value. This advantage of privacy may, even for routine tasks, be more important to worker satisfaction and performance than the benefits of social contacts provided in less private spaces.

It is clear that visual and acoustical privacy are still significant problems associated with open-office planning. In another Sundstrom study (1982), the sound-masking system, carpeting, and semi-sound-absorbing panels were not sufficient to control sound reflections, particularly in special situations, such as when offices were adjacent to a window wall. Factors that contribute to this "weak link" in achieving visual and acoustical privacy and ways to eliminate or offset these factors need further investigation.

Status Indicators

A factor suggested by the work of Sundstrom and associates (1980) and that of Konar, Sundstrom, Brady, Mandel, and Rice (1982) is the potentially overriding importance of status indicators. The traditional office with four walls and a door is an indicator of status in an organization. Research by Konar and associates (1982) and Steele (1973) indicates the importance of fit between status indicators and perceived position within the organizational hierarchy. A worker who perceives four walls and a door as the appropriate status reward for a person of his or her position may express dissatisfaction and exhibit reduced performance under open-office conditions. Status incongruence has been associated in a number of studies of office workers with mental and physical ill-health (Berry 1966; Brook 1973; Erikson, Pugh, and Gunderson 1972; 1973; Kahn and French 1970; Kasl and Cobb 1967).

What Is an Appropriate Choice?

Clearly, open-office furnishing systems have substantial advantages to the organization. As described previously, these systems are cost-effective, provide flexibility, and accommodate a greater number of workers in a given square-foot area. For the worker, research indicates that open-office systems have not been as successful as anticipated. Greater effort is needed to respond more effectively to the behavioral requirements of workers. The current literature in this field suggests a number of critical areas for further research.

Product Testing

Further research into methods of sound masking and sound absorption is needed. Product testing should be conducted in field settings to account for the variety of confounding factors, such as the problem of sound reflection from glass surfaces in offices areas located along a window wall. Sundstrom and associates (1982) and Wineman (1980) have suggested the mock-up (often constructed within an existing office setting) as a controlled technique for such testing.

Partition Height

A question arises about the height of partitions in open-office settings. Sundstrom and associates (1982) found a direct link between physical enclosure and satisfaction with privacy. However, their research shows that perceived privacy decreased more sharply for office workers with 78-inch partitions than for those with 60-inch ones. Objective measures indicated that the workers with higher partitions had more acoustical privacy, but their perceptions of privacy were lower. (A confounding factor in these results is that these two groups of workers were at different job levels.) The work of Goodrich (1982) implies that higher partitions may make noises more disturbing since the worker is unaware (visually) of the presence of the noise source. The privacy afforded by partitions of various heights should be investigated by job type.

Acoustical Disturbances

Further research would be useful on the types of acoustical privacy problems that are most bothersome to office workers. The work of Sundstrom and associates (1982) indicated that workers found the inability to hold confidential conversations to be a greater problem than other aspects of privacy, and this was especially a problem for managerial employees. Research by Hedge (this volume), Wineman (1981), and others has shown conversations of colleagues and telephone conversations to be most bothersome to office workers. Acoustical disturbances should therefore be looked at by job level and job task.

Size of Space

Adequate space is an important factor affecting worker satisfaction with their workspace (Brill, Mandel, and Quinan 1982; Louis Harris and Associates 1980; Marans and Spreckelmeyer 1982). Open-office systems, with their efficient storage capabilities and integral work surfaces, shelving, files, and so forth, allow a greater number of workers to be housed in a given area without decreasing the amount of open floor space per worker. However, unless the acoustical effects of this increased density are offset through the effective use of sound-masking systems and sound-absorbing materials and furnishings, satisfaction with acoustical privacy would be expected to decrease.

It is unclear whether office workers perceive a decrease in the overall size of open-office spaces. If so, this dissatisfaction may influence their perceptions of other aspects of the workspace and affect overall satisfaction.

Job Level/Job Tasks

Throughout this discussion it has been observed that many of the factors influencing worker satisfaction and performance may vary in importance, depending upon job level and the worker's particular job tasks. Office research to date, however, has not provided the depth of analysis necessary to draw appropriate conclusions in this respect.

For example, intuitively it would seem that for jobs involving tasks requiring concentration, the workspace requirements for visual and acoustical privacy would be much more stringent than for jobs involving routine tasks, where visual and acoustical relief might be welcomed. As described previously, this hypothesis was tested by Sundstrom and his associates (1980), who found that more private space was preferred irrespective of job tasks; and, in fact, job performance was found to be higher in the more private spaces. Sundstrom and his associates offer a number of potential explanations for the results: (1) In private space, one is less vulnerable to noise and distraction; (2) enclosure and visual privacy may reduce the pressure to maintain appearances; and (3) people may prefer private workspaces because of their symbolic status value. It may also be a learned response to seek privacy when one wishes to carry out work tasks. These advantages of privacy may, even for routine tasks, be of overriding importance to worker satisfaction and performance.

These results underscore the complexity of the work environment system, and the need for research that responds to these interacting environmental factors. The open plan should be considered as just one potential office layout. As emphasized by Duffy (1974a, 1974b), who has developed a taxonomy of office types, the most suitable office design should be selected on the basis of such organizational factors as organizational structure, management style, and work type (see also Hedge, this volume), as well as in response to worker needs.

FUTURE DIRECTIONS IN OFFICE DESIGN

Throughout the chapters in this book, four issues continually reappear. These are the needs for: (1) individual choice and control; (2) environmental diversity; (3) worker participation; and (4) closer liaison between professionals in the field.

Design and management professionals strive for control over environmental quality. This is exemplified by the mechanical engineer's desire for a closed system (i.e., no opening windows) for better heating, ventilation, and air-conditioning control. With a high-performance system, which is clearly the design goal, these conditions are optimal. However, what happens, as is so often the case, when the system under actual conditions does not perform as expected, or when natural conditions (heat or cold, for example) stray beyond the expected norms? To workers, individual control takes on increasing significance. Similarly, many office managers or administrators strive to perfect an orderly and efficient organizational image that entails uniformity of work stations. Again, the worker is left with little opportunity to adapt the workspace to his or her particular needs or to personalize the space for a feeling of at least temporary ownership or "belonging" to that particular space. There is a need in office settings to return some amount of choice and control to the workers.

It has been demonstrated in numerous studies (Baron and Rodin 1978; Seligman 1975; Strickland 1977) that the ability to exert some amount of control over one's environment can reduce the negative effects of such environmental factors as crowding and noise. Research indicates that increased actual and perceived control (the availability of control even if it is not utilized) will increase satisfaction, reduce stress, and enhance task performance (Averill 1973; Barnes 1980; Baron and Rodin 1978).

Office workers may exert control over the physical workspace in two ways. If an environment is perceived to be unsatisfactory, it may be changed directly by altering temperature, switching lights on and off, opening or closing windows and shades, opening or closing doors, rearranging furnishings, or personalizing the space. In an office space where flexible control of the boundaries is more difficult, such as in an open-plan setting, a worker may exert control indirectly by moving to a more appropriate space. For example, a worker may use an adjacent conference room for private telephone calls or conversations with clients or colleagues. Thus, the availability of and ability to use alterative settings and mechanisms of control (thermostat, doors, opening windows, and so on) become important determinants of satisfaction.

Within the work setting, greater attention should be paid to providing opportunities for choice and control by individual workers. For example, a narrow, rectangular floor plan rather than the large, undifferentiated floor areas of today's office buildings, would allow greater individual control. Workers would be closer to windows for controlled natural lighting and exterior views; potentially operable windows would allow control over temperature and ventilation (Grey 1983).

To maximize choice and control, environmental differentiation should be enhanced. Under open-plan conditions, workers should have the choice to move to more private space for private conversation or tasks requiring a high degree of concentration. As an alternative to the large, anonymous conference space, smaller private spaces (to accommodate two to four persons) could be provided adjacent to working groups to increase a perception of accessibility and territorial control.

In private office arrangements, the problem is of a contrasting nature. Here, there is a need to enhance opportunities for interaction and communication. Szilagyi and Holland (1980) reported on a study of highly skilled professionals in a petroleum-related organization. The workers were involved in a move to a new office space in which the level of privacy was retained but social density (people within a 50-foot walking distance) increased. Results indicated significant increases in job feedback, friendship opportunities, work satisfaction, information exchange, and task facilitation. (Perceptions of job autonomy were found to decrease.) There are a number of cautions, however, that go along with interpretation of these results. They are from a single study of a select sample of office workers (highly skilled professionals) and therefore may not be applicable to other organizations or other job levels. It is also important to clearly differentiate between social density and physical density. As previously mentioned, increases in physical density (people per square foot) may be accompanied by numerous other problems, such as noise and crowding. Social density may be increased while keeping physical density constant by careful planning of circulation pathways, entries, and exitways such that workers come into contact with each other more easily. Spaces should also be planned to enhance such encounters. For example, places for casual conversation should be provided along circulation paths and in places where workers may gather for the use of support services, such as duplicators, files, or coffee machines.

As office organizations increase in complexity, design and management personnel look for ways to achieve standardization. Clearly this must be achieved to bring a complex task into the realm of manageability. However, efforts at standardization reduce variation within the office setting. Diversity is a valued quality in and of itself (Kaplan and Kaplan 1978) and predicts the ability of the environment to meet the diversity of workers' needs. In addition to allowing greater freedom of choice, environmental variation provides visual relief. Perhaps this is why views outside and the variability of natural lighting are apparently so highly valued by office workers.

Typically, office standards are based upon assumptions about the range of tasks performed at various job levels and factors such as status demarcation. There is a need to broaden the basis upon which these standards are conceived to respond more directly to both individual and task performance differences.

Research demonstrates that worker involvement is directly related to satisfaction. The work of Davis and Szigeti (this volume) emphasizes the importance of worker participation in the programming of office space. Ellis's research (this volume) indicates that the acceptance of innovation in office settings may be dependent upon user involvement. Participation in the process appears to be important whether participation results in change or not.

Finally, the complexity of the office setting suggests the need for a closer liaison among professionals. Zeisel (1983) has emphasized the need for this kind of interaction among the design professionals, systems engineers, and other participants in the planning and design of settings to eliminate what he has called "unidisciplinary problem solving," the process through which decisions are made in one discipline without regard for their impacts in other areas. For example, an interior designer might specify 6-foot partitions without consideration for the resultant effects on air circulation within the workspaces. Hedge (this volume) advocates the closer cooperation among designers, behavioral researchers, and other professions involved in the operational management of offices.

In conclusion, it appears that the increasing complexity of office organizations has promoted trends of office design and management that may lead to worker dissatisfaction and a loss of productivity. To reverse these potentially damaging trends, there is a need to enhance professional collaboration in design and management decision-making processes, to involve workers in these processes, and to enhance opportunities for environmental choice and control.

References

Allen, T. J., and P. G. Gerstberger. 1973. A field experiment to improve communication in a product engineering department: The nonterritorial office. *Human Factors* 15: 487–498.

American Productivity Center. 1983. *Blue Cross and Blue Shield case study*. Grand Rapids, MI: Steelcase Inc.

Aston, S. M., and H. E. Bellchambers. 1969. Illumination, colour rendering and visual clarity. *Lighting Research and Technology* 1 (4): 259–261.

Averill, J. R. 1973. Personal control over aversive stimuli and its relationship to stress. *Psychological Bulletin* 80: 286–303.

Barnaby, J. F. 1980. Lighting for productivity gains. *Lighting Design & Application* (February): 20–28.

Barnes, R. D. 1980. Perceived freedom and control and the built environment. In J. Harvey (Ed.), *Cognition, social behavior and the designed environment*. Hillsdale, NJ: Erlbaum.

Baron, R. and J. Rodin. 1978. Personal control as a mediator of crowding. In A. Baum, J. E. Singer, and S. Valins (Eds.), *Advances in environmental psychology* Vol. 1: *The urban environment*. Hillsdale, NJ: Erlbaum.

Berry, K. J. 1966. Status integration and morbidity. Unpublished doctoral dissertation, University of Oregon.

Boyce, P. R. 1974. User's assessments of a landscaped office. *Journal of Architectural Research* 3 (3): 44–62.

Brill, M., D. Mandel, and M. Quinan. 1982. *The office environment as a tool to increase productivity and the quality of work life*. Buffalo, NY: BOSTI.

Brook, A. 1973. Mental stress at work. *Practitioner* 210: 373–391.

Brookes, M. J., and A. Kaplan. 1972. The office environment: Space planning and affective behavior. *Human Factors* 14: 373–391.

Crouch, C. L. 1978. Lighting for seeing. In G. C. Clayton and F. E. Clayton (Eds.), *Patty's industrious hygiene and toxicology* Vol. 1. New York: John Wiley & Sons.

Duffy, F. 1974a. Office design and organizations: 1.Theoretical basis. *Environment and Planning B* 1: 105–118.

Duffy, F. 1974b. Office design and organizations: 2. The testing of a hypothetical model. *Environment and Planning B* 1: 217–235.

Elder, J., and R. L. Tibbott. 1981. *User acceptance of an energy efficient office building: A study of the Norris Cotton Federal Office Building*. Washington, DC: U.S. Government Printing Office.

Elder, J., G. E. Turner, and A. I. Rubin. 1979. *Post-occupancy evaluation: A case study of the evaluation process*. Washington, DC: U.S. Government Printing Office.

Erikson, J., D. Edwards, and E. K. Gunderson. Status congruency and mental health. *Psychological Reports* 33: 395–401.

Erikson, J., W. M. Pugh, and E. K. Gunderson. 1972. Status congruency as a predictor of job satisfaction and life stress. *Journal of Applied Psychology* 56: 523–525.

Evans, G. W. 1979a. Behavioral and physiological consequences of crowding in humans. *Journal of Applied Social Psychology* 9: 27–46.

Evans, G. W. 1979b. Design implications of spatial research. In J. Aiello and A. Baum (Eds.), *Residential crowding and design.* New York: Plenum Publishing.

Evans, G. W., and S. V. Jacobs. 1982. Air pollution and human behavior. In G. Evans (Ed.), *Environmental stress.* New York: Cambridge University Press.

Farrenkopf, T., and V. Roth. 1980. The university faculty office as an environment. *Environment and Behavior* 12: 467–477.

Flynn, J. E. 1977. The effects of light source color on user impression and satisfaction. *Journal of Illuminating Engineering Society* 6 (3): 167–179.

Goodrich, R. 1982. Seven office evaluations: A review. *Environment and Behavior* 14 (May): 353–378.

Goodrich, R. 1979. *How people perceive their office environment.* New York: Citibank.

Grey, J. Pers. comm., October 21, 1983.

Hardy, A. C. 1974. A case for reduced window areas. *International Lighting Review* 25 (3): 90–92.

Hawkes, R. J., D. L. Loe, and E. Rowlands. 1979. A note towards the understanding of lighting quality. *Journal of the Illuminating Engineering Society* 8 (2): 111–120.

Hedge, A. 1983. Office design and office workers' health. Paper presented at 3rd Annual Irvine Symposium on Environmental Psychology, University of California at Irvine, April 28–29, 1983.

Holahan, C. J. 1982. *Environmental psychology.* New York: Random House.

Hughes, P. C. 1981. School lighting for the total person: A psychobiological approach. *Council of Educational Facility Planners Journal* (March–April): 4–6.

Hughes, P. C. 1980. The use of light and color in health. In A. C. Hasings, J. Fadiman, and J. S. Gordon (Eds.), *Health for the whole person: The complete guide to holistic medicine.* Boulder, CO: Westview Press.

Hughes, P. C., and J. F. McNelis. 1978. Lighting, productivity and the work environment. *Lighting Design and Application* (December): 32–40.

Hundert, A. T., and N. Greenfield. 1969. Physical space and organizational behavior: A study of office landscape. *Proceedings of 77th Annual Convention of the American Psychological Association* 1: 601–602.

Ives, R. S., and R. Ferdinands. 1974. Working in a landscaped office. *Personnel Practice Bulletin* 30(2): 126–141.

Kahn, R. L., and J. R. P. French. 1970. Status and conflict: Two themes in the study of stress. In J. McGrath (Ed.), *Social and psychological factors in stress.* New York: Holt, Rinehart & Winston.

Kaplan, S., and R. Kaplan. 1978. *Humanscape: Environments for people.* North Scituate, MA: Duxbury Press.

Kasl, S. V., and S. Cobb. 1967. Effects of parental status incongruence and discrepancy in physical and mental health of adult offspring. *Journal of Personality and Social Psychology Monograph* 7 (2), Part 2 of 2 parts (whole No. 642), 1–15.

Konar, E., E. Sundstrom, E. S. Brady, D. Mandel, and R. W. Rice. 1982. Status demarcation in the office. *Environment and Behavior* (14) (September): 561–580.

Kraemer, Sieverts & Partners. *Open-plan offices* (J. L. Ritchie, Trans.). New York: McGraw-Hill.

Louis Harris and Associates. 1980. *The Steelcase national study of office environments, No. II: Comfort and productivity in the office of the 80's.* Grand Rapids, MI: Steelcase, Inc.

Louis Harris and Associates. 1978. *The Steelcase national study of office environments: Do they work?* Grand Rapids, MI: Steelcase, Inc.

Maas, J. B., J. K. Jayson, and D. A. Kleiber. 1974. Effects of spectral difference in illumination on fatigue. *Journal of Applied Psychology* 59: 524–526.

Marans, R. W., and K. F. Spreckelmeyer. 1982. Evaluating open and conventional office design. *Environment and Behavior* 14 (May): 333–351.

Mehrabian, A., and J. A. Russell. 1974. *An approach to environmental psychology.* Cambridge: MIT Press.

National Research Council Committee on Indoor Pollutants. 1981. *Indoor pollutants.* Washington, DC: National Academy Press.

Nemecek, J., and E. Grandjean. 1973. Results of an ergonomic investigation of large-space offices. *Human Factors* 15: 111–124.

Oldham, G. R., and D. J. Brass. 1979. Employee reactions to an open-plan office: A naturally occurring quasi-experiment. *Administrative Science Quarterly* 24: 267–284.

Palmer, A. E., and S. M. Lewis. 1977. *Planning the office landscape.* New York: McGraw-Hill.

Parsons, H. M. 1976. Work environments. In I. Altman and J. F. Wohlwill (Eds.), *Human behavior and environment: Advances in theory and research,* Vol. 1. New York: Plenum Publishing.

Seligman, M. 1975. *Helplessness: On depression, development and death.* San Francisco: Freeman.

Shoshkes, L. 1976. *Space planning: Designing the office environment.* New York: Architectural Record Books.

Spencer, T., J. E. Flynn, C. Hendrick, T. Spencer, and D. Martyniuk. 1979. A guide to methodology procedures for measuring subjective impressions in lighting. *Journal of the Illuminating Engineering Society* 8 (2): 95–110.

Steele, F. I. 1973. *Physical settings and organizational development.* Reading, MA: Addison-Wesley.

Stellman, J. M. 1977. *Women's work, women's health.* New York: Pantheon.

Sterling, E., and T. Sterling. 1981. The impact of different ventilation and lighting levels on building illness: An experimental study. (Research report). Vancouver, B.C.: TDS Limited.

Strickland, B. R. 1977. Internal-external control of reinforcement. In T. Blass (Ed.), *Personality and social behaviors.* Hillsdale, NJ: Erlbaum.

Sundstrom, E., R. Burt, and D. Kamp. 1980. Privacy at work: Architectural correlates of job satisfaction and job performance. *Academy & Management Journal* 23: 101–117.

Sundstrom, E., R. K. Herbert, and D. W. Brown. 1982. Privacy and communication in an open-plan office: A case study. *Environment and Behavior* 14 (May): 379–392.

Szilagyi, A., and W. Holland. 1980. Changes in social density: Relationships with functional interaction and perceptions of job characteristics, role stress, and work satisfaction. *Journal of Applied Psychology* 65 (1): 28–33.

Turiel, I., C. D. Hollowell, R. R. Miksch, J. V. Rudy, and R. A. Young. 1983. The effects of reduced ventilation on indoor air quality in an office building. *Atmospheric Environment* 17: 51–64.

U.S. Department of Health, Education and Welfare. 1973. *Industrial exposure to ozone.* NIOSH pamphlet #74-118.

Wells, B. 1965. Subjective responses to the lighting installation in a modern office building and their design implications. *Building Science* 1: 57–67.

Wheeler, L. 1969. *The office environment*. Chicago: Interior Space Designers Inc.

Williams, H. G. 1975. High pressure sodium lighting in offices for reduced energy use. *Industry Applications Society (IAS) Meeting*, pp. 81–87.

Wineman, J. 1983a. Techniques for user involvement in programming and evaluation. Paper presented at 3rd Annual Irvine Symposium on Environmental Psychology, University of California at Irvine, April 28–29.

Wineman, J. 1983. Environmental factors pose a threat to office workers. Paper presented at 3rd Annual Irvine Symposium on Environmental Psychology, University of California at Irvine, April 28–29.

Wineman, J. 1982. The office environment as a source of stress. In G. Evans (Ed.), *Environmental stress*. New York: Cambridge University Press.

Wineman, J. 1981. Office evaluation research: Issues and applications. Paper presented at the Center for Building Technology Federal Workshop Series on Building Science and Technology. The office as a work environment: The measurement and evaluation of performance. Gaithersburg, MD: National Bureau of Standards, February 1981.

Wineman, J. 1980. Evaluation of the office work environment. Paper presented at the American Psychological Association Annual Convention, Montreal, Canada, September 1980.

Wineman, J. 1978. Building evaluation research: Lighting evaluation. Research report prepared for Applied Environmental Research Divison of Smith, Hinchman & Grylls, Ann Arbor, MI, February 1978.

Working Women. 1981. Warning: Health hazards for office workers—An overview of problems and solutions in occupational health in the office. Cleveland, OH: Working Women Education Funds.

Wurtman, R. J. 1975. The effects of light on the human body. *Scientific American*. 233: 68–77.

Zeisel, J. 1983. Energy and occupancy: A total building performance model. Paper presented at the Energy Use Conference, Cambridge University, England.

APPENDIX

Annotated Bibliography

KATHRYN MAIER-BRUWELHEIDE
GLENN S. FERGUSON

Alessi, D., M. Brill, and D. Fowles. 1979. Productivity, job satisfaction and the office workspace. *Civil Service Journal* 19: 14–19.

Because productivity level in the office setting is of major concern, the physical environment of the office may be seen as somewhat of a mold, with the power to shape the activities and behaviors that take place there. Intervention through that physical environment is reviewed as affecting both job accomplishment and job satisfaction.

Allen, T. J., and P. G. Gerstberger. 1973. A field experiment to improve communications in a product engineering department: The nonterritorial office. *Human Factors* 15(5): 487–498.

A total of 24 product engineers were moved from a conventional office plan to a nonterritorial office, which utilized no walls and no permanent work stations. The new office was designed with the intention of fostering communication between workers and departments. Communication and productivity were monitored for one year to determine effects of the new setting. Results showed satisfaction with the setting, but no improved productivity levels.

Alsleben, K. 1965. The office landscape and its subjective spaces. *Kommunikation* 1(November): 75–82.

This review of the open plan discusses significant problems as well as advantages. Sample situations illustrate solutions through design to portray the complexity involved in office designing.

Altman, M. A. 1965. Revisiting law office layout and design. *American Bar Association Journal* 65(November): 1644–1648.

Many of the conventional decisions in office designing must be considered in a different light when planning the law office. Space needs for books, papers, and meetings must be carefully planned for the lawyer and his or her office space. Desks and furniture in general are of great importance in these offices.

Armstrong, D., and C. Nuttall. 1981. Managing the efficient automated workplace. *Best's Review* 82(May): 48.

Managing the automated workplace involves new skills for managers. This review of the facility as a "productivity-enhancing tool" points out the potential of the automated office when both the worker and the manager know how to utilize it.

Bach, F. W. 1965. The whos and wherefores of the open plan office. *Kommunikation* 1(November): 103–105.

Specific organizational rationales are provided for functional use of the open plan. Approximated costs per workplace and building costs in general are illustrated in chart form.

Barkman, A. P. 1982. Open-plan offices need an acoustical design. *Office* 95(March): 118–119.

The importance of acoustical control in the open-plan office is based upon two needs: control of noise level and speech privacy. Performance criteria for open-plan interiors include sound-reflectant materials and lead to analysis of a noise reduction coefficient.

Barnaby, J. F. 1980. Lighting for productivity gains. *Lighting Design and Application* 10(February): 20–28.

An on-site lighting study in an insurance firm illustrates a positive correlation between lighting levels and performance accuracy. Lighting levels are quantified in reference to task performance, and illumination levels are discussed. Further, a cost analysis is done with the intention of determining the monetary benefits of increased lighting levels in reference to productivity.

Becker, F. D. 1981. *Workspace: Creating environments in organizations.* New York: Praeger Publishers.

Facility planning and management is a crucial process in the design of offices. What makes the process more difficult is the existence and significance of a distinct relationship between environmental variables and the individual's motivation and productivity level. The environment, or physical setting, is referred to as a catalyst, as a prosthesis, as a social process, and much more, all in reference to the workspace.

Bell Canada's office landscape experience. 1980. *Administrative Management* 41(September): 48–51.

After adopting a "construction management" approach, Bell constructed a new office building, depending a great deal on its own employees. Traffic patterns, information exchange, and aesthetics were some of the elements considered in planning stages.

Bell, F. A. 1981. Employee productivity in the open plan office. *Buildings* 15(August): 54.

A study of three open offices investigated the validity of the open plan as a method of office planning in reference to the need for higher productivity levels and persistent complaints about the open plan. Using Time Measurement analysis, a productivity improvement was calculated as a result of a new office layout. Other improvements were found in noise level, motivation, and morale, as a result of the open-office furniture systems.

Ben-Porat, A. 1981. Satisfaction from office environmental change. *Psychology, A Quarterly Journal of Human Behavior* 18(1): 17–23.

The variables job context, job content, privacy, and satisfaction composed a model of job satisfaction by which the adjustment of 31 employees to a new open-office design was examined. The subjects responded to a questionnaire only after the move, and a multiple regression analysis was done on the data. The goal of the study was based upon satisfaction as an indicator of adjustment.

Beranek, L. L. 1956. Criteria for office quieting based on questionnaire rating studies. *Journal of the Acoustical Society of America* 28: 833–852.

A study of noise conditions and reactions involving 184 executive and lower-level employees at a large Air Force base illustrates differences in noise tolerance. Questionnaire and observation methods were employed to assess the workers' ability for conversation and use of the telephone at differing levels of sound or speech interference. Results did illustrate a difference in noise level toleration between the two job levels.

Binkley, J. L., and J. A. Parker. 1978. Specifying for user needs in office environments. In W. Preiser (Ed.), *Facilities programming: Methods and applications.* Stroudsburg, PA: Dowden, Hutchinson and Ross.

The defining and utilization of performance specifications provide the bases of design for the office. User needs provide a foundation for the development of a physical connection or link between users and work systems.

Black, F. W. 1964. Desirable temperatures in offices: A study of occupant reaction to the heating provided. *Journal of the Institution of Heating and Ventilation Engineers* (November): 319–328.

A study comparing two types of heating systems in an office finds no real difference. Both objective and subjective evaluations of heating conditions were utilized. Differences between temperature evaluations by men and women are mentioned and implications for office design discussed.

Block, G. E., and R. C. Block. 1972. Office landscaping. *Personnel Practice Bulletin* 28(1): 46–57.

To bridge the gap between the corridor office and the open-plan office, the landscaped office was developed. The functional physical elements of this style of office plan are discussed in terms of ideal levels. Strengths as well as weaknesses of the system are offered, with emphasis on the benefits.

Bobele, H. K., and P. J. Buchanan. 1979. Building a more productive environment. *Management World* (January): 8–10.

In their efforts to inspire workers to be more productive, managers very often overlook the obvious: the importance of altering the physical space around and between the workers. The concepts of "differentiation" and "integration" are defined and applied to particular situations as examples. Physical space is manipulated to deal with managerial and organizational goals.

Boje, A. 1971. *Open-plan offices* (B. H. Walley, Ed. and Trans.). London: Business Books. (Originally published, 1968.)

The open-plan office is described as including many optimum features, ideal for some businesses. Organization and management of the open plan is discussed at every level of business. If suitable, this design may provide higher morale and productivity levels. A symposium of papers and different office design styles is included.

Bomberg, H. 1979. The liberated office. *Management World* (January): 11–13.

The evolution of the office requires a flexible structure that can respond to constant change. The open plan is reported to be such a system. Applied examples are given, as are questions to be considered for every workspace to determine functionality.

Bomberg, H. 1981. Open plan: Flexibility for the future. *Management World* 10(December): 14.

The open plan is briefly compared to the conventional office, and drastic advantages with the open plan are illustrated.

Boyce, P. R. 1974. Users' assessments of a landscaped office. *Journal of Architectural Research* 3(3): 44–62.

Approximately 300 workers were surveyed once before and twice after a move to a somewhat "typical" office landscape from several different buildings employing closed-plan offices. The three surveys were designed to examine changes in attitude after the move, as well as satisfaction with specifics of the new setting. The main advantage as a result of the move was improved communications; disadvantages included ventilation problems and high noise levels.

Brookes, M. J. 1969. A maze of contradictions. *Progressive Architecture* 50(11): 130–131.

A review of the open-plan "boom" reveals realistic consequences of this design. The problem lies in the architect's lack of understanding of the implications of an office design. Where productivity and morale were expected to flourish, in the open plan they did not. Architects and space planners must understand the consequences of design decisions before implementation occurs.

Brookes, M. J. 1972. Changes in employee attitudes and work practices in an office landscape. In W. J. Mitchell (Ed.), *Environmental design: Research and practice,* Proceedings of the Environmental Design Research Association (No. 3)/Architectural Research (No. 8) Conference. Los Angeles: University of California.

For a discussion of field study, see Brookes and Kaplan 1972.

Brookes, M. J. 1972. Office landscape: Does it work? *Applied Ergonomics* 3(4): 224–236.

For a discussion of field study, see Brookes and Kaplan 1972.

Brookes, M. J., and A. Kaplan. 1972. The office environment: Space planning and affective behavior. *Human Factors* 14: 373–391.

The current state of expertise in office and space planning is discussed. A debate between researchers exists about the actual benefits of the office landscape, thus inspiring a field study to investigate the gap between assumptions and research findings. The field study, utilizing a semantic scaling instrument, investigated the attitudes of 120 employees relocated from a combination bull pen and cubicle layout to an open-office landscape. The use of factor analyses on 45 descriptors illustrates relationships between ratings and satisfaction, general effects of office change, and overlap between workspace satisfaction and satisfaction with the environment as a whole.

Building Programs International & Interior Facilities Associates. 1979. *How people perceive their office environment*. New York: Citibank.

This review of a post-occupancy survey of employees' reactions to a newly designed office environment illustrates a relationship between overall design opinion and personal workspace opinion. The improvement of the physical work environment implies concern on the part of the company for the workers. The design of the study was based upon questionnaire data.

Burger, J. M. 1981. Verbal message inhibition through nonverbal communication within an open-space office: An application of equilibrium theory to organizational contexts. Paper presented at the meeting of the American Psychological Association. Los Angeles, August 1981.

This field study employed 23 office employees to investigate the applicability of equilibrium theory to the regulation of communication in the office setting. Relationships between self- and other-initiated communications and the use of desktop objects was investigated. The use of such nonverbal cues was found to be related to the initiation of communication as well as to the length of it.

Business Equipment Manufacturers Association. 1967. *Developing the total office environment* (BEMA Business Equipment Conference, Chicago, 1966). Washington, DC: Thompson Book.

See Lerner 1967; Powell 1967; Steele 1967; Waddell 1967.

Business Equipment Manufacturers Association. 1968. *New concepts in office design* (BEMA Management Conference, New York, 1967). Elmhurst, IL: Business Press.

See Johnson 1968; Mogulescu 1968; Rodgers 1968; Schindler 1968; Torgeson 1968.

Business Equipment Manufacturers Association. 1969. *Improving office environment* (BEMA Management Conference, Chicago 1968). Elmhurst, IL: Business Press.

This is a collection of seven articles on office environment presented at a BEMA conference in 1968. Article topics are: designing for American employees; systems office landscape; individual view of a landscape office; a bank's view of its office needs; the designer's challenge; the need for a professional designer; and inside staff designers. The audience for these presentations was that of the manager, now interested in the role of the office designer. See DeHaan 1969; Jaeger 1969; Miller 1969.

Campbell, D. E. 1978. *Interior office design and visitor response*. Paper presented at the meeting of the American Psychological Association, Toronto, August 1978.

A total of 251 students participated in a simulation study investigating the effects that furniture arrangement and the presence of living things, aesthetics, and neatness in an office have on visitors. Through the use of slides, the subjects rated each scene in terms of visitor comfort, visitors' feelings of being welcome, and so on. Results showed positive effects for living things, aesthetics, and neatness, but not for furniture arrangement.

Campbell, D. E. 1979. Interior office design and visitor response. *Journal of Applied Psychology* 64(6): 648–653.

See Campbell 1978.

Canter, D. 1968. Office size: An example of psychological research in architecture. *Architects' Journal* (April 24): 881–888.

The problem of the utilization of psychological research findings by architects has always plagued the field of environmental psychology. Specifically, the psychological implications of design are what need to be conveyed. The implications of design and psychological research behind any knowledge in this area are often difficult for the designer to understand. Therefore, the problem is one of communication. The strategies involved in investigating the effects of office size are discussed in detail.

Canter, D. 1977. Priorities in building evaluation: Some methodological considerations. *Journal of Architectural Research* 6(1): 38–40.

A discussion of the many experts involved in environmental design and the expressed priorities of each seeks the solution of how the relative impact of different aspects of the environment can be determined. Five strategies for determining priorities are identified and discussed: user ratings, variance proportions, criterion correlation, complaints, and relationship with physical variables.

Canter, D. V. 1969. The psychological implications of office size. Doctoral dissertation, University of Liverpool.

Unavailable for review.

Canter, D. V. 1972. Reactions to open plan offices. *Built Environment* 1(October): 465–467.

Even though assumptions of the effects of open-office planning have been optimistic in the past, research does not support this optimism. This review article points to research that illustrates the relatively little effect environment has upon clerical workers, and discusses lack of satisfaction with the workplace and increased distractions.

Ceiling-high wall partitions. 1982. *Buildings* 76(4): 41.

The many advantages of ceiling-high partitions, as opposed to conventional walls, are discussed. This particular method of vertical construction is not only cost efficient, but also anticipatory of future needs through flexibility, while providing a sense of permanence; obsolescence does not become a problem.

Centraal Beheer Offices, Apeldoorn, Holland. *Architects' Journal* 162(October 1975): 893–904.

The Centraal Beheer Offices, designed by Hertzberger, are seen as a reflection of his philosophy. The philosophical views of Hertzberger are based upon a view of architectural form as a catalyst for stimulation of imagination. Evaluation of the offices as reflective of Hertzberger's original intentions and style illustrate success. Through a combination of his design and the organization itself, the company has been very successful.

Clearwater, Y. A. W. 1980. Social-environmental relationships in open and closed offices. Doctoral dissertation, University of California, Davis, 1979. *Dissertation Abstracts International*, 1980, 40, 5072B (University Microfilms No. 80-09527).

Attitudinal measures were used to investigate the reactions of 400 employees to a new office setting. The measures were aimed at environmental satisfaction, employee morale, interpersonal relations, and productivity. Results, discussion, and extensive coverage of the issues provide for complete discussion at significant points.

Cohen, A., and E. Cohen. 1980. Behavioral aspects of space. *Real Estate Today* 13(5): 55.

Even though there are three important factors involved in the planning of an office—the aesthetic, the functional, and the behavioral—the last is the least understood. The main objective of office planning is relative to that particular organization and its workers.

Collons, R. 1981. The effectiveness of office layout. *Best's Review* 81(February): 86.

Office layout, as well as leadership effectiveness, has an important effect upon the functioning of the organization. A review of an earlier study on physical layout and situational control illustrates that alterations in physical space and distance between work groups may have significant effects upon successful organizational workings.

Connell, J. J. 1980. The need for new office research. *Management World* 9(January): 24.

Because new elements of office technology offer possibilities for improvement in productivity levels, these new products should be researched before being put on the market. New office technologies are more often concerned with communicating information than processing it, so these technologies must be adaptable to the varying communication styles of managers.

Cumpston, C. 1973. Partitions and screens gaining overdue acceptance as prominent fixtures in the modern office environment. *Administrative Management:* 34(January): 30–33.

Partitions and screens are discussed as a functional element of the office. Characteristics common to all partitions are noted, along with applied examples to illustrate flexibility and dependability.

Curtis, J. 1981. Computer program for acoustical privacy in any office space. *Office* 94(September): 49.

A computer program, Opland, is introduced. This program, as it is stated, can predict reactions of office employees to acoustical privacy provided by a particular office design. The program replicates the chosen office layout as well as other materials of the office, thus allowing the designer to foresee the acoustical effects of each design. Even though many preliminary stages are involved, cost efficiency in choosing the best layout is a benefit.

Daroff, K. 1980. Office environments in the 1980's. *Industrial Development* 149(2): 11–14.

Even though the importance of technological advances in the office are increasing, the human-technology interface is still the most important resource and will remain so for quite some time. This summary article describes seven major guidelines for the successful planning of an office. The design of the interior space of a building is the most crucial step.

Davis, G. 1972. People in the work-place. *Building Research* (April/June): 3–8.

This discussion article identifies the ecological system of the workplace and its components, emphasizing the individual as the most complex and most important element in the system. Whatever form any of the other elements take, they will affect the human element. User participation in the design process then becomes crucial in creating the workplace, and the adaptable workplace is the most functional one.

Davis, G. 1972. Using interviews of present office workers in planning new offices. In W. Mitchell (Ed.), *Environmental design: Research and practice*, Proceedings of the Environmental Design Research Association (No. 3)/Architectural Research (No. 8) Conference. Los Angeles: University of California.

The development of a design program to be used by architects is discussed. The use of interview methods as well as sample and field work provided data, translated into architectural criteria, to be directly used by the architect. Perceptions, feelings, and space and facilities use levels were considered and are discussed in great detail. Problems with research and analysis in this kind of programming project are discussed.

Davis, G. 1973. FREEFIT: A "second generation" development out of office landscape experience. Paper presented to the Office Landscape Symposium of the Administrative Management Society, New York, April 1973.

The ecological system of the workplace provides the basis for a "second generation" solution to the conflict between the needs of the individual and those of the organization in designing an office. Specific needs are explained and translated into the FREEFIT solution.

Davis, G. 1974. Applying a planned design process and specific research to the planning of offices. Unpublished manuscript. (Available from The Environmental Analysis Group, Ltd., Ottawa, Canada.)

Through years of research and experience, planning has become known as a process, not just one written program. The final product, besides being part of an ongoing process, provides a degree of flexibility in the planning, and a balance between complicated and often conflicting objectives. A detailed process of planning that incorporates the mentioned research and experience is presented.

Davis, G. 1978. A process for adapting existing buildings for new office uses. In W. Preiser (Ed.), *Facility programming: Methods and applications.* Stroudsburg, PA: Dowden, Hutchinson and Ross.

A case study is used to illustrate the process of programming involved in the conversion of an existing building into office space. All involved elements are discussed, from preliminary discussions and the beginning phases of programming to occupancy and feedback. A model of the main tasks involved and their sequencing is provided.

Davis, G., and I. Altman. 1976. Territories at the work-place. Theory into design guidelines. *Man-Environment Systems* 6(1): 46–53.

Fundamental steps in determining the layout and design of an office environment are presented. The main issues to be considered—territories, privacy, and control of boundaries—are discussed and presented in tables.

Davis, G., and G. Shuttleworth. 1973. *Creating an effective office environment.* Vancouver, British Columbia, Canada: The Environmental Analysis Group.

A discussion of general principles used in planning office buildings, and the ecological system involved, leads to a complete summary of the complex and many needs that must be considered. The different types of office layout are presented and analyzed in terms of how they meet the needs of the organization.

Davis, G., and F. Szigeti. 1982. Programming, space planning and office design. *Environment and Behavior* 14: 299–317.

Defining specific user needs and the type of project being considered are the two major determiners of not only the final design of an office, but also the design process. Deciding upon physical requirements of an office, the generation of user-oriented requirements, and arising programming processes are the basic elements of the article.

Dean, A. O. 1977. The pros and cons and future prospects of open landscaping. *AIA Journal*: (July): 46–47, 82.

Both positive and negative aspects of open-office landscaping are presented, based upon actual setting application. Comprehensive planning and continuous surveillance have become an important phase in any successful office planning, from cost efficiency to loss of privacy. Future ideas in successful planning are presented.

Dean, A. O. 1980. Workplaces: The open office revisited. *AIA Journal* (July): 50–56.

A summary of the increasing number of large companies now employing the use of the open plan and systems furniture illustrates a variety of choices. Most successful offices provide various kinds of spaces, from totally closed to totally open. Issues of status, interaction, privacy, and technology are paramount and tend to dictate the types of spaces provided.

DeChiara, J., and J. H. Callender (Eds.). 1980. *Time-saver standards for building types.* 2nd ed. New York: McGraw-Hill.

Over 100 types of buildings are discussed and illustrated in terms of design criteria and problems in planning and design. Human dimensions, furniture dimensions, and all kinds of interior spaces are explained in reference to job and role needs. Specifically, offices are treated as they occur in many different settings, such as dental, insurance, and industrial.

DeHaan, N. R. 1969. Yes! You do need the help of a professional interior designer. In *Improving office environment* (Business Equipment Manufacturers Association Management Conference, Chicago, 1968). Elmhurst, IL: Business Press.

Rationales for the employment of a professional designer are discussed, based upon four areas: physical space, manpower, initial and maintenance costs, and aesthetics. Support for this argument relies heavily upon the refined skills of the professional space planner as opposed to general in-house management staff.

Duffy, F. 1976. Buildings never lie. *Architectural Design* 46(2): 105–106.

Architecture tends to reflect the current values of society, and this is especially true of office interiors. Further, the relationship between the individual and the organization is well reflected in the design of the office. Therefore, the role of the architect is described as mediator, through design, of individual and institutional values.

Duffy, F. 1979. Future of office planning. *Architectural Review* 165(988): 365–366.

Architecture, in and of itself, can no longer expect to solve design problems. This discussion of the issue simply states the difference and at the same time the relationship between the shell of a building and its interior space. The architect must understand the difference between the two as well as user needs.

Duffy, F. 1969. A method of analyzing and charting relationships in the office. *Architects' Journal* 149(11): 693–699.

The basis of any design by an architect should be the data concerning the users. Even though lack of methods has prevented such practices in the past, this paper addresses the issue and presents a method. Different charting methods used to outline office activities are explained; using these, the architect should be able to understand existing interrelationships. Case studies are used as examples.

Duffy, F. 1980. Office buildings and organizational change. In A. D. King (Ed.), *Buildings and society: Essays on the social development of the built environment.* London: Routledge & Kegan Paul.

Four major issues inherent to the office and its building—social relationships, technology, building construction, and internal factors of design—are examined in a comparison of three pairs of buildings. A conflict between internal organizational factors and external factors existed in the past and is said to exist now.

Duffy, F. 1969. *Office landscaping: A new approach to office planning*, 2nd ed. London: Anbar.

Based upon the belief that good work cannot be done in "bad" offices, this explanation and support for office landscaping explains how the needs of the workers can be met with this design. Office landscaping, originated and developed in Germany, rejects both the conventional office plan and the open plan. Sample floor plans are provided.

Duffy, F. 1969. Role and status in the office. *Architectural Association Quarterly* 1(4): 4–13.

Role and status are distinguished from each other, and their importance in the office setting is discussed. Status is often exhibited in the design of an office, and examples of this are given. The interaction between the two conflicts that may arise are affected by architectural design, but affect design as well.

Duffy, F. 1974. Office design and organizations: 1. Theoretical basis. *Environment and Planning B* 1: 105–118.

The reciprocal interaction between the organization and the design of the office is discussed. Influence is never unidirectional. A thorough discussion of research in this area illustrates a large degree of variance in conclusions drawn. A theoretical model is developed.

Duffy, F. 1974. Office design and organizations: 2. The testing of a hypothetical model. *Environment and Planning B* 1: 217–235.

This article discusses the testing of a hypothetical model that attempts to draw a relationship between office layout and organization. The question of office layout as a reflection of the style of organization is challenged. Level of bureaucracy in an organization has become an important factor in hypothesizing about expected behavior.

Duffy, F., C. Cave, and J. Worthington (Eds.). 1976. *Planning office space*. London: Architectural Press.

The importance of office planning now lies in the ability of the architect and the client to collaborate on design in order to fit the needs of the office shell as well as the needs involved in managing the space. Many photographs and sketches are used to illustrate the existent as well as the projected office design. Several examples of differing office styles are provided.

Duffy, F., and J. Worthington. 1977. Organizational design. *Journal of Architectural Research* 6(1): 4–9.

This article discusses the relationship of organizational design to office layout and design and addresses the issue within a sociological framework. Through a discussion of the brief (program) the article explains how the changing organization must be fit into a changing space. It stresses that physical and organizational options should be investigated and fit together for maximum performance.

Durand, D. E. 1977. Power as a function of office space and physiognomy: Two studies of influence. *Psychological Report* 40(June): 755–760.

Two studies empirically investigate relationships between organizational power and office size, and personal power and physical characteristics. A significant correlation is shown to exist between office size and organizational power in this particular study.

Elder, J., G. E. Turner, and A. I. Rubin. 1979. *Post-occupancy evaluation: A case study of the evaluation process* (NBSIR 79-1780). Washington, DC: Center for Building Technology, National Bureau of Standards, July 1979.

A case study of a courthouse and a federal building illustrates steps taken in the design process. Emphasis is put upon the accumulation and utilization of user information in the design process, as well as on the significance of evaluation before and after design. Specific design decisions are discussed as they were made, and oftentimes changed, at each stage. Problems with the planning and design process are reviewed.

Ellis, P., and F. Duffy. 1980. Lost office landscapes. *Management Today* (May): 47.

On-site evaluations of four offices in European cities were held to provide individual worker feedback and professional feedback for the office landscape. Disturbance was a primary complaint and lower-level workers were better able to tolerate it. On the other hand, communications were found to have improved. Cultural differences are discussed in reference to design and layout preferences.

Ellwood, H. 1979. Offices. In P. Tutt and D. Adler (Eds.), *VNR metric handbook of architectural standards*. New York: Van Nostrand Reinhold.

Specific physical proposals are offered for every element level of the office building, from the shell to small-scale services. In addition, different types of building shells (and office layouts) are analyzed for different kinds of organizations. Finally, many tables and charts are used to illustrate dimensions and relationships of particular spaces within the shell.

Farbstein, J., and M. Goldman. 1981. *The impact of the office environment on its users*. San Luis Obispo, CA: Farbstein/Williams & Associates.

Specific environmental conditions are discussed in terms of their impact upon office workers, the workers' comfort, and their level of productivity. Activities and worker movement are often determiners of office layout; in this sense, there is a need for flexibility in regard to the functioning of the organization. The final consideration in office planning is often the image projected by the physical design.

Farrenkopf, T., and V. Roth. 1980. The university faculty office as an environment. *Environment and Behavior* 12(4): 467–477.

This study of 71 faculty members used an interview of each subject to determine the importance of such office-related issues as location, privacy, and aesthetics. Because so much of the faculty members' time is spent in face-to-face interaction, issues such as privacy and space were important. The findings have implications for the design and location of faculty offices.

Finnegan, M. C., and L. Z. Solomon. 1981. Work attitudes in windowed vs. windowless environments. *Journal of Social Psychology* 15(December): 291–292.

A study conducted in an office setting used a 33-item questionnaire to discover the feelings of office workers in windowed vs. windowless offices. A positive relationship was found between overall job satisfaction and having a windowed office.

Fritsche, R. E. 1979. Office landscape: The productive environment. *Best's Review* 79(January): 79–80.

The monetary benefits of a productive work environment are discussed. In the case presented, an insurance firm, the open-plan design provides a productive work environment. Flexibility and low maintenance costs are two of the proclaimed advantages of the open plan here.

From grid to growth. 1969. *Progressive Architecture* 50(11): 100–109.

The outdated grid design of offices is slowly being replaced with a more flexible, adaptable system. The office is seen as being organic and so its design must fit it. The office landscape, originated by a group of management consultants, is based upon the philosophy that form follows function. The spatial configuration of the office layout must be reflective of the work and communication processes that go on.

Fucigna, J. T. 1967. The ergonomics of offices. *Ergonomics* 10(5): 589–604.

Following a brief overview of the field of ergonomics, a study of the effectiveness of the Action Office is described. A daily log of activities, kept for each one of a small number of subjects, investigated opinions, daily plans, and impact on the job. As a result, the Action Office was found to be superior to the conventional office in meeting the physical requirements of the subjects. The problem of empirical validation of findings now exists.

Gaskie, M. F. 1980. Toward workability of the workplace. *Architectural Record* (Mid-August): 70–75.

This ongoing survey of office environments by the Buffalo Organization for Social and Technological Innovation is in search of objective and quantifiable data that can be utilized by the architect to design the productive office environment. With the use of before and after office relocation measures, the survey is intended to determine the environmental impact of the office on job satisfaction. Many general trends are definable at this point in time.

Gensler, M. A., Jr., and P. B. Brandt. 1978. *A rational approach to office planning.* New York: AMACOM.

The success of any office planning depends upon the degree of client involvement. Specific components of planning and programming, design and space planning, and construction are discussed. Some problems that may arise in the process are pointed out.

Goldfield, R. 1981. A change of space: Open forum on open plan. *Inc.* 3(February): 127.

The economic advantage of the open-plan office is no justification for unsatisfied and uncomfortable workers. Opposing opinions concerning the open plan illustrate that the advantages and disadvantages can be determined by asking the employees themselves. Obviously, degree of success depends upon individual people and individual organizations.

Goodrich, R. 1978. Office environment: Post-occupancy evaluation. *Man-Environment Systems.* 8(4): 175–190.

A postoccupancy evaluation, through questionnaire, distinguishes different work station types, described as "self-contained offices." Issues such as work effectiveness, self-fulfillment, psychological climate, equipment, privacy, and orientation are investigated. Results illustrate explicit differences between the work stations; a summary of all results is provided.

Goodrich, R. 1982. Seven office evaluations: A review. *Environment and Behavior* 14: 353–378.

Several studies of organizations and their office designs are cited to illustrate the importance of the designed environment and how it inhibits or facilitates desired levels of privacy. The responsive environment must support all activities and needs of the individual users in order to be successful. Therefore, there is no one ultimate office design.

Gottschalk, O. 1967. Complexity in planning office buildings. *Kommunikation* 3: 84–87.

The planning of an office is recognized as a simultaneous, cooperative effort between several individuals. A bubble diagram, a planning flow chart, and other graphics are used to illustrate important factors influencing the planning process.

Gottschalk, O., and H. J. Lorenzen. 1966. The new shape of office buildings. *Kommunikation* 2(February): 159–180.

Varied graphic methods are used to determine frequency of communication, physical components of the work environment, and sociological elements. Three layout types are illustrated and discussed in terms of these and other aspects of the office environment. Actual examples are discussed to emphasize points.

Hansen, R. A. 1974. Unintelligibility, not audibility, determines acoustical privacy in an open plan. *Contract* 15(2): 43–47.

Important acoustical issues for the open-plan office are discussed. Because privacy of speech is crucial in the open plan, a distinction is made between Class A and Class B speech privacy. The distinctions between speech audibility and intelligibility are of primary importance as well. Physical elements of the office environment used to control speech privacy are discussed in detail.

Harris, D. A., A. E. Palmer, M. S. Lewis, D. L. Munson, G. Meckler, and R. Gerdes. 1981. *Planning and designing the office environment*. New York: Van Nostrand Reinhold.

Office planning, as a creative process, begins and ends with the systematic use of data collected on the particular environment to be designed. Planning an office environment involves a merging of several disciplines, such as architecture, interior design, and furniture manufacturing, as well as an understanding of the individuals and tasks as they are evaluated by each discipline. Defining the project according to the data collected and the needs specified is a crucial step toward a successful office design.

Hedge, A. 1982. The open-plan office: A systematic investigation of employee reactions to their work environment. *Environment and Behavior* 14(5): 519–542.

A survey of employees in a warehouse converted to an office building emphasizes many of the problems inherent in the open-plan office style. No evidence was found in this study to support the open plan. Among the more significant problems were privacy and distractions, especially in higher-level groups.

Henrich, C. 1980. Facilities management: Energizing the work environment. *Buildings* (October).

The importance of constant management of a facility is emphasized. The facility manager is seen as an active participant in the office environment, keeping that environment dynamic. This discussion of facilities management stresses the importance of the role.

Herbert, R. K. 1980. Noise control in the open plan. *Administrative Management* 41(December): 27–29.

Acoustical control in the open-plan office depends upon a balance between control of distracting noises among offices and the level of background noise, or masking sound. A guide to noise control terminology is provided for better understanding of the varying degrees of sound. The degree of acoustical privacy achieved is dependent upon physical elements provided by the office itself.

Hohl, R. 1968. *Office buildings: An international survey*. New York: Praeger Publishers.

The successful functioning of an organization is represented by an electric circuiting diagram, involving steady voltages, working impulses, and a productive power output. Even though producing a psychologically supportive work environment is the responsibility of the architect, his or her conferences with the client as well as limitations provided by building regulations make this a more challenging job.

Howard, P. 1972. Office landscaping revisited. *Design and Environment* 3(3): 40–47.

The importance of the open plan is seen in its facilitation of communication and work processes. Through manipulation of office layout and systems furniture, the workplace can be made supportive of the needs of the worker. This discussion of the office landscape and the importance of furniture emphasizes the worker as the crucial element.

Hughes, P. C., and J. F. McNelis. 1979. Lighting, productivity, and the work environment. *Lighting Design and Application* 8(December): 32–40.

Cost effectiveness of higher lighting levels is illustrated through study of preferred lighting level and actual productivity level of visual search. Two tasks, chosen because of their similarity to clerical tasks, were completed under three lighting levels. Results illustrate a preference for and decreasing eye discomfort with the higher illumination level in both age groups.

Hundert, A. T., and N. Greenfield. 1969. Physical space and organizational behavior: A study of an office landscape. *Proceedings of the 77th Annual Convention of the American Psychological Association* 4: 601–602.

An empirical study using a total of 63 subjects investigated hypothesized advantages of the office landscape over the conventional office. Results supported only the phenomenon of improved information flow in the office landscape. Because there are risks involved in the method used, flaws in dependence upon only one or two styles of data collection, questionnaire and interview, become apparent.

The interior designer as tenant. 1971. *Progressive Architecture* (March): 74.

A description and brief discussion of the office space occupied by a space-planning firm addresses issues from conference rooms to proxemics. Office arrangement is determined by work patterns and space needs.

ISD Incorporated. 1969. *The office environment*. Chicago: ISD Incorporated.

This article reviews pleasing and annoying elements that exist in the office environment of the professional as well as the non-professional. Four elements of the environments were defined and rated: spatial, equipment, functional, and interaction. Twelve major conclusions, including worker adaptation and micro and macro environmental differences, are drawn from the study.

Ives, R. S., and R. Ferdinands. 1974. Working in a landscaped office. *Personnel Practice Bulletin* 30(2): 126–141.

Fifty-five relocated office workers of a city council were interviewed to determine whether they preferred the conventional office or the new landscaped one. Differences were found to exist between job levels: senior council officers, supervisors, and staff.

Jacobi, P., and H. Niewerth. 1965. Relaxation during office hours. *Kommunikation* 1(September): 99–101.

Observation of specific behaviors, and their hypothesized rationale, provides a basis for design. Specific suggestions are offered in response to observations.

Jaeger, D. 1969. Office landscape: A systems concept. In *Improving office environment* (BEMA Management Conference, Chicago, 1968). Elmhurst, IL: Business Press.

The advantages of the office landscape system as approached by The Quickborner Team are investigated. Such issues as functional, sociological, and economical elements are discussed. The cybernetics, or information processes, that exist in an office setting are of critical importance to the planning of the work environment. The actual working structure and links of communication flow vary from the formal lines and structures to the informal.

Johnson, K. E. 1968. Individual choices versus conformity to standards in design of private offices. In *New concepts in office design* (BEMA Management Conference, New York, 1967). Elmhurst, IL: Business Press.

Individuality in the design of private offices and an overall harmoniousness of design are discussed as the most important issues in office design. Also, it is pointed out that more research is needed in the ecology of office design.

Johnson, K. E. 1970. The office environment people prefer. *AIA Journal* (February): 56–58.

Three hundred and fifty-eight office workers were questioned on their feelings about their offices. Many environmental factors were investigated, grouped into four categories: spatial, equipment, functional, and interaction. Findings indicate that people will adapt to less than optimal conditions, even though they are strongly opinionated about office conditions.

Joiner, D. 1971. Office territory. *New Society* 18: 660–663.

The issues of territoriality and preferred space are discussed in reference to the office. Position, distance, and symbolic decoration are noted as the three important spatial determiners. Placement of desks and chairs in relation to doors can often be one of the most important territorial signals.

Joiner, D. 1971. Social ritual and architectural space. *Architectural Research and Teaching* 1(3): 11–22.

The office setting is explained in reference to such principles as territoriality, personal space, barriers, status symbols, and furniture arrangement. Cultural variations and types of organizations are discussed in reference to furniture arrangement, but, generally, no major conclusions are drawn. The significance of the article lies in its emphasis upon these factors affecting settings that go beyond the physical.

Justa, F. C., and M. B. Golan. 1977. Office design: Is privacy still a problem? *Journal of Architectural Research* 6(2): 5–12.

Privacy needs are determined and met by a combination of sociophysical elements in any particular environment. This study used interviews, observations, and questionnaires in the investigation of factors influencing privacy in four different companies. Results of the study illustrate that achieving desired privacy levels depends upon many factors, including what is available and acceptable in terms of privacy regulation.

Kaplan, A. 1977. Human needs in the work environment. *Modern Office Procedures* (September): 132–133.

Maslow's hierarchy of needs is illustrated and discussed in the development of guidelines for the design of work environments. The satisfaction of biological, social, and psychological behavior needs is feasible through the design of the office environment. The satisfaction of these needs is facilitated through climatic, ambient, and other environmental factors.

Kaplan, A. 1979. Programming for office planning and design. *Modern Office Procedures* 24 (December): 86.

Programming, when used as a tool to outline the course of action to be taken in the planning and design of an office, is an important step in the overall planning process. It is an attempt to define and understand all of the individuals, behaviors, and interactive aspects of the organization as well as the workers and the surrounding environment. The final program, then, is the decoding of all the data and the statement of specific criteria to guide the design of the office.

Katz, R. L. 1981. Acoustical design. *Navy Civil Engineering* 21(3): 9–12.

An effective acoustical design is needed in the open-plan office to control distraction and speech privacy. Many effective uses of sound-absorbent materials are mentioned.

Keighley, E. C. 1970. Acceptability criteria for noise in large offices. *Journal of Sound Variation* 11(1): 83–93.

A questionnaire was administered to a total of 1,902 office workers in 40 offices to determine the subjective effects of noise. The average dB level was assessed for each office and correlated with subjective questionnaire results. Problems involved in the measuring of noise as it changes in an office setting are discussed.

Klebanoff, S. 1978. The art of OP. *Across the Board* 15(May): 42–47.

This brief review of the history of the open plan discusses two major types: office landscape, and the more popular modular approach. A modified version of the open plan, the "American plan," has been adopted by many organizations. Pros and cons of the open plan are illustrated through user responses.

Kleeman, W., Jr. 1974. Humanizing offices by participatory design. In R. P. Fairfield (Ed.), *Humanizing the workplace*. Buffalo, NY: Prometheus.

The importance of worker participation in office design is discussed. The use of a questionnaire can help the designer to satisfy worker needs in the office space. Each part of the workplace is designed in terms of ergonomic criteria.

Kleeman, W. B., Jr. 1982. The need for ergonomics expertise in office design. *Applied Ergonomics* 13(2): 125–127.

Two book reviews and two ongoing office worker survey reviews illustrate some common and some not so common findings uncovered in worker safety and satisfaction research. The main conclusion provided concerns user participation in the planning stages of design. Worker participation in this sense has been successful in the past, especially in Japan.

Kleinschrod, W. A. 1968. Discord in the garden of landscape. *Administrative Management* 29(12): 30–32.

The issue of the actual uniqueness of the office landscape and its flexibility is discussed.

Supporters of the design argue that the building in which the office is housed is of major importance. The argument of economy may have become more important than the one of communications.

Klimoski, R. J. 1979. Work place design and worker behavior. Paper presented at the meeting of the American Psychological Association. New York, September 1979.

A link between a theory of motivation and effects of office design on employee behavior is made. Architectural determinism as a unidirectional phenomenon is discussed in that it may be defined bidirectionally: workplace design may affect behavior, but behavior affects the design of the workplace as well. Some comments on existing research in the area are made.

Konar, E., E. Sundstrom, C. Brady, D. Mandel, and R. W. Rice. 1982. Status demarcation in the office. *Environment and Behavior* 14(5): 561–580.

This summary of an empirical study illustrates the existence of a relationship between status demarcation and satisfaction with the work setting. These status markers provide a sense of support for the individual, depending upon his or her rank in the organization. Hypotheses concerning rank and status, traditional status markers, and environmental status support were investigated.

Kraemer, Sieverts & Partners. 1977. *Open-plan offices: New ideas, experience and improvements* (J. L. Ritchie, Trans.). London: McGraw-Hill. (Originally published, 1975).

This report on a study of 20 German open-plan offices begins with the somewhat common pros and cons of the open-plan office. Data were gathered on elements such as floor area, rest areas, and lighting, and employees' opinions were recorded through a questionnaire. Detailed discussions of all facets of the study provide a basis for conclusions or recommendations offered.

Krieks, H. 1980. We are witnessing the beginning of the end of the office landscape. *Interiors* (February): 82; 86.

The expression of some very definite views on the open-plan office design, and comments about its durability, arouse strong feelings in respondents. Although responses are both positive and negative, a variety of views are presented.

Langdon, F. J. 1963. The design of mechanised offices: 1. A user study. *Architects' Journal* 137(21): 943–947.

A survey of offices using automatic data-processing equipment illustrates design problems in such offices. Worker satisfaction was investigated, revealing problems of noise and ventilation especially. Conclusions stress the need for investigative space planning for such equipment.

Langdon, F. J. 1963. The design of mechanised offices: 2. Space layout and storage. *Architects' Journal* 137(21): 1081–1086.

The issues of storage space and layout in an office are discussed. Recommendations and relevant issues are based upon results of the survey designed to address these layout problems. Objective methods of space storage are explained.

Langdon, F. J. 1965. A study of annoyance caused by noise in automatic data processing offices. *Building Science* 1: 69–78.

A questionnaire was given to office workers in seven offices in order to assess the distractability of noise in those offices. Both open- and closed-ended questions were used to allow respondents to assess noise levels as well as comment upon them.

Page 332

Results illustrate that noise is the most significant source of annoyance, yet variances were found between job levels.

Langdon, F. J. 1966. *Modern offices: A user survey* (National Building Studies Research Paper 41) London: HMSO.

A survey of overall office conditions and an estimate of standards of office space covers issues from architecture to ventilation. Data were collected through the use of inventory and questionnaire. A detailed discussion of satisfaction and dissatisfaction with physical and psychological elements of the office setting provides extensive information about offices in general.

Langdon, F. J., and E. C. Keighley. 1964. User research in office design. *Architects' Journal* (February 5): 333–339.

User satisfaction surveys have prevailed for determining efficiency and cost in terms of administrative activities in the office setting. Because of the importance of workers' reactions in this setting, other attempts to research and define an optimal office setting have been weak. The article reviews many environmental attributes of the modern office, and user satisfaction with these settings.

Lautzenheiser, T. 1981. A decision model for office lighting design. *Lighting Design and Application* 11(November): 33–38.

Lighting systems have become an important part of the design of the office, or any workspace. Because of the many kinds of lighting available, a decision model is presented. The process of decision making in the area of lighting is based mainly upon ambience and upon the work being done.

Lebus, P. 1979. The English manager's castle. *Management Today* (November): 148.

A brief statement of international differences in approach to office design points out America's emphasis on strong corporate image. Layout selection is a two-part problem, based on the needs of the job, overall company policy, and the particular layout profile (and its seven elements).

Leibson, D. E. 1981. How Corning designed a "talking" building to spur productivity. *Management Review* 70(September): 8–13.

Facing a productivity and idea-generation problem, Corning employed an engineering expert to find a solution. The solution was found through manipulation of the physical setting. It was found that vertical separation hinders communication more than horizontal separation does.

Leonard, W. M. 1981. Start now to think about new office space. *Administrative Management* 42(December) 24–28.

An involved process of planning stages is presented. Designing the office, specifically, is listed as fifth out of six stages. Interviews as well as different kinds of analyses of the choice of an office design are mentioned.

Lerner, L. 1967. Projecting the corporate image through office facilities. In *Developing the total office environment* (BEMA Business Equipment Conference, Chicago, 1966). Washington, DC: Thompson Book.

A look at a relationship between architecture and the corporate image expresses the need for direct communication. In this relationship, the individual needs of each company are reflected in its office design. Many illustrations are offered as examples.

Lewis, P. T., and P. E. O'Sullivan. 1974. Acoustic privacy in office design. *Journal of Architectural Research* 3(1): 48–51.

Acoustic problems in open-plan offices are based upon the need for both privacy and ease of communication in the same office space. Acoustic solutions for the two conditions are different for the cellular office and the open-plan office. Solving acoustic problems is guided by the needs of the client, as well as the design of the particular office.

Lipman, A., I. Cooper, R. Harris, and R. Tranter. 1978. Power, a neglected concept in office design? *Journal of Architectural Research* 6(3): 28–37.

This exploration of the design and use of office space studies the relationship between the office space and the office organization. Field studies of the office space as a functional setting involved a literature search and interviews. The goal of productive efficiency is reviewed. Implications for research are mentioned.

Lorenzen, H. J. 1967. Organizational aspects in planning office buildings. *Kommunikation* 3(1): 14–26.

Because the staff of a business can be seen as an information-processing unit housed within a building reflective of its own internal system, the connecting links of that system are most important. Input and output in the form of communication is crucial for any information system. The design of office space, then, must be adaptable to the changing needs of such an organization.

Lorenzen, H. J., and D. Jaeger. 1968. The office landscape: A "systems" concept. *Contract* 9: 164–173.

Office landscape systems are discussed in terms of the need for teamwork between specialists. To meet the needs of office personnel, these specialists must fully understand the cybernetics, or the information processes, that exist in the organization. The office building itself and its spatial arrangement become tools for successful communication flow.

Maddox, E. 1979. Managing without obstacles: A look at the open office. *Supervisory Management* 24(4): 15–22.

Both communication needs and those of adjacency of location are primary considerations in the design of the successful open-plan office. The open plan, in general, is presented as supporting staff needs.

Magnus, M. 1981. Work environment: Its design and implications. *Personnel Journal* (January): 27–28; 30–31.

The effect office design has on its personnel is discussed in terms of the many factors that influence office systems. Employee participation in the design process is considered important, although the design of an office should not be expected to solve all problems. Much emphasis is put upon the involvement of personnel in planning and designing.

Making office walls come tumbling down. 1968. *Business Week* (May 11): 56–58.

Arguments against the office landscape are based upon the need for privacy and status. One of the basic claims of the office landscape is the need for the spatial arrangement in an office to follow the lines of communication. Also, flexibility in space requirements and arrangements is necessary and can be found with the office landscape.

Manning, P. 1970. Office design: A study of environment. In H. M. Proshansky, W. H. Ittelson, and L. G. Rivlin (Eds.), *Environmental psychology: Man and his physical setting*. New York: Holt, Rinehart & Winston.

Theoretical principles of the office or building environment are translated into applied principles. Issues such as space, light, thermal conditions, and noise are discussed and, as criteria, become the bases of particular design features. Different techniques of investigating the setting are used and discussed. Emphasis is placed upon the multidisciplinary requirements of the environmental design process.

Marans, R. W., and K. F. Spreckelmeyer. 1980. An organizational framework for conducting evaluations of built environments. Unpublished manuscript. University of Michigan. Architectural Research Laboratory.

The evaluation and design of a particular building consisted of four specific stages: information gathering, design phase, data collection, and documentation. Methods of investigation and data gathering are discussed in detail. This model, as a framework, allows applicability to other similar investigations.

Marans, R. W., and K. F. Spreckelmeyer. 1981. *Evaluating built environments: A behavioral approach*. Ann Arbor, MI: University of Michigan.

A total of 239 federal employees completed a questionnaire as an evaluation of their work environment. Even though the building itself has been recognized for design excellence by architects, one-third of the workers in the building expressed discontent with their workplace. This study was designed with the intention of determining whether designed environments actually operate as they were intended.

Marans, R. W., and K. F. Spreckelmeyer. 1982. Evaluating open and conventional office design. *Environment and Behavior* 14: 333–351.

Because postoccupancy evaluations of office settings may often be seen as weak, a model was presented here to guide the collection and evaluation of such data. Findings from a study of a federal office building were analyzed in reference to the model provided. The model, which illustrates relationships between environmental conditions and subjective responses to them, has implications for environmental satisfaction as well.

Maskovsky, G. S. 1981. Strategic planning for tomorrow's office. *Office* 93(March): 34.

The proposed office of the future automatically employs consideration of five functional areas: work processing, reproduction, distribution, records management, and administrative support. In order to meet the needs of these areas successfully, a plan must involve statement of existing circumstances, statement of goals, and activities required to meet those goals.

Mazo, W. S. 1982. Facilities planner and the office of the future. *Industrial Development* 151(2): 36.

The millions of people who now work in offices are not prepared, or educated, to accept the overload that will probably be produced by the technology of the office of the future and resistance will have to be met. Flexibility is a critical element of the design of the future office.

Mazo, W. S. 1980. The impact of future office systems on facilities planning. *Industrial Development* 149(2): 6–11.

Technological changes in the office are an important element for the facilities planner to consider. Facilities must now include new equipment and much of this is described and explained. With this new equipment, the office of the future will link together the many electronic systems.

McCarrey, M. W., L. Peterson, S. Edwards, and P. VonKulmiz. 1974. Landscape office attitudes: Reflections of perceived degree of control over transactions with the environment. *Journal of Applied Psychology* 54: 401–403.

Attitude data from 600 office workers was analyzed to identify elements of personal control in the open or landscaped office. It was hypothesized that negative or positive office landscape evaluation was based upon the individual's degree of perceived control over the environment.

McElroy, J. C., and P. C. Morrow. 1982. Desk placement in the faculty office. *Psychological Reports* 50(2): 675–678.

The experiment, which utilized simulation methods, reported operationalized office design. Significance of different informational cues varies with seating and doorway position. This replication of an earlier study illustrates the importance of desk placement to the active visitor vs. the casual observer.

Mercer, A. 1979. Office environments and clerical behaviour. *Environment and Planning B* 6: 29–39.

This study of clerical workers in three different styles of office involved direct observation and performance measurement. The phenomena of convenience and comfort are related to environment and to activity. Pros and cons of noise and comfort are discussed for the traditional office, the open-plan office, and the Action Office 2 (created by panels).

Meroney, J. W. 1982. Ergonomic work station design adds to efficiency. *Office* 96(6): 92.

This brief summary of work station design emphasizes several issues that should be considered in the design and placement of the workspace—from size and location to privacy and psychological disorders.

Miller, L. G. 1969. Designing environments for American industry and its employees. In *Improving office environment* (BEMA Management Conference, Chicago, 1968). Elmhurst, IL: Business Press.

Physical elements and functionings of an office have been dealt with sufficiently. Human and social factors, such as emotional health, are issues to be considered in the office today. Open-office planning at DuPont is discussed in terms of the psychological needs of employees.

Mogulescu, M. H. 1968. Determining whether to move or modernize. In *New concepts in office design* (BEMA Management Conference, New York, 1967). Elmhurst, IL: Business Press.

Criteria to consider when making the decision whether to relocate or modernize an office, including shape and size of floor, mechanical elements, space usage, flexibility, and costs, are discussed. A specific example is given.

Mogulescu, M. 1970. *Profit through design*. New York: American Management Association.

The increasing number of white-collar workers has greatly affected effective communication and functioning within the office. Management is faced with many alternatives when trying to optimize productivity. Several case studies are provided to illustrate problems and their solutions utilizing different office plans.

Moleski, W. H. 1974. Behavioral analysis and environmental programming for offices. In J. Lang, C. Burnette, W. Moleski, and D. Vachon (Eds.), *Designing for human behavior: Architecture and the behavioral sciences*. Stroudsburg, PA: Dowden, Hutchinson and Ross.

The task of developing an environmental program for the interior design of a large office includes behavioral contingencies as a vital element of the design solution. Beginning with user needs and then translating these into design possibilities is fundamental to the process. An analytical programming model is described; it discusses the physical system to support the behavioral system.

Moleski, W. H., and R. J. Goodrich. 1972. The analysis of behavioral requirements in office settings. In W. Mitchell (Ed.), *Environmental design: Research and practice*, Proceedings of the Environmental Design Research Association (No. 3)/Architectural Research (No. 8) Conference. Los Angeles: University of California.

The organization, a complex ecological unit, is explained as a determinant of the environment through the activities that take place within it. Interview, questionnaire, and user survey were used in combination to identify factors of the work setting related to the behavioral-environmental interface. The organization is described as an activity system composed of different levels of activity.

Moleski, W. H., and J. T. Lang. 1982. Organizational needs and human values in office planning. *Environment and Behavior* 14: 319–332.

The accomplishment of particular organizational goals may often be either facilitated or hindered by the layout of the office. Communication networks, collaboration, and compatibility of activities are some of the organizational needs that guide facility design. An information and interaction exchange must take place between the designer, the user, and the space so that environmental planning will encompass these needs, as well as needs for future growth and change.

Nemecek, J., and E. Grandjean. 1973. Noise in landscaped offices. *Applied Ergonomics*. 4(1): 19–22.

The subject of noise and its effects, part of an extensive study employing many ergonomic measurements in 15 landscaped offices, is discussed. Questionnaire responses indicated that employees were most distracted by conversation. The use of a background noise is suggested for the office environment.

Nemecek, J., and E. Grandjean. 1973. Results of an ergonomic investigation of large-space offices. *Human Factors* 15(2): 111–124.

Ergonomic measurements were made in 15 offices to determine advantages and disadvantages of the large-space office (20 to 120 persons). The elements investigated were noise, lighting, and room climate. Advantages defined in the study included better personal contacts and more rational work flow.

New office concept geared to people and productivity. 1982. *Office* 95(June): 19.

New computer systems as a means of providing efficiency in everyday task-work are introduced. The advancing technology calls for expert consultants, few of whom exist at this time. The workers and their functioning remain the key to office planning.

Niewerth, H. 1968. Administration in an open plan office. *Kommunikation* (November).

A postoccupancy evaluation conducted on a German office building, including a summary of the preplanning process, is explained. Issues ranging from space availability and employee placement to physical descriptions of the building and its elements are included in this detailed and specific summary statement of a work environment.

Office landscape. Interior design data. 1964. *Progressive Architecture* 45(9): 201–203.

The German system of office design. *Bürolandschaft* or office landscape, is discussed. This method is based on work flow, communication, and circulation, as much American office planning is. This free-form layout style, determined mainly by traffic flow, regulates acoustics through the use of carpeting. One important element of this system is the understanding among all workers that they are part of a team.

Office lighting, comfort and productivity: How the workers feel. 1980. *Lighting Design and Application* 10(July) 35–39.

The importance of lighting in worker comfort and productivity is investigated in this follow-up survey to the 1978 Louis Harris office study. Lighting was found to be important for comfort, and comfort for productivity, but no direct relationships between these two factors were found.

Oldham, G. R., and D. J. Brass. 1979. Employee reactions to an open-plan office: A naturally occurring quasi-experiment. *Administrative Science Quarterly* 24: 267–284.

Two approaches attempt to explain how the open-plan influences reactions of employees toward work: The research discussed investigated hypotheses for both these positions in a study of worker reactions before and after a move from a conventional office to an open-plan one.

Oler, W. H. 1981. Comfort, function, and beauty are important ingredients for improving worker productivity. *Administrative Management* (September): 110.

A positive attitude toward the work environment is an important factor in worker satisfaction and, in turn, productivity. Good design projects an image to others and can improve the flexibility of an office setting.

Palmer, A. E., and M. S. Lewis. 1977. *Planning the office landscape*. New York: McGraw-Hill.

Office landscaping as an approach to office planning is not synonymous with the open-plan concept. Worktime, paperflow, communication, and other phenomena are investigated and solutions are proposed to illustrate principles of office landscaping.

Panero, J., and M. Zelnik. 1979. *Human dimension and interior space: A source book of design reference standards*. New York: Whitney Library of Design.

This exploration of the issue of anthropometrics in workspace design includes theory and application, illustrations, and exact physical relationships and provides complete coverage of this issue. Because no "average" can be assumed in anthropometrics, many varying dimensions come into play. The book, which is aimed at both furniture designers and builders, focuses on the idea of adjustability in interior design, which, until now, has not been fully explored.

Parker, K. 1977. Checkpoints for moving and modernizing the office. *The Office* 85(February): 52.

Space planning, as the key to office design, should begin before property is purchased. Questionnaires, patterned for each individual business, provide information about the issues of staff responsibilities, work flow, traffic, visitor rate, and projected growth.

Parson, H. M. 1976. Work environments. In I. Altman and J. F. Wohlwill (Eds.), *Human behavior and environment: Advances in theory and research,* Vol. 1. New York: Plenum Publishing.

Work settings in general are considered in regard to the worker, the dependent variable.

In-depth discussions of two work environments in particular, the industrial setting and the business office, illustrate how the external elements of the environments affect the individuals in them and the many differences that may occur between two slightly different settings.

Pascaris, P., and M. S. Graham. 1981. *Bell Scarborough Administration Centre: A case study*. Toronto, Canada: Bell Canada.

The development of an office landscape for one of Bell Canada's administrative offices is discussed in a step-wise fashion. This building was built to meet the needs of the changing work population. Block and space planning are two important stages in this example.

Pile, J. 1980. Does office comfort increase productivity? *Interiors* (June): 52.

A brief review of two Louis Harris studies on offices suggests insufficiencies. Because no true cost/benefit study was made in regard to the influence of the office itself on work performance, survey data will have to suffice.

Pile, J. F. 1969. The nature of office landscaping. *American Institute of Architects' Journal* 52(1): 40–48.

The fundamental ideas of office landscaping as a process are discussed. The steps as well as the problems inherent in this process are explained in detail and conclusions, many of which detail advantages (such as cost), are provided.

Pile, J. F. 1977. The open office: Does it work? *Progressive Architecture* (June): 68–81.

The pros and cons of the open office are discussed in search of an explanation for its mediocre status. The issues of privacy, acoustics, status, and resistance to the open plan as a new idea are detailed. Physical elements such as furniture, wiring, and lighting are discussed and illustrated.

Pile, J. F. 1978. *Open office planning: A handbook for interior designers and architects*. New York: Whitney Library of Design.

A history of office landscaping, based upon the concept of the open plan without partitions, is presented. The many steps involved in the preplanning and planning stages of office design are explained, diagrammed, listed, and illustrated (in floor plans). The building shell, interior equipment, and privacy are some of the issues addressed in this presentation of an explicit approach to the planning of offices.

Pilkington Research Unit (P. Manning, Ed.). 1965. *Office design: A study of environment*. Liverpool, England: Pilkington Research Unit, Department of Building Science, University of Liverpool.

This overall survey of the office environment, including the interior office, the office building, and the attitudes of the users, is broken down into the many smaller environments involved. Spatial, visual, thermal, aural, and social aspects of the office are discussed.

Planas, R. E. 1978. Perfect open plan priority: The human element. *Buildings* (March): 74–75.

The evolution of the office as an environment is emphasized in reference to the worker-physical element interaction. Education of the user and the manager is an important part of a successful office environment.

Powell, D. D. 1967. Concepts and facilities for increasing clerical productivity. In *Developing the total office environment* (BEMA Business Equipment Conference, Chicago, 1966). Washington, DC: Thompson Book.

Many of the productivity problems in secretarial work are due to the design of the office, from the desk itself to the communication system utilized. Specific solutions to problems are illustrated and discussed.

Prince, J. 1980. Taking the modular office one step further. *Administrative Management* 41(July): 51.

The individual worker and his or her space requirements are primary considerations in designing the interior office. The "ultimate system" is introduced as the solution to the interchangeable, reusable, completely portable office.

Pritchard, G. 1981. Use the office experts. *Accountant* 185 (November 5): 565–566.

Specific explanations of the individuals involved in office planning and design, in particular the roles of architects and design consultants, supplement a brief discussion of the stages of such a process.

Privacy in the office. 1982. *Journal of Systems Management* 33(June): 6–10.

Two questionnaires are provided in this discussion of privacy in the office. These distinguish between subjective and objective privacy. In a comparison of the open office to the closed office, suggestions are provided on how to indicate private territory to others. Reducing unwanted stimulation and distractions are discussed as well.

Propst, R. 1968. *The office: A facility based on change.* Ann Arbor, MI: Herman Miller Research Corporation.

A discussion of the history of the office and the changes it has undergone provides a basis for an explanation of the office in its current state. Conflicts, planning, and change are all important to the design of an office.

Propst, R. L. 1972. Office function and equipment. *Building Research* 9(2): 16–19.

One of the most important issues to be considered in office design is the office function and the business in which it functions. The costs and consequences of redesign and change are discussed in regard to their negative and positive effects.

Propst, R., J. Adams, and C. Nuttall. 1977. *The department of social services office innovation project.* Ann Arbor, MI: Herman Miller Research Corporation.

Physical problems in a welfare office are investigated. Facility problems, objectives, planning, layout implementation, and evaluation are discussed in detail, emphasizing the importance of each stage in such a project. Each individual problem is dealt with in terms of the physical structure and its implications.

Pulgram, W. L. 1979. Environment and human: The link is strong. *Office* 90: 141–145.

The building blocks of a recycled office, or of a new office, must be based upon a people-oriented design. It is imperative for efficiency and economy that the work environment be directly related to the purpose (and functioning) of the organization. Productivity must be environmentally supported at all levels.

Quickie offices: Affordable, transportable and ready for immediate use. 1981. *Administrative Management* 42(November): 34–36.

The basic characteristics of a preengineered relocatable office module are compared to those of a permanent structure. Flexibility, convenience, and economics are some of the emphasized advantages of the modular office building.

Rader, M., and J. Gilsdorf. 1981. Preventing environmental stress in the open office. *Journal of Systems Management* 32(3): 25.

A nonempirical relationship is suggested between factors in the office setting initiated by the open plan, and issues of stress and low productivity. A number of nontechnical solutions are offered to meet the needs of office layout.

Riland, L. H., and J. Z. Falk. 1972. *Employee reactions to office landscape environment.* Rochester, NY: Relations Department, Eastman Kodak Company, April 1972.

A study of employee reactions to the office landscape at Eastman Kodak involved two phases: initial studies of the original 1968 installations and later studies involving pre-move and post-move surveys. The article concentrates mainly on reactions of employees to different aspects of the office design.

Ripnen, K. H. 1960. *Office building and office layout planning.* New York: McGraw-Hill.

The task of providing the most functional, comfortable, efficient office begins with the work of the office space administrator, from surveying individual space usage to charting the organization work relations. The roles of the architect and the engineer involve the more structural and mechanical aspects of the process. Full descriptions, working drawings, and specifications provide explanations of every step in the process.

Rodgers, S. G. 1968. Modularity versus free-form clustering. In *New concepts in office design* (BEMA Management Conference, New York, 1967). Elmhurst, IL: Business Press.

The difference between the cellular office plan and "free form clustering" is discussed in terms of flexibility and communication. Spacing, visual and aural privacy, and distracting noise levels are discussed in terms of the office landscape.

Rout, L. 1980. Designers modify the open office to meet complaints of workers. *Wall Street Journal* (November 5): 1.

Even though the open office gained popularity very quickly when it was first introduced, its definition is being modified. Offices employing this design have altered the original physical elements in terms of partition height or space allocation.

Ruys, T. 1971. Windowless offices. *Man-Environment Systems* (January): 49.

A study interviewing 139 occupants of windowless offices points out that workers are able to perform as well without windows, although they prefer them. Psychological reasons (claustrophobia, depression) for having windows weighed more heavily than physical ones (light, ventilation).

Sachs, R. T. 1981. Workstations for the open plan. *Administrative Management* 42(October): 55.

Ergonomics, limited flexibility, and individual work styles are seen as the basis for work station design in this review of current work station and systems furniture components. Issues such as visual and acoustical privacy are discussed in terms of specific furniture elements.

Saphier, M. 1968. *Office planning and design*. New York: McGraw-Hill.

This modified textbook presents the steps involved in space planning and design in a logical, sequential order. Space planning is seen as a step-wise procedure that varies with each particular setting and with the individuals involved. Full understanding of the problem and its many elements is of primary importance in the planning process if the utilization of interior space is to be maximized.

Saphier, M. 1978. *Planning the new office*. New York: McGraw-Hill.

The decision-making process is a fundamental yet dynamic part of office planning. Much preplanning decision making is involved in space planning. Varied consultants are employed when necessary, as are contractors.

Scala, B. 1977. Building blocks of the open office. *Administrative Management* (38)(June) 39–54.

Needs of the new office concept are discussed. Functionality of work stations, task lighting as an energy saver, and seating are considerations that guide the decision-making process. The open-plan office can be only as successful as its elements.

Schaff, F. D. 1972. Office space in a time of change. *Building Research* 9(2): 20–22.

The benefits of planning office spaces with professional space planners are discussed. It is pointed out that managers should not be the main decision makers in the process. Managers should, however, provide space planners with background information and job requirements.

Schindler, B. 1968. Principles for planning a new business home. In *New concepts in office design* (BEMA Management Conference, New York, 1967). Elmhurst, IL: Business Press.

The work environment may be seen as a business "home," and space planners should make it as efficient and productive as possible. Major areas of the successful work environment—functional layout, full-time air conditioning, good lighting, good acoustical qualities, and overall good design—are discussed. Good planning must be based on usable information.

Schmertz, M. F. (Ed.). 1975. *Office building design*, 2nd ed. New York: McGraw-Hill.

Office buildings and their floor space are discussed and specific examples and visual illustrations are provided. The discussion is basically about structure, dealing with different sizes of office buildings; only one chapter is devoted to interiors.

Schuler, R. S., L. P. Ritzman, and V. Davis. 1980. *Merging prescriptive and sociopsychological approaches for office layout* (WPS 80-27). Columbus, OH: Ohio State University, College of Aministrative Science, April 1980.

The fusion of two themes dominant in spatial arrangement literature, a prescriptive one and a sociopsychological one, is discussed. A study of 332 employees tested hypotheses of relationships between employee accessibility, satisfaction, and perceptions of job conditions, and perceptions of role conflict. Results illustrate, among other things, a strong relationship between privacy and satisfaction with supervisors.

Schumann, A. 1981. How to develop a useful work station analysis. *Office* 93: 122.

A brief description of the steps involved in a work station analysis are reviewed.

Analysis of worker habits and space needs in combination with interview data provide the basis for the investigation.

Shelton, S. J. 1969. Landscaped offices. *Architects' Journal* (March 5): 655–663.

The specifics of the landscaped office are discussed in detail, from space and furniture to air conditioning. Methods for determining the needs of a business in a landscaped office are offered. The landscaped office is described as the reasonable compromise between the conventional and the open-plan office.

Shiff, R. A. 1979. Satellite administrative zones. *Information and Records Management* 6(2): 10–12.

Satellite administrative zones are part of today's office. These zones allow the open or landscaped office to centralize information for easy access, improved communication, and space saving. Administrative zones, usually set up when a business moves or renovates, concentrate on efficiency.

Shoshkes, L. 1976. *Space planning: Designing the office environment.* New York: Architectural Record.

A brief history of offices and their different layout styles introduces the many theories of office design. Planning for design change includes issues such as flexibility needs, work group and communication needs, and the desire for change. Physical aspects that support the needs of the workers are explained in detail.

Shuttleworth, G. N. 1972. Convertible space in office buildings. *Building Research*. 9(2): 9–15.

Office landscaping is seen as a concept important to the corporation. The office landscape, as convertible space, must meet corporate needs, such as flexibility and communication, as well as the individual worker's needs, such as privacy and permanence. How these needs are specifically met are dealt with in detail.

Siegel, A. I., J. J. Wolf, and J. Pilitsis. 1982. A new method for the scientific layout of workspaces. *Applied Ergonomics* 13(2): 87–90.

With the aid of a multidimensional scaling computer program, a new system of layout design has been developed. This system, called SPACE, is based upon placement of "objects" (people or equipment) in facilities. Application of the technique involves managers who are familiar with the objects of the space, and the manager's functions. Validity tests have been done on this method to illustrate that it yields results equal to or better than current space-planning methods.

Sloan, S. A. 1972. Translating psycho-social criteria into design determinants. In W. Mitchell (Ed.), *Environmental design: Research and Practice*, Proceedings of the Environmental Design Research Association (No. 3)/Architectural Research (No. 8) Conference. Los Angeles, CA: University of California.

Social and psychological issues important to the worker are seen as crucial to a successful office design. Proxemics, aggression, privacy, and happiness are phenomena that must be considered by the design staff. The social science data obtained for the study was grouped into three categories: sociability, territoriality, and aggression.

Socrates, G. 1978. Layout design for safe and productive working. *Management Services* 22(May): 56–57.

Layout and design of the workplace affect the comfort, and thus productivity, of the employee. A complete description of worker needs and behaviors is necessary to avoid possible health hazards and to facilitate worker comfort.

Sommer, R. 1974. *Tight spaces: Hard architecture and how to humanize it*. Englewood Cliffs: Prentice-Hall.

The issue of the office landscape is addressed in the chapter entitled "Alien Buildings." The problems inherent in openness and flexibility are emphasized, and a complete discussion of personalization is included. The unchanging and unmanageable effects of "hard architecture" are considered, as are feeble attempts to combat such permanency.

Sorensen, R. S., and J. M. Hemphill. 1981. Purdue revisited: The soundness of the open plan. *Administrative Management* (January): 28–31, 74.

Specific alterations in sound, space, lighting, and other elements are discussed in reference to a specific example. Because the process of office landscaping is constantly evolving, changes must be made, as must plans for the future.

Spivack, M. 1981. A change of space: Draft a proper fit. *Inc.* 3(February): 109–110.

The importance of the use of a predesign process in redesigning an old office or designing a new one is emphasized. This program is basically a careful description of the needs and functions of office personnel and is used to formulate an effective final design. Once the design itself is formalized and instigated, the evaluation is paramount, especially since it is based upon the predesign program itself.

Stea, D. 1965. Space, territory and human movements. *Landscape* 15(1): 13–16.

The idea that territoriality in man is modified by the designed environment is discussed. Changing the defining characteristics of a territory or environment changes the behavior that takes place within it. The importance of the design of an office and of the barriers that define that space then becomes clear.

Steelcase Inc. 1978. *The Steelcase national study of office environments: Do they work?* Grand Rapids, MI: Steelcase Inc.

This original study, designed to investigate the attitudes of office workers as well as professional office planners, was conducted by Louis Harris and Associates, Inc. Issues such as job satisfaction, participation in office planning, and offices of the future were investigated through interviews. The report includes detailed explanations of methods used, responses received, and specific and overall conclusions of the study.

Steelcase Inc. 1980. *The Steelcase national study of office environments, No. II: Comfort and productivity in the office of the 80's*. Grand Rapids, MI: Steelcase Inc.

This investigation of attitudes of workers toward comfort and productivity is based upon an earlier study, done for Steelcase, of office workers and their environments. The design of the study was based upon interviews in the homes of 1,004 office workers and 203 executives. Eight major findings of the study are discussed, interview responses are presented, and all elements of the office environment influencing the workers' perceptions of comfort are dealt with in detail.

Steelcase Inc./The American Productivity Center. 1982. *White-collar productivity: The national challenge*. Grand Rapids, MI: Steelcase, Inc.

Inspired by two previous studies done for Steelcase, this study was designed to determine which techniques of design have led to increased productivity in American offices. A survey of 685 firms was used to identify current efforts used to improve productivity and to determine which of these are successful.

Steele, F. I. 1973. *Physical settings and organization development*. Reading, MA: Addison-Wesley.

This extensive discussion of environment and behavior, in particular their influence on organizational change, is based upon a new area of thought called, among other things, "environmental organizational change." The importance of the physical environment on individual behavior is discussed in detail. The process of development and design of the physical elements surrounding the individuals and user involvement in this process is stressed.

Steele, R. J. 1967. The critical path in the office: The flow of paper and data. In *Developing the total office environment* (BEMA Business Equipment Conference, Chicago, 1966). Washington, D.C.: Thompson Book.

The benefits of using the critical path (PERT) method, or flow charting, for projects such as office planning are discussed. Mathematical modeling techniques are also explained, but not as a substitute for PERT or flow charting. The three vary as far as degree of detail examined.

Sternberg, R. H. 1981. What's new in the office environment. *Management World* 10(December): 8–10.

This review of the benefits of the open-plan office also includes projected cost savings. Several examples for functionality and flexibility in the new office are given.

Sundstrom, E., R. E. Burt, and D. Kamp. 1980. Privacy at work: Architectural correlates of job satisfaction and job performance. *Academy of Management Journal* 23(1): 101–117.

The definitions of psychological privacy and architectural privacy guide three correlational studies in work environments. Issues investigated, such as job satisfaction and performance, distractions, crowding, and privacy, were compared in the work setting for individuals at different job levels.

Sundstrom, E., R. K. Herbert, and D. W. Brown. 1982. Privacy and communication in an open-plan office: A case study. *Environment and Behavior* 14: 379–392.

A study was done of a group of employees (at four job levels) before and after office relocation on the assumption that perceived privacy is correlated with actual physical enclosure, and that privacy needs increase with job level. Based upon questionnaire, acoustical, and space measurement data, results indicate that the move to the open-plan office included a decline in privacy of all kinds, mainly with those who had moved from an enclosed office. Findings of the acoustical data indicated insufficient sound control in the open plan.

Sundstrom, E., G. Picasso, and D. W. Brown. 1981. Privacy and communication in an open-plan office: A case study. Unpublished manuscript, University of Tennessee.

See Sundstrom, Herbert, & Brown, 1982.

Sundstrom, E., J. P. Town, D. W. Brown, A. Forman, and C. McGee. 1982. Physical enclosure, type of job, and privacy in the office. *Environment and Behavior* 14(5): 543–559.

Relationships between workspace size, job complexity, perceived privacy, and workspace and job satisfaction were investigated through the use of questionnaire data and objective space measurement. Because this study was inspired by an earlier study of perceived and physical privacy, its results support the earlier findings of a relationship between the two. No relationship was found, however, between workspace and job satisfaction, and increasingly complex job duties.

Szilagyi, A. D., and W. E. Holland. 1980. Changes in social density: Relationships with functional interaction and perceptions of job characteristics, role stress, and work satisfaction. *Journal of Applied Psychology* 65: 28–33.

The effects of social density on stress, satisfaction, and interaction for 96 professional employees was investigated. Measures employed in the study were questionnaire, measures of social density, and measures of functional interaction. Contrary to results of earlier studies, it was shown that increased social density brought about positive changes in employee stress, satisfaction, interaction, and job characteristics.

Szilagyi, A. D., W. E. Holland, and C. Oliver. 1979. Keys to success with open plan offices. *Management Review* (August): 26–28; 38–41.

When changing the layout of an office to an open plan, the organization, and the designer, must fully understand how the structural alteration will affect any behavioral change in the workers. The effectiveness of a design is largely due to employee morale in that setting. Steps to aid in the successful planning of an office are provided.

Tierney, E. T. 1972. Five steps to better office layout. *Administrative Management* 33(September): 28–31.

A functional description of one method of office analysis is provided. Included are a template office layout diagram, charts, and a physical location diagram to illustrate space needs and activity and departmental relationships. The article stresses the significance of the sequence of steps used in determining the structure, function, space needs, and the reallocation.

Torgeson, T. W. 1969. The inside staff professional designers can do the best job. In *Improving office environment* (BEMA Management Conference. Chicago, 1968). Elmhurst, IL: Business Press.

The issue of whether to employ in-house or outside design staff is discussed. The importance of design control, design continuity, follow-through, and other components of the continued design process is explained in terms of both kinds of consultants.

The trouble with open offices. 1978. *Business Week* (August 7): 84–88.

The open-plan office is not an easy solution to every business's problems. Even though many open-plan offices have been successful, problems with status and privacy often arise, leaving the workers dissatisfied. The basic idea of open planning may be simple, but the concepts that make it successful are complicated.

Urban Land Institute. 1982. *Office development handbook*. Washington, D.C.: Urban Land Institute.

This office development handbook geared toward the design professional, the manager, and the public offers a discussion of every element to be considered when developing an office or an office building. An extensive array of illustrations, charts, and graphics, from the exterior to the interior, aid in the understanding of office and building design.

The discussion of interior design elements emphasizes the space and its occupants as well as energy efficiency and change.

Underground storage area becomes attractive, economical office. 1979. *Lighting Design and Application* 9(August): 40–41.

An actual example of a lighting design challenge illustrates the specifics of satisfactory lighting in an underground open-office plan. Because of successes in areas such as lighting, companies are better able to be worker efficient.

Waddell, W. C. 1967. Effective space utilization and its meaning to employee morale. In *Developing the total office environment* (BEMA Business Equipment Conference, Chicago, 1966). Washington, D.C.: Thompson Book.

The use of space in an office setting is discussed in terms of issues important to the worker, such as status, partitioning, noise control, ventilation, and lighting. Space planning and space allocation must take these phenomena into consideration because they directly affect worker morale. Work flow and processes may be one effective way of determining space utilization needs.

Waller, R. A. 1969. Office acoustics: Effects of background noise. *Applied Acoustics* 2: 121–130.

Support for the use of an electronic masking sound system is presented. It is pointed out that sound produced by ventilation or air-conditioning systems is unreliable and often annoying. Communication privacy is considered to be the most important reason for installation of "deliberate noise."

Wankum, A. 1969. *Layout planning in the landscaped office*. London: Anbar.

This discussion of furniture layout in a landscaped office is based upon analysis of working groups. The specifics and graphics of such an analysis are described and illustrated. Zoning, models, and basic rules of offices are supplemented by symbols and illustrations.

Warnock, A. C. C. 1973. Acoustical privacy in the landscaped office. *The Journal of the Acoustical Society of America* 53(6): 1535–1543.

The value of acoustical privacy provided by the use of masking noise in an open-plan office is investigated. Even though lack of privacy can cause dissatisfaction in the office, the findings of this study imply that in some cases aural privacy may not be of crucial importance. The use of sound-absorbent building materials rather than masking sound is recommended.

Wells, B. W. P. 1964. A psychological study with office design implications. *Architects' Journal* 140(16): 877–882.

Advantages of block buildings as opposed to slab buildings in terms of the open-office design (on the visual, thermal, and aural environments) are discussed. The particular design of an office, however, depends upon the needs of the corporation. Lighting—natural vs. artificial—is an important issue in this discussion.

Wells, B. W. P. 1965. The psycho-social influence of building environment: Sociometric findings in large and small office spaces. *Building Science* 1: 153–165.

A study of the psychosocial effects of large and small offices affords hypotheses concerning friendship development within these spaces. A total of 295 subjects employed in different job levels were asked to respond to visual and verbal stimuli, including feelings about their office size. A sociometric analysis was utilized to illustrate a relationship between smaller offices and group cohesion.

Wells, B. W. P. 1965. Subjective responses to the lighting installations in a modern office building and their design implications. *Building Science* 1: 57–68.

A study of office workers' lighting preferences tested three hypotheses dealing with amount of daylight estimation, the belief that natural light is better to work by, and the importance of being able to see out a window. The method of study included both questionnaire and physical measurement. From the study a weak relationship was found between amount of actual daylight present and the workers' estimations of amount of daylight; in other words, artificial lighting may oftentimes be as sufficient as natural light regardless of the workers' beliefs.

What about the workers? 1978. *Architects' Journal* (October 4): 627–633.

The spatial layout of an office environment is seen to have a direct effect on productivity and efficiency. Because management has some influence over the physical office environment, it has at least that much power over the workers. Office planning and design guidance are considered to be very important to the power relationship existing in the office setting.

Wheeler-Nicholson, D. 1969. Maybe: An Americanization of the open plan. *Office* 70(1).

Open planning and office landscaping are each seen as a systems approach to overall work accomplishment. Americanized open planning is geared toward the individual worker and his or her particular job and personal needs. The problem lies in accommodating a variety of workers with a variety of needs.

Wineman, J. D. 1980. Evaluation of the office work environment. Paper presented at the meeting of the American Psychological Association, Montreal, September 1980.

Satisfaction with the workspace, as well as control over social interaction, is seen to be of great importance to performance. Simple surveys of workers in open offices suggest that the open office, as an office design, should be reevaluated, especially in terms of privacy considerations.

Wineman, J. D. 1981. Office evaluation research: Issues and applications. Paper presented at the Federal Workshop Series on Building Science and Technology, Center for Building Technology, National Bureau of Standards, Washington, D.C., February 1981.

Acoustical privacy and lighting are discussed as two of the most important office setting elements affecting worker satisfaction. The state of research in these areas, as applied to open-office planning, is explained.

Wineman, J. D. 1982. Office design and evaluation: An overview. *Environment and Behavior* 14: 271–298.

The relationship between worker perceptions of the office environment and job performance is the basis for this review of current research in this area. Ambience, ergonomics, lighting, privacy, and symbolic identification are areas that have been investigated in the research. The measurement of subjective and objective factors in the office environment is considered to be a general problem in this kind of research.

Wineman, J. D. 1982. The office environment as a source of stress. In G. W. Evans (Ed.), *Environmental stress*. New York: Cambridge University Press.

This in-depth discussion of environmental stressors and environmental mediators in the office setting considers many factors, from ergonomics to privacy. Social/psychological factors are discussed in reference to the harmful consequences of stressors in the office. The mediating ability of environmental perception allows individuals to respond to stress in different ways.

Wise, J. A., J. W. Skirvin, D. Fey, and E. Valbert. 1979. Human factors applications to the design of legal offices. *Proceedings of the 23rd annual meeting of the Human Factors Society*, pp. 106–110.

The steps of a functional programming study of a legal firm are discussed. Activities and behavioral patterns are the basis for such a study. The threat of design errors that are not immediately visible is discussed.

Witten, M. 1978. Towards the liberated office. *Canadian Business* 51(June): 61.

This discussion of organizational control over offices stresses the importance of personalization of the workspace, as well as employee involvement in the design process. Prior input by and an understanding of the employees themselves facilitates successful design.

Wolin, B. R. 1982. Managing the open plan. *Administrative Management* 43(January): 34–36.

This discussion of the functioning of office systems within an organization emphasizes use of space and building design. Within these two major issues lies the consideration of many individual/productivity problems.

Woodson, W. E. 1981. *Human factors design handbook.* New York: McGraw-Hill.

The architectural systems of office buildings are discussed in terms of the human element and related needs. Figures aid in the illustration of important issues, from site selection to interior layout, and from reception areas to window spaces. Approximate measurements of optimal office furniture are presented and specific guidelines for design are listed.

Young, H. H., and G. L. Berry. 1979. The impact of environment on the productivity attitudes of intellectually challenged office workers. *Human Factors* 21(4): 399–407.

This empirical study relying upon subjective reports supports its hypotheses that music or nature sounds are preferred to a totally quiet office, but are undesirable in combination with random noise or distractions. An "artificial window" was used to illustrate that the use of imitations at natural stimulation was almost as desirable as the real thing.

Yuan, S. M., and C. A. Bennett. 1980. The acceptability of HID task-ambient lighting for offices. *Lighting and Design Application* 10(November): 50–56.

This empirical study engaging acuity and color discrimination tasks with independent groups illustrates that the different light sources used were equally acceptable. Basically, the aim of the study was to measure functional differences between task-ambient lighting and higher efficacy, high-intensity discharge (HID) sources.

Zeitlin, L. R. 1969. *A comparison of employee attitudes toward the conventional office and the landscaped office.* New York: Organization and Procedures Department, Port Authority of New York, April 1969.

Worker acceptability of a new design, the landscaped office, was investigated through a questionnaire for the New York Port Authority. The study focused mainly on effects of layout on interaction, supervision, work methods, and job satisfaction. Results indicate overall satisfaction with the landscaped office, even though it is implied that job performance and satisfaction cannot be facilitated by office layout.

Zweigenhaft, R. L. 1976. Personal space in the faculty office: Desk placement and the student-faculty interaction. *Journal of Applied Psychology* 61(4): 529–532.

The importance of architectural features in promoting social interaction is discussed in terms of the faculty office and the individual instructor. A comparison of faculty age, status, and sex with use of office furniture illustrate some interesting relationships. Data included observed seating patterns and students' ratings.

Index

218, 272, 273, 279, 281, 284, 285, 286–87, 307
Duncan, O. D., 97, 101, 102
Duquesne Corp., and perceived work environment, 112 (table)

Eastman Kodak Company, 266, 269
Edwards, S., 90
Effectiveness. *See* Organizational effectiveness
Elder, J., 295, 297, 298, 302
Electronic mail, 267–68
Electrostatic conditions, 149
Eleftherakis, E., 149
Elfstrom, G., 255
Ellis, L., 41
Ellis, Peter, 136, 140, 225, 285, 296, 297, 309
Employment economy, 279
Environment-behavior system, 86–88
Environmental Design Research Association (EDRA), 39
Environmental Research Group (ERG), 9
Equity theory, 215–16
Erikson, J., 305
Estimation model of satisfaction, 85–97
Ethernet network, 269
Evaluation of work environments, 65–66
    model for, 68–73
    postoccupancy, 26, 29, 39, 83
    test cases of model and results, 73–83
Evans, G. W., 298, 299
Events and settings, 50–52
Executive function, 9
Expectancy theory, 216–17
Extrinsic rewards, xi, xii (fig.), xiv (fig.), 294
Exxon Corp., 275

Factor analysis of response to work environment, 153–56, 167–70
Fairbanks, K., 236
Falk, J. Z., 87, 89, 180
Falluchi, A., 251
Fanuc, Fujitsu, 271
Farrell, W. R., 178
Farrenkopf, T., 295, 297, 302
Federal Aviation Administration, 285
Federal Express Corp., 275
Federal-Moguel, 263–64
Ferdinands, R., 91, 302
Ferguson, Glenn S., xiv, 66, 85, 294, 295
Festinger, L., 119
Fiedler, F. E., 28, 37
Fleming, A. M., 151
Flynn, J. E., 296, 297
Ford, R. N., 4, 18
Forman, A., 102, 140, 141, 181
Fraser, L., 262
French, J. R. P., 305
Furniture, 125, 129–30, 136
    for computer terminals, 253–66
    as status marker, 206–8
Future. *See* Offices in the future

Galbraith, J., 6
Gallese, L. R., 272
Gange, J. J., 181
Gans, Herbert J., 7, 228
Geen, R. G., 181
General Electric, 270
General Motors, 271
Gerstberger, P. G., 67, 302
Glover, M., 23
GMFanuc Robotics Corporation, 271
Golan, M. B., 87, 121, 178
Goodrich, Ronald, 66, 295, 297, 302, 305
Grandjean, E., 87, 89, 90, 91, 140, 179, 252, 254, 255, 256, 260, 304
Greenfield, N., 90, 179, 302, 304

concept of, 177–78
and job type, 181–82, 187 (fig.),
    188 (table), 189 (table)
and noise, 194–98
in open vs. conventional of-
    fices, 140, 150–51, 162–63
    179–80
perceived, and satisfaction, 90,
    94 (table)
and the physical environment,
    178–79, 184, 185–87
and satisfaction, 180–81
and status, 209
Processes for planning and design-
    ing offices, 26–33
    roles for, 28 (table)
    use of methods and, 29 (table)
    user involvement in, 27 (table)
    variables affecting choice of,
        33–39
Procter & Gamble Corp., 275
    and perceived work environ-
        ment, 112 (table), 120, 122,
        124
Production function, 9
Productivity among office workers,
    ix–x
    and furniture, 262–66
    open vs. conventional office
        and, 171
    and satisfaction, x–xiii, 293
Properties, 87–88
    architectural, xiv
    organizational, xiv–xv
*Property and Information Technol-
ogy,* 279
Proshansky, H. M., 6, 86, 121
Power, 43–44
    problems of, and settings, 60–
        61
    settings as elements of, 48–52
    settings as symbols of, 44–52
    and settings usage, 47–48
Pugh, W. M., 305
Pye, R., 272, 284

Quality circles, 286
Quality of work life, 4, 70
Quinan, M., xiii, 306

Raynolds, P. A., 37
RCA Corp., 275
Recognition as a motivator, xi
Rees, K., 70
Reinartz, G., 140
Research on work environments, ix,
    38–39, 85–86, 92. *See also* User-
    needs research
    current concerns, 295–307
    directions in, xv–xvi
    directives applied, xvi–xviii
    future directions in, 307–10
    and lighting, 246–48
    methodological limitations, 294–
        95
    and open offices, 140–42, 179–
        80
    and privacy, 179–80
    and user surveys, 172–74
Residential environments, 69–70
Responses to work environment, xi,
    xiii, 70–73, 88, 140–41. *See also*
    Perceived work environment
    and ambient conditions, 146
        (table), 160 (tables), 161
        (table), 163 (table)
    and disturbances, 150 (table)
    factor analysis of, 154–55 (ta-
        ble), 168–69 (table)
    and health issues, 153 (table),
        166 (table)
    and lighting, 148 (table), 162
        (table)
    models of, 98 (fig.), 99 (fig.),
        101 (fig.)
    and privacy, 151 (table), 163
        (table)
    related to work tasks, 152 (ta-
        ble), 164 (tables), 165 (table)
Responsibility as a motivator, xi